Triumph of the People

The Sandinista Revolution in Nicaragua

George Black

Zed Press, 57 Caledonian Road, London N1 9DN

Triumph of the People was first published by
Zed Press, 57 Caledonian Road, London
N1 9DN in October 1981.

Copyright © George Black, 1981

ISBN 0 86232 036 4 Pb
ISBN 0 86232 092 5 Hb

Copyedited by Mandy Macdonald
Typeset by Margaret Cole
Proofread by Penelope Fryxell
Cover design by Jan Brown
Cover photo by Camera Press
Printed by Krips Repro, Meppel, Holland

U.S. Distributor:
Lawrence Hill & Co., 520 Riverside Avenue,
Westport, Conn. 06880, U.S.A.

**British Library Cataloguing in Publication
Data**

Black, George
    Triumph of the people: the Sandinista
    revolution in Nicaragua.
    1. Nicaragua — Politics and government
    — 1979 —
    I. Title
    972.85'052   F1527

    ISBN 0 86232 036 4 Pb
    ISBN 0 86232 092 5 Hb

When we came out of the trenches we began to take on the role of national leaders: statesmen, as they say. The task really frightened us, but governing is an art and not an idea with which you are born, already planted in your head. We handled the war successfully and we were not soldiers. We became *guerrilleros* — we were not born *guerrilleros*. We were not born as politicians either. It is our revolution, our people, which has created our role for us.

Comandante Henry Ruiz 'Modesto'
21 December 1979

It is realists who make the best revolutions, the best and most profound revolutions.

Fidel Castro
26 July 1979

Note to Readers

Due to the technical limitations of the typesetting system used in the production of this book we have been unable to include accents on Spanish words in the text.

Acknowledgements

Whether consciously or unconsciously, many people have helped over the last two years to make this project a reality. In some cases, it has been the result of long friendship and constant advice; in others, a single conversation has been enough. My thanks, then, to the following people: Humberto Arguello, Tomas Arguello and Gonzalo Murillo of the Nicaraguan embassies in London and Brussels; Raul Guerra, Sylvia McEwan and other *companeros* of the FSLN Department of International Relations, for the proof that solidarity is a two-way process; Comandante Carlos Nunez and *companeros* of the FSLN Department of Propaganda and Political Education, for reading the manuscript and offering invariably helpful comments; Fernando Cardenal, Sonia de Chamorro, Katerina Grigsby, Roberto Saenz and many others for the inspiration of the Literacy Crusade; Angel Barrajon, Enrique Schmidt and Marivi Schmidt — the FSLN 'old guard' in Europe; Fatima Caldera of AMNLAE, Carlos Fernando Chamorro of *Barricada*, Jose Duley of the EPS, Miriam Guevara and Olivia de Guevara of Solentiname, Uriel Guzman of the Monimbo CDS, Julio Lopez of Esteli, Salomon Ramirez of Bonanza, Jose Antonio Sanjines of the Frente Sur, Miriam Villaneuva of Rivas, and Ivan of the EPA; Hans Langenberg, Klaas Wellinga and other European solidarity workers; John Bevan, Richard Furtado and other comrades and friends of the Nicaragua Solidarity Campaign in London; colleagues at work for giving me the informal equivalent of a two year sabbatical; Robert Molteno at Zed Press for efficiently and sympathetically dealing with an overlong manuscript; Nadine Abarca, Colin Cameron, Amalia Chamorro, Peter Chapman, Patricio Cranshaw, Ligia Elizondo, Alma Guillermoprieto, Phil Gunson, Hermione Harris, Alicia Hinojosa, Martin and Mora Lopez, Tommie Sue Montgomery, Reggie Norton, Biddy Richards, Sonia Roa Suazo, Pete Utting, Raul Vergara. And above all, Christine Czechowski.

At a level beyond individual thanks, however, whatever merit this book may possess is due entirely to the people of Nicaragua, for their militant courage and inexhaustible generosity.

George Black
May 1981
London

Map A: Principal Place-names mentioned in the text

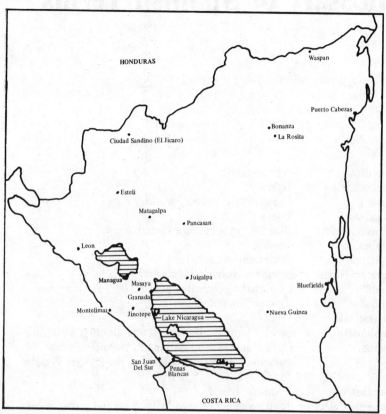

Map B: Regional

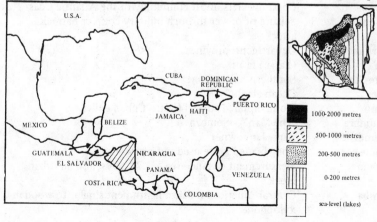

Map C: Topography

Glossary of Spanish Terms

Acuerdos	Agreements
Alfabetizacion	Literacy
Barrio	Urban district, usually working-class
Brigadista	Literacy teacher
Camisas Azules	Blue Shirts (Somocista Fascist Youth)
Campesino	Peasant
Capitalino	Inhabitant of capital city
Carretera Norte	Northern Highway (Managua)
Caudillo	Charismatic personalist political leader, strongman
Central	Trade union federation
Comerciante	Trader
Comisariato	Store, normally attached to farm or other workplace
Compa	(Affectionate) abbreviation of *companero,* most commonly applied to soldiers in the Ejercito Popular Sandinista
Companero	Comrade, friend
Convenio Colectivo	Joint agreement signed by workers and management
Cordoba	National currency of Nicaragua, value (1980) 10 US cents
Costenos	Coast dwellers, most commonly of the Atlantic Coast
Cuartelazo	Seizure of power through military coup or barracks attack
Departamento	Department, province
Finca	(Large) farm
Frente Sur	Southern battle front
Guaro	Cheap alcohol
Gusano	Worm; applied to anti-Castro Cuban exiles
'El Hombre'	'The Man' – Somoza
Latifundista	Large landowner
Machete	Long-bladed knife used in farm work
Manzana	Measurement of land area = 1.72 acres; also an urban block
Marimba	Central American musical instrument similar to wooden xylophone

Mestizo	Of mixed descent (Indian and Spanish)
Muchachos	Kids, boys, used of young combatants of the FSLN
Nacatamales	Nicaraguan delicacy of ground maize and meat
Oreja	Literally, 'ear': word used for Somocista informer
Pepena	Final stage of coffee hargest, when late and fallen berries are picked
Reparto	Urban housing area
Rojinegro	Red and black flag of the FSLN
Sindicato	Trade Union
Tortilla	Flat maize pancake: staple food in Central America
Treceavo Mes	'Thirteenth month', extra month's salary paid to workers in December

Glossary of Organisations

Nicaraguan politics are a labyrinth of initials and abbreviations. Listed here are those which occur most frequently in the text. Less important organisations are generally spelt out in full whenever mentioned.

AMNLAE	Asociacion de Mujeres Nicaraguenses 'Luisa Amanda Espinoza'	Association of Nicaraguan Women 'Luisa Amanda Espinoza'
AMPRONAC	Asociacion de Mujeres Ante la Problematica Nacional	Association of Women Confronting the National Problem
AMROCS	Asociacion de Militares Retirados, Obreros y Campesinos Somocistas	Association of Somocista Retired Soldiers, Workers and Peasants
ANCLEN	Asociacion Nacional del Clero Nicaraguense	National Association of Nicaraguan Clergy
ANDEN	Asociacion Nacional de Educadores Nicaraguenses	National Association of Nicaraguan Teachers
APP	Area de Propiedad del Pueblo	Area of Public Ownership
ARE	Asamblea de Reactivacion Economica	Economic Reactivation Assembly
ATC	Asociacion de Trabajadores del Campo	Rural Workers' Association
BECAT	Brigadas Especiales Contra Actos de Terrorismo	Special Brigades Against Acts of Terrorism (National Guard)
CADIN	Camara de Industrias de Nicaragua	Nicaraguan Chamber of Industries
CAS	Cooperativa Agricola Sandinista	Sandinista Agricultural Cooperative
CAUS	Central de Accion y Unidad Sindical	Federation of Trade Union Action and Unity (Communist)

CBS (1)	Comite de Barrio Sandinista	Sandinista Barrio Committee
CBS (2)	Comite de Base Sandinista	Sandinista Base Committee
CCS	Cooperativa de Credito y Servicios	Credit and Service Cooperative
CDC	Comite de Defensa Civil	Civil Defence Committee
CDD	Comite de Direccion Departamental	Departmental Leadership Committee
CDS	Comite de Defensa Sandinista	Sandinista Defence Committee
CEP (1)	Colectivo de Educacion Popular	People's Education Collective
CEP (2)	Colectivo Estatal de Produccion	State Production Collective
CGT-I	Confederacion General de Trabajo — Independiente	General Confederation of Labour — Independent (Socialist)
CLT	Comite de Lucha de los Trabajadores	Workers' Fighting Committee
COIP	Corporacion Industrial del Pueblo	People's Industrial Corporation
CONDECA	Consejo de Defensa Centroamericana	Central American Defence Council
COR	Comite Obrero Revolucionario	Revolutionary Workers' Committee
COSEP	Consejo Superior de la Empresa Privada	Higher Council of Private Enterprise
CNI	Comision Nacional Intersindical	National Inter-Union Commission
CPDH	Comision Permanente de Derechos Humanos	Permanent Human Rights Commission
CST	Central Sandinista de Trabajadores	Sandinista Workers' Federation
CTN	Central de Trabajadores de Nicaragua	Workers' Federation of Nicaragua (Social Christian)
CUS	Consejo de Unificacion Sindical	Council of Trade Union Unification
EDSN	Ejercito Defensor de la Soberania Nacional	Army for the Defence of National Sovereignty (Sandino)
EEBI	Escuela de Entrenamiento Basico de Infanteria	Basic Infantry Training School (National Guard)
ENABAS	Empresa Nicaraguense de	Nicaraguan Institute of

	Alimentos Basicos	Basic Foodstuffs
EPA	Ejercito Popular de Alfabetizacion	People's Literacy Army
EPS	Ajercito Popular Sandinista	Sandinista People's Army
FAD	Fuerzas Armadas Democraticas	Democratic Armed Forces (Somocista)
FAN	Fuerza Aerea de Nicaragua	Nicaraguan Air Force
FAO	Frente Amplio Opositor	Broad Opposition Front
FARAC	Fuerzas Armadas Anticomunistas	Anti-Communist Armed Forces (Somocista)
FARN	Fuerzas Armadas Revolucionarias de Nicaragua	Revolutionary Armed Forces of Nicaragua (Somocista)
FER	Frente Estudiantil Revolucionario	Revolutionary Students' Front
FETSALUD	Federacion de Trabajadores de la Salud	Health Workers' Federation
FIR	Fondo Internacional de Reconstruccion	International Reconstruction Fund
FPN	Frente Patriotico Nacional	National Patriotic Front
FPR	Frente Patriotico de la Revolucion	Patriotic Front of the Revolution
FREPA	Frente Patriotico Anticomunista	Patriotic Anti-Communist Front (Somocista)
FSLN	Frente Sandinista de Liberacion Nacional	Sandinista National Liberation Front
GPP	Guerra Popular Prolongada	Prolonged Popular War (FSLN Tendency)
IAN	Instituto Agrario Nicaraguense	Nicaraguan Agrarian Institute (Somoza)
INDE	Instituto de Desarrollo Nicaraguense	Nicaraguan Development Institute
INRA	Instityto Nicaraguense de Agraria	Nicaraguan Agrarian Reform Institute
INVIERNO	Instituto de Bienestar Campesino	Peasant Welfare Institute (Somoza)
MAP-FO	Movimiento de Accion Popular – Frente Obrero	People's Action Movement – Workers' Front
MCCA	Mercado Comun	Central American Common

	Centroamericano	Market
MDN	Movimiento Democratico Nicaraguense	Nicaraguan Democratic Movement
MICOIN	Ministerio de Comercio Interior	Ministry of Internal Trade
MIDA	Ministerio de Desarrollo Agropecuario	Ministry of Agricultural Development
MILPAS	Milicias Populares Antisomocistas	Anti-Somocista People's Militias
MISURASATA	Miskito, Sumo, Rama, Sandinista, Asla Takanka	Miskito, Sumo, Rama, Sandinista, All Together
MLC	Movimiento Liberal Constitucionalista	Constitutionalist Liberal Movement
MORE	Movimiento Obrero Revolucionario	Revolution Workers' Movement
MPS	Milicias Populares Sandinistas	Sandinista People's Militias
MPU	Movimiento Pueblo Unido	United People's Movement
OAS		Organisation of American States
OSN	Oficina de Seguridad Nacional	National Security Office (Somoza)
PCD	Partido Conservador Democrata	Democratic Conservative Party
PCN	Partido Comunista de Nicaragua	Communist Party of Nicaragua
PLI	Partido Liberal Independiente	Independent Liberal Party
PLN	Partido Liberal Nacionalista	Nationalist Liberal Party (Somoza)
PPSC	Partido Popular Socialcristiano	People's Social Christian Party
PSC	Partido Socialcristiano	Social Christian Party
PSD	Partido Socialdemocrata	Social Democratic Party
PSN	Partido Socialista Nicaraguense	Nicaraguan Socialist Party
SCAAS	Sindicato de Carpinteros, Albaniles, Armadores y Similares	Union of Carpenters, Bricklayers, Assembly Workers and Allied Trades
SENAPEP	Secretaria Nacional de Propaganda y Educacion	National Propaganda and Political Education

	Politica	Secretariat (FSLN)
UCA	Universidad Centroamericana	Central American University
UDEL	Union Democratica de Liberacion	Democratic Union of Liberation
UDN	Union Democratica de Nicaragua	Democratic Union of Nicaragua (right wing in exile)
UNAN	Universidad Nacional Autonoma de Nicaragua	National Autonomous University of Nicaragua
UPANIC	Union de Productores Agricolas de Nicaragua	Union of Agricultural Producers of Nicaragua
UPE	Unidad de Produccion Estatal	States Production Unit

Contents

PART 1
Somocismo and Sandinismo

1. The Weakness of the Nicaraguan State

From the top of a small hill, the Loma de Tiscapa, the whole of Managua is visible. The sprawling capital of Nicaragua, its centre devastated by the 1972 earthquake, its industrial zones and working-class *barrios* still scarred by the bombing raids of General Anastasio Somoza Debayle's airforce during the 1979 war of liberation. On Somoza's maps, the *Loma* and the area below it had appeared simply as '*Zona Militar*'. When the people of Managua arrived there on the morning of 19 July 1979, followed by the first victorious units of their vanguard, the Frente Sandinista de Liberacion Nacional (FSLN), they broke open the armouries of the defeated National Guard, taking possession of an area no more than one kilometre square in which the whole military strength of the Somoza dictatorship had been concentrated for over 40 years.

In the time of Somoza's father, Anastasio Somoza Garcia, founder of the dynasty, all the military installations had been opened with a single master key. On the roof of the old Presidential Palace, damaged in the earthquake, were anti-aircraft batteries. Next to the kitchens, 60 handpicked soldiers slept, the personal bodyguard of the dictator, on 24-hour alert. Beneath the Palace were the cells where political prisoners were tortured, on top of stores of explosives which would guarantee the death of opponents in the event of sabotage. When the Sandinistas came to power, the zone contained the Military Academy, artillery emplacements, the 'General Somoza' Armoured Battalion, the Basic Infantry Training School (EEBI) commanded by the dictator's son Anastasio Somoza Portocarrero, the National Guard telecommunications centre, the country's main military stores, the headquarters of the Office of Security. To the rear of the hill, rendered impregnable by the deep crater-lake at its foot, is the large military hospital; to the east side, set into the base of the hill, the massively fortified air-conditioned bunker from which the third Somoza directed his military operations against the FSLN.

A Colombian journalist once asked Somoza Debayle if he had read Gabriel Garcia Marquez's *Autumn of the Patriarch*,[1] the magnificent portrait of a monstrous, decaying Latin American dictator. Potent myths surround dictators. And in a year which also saw the collapse of Amin in Uganda and the Shah in Iran, much bad journalism attempted to anatomise the vicious-

3

ness and corruption of the Somoza family, as if the members of a dynasty which had amassed such concentrated economic, political and military power, running Nicaragua like a private estate, were fictional characters unrelated to the history which first made them possible, then sustained them, and finally swept them away.

The Somoza dictatorship came to power in two stages, with Anastasio Somoza Garcia assuming control of the US-created National Guard in 1933, and then taking over the presidency of Nicaragua three years later. He did so at a time of crisis for United States domination of the country. US intervention and occupation had been almost continuous for a quarter of a century, and US troops — fought to a standstill in Latin America's first major guerrilla war by Augusto Cesar Sandino, from whom the FSLN takes its name — no longer had the will or the capacity to prolong direct military rule. Instead, they sought in the Somoza family a local instrument of domination. Its power would rest on the historic debility (even by Central American standards) of the Nicaraguan state, torn apart by intra-oligarchical disputes throughout the 19th century, and further undermined by repeated foreign intervention and belated insertion into world capitalist markets. The Nicaraguan bourgeoisie, economically and politically weak as a result, and further hit by the worldwide economic crisis of the 1930s, could offer little resistance to Somoza, while the popular movement was decapitated in 1934 after the massacre of Sandino and his followers on Somoza's orders. For the 45 years which followed, Somocista power rested on this combination of factors, and was sustained by a repressive apparatus unique in Latin America, turned astutely into a praetorian guard at the service of a single family, and by the guarantee of continuous support from the United States.

Independence: The Uncertain Beginning

The atrophied national state which allowed Somoza's rise to power and explains much of the subsequent class struggle in Nicaragua dates back to the country's independence from the Spanish Empire. With no organised opposition to Spanish rule — only the quarrels of tiny elites — and in the absence of a traditional colonial economy geared to mining or agriculture, no solid economic base developed in the 19th century, and no powerful social group emerged linked to a particular economic activity or political history. When the Spaniards abandoned Central America quietly in 1821, they left a power vacuum filled erratically by warring landowners and merchants, soldiers, clergy and foreign adventurers. The factions crystallised into the two antagonistic political parties which dominated Nicaraguan politics for the next 150 years: the Conservatives of Granada and the Liberals of Leon. The Conservatives were aristocratic landowners, cattle ranchers and large merchants, descendants of the colonial military and bureaucratic elites, backed by the Church hierarchy. The Liberals, small landowners and artisans, less influential than their counterparts in the rest of Central America, were part of a regional wave of Liberalism influenced by English notions of free trade, which had sought briefly and ineffectively to create a Central American federation which would break with colonial stagnation and develop wider export markets. The emergent mercantile class in Nicaragua was ambiguous, tending to Liberalism in its demands for free trade but leaning to the Conservatives as the first banking and moneylending institutions grew up.[2]

These traditional regional conflicts were particularly acute in Nicaragua, which has the lowest population density of the Central American republics, and did much to prevent the development of a strong and unified national bourgeoisie. The two cities developed independent power structures and economies, using their own separate ports for foreign trade. 'Both cities were like substitutes for a non-existent national state.'[3] Their introverted political development assured an extraordinary continuity of ruling families, many of whom — like the Chamorros of Granada — figure prominently even now in revolutionary Nicaragua. The lack of a national economic base was made worse by the frequent armed conflicts between oligarchical groups, preventing the progressive expansion of agriculture favouring major export crops like coffee. By the middle of the century, the Liberals were discredited by their association with the North American 'filibuster' William Walker. Walker, an obscure Tennessee adventurer who tried in the 1850s to take personal control of Central America, was brought into Nicaragua to aid the Liberal cause but soon routed by joint Central American resistance. But the Liberals' flirtation with him opened the way for 36 years of uninterrupted Conservative rule from 1857 to 1893, during which affairs of state were conducted in the Club de Granada, the economy stagnated further and the peasant majority were kept in misery by repressive legislation or forced to fight for landowners in useless, unending civil wars.

And once foreign eyes began to turn again towards Nicaragua, attracted by the possibilities of a canal between the Atlantic and Pacific Oceans, the Conservative Government turned the country into a state at the service of foreign interests. Each intervention, whether British, German or North American, appealed to the Conservatives as a source of commercial spinoffs, while the accompanying treaties and agreements sold off more and more of Nicaragua's sovereignty. The navigable Rio San Juan, which connected with Lake Nicaragua and left only a narrow strip of territory on the Costa Rican border to be excavated, had already appealed to Spanish colonial engineers as a promising site for a canal to export products from Peru and compete for trade with the Far East. To the US Government of the late 19th century, the strategic importance of a canal through the Central American isthmus was clear: it guaranteed political and economic dominance over the whole of Latin America. Although a canal commission appointed by President McKinley opted unanimously for the Nicaraguan site, the USA chose Panama instead in 1903. Nonetheless, Nicaragua's proximity to Panama, and the notorious instability of its governments, kept it prominent among the USA's strategic interests.

Intervention and the Loss of Statehood

While the Conservatives sought allies in Honduras and El Salvador, the Liberals found military support by recruiting William Walker with offers of land and gold. Having headed a similar military expedition against Northern Mexico in 1853, Walker arrived in Nicaragua two years later with his 58-man 'American Phalanx of Immortals', routing Conservative troops in Granada and then turning on his Liberal paymasters with equal ease, demonstrating the incapacity of any Nicaraguan government to defend itself against foreign aggression. Walker installed himself unilaterally as president, contracting foreign loans which used the territory of Nicaragua as collateral, reinstituting slavery, confiscating Nicaraguan landholdings for redistribution to US citizens, and declaring English the official language. Although Walker acted essentially as an individual, he received powerful backing from the Southern slave states and immediate diplomatic recognition from the United States Government. But within two years he was overthrown after a series of up-risings in Nicaragua and the assembly of a joint force of other Central Americans and the American railroad magnate Cornelius Vanderbilt, whose Accessory Transit Company had been granted rights of passage through the likely canal route by the Nicaraguan Government in 1849.

The English too joined in the effort to oust Walker. Rushing to fill the vacuum left by the departing Spaniards, England extended its military and commercial domination of the Caribbean to the adjacent coasts of Central America, seizing the Guatemalan province of Belize (British Honduras) and occupying the eastern parts of Honduras and Nicaragua. Here it established the 'Mosquito Kingdom' protectorate in 1847, ruled by locally appointed 'kings' but with a British superintendent resident in the Atlantic port town of Bluefields. The pound, not the dollar, was the first currency of foreign domination in post-colonial Nicaragua, both through loans to the government and the uncontrolled influx of English manufactured goods. Although British cultural influences remain strong on the Costa Atlantica, outright colonial aspirations on the part of Britain ended by the 1890s, falling foul of the Monroe Doctrine of 1823, which claimed the Americas as an exclusive target for US expansionism in exchange for non-intervention in the colonial affairs of the European powers. The British also came up against a new current of Liberal nationalism at the end of the century; and although they briefly asserted their claims to the Mosquito Coast by landing Royal Marines in Bluefields and the Rio San Juan in 1893, they were ignominiously despatched by Nicaraguan troops of the Liberal president Jose Santos Zelaya.[4]

The Monroe Doctrine came into its own. After the slaughter of the North American Indians, the annexation from Mexico of the states of Arizona, California, Nevada, New Mexico, Texas and Utah, and the discovery of gold in the Sacramento Valley in 1849, it was inevitable that the private commercial ambitions of North American speculators — like the consortium of New York bankers and businessmen who backed Vanderbilt — should yield to the ambitions of an expansionist US Government. The feeble state of Nicaragua was a fine opportunity to put muscle into the Monroe Doctrine, and British claims to the Caribbean Coast were perceived as an open threat to nascent American imperialism. Naturally, US military adventures and commercial objectives were formalised in a series of treaties, which – with the acquiescence of the Conservatives – placed the country's sovereignty in foreign hands. The 1850 Clayton-Bulwer Treaty, over which the Nicaraguan Government was not even consulted, allowed for joint US-UK control of any future canal zone, while the subsequent Cass-Irisarri (1858) and Dickinson-Ayon (1867) Treaties extended US rights of free transit through Nicaragua, coinciding with the expansion of the US plantation system throughout Central America and the first stirrings of the giant fruit multinationals like the Standard and United Fruit Companies.

Liberal Reform and the US Response

The 19th-century seignorial rule of the Conservatives, who pursued this anti-nationalist course until 1893, was incapable of providing the major structural reforms needed to respond to the new demands of the Nicaraguan economy. The agricultural base of the economy, centred on coffee, had finally expanded towards the end of the 19th century, bringing with it the ascent of a new class unwilling to be stifled by the archaic Conservative state. The contradiction was resolved after a Liberal revolt led by Jose Santos Zelaya in 1893, opening the way for sixteen years of national development headed by this relatively dynamic new agroexporting bourgeoisie. Zelaya was no democrat (it was reported that in the farcical elections which sustained his dictatoriship, 'campesino' voters were given the choice of three candidates: Jose, Santos or Zelaya'[5]) but he modernised the state, opening roads, railways, port facilities and improved communications networks, in a way which would efficiently serve the new requirements of an economy oriented to agricultural exports. Zelaya's nationalism and the first attempts to weld together a coherent state in Nicaragua soon came into open conflict with US policies. When the Panama Canal was built in 1903, Zelaya investigated ways of having a second canal dug in Nicaragua, infuriating the USA. His hostility to reactionary Central American governments friendly to Washington made matters worse, and when he began to make significant commercial overtures to Great Britain and Japan, the North Americans began to look for ways of bringing about his downfall. In 1908, Zelaya contracted a large loan from the British Ethelburg finance syndicate to construct a railway, against the direct opposition of US Secretary of State Knox, and Washington accused Zelaya of infringing the Monroe Doctrine by entering into such close relationships with foreign powers. The following year, Zelaya went too far: a Conservative uprising in the Atlantic port of Bluefields engaged two Americans to sabotage government ships. The two were captured and executed, giving the USA the pretext it needed. Knox issued a furious note condemning Zelaya for 'undermining the democratic institutions' of Nicaragua and broke off diplomatic relations. Four hundred US Marines moved in to protect the Conservative revolt, and American military and diplomatic pressure brought the Liberal experiment to an end.

The Knox Note made explicit the US right to intervene directly in Nicaraguan affairs. The era of the Monroe Doctrine had given way to 'big stick' diplomacy. When the Marines landed in Bluefields, the Americans were following a new pattern of intervention already established in Cuba and Puerto Rico (1898), continued in Honduras (1905) and Panama (1908), and intensified with the successful Mexican Revolution of 1910 and the resulting US obsession with having reliable anti-Mexican friends in the Central American isthmus.

The overthrow of Zelaya's presidency was achieved with a spectacular blend of diplomatic offensive, military strength and North American private capital. The Conservative uprising had requested, and received, armed support in the form of 400 Marines, who arrived – in the time-honoured phrase – to 'protect American lives and property'. It was additionally financed by $1 million from American businessmen, including substantial contributions from the US-owned Rosario and Light Mines Company, for whom Secretary of State Knox – curiously enough – was legal counsel. The USA refused to grant recognition to the Liberal Government of Jose Madriz, which succeeded that of Zelaya. Madriz's resignation was forced within the year by the mere presence of US troops, without a shot being fired, and Washington duly installed Adolfo Diaz, a Conservative accountant employed by the same US-owned Rosario and Light Mines Company, as president of Nicaragua. Washington was well aware of the weakness of its designated puppet, and through his regime American penetration of Nicaragua was child's play.

The Liberal reform had destroyed the relevance of the Conservative oligarchy as a class, and its reinstallation in power defied history. The expansion of coffee production had meant a radical reorganisation of agriculture and thus new patterns of land ownership. Coffee brought institutional and political reforms which guaranteed the continuity of foreign trading links, and Conservative economic interests were unable to sustain the dynamic of an economy now geared to providing raw materials for the industrial world.[6] Any pretence that intervention had been designed to prevent renewed Conservative-Liberal civil war was soon shattered, and after the stability of the Zelaya regime open conflict again broke out. By the end of 1911, Diaz was incapable of controlling Liberal and nationalist opposition and claims for limited bourgeois democracy, and he invoked his only real power base in a note to the US Embassy: 'The serious dangers which beset us can only be destroyed by skilful and efficient aid from the United States, like that which produced such good results in Cuba. For this reason it is my intention, through a treaty with the American Government, to modify or enlarge the Constitution . . . permitting the United States to intervene in our internal affairs in order to maintain peace.'[7] His impotence, and that of the Conservatives as a class, made ever deeper American penetration of Nicaraguan affairs inevitable. Those who benefited most directly from the Diaz regime were US bankers, who rapidly assumed control of the country's finances. In the same year, a group of New York bankers granted Diaz a loan to pay off his British creditors, spinning Nicaragua deeper into the web of economic dependency and simultaneously staving off the threat of renewed British involvement.

The US-backed Conservative order was brutally reasserted in 1912, when General Benjamin Zeledon, formerly a minister in Zelaya's cabinet, led a rebellion against Diaz. Again Diaz called in the Marines. When they arrived, they found in Zeledon's movement an entirely new phenomenon: the embryo of popular resistance, an army of patriots largely composed of peasants and poor artisans. Zeledon quickly controlled the towns of Masaya, Jinotepe and Leon, and even laid siege to Managua before betrayal by a Conservative general cornered his troops in the hilltop fortress of El Coyotepe above Masaya. North American troops stormed the hill, killing 'El Indio' Zeledon and, according to Gregorio Selser, massacring more than 600 of his followers.[8] The example of Zeledon's resistance was not forgotten by the FSLN, who gave his name to their *Frente Sur* (Southern Front) during the offensive against Somoza.

With *Pax Americana* again imposed at gunpoint, most of the US Marines (who by this time had grown to an occupation force of 2,700) returned home, leaving a small Legation Guard of 100, sufficient reminder of who was running the country. The economic implications of American rule also became clear. As well as having its European debts cancelled by new loans, the Diaz government received working capital and stood by while the Americans appointed a controller of customs revenues and assumed effective control of Nicaraguan finances, handing over US-stipulated sums to the Nicaraguan Government on a monthly basis. Customs revenues, the railways, and the national steamship company were offered as security against loans contracted at punitive rates from the US banking house of Brown Brothers and Seligman, and American administrators were duly appointed to each of these utilities. 51% of shares in the Banco Nacional were handed over to US bankers, and the tax laws and currency overhauled according to Washington's wishes. By the time of the presidency of General Emiliano Chamorro, who came to power in 1916, financial control had been neatly formalised in a three-man committee composed of the Nicaraguan Minister of Finance and two North Americans, of whom one was a State Department nominee. The arrangement was known as the 'Lansing Plan'. Even this paled, however, by comparison with the latest canal treaty. Rarely can any government had been party to such a humiliating document as the 1916 Chamorro-Bryan Treaty, which gave the United States exclusive rights in perpetuity to construct a canal on Nicaraguan territory, as well as a renewable 99-year lease on the Corn Islands off the Atlantic Coast and rights to build a naval base in the Gulf of Fonseca, which separates Nicaragua, Honduras and El Salvador. In exchange the Nicaraguan Conservatives received $3 million, which went

straight to New York to pay off interest on loans. The handover of
Nicaragua was complete.

The United States wanted more, however. When Emiliano Chamorro
showed political ambitions of his own, attempting to bypass the Constitution
and have himself elected to a second presidential term in 1920, his plans were
vetoed by the State Department, which sent in an academic from Princeton
University to redraft the country's electoral laws. Under US supervision,
electoral fraud worked smoothly in 1925, but instead of restoring the
Conservative Party to power the election brought in an unstable coalition of
dissident Conservatives and Liberals. The new president was the Conservative
Carlos Solorzano, and his deputy the Liberal Juan Bautista Sacasa. Among
the supporters of Sacasa's candidature was an emergent Liberal called
Anastasio Somoza Garcia. As soon as the new government came to office,
the military weakness of Solorzano and the fragility of his regime moved
the United States to remind the new president of an agreement made with
his predecessor: the creation of a small and efficient US-trained military
force, similar to those being set up under US supervision in Haiti, the Philippines and the Dominican Republic. It would be known as the National Guard.

The Nicaraguan Economy Before Somoza·

The economy and class structure of mid-1920s Nicaragua was strongly
influenced by the development of a single export crop: coffee. Basing itself
on the development of coffee, the agroexporting bourgeoisie had finally
enabled Nicaragua to make its late entry into the world capitalist economy.
Production had in fact begun in the middle of the previous century but had
grown slowly in comparison to other Central American countries. Even so,
it grew to represent 50% of Nicaragua's export earnings in the two decades
between 1920 and 1940, and the economic power of the traditional
monopolistic traders of Granada was no match for the potential vitality of
the 'coffee bourgeoisie'. Their first market was Great Britain, later superseded
by the USA, although Britain continued to exert indirect influence until
the 1930s by virtue of its role in determining world market prices. Not only
was coffee Nicaragua's main export earner until the 1940s; it was also the
only substantial economic activity which generated capital within the
country. The other main raw materials — bananas, rubber and gold — were
produced in enclaves owned by US capital, and their sale remained separate
from the national economy, weakening its base still further. In the whole
of Central America, the banana companies operated as states within the
state, with their own police force, shops and even currency.[9] They enjoyed
their own independent transport infrastructure and distribution network. The
participation of local capital was insignificant, the companies' operations
were tax-free and their decision-making centred abroad, unconnected to
either the productive or the political apparatus of the Nicaraguan state.

Such a mono-product economy was of course vulnerable to world price fluctuations, acutely so in the case of Nicaragua, where the world capitalist depression coincided with the internal crisis of civil war. Coffee prices plummeted from $458 per ton in 1926 to $142 in 1938. The reaction of the coffee bourgeoisie was to slash production costs, mainly by cutting wages or replacing them with payment in kind, and simultaneously to increase the land area under cultivation to compensate for falling prices. The drastic measures required to maintain profits brought economic collapse and universal misery for the rural masses. The demands of a collapsing market emphasised too the peculiarity of all Central American rural societies. Capitalist expansion meant, paradoxically, turning the clock back to impose semi-feudal social relations between the landowner and the rural workforce, relations which remained the norm in much of the Nicaraguan countryside until the 1979 Revolution. Extending land use meant accelerating the expulsion of peasants from prime agricultural land, continuing a cycle formalised in law by Conservative regimes of the 1870s and 1880s. Coffee owners, having stolen the peasants' land, now needed a large plantation workforce permanently on hand. So these workers were partly salaried and partly paid in kind, and given small subsistence plots to work. The combination left them tied to the land and to the *patron* for life.[10]

The importance of coffee also reinforced the unequal development of Nicaragua. The already distorted concentration of population, power and state infrastructure was made worse because the climate and fertile soils best suited to coffee production were also centred on the Pacific coastal belt and the highlands of the *Norte Central*. Coffee growing spread through the mountainous *departamentos* of Jinotega and Matagalpa, while the highest yields were in Carazo, Granada and Masaya, heavily populated areas close to Managua. By the late 1920s Nicaragua's fate as a supplier of agricultural exports to United States capitalism was sealed.

This economic model produced a backward dependent capitalism, where power rested with a small bourgeoisie whose economic interests coincided at the local level with US designs for Nicaragua. It meant of course that the model imposed by American control carried with it many of the seeds of later problems for US foreign policy. The political aspirations of a class which might have injected dynamic capitalist growth into Nicaragua — expressed by the Zelaya Liberal Government — had been shown to be by definition incompatible with American interests, and had promptly been aborted. Zelaya's very nationalism, given US intervention, only guaranteed the further anti-national development of the economy and debility of the state.

By the mid 1920s renewed civil war was imminent. With the subversion of bourgeois nationalism, the war would bring forth Nicaragua's first real experience of radical nationalism, the first popular alternative to imperialism and local domination. It would however end with the installation of *Somocismo*. The Somoza dictatorship which followed the war was a product, not a cause, of foreign domination.[11] Or in the words of one FSLN militant: 'Somoza didn't bring in the *yanquis*. The *yanquis* brought in Somoza.' Dictatorial capitalism was secondary, a necessary instrument of imperialist

11

control. By this logic, and the related internal logic which made super-exploitation of the workforce the only possible response for a bourgeoisie robbed of 'normal development', dictatorship became the only workable form of capitalism in Nicaragua.[12] And throughout the long nightmare of *Somocismo*, Nicaragua's dominant classes passively accepted the economic and strategic role mapped out for them by the United States. First, however, a seven-year long war had to be fought.

Liberals, Conservatives, and the Marines

The coalition government of Solorzano and Sacasa was an unworkable marriage of conflicting class interests, in effect no more than a holding operation to stave off the inevitable civil war. As the government quickly foundered, Emiliano Chamorro returned in October 1925 to overthrow Solorzano, purging the regime of Liberals and trying to set up a 'pure' Conservative Government of traditional cut. But this style of Conservatism was no longer appealing to Washington, and Chamorro made the fatal error of attempting to bring the fledgling National Guard under his personal control. The move incurred Washington's rage, and the USA invoked its Peace and Friendship Treaty with Central America, which refused to recognise governments which had seized power through a *coup d'etat*. As before, the withdrawal of American support guaranteed the downfall of a Nicaraguan government. In its place, the United States resurrected Adolfo Diaz, the mining accountant and president of a decade earlier, in their efforts to restore a working model of Conservatism; but by this time the country was in open crisis. Local Liberal revolts sprang up in different parts of the country, one of them headed by Anastasio Somoza Garcia, who had now adopted the title of 'General'. On Diaz's appointment, the Liberals promptly set up a 'constitutional' government in the Atlantic port of Puerto Cabezas in December 1926. The *'Guerra Constitucionalista'*, as the war became known, assured the final submersion of the Conservative oligarchy as a significant political force. Henceforth their influence would be restricted to that of acquiescent minority opposition to the Somoza dynasty, and the economic power of those great Conservative families which had amassed durable fortunes.

Fearing Mexican 'Bolshevism' and possible support for the Liberal rebels, the USA decided that Nicaragua was a test case for regional geopolitics. Early in 1927 Coolidge assured Congress that he had conclusive evidence of Mexican involvement, and repeated that no power except the USA had the right to exert influence in Central America. There was only one possible response; and US Marines duly disembarked at Corinto in January. This time the force was a large one: 215 officers commanding 865 Marines and 3,900 soldiers, accompanied by arms supplies to the Diaz Government. But the Americans recognised that they were backing a loser in the Conservative Party. With the Zelaya model of Liberalism equally unpalatable, their strategy depended on fostering the division which now existed within the ranks of the

Liberal opposition, weeding out the nationalist traditions inherited from Zelaya, and building a Liberal pattern of economic development compatible with US interests. The trick was to identify specific sectors of the Liberal leadership who would prove amenable, and they found their man in Sacasa, the head of the 'constitutional' government, and Jose Maria Moncada. Moncada had sided in 1909 with the Conservative overthrow of Zelaya and now took charge of denationalising the Liberal Party. Sacasa too placed himself at the orders of the US Government.

In one essential aspect the Constitutionalist War was not a simple re-run of earlier Liberal-Conservative conflicts. The Liberal army was composed on one hand of elements of the bourgeoisie, and on the other of a sizeable group of workers and peasants. This group had the elements of a new class consciousness, and prominent among them were the mineworkers of the north-east, the most coherent sector of a still undeveloped working class. It was the presence of these forces which created the conditions for transforming the conflict into an anti-imperialist war of national liberation. The Americans appreciated this nascent working-class and peasant militancy, and their strategy rested on the ability of Sacasa and Moncada to stifle it.

By 1927, not even US military support was able or willing to prop up the Conservatives. Instead, the Americans resorted to a pact between the two parties. A special presidential envoy named Henry L. Stimson arrived from Washington to impose terms: a ceasefire; general amnesty; the handover of all arms to the US Marines until such time as they could organise the Nicaraguan Guard efficiently under US supervision and with US officers; and US-supervised elections in the following year.[13] Diaz and Moncada promptly signed the Pact of Espino Negro and both of Nicaragua's political parties accepted subservience to United States domination. At that moment the Constitutionalist War became a class-based revolutionary war, led by the only Liberal officer to reject the Pact and recognise that United States imperialism was at the heart of Nicaragua's crisis. He was the 31-year-old Augusto Cesar Sandino. Sandino's vision of the war had remained constant since his decision to fight in May 1926, on his return to Nicaragua after several years of working abroad. His experience was vital to the formation of his class consciousness: as a warehouseman at the Montecristo sugar mill in Honduras, owned by the Honduras Sugar and Distilling Company; as a banana plantation worker for the United Fruit Company in Guatemala; and as an oilfield worker for the South Pennsylvania Oil Company and the Huasteca Petroleum Company, both in Mexico. It had given him firsthand knowledge of the reality of American imperialism in Central America.[14] Under Sandino's leadership, the war against US intervention was Nicaragua's first organised questioning of bourgeois power structures, and gave shape for the first time to a long — if sporadic — tradition of spontaneous popular revolt.

Notes

1. Gabriel Garcia Marquez, *The Autumn of the Patriarch*, trans. Gregory Rabassa; (London, Jonathan Cape, 1977).
2. Edelberto Torres, *Interpretacion del Desarrollo Social Centroamericano* (San Jose, Costa Rica, EDUCA, 5th edn, 1977), pp. 38-43, 46-51.
3. Sergio Ramirez, *El Pensamiento Vivo de Sandino* (San Jose, EDUCA, 5th edn, 1980), p. vii.
4. Torres, *op. cit.*, pp. 44–6.
5. Quoted in Richard Millett, *Guardianes de la Dinastia* (San Jose, EDUCA, 1979), p. 36.
6. Torres, *op. cit.*, pp. 62–7.
7. Quoted in Jaime Wheelock Roman, *Imperialismo y Dictadura – Crisis de una Formacion Social* (Mexico City, Siglo XXI, 1975), p. 110.
8. Gregorio Selser, *El Pre-Sandino – Benjamin Zeledon* (Havana, Casa de las Americas No. 117, 1979), p. 59.
9. Ramirez, *op. cit.*, p. xiv.
10. Torres, *op. cit.*, pp. 80–2.
11. Humberto Ortega, *50 Anos de Lucha Sandinista* (Mimeo, n.p., 1976), pp. 75–7.
12. Julio Lopez, Orlando Nunez, Carlos Fernando Chamorro, and P. Brenes, *La Caida del Somocismo y la Lucha Sandinista en Nicaragua* (San Jose, EDUCA, 1979), pp. 18–19.
13. Millett, *op. cit.*, p. 77.
14. Ramirez, *op. cit.*, p. xxxi.

2. Sandino and the Tradition of Resistance

Sandino's Predecessors

Only 4% of modern Nicaraguans are pure-blooded Indians. By contrast, the *mestizos* — those of mixed Spanish and Indian blood — account for three-quarters of the population. The growth of *mestizaje* was rapid in the colonial period, and was used by the Spanish colonisers as an instrument of 'class conciliation' to legitimise 300 years of segregation, slavery and brutal exploitation of Nicaragua's original inhabitants.[1] Today, only two Indian settlements remain in the country's principal towns: the *barrios* of Monimbo in Masaya and Subtiava in Leon; and it was no accident that these were the first centres of popular insurrection against Somoza in 1978. They were inheriting a militant tradition recognised earlier by Sandino: 'I am a Nicaraguan and I feel proud that Indian American blood runs in my veins.'

The Spanish Empire had tried to turn the militancy of Nicaragua's Indians to its own advantage, drafting thousands of them to fight in the conquest of the Andean countries. But the Indians remained intractable to the brutal discipline of colonial rule. Although their revolts were primarily local, and did not represent a movement capable of dislodging Spanish rule, they were marked by an insurrectional character rooted in the most exploited classes, and therefore quite distinct from the cabalistic opposition of emergent elites. The Subtiava Indians fought the Spaniards in the 17th and 18th centuries, and in 1811-12 Indian insurrections, armed with sticks and machetes, became generalised in Leon, Masaya, Granada and Rivas. In both the 1820s and 1840s Indian uprisings continued. By the middle of the century there were stirrings of guerrilla activity in the northern mountains of Las Segovias, where Sandino later fought; in 1856 insurrections in Ometepe and elsewhere against Walker's filibusters; in 1881 a prolonged offensive by peasants around Matagalpa against the theft of traditional farmlands by the oligarchy. And finally, Sandino's most recent inspiration: the resistance of 'El Indio' Zeledon in Masaya against vastly superior US forces. When Zeledon was killed in 1912, his body was paraded in public. The 17-year-old Sandino saw the procession as it passed near his home village of Niquinohomo. The sight left a profound impression on him.

During the United States military occupation, the insurrectional tradition grew. Between 1913 and 1924, there were ten or more armed uprisings against Conservative rule, and on each occasion US troops imposed martial law. In the same period, incipient working-class organisation added a new dimension to the struggle. The first major strikes took place against US-owned companies: the Cuyamel Fruit Company in 1921 and the Cukra Development Company in 1922-3, both of which ended in massacres of workers; later there were strikes in the Bragman's Bluff Lumber Company and the mining enterprises of Siuna and Bonanza in the north-east. In 1926, strikes against the banana companies of the Atlantic Coast turned into full-scale armed uprisings. Each North American economic enclave was hit.

To grasp one reason for the success of the class alliances formed by the FSLN in the late 1970s, it is essential to dispel the myth that all the anti-Conservative uprisings stemmed from the exploited classes. The Liberal bourgeoisie also resorted to arms after the overthrow of Zelaya and the artificial imposition of Conservative rule. Later, when the Somocista mutation of Liberalism assumed power, Conservative dissidents also took up arms. The frustration of democratic openings by the USA made armed insurrection a historical possibility for important sectors of the Nicaraguan bourgeoisie.

The Crazy Little Army[2]

4 May 1980 saw the inauguration of the Council of State in Nicaragua, the legislative body installed by the Sandinista Government as the 'solid political expression of national unity', in which 'the popular masses and their organised struggle continue to be the principal source of power and revolutionary change'.[3] The date was designated *Dia de la Dignidad Nacional* (Day of National Dignity), the date on which Sandino had rejected the pact signed by Stimson and Moncada at Espino Negro in 1927.

On his arrival, Stimson (who had served as Secretary of War in the cabinet of President Taft) made his position clear. He confessed that he found military men easier to understand than politicians and declared that Nicaraguan politicians were no longer capable of running their country. In the soldier Moncada he had an ideal instrument for guaranteeing American interests in Nicaragua. Although the Somoza regime was still nine years away, the pact of Espino Negro signified the establishment of a military dictatorship with no social base. Moncada was the man who prepared the ground for *Somocismo*.

Sandino had left his job in Mexico almost a year earlier, in May 1926. He made his way immediately to the northern mines of San Albino, assembling the 30-man nucleus of his army, adding another 45 sympathisers from the banana fields of Puerto Cabezas and Prinzapolca on the Atlantic Coast, and using his savings to equip his force with rudimentary arms. His arrival also coincided with the armed uprising of other Atlantic Coast banana workers, who seized the Conservative barracks at Bluefields.

In this first, 'Constitutionalist' phase of the war, Sandino employed the conventional tactics of a regular army, but early military defeats and the terrain in which he was fighting led him to adopt — and master — the tactics of guerrilla warfare. After his rejection of Espino Negro, he withdrew to his mountain stronghold of El Chipote, and on 2 September 1927 put his name to the founding document of his 'crazy little army', the Ejercito Defensor de la Soberania Nacional de Nicaragua (Army in Defence of the National Sovereignty of Nicaragua: EDSN). His signature was followed by that of hundreds of other literate soldiers, now highly disciplined in columns commanded by generals, mostly natives of the northern mountains of Las Segovias, but with a sprinkling of Central American internationalists.

El Chipote was an inaccessible mountain peak, permanently wreathed in cloud, surrounded by ravines and with no visible paths of access that the American troops could detect. Here Sandino built a complex of palm-thatch living quarters, food and armament stores, corrals for horses and livestock, tailors' shops and bootmakers, munitions and arms workshops. Danli, a small town just across the nearby Honduran border, served as a communications centre with the outside world. It was from El Chipote that Sandino's first frontal military attacks were launched.

The first major offensive after Espino Negro was an assault on the northern garrison of Ocotal in July, where troops of the newly formed National Guard were entrenched. By this time, Sandino could already rally a force of several hundred for a single attack, but arms were still lacking. Many carried only machetes. After a twelve-hour siege, the most powerful US weapon was called in: aerial bombing destroyed much of Ocotal and inflicted heavy losses on Sandino's men. The Americans found Sandino's increasing control over the north impossible to tolerate and ordered the destruction of El Chipote. Massive air strikes were launched against the hill, which was surrounded by Marines and National Guardsmen, but when US forces reached the summit they found nothing but a ring of straw dummies wearing the red and black kerchieves of the EDSN.

After Ocotal and the later military reverse of Telpaneca, Sandino realised that the United States possessed a number of weapons which made regular warfare difficult: superior arms, sophisticated military tactics and airpower. But to compensate for this, Sandino could count on a weapon which the Americans could never possess: an intimate knowledge of his chosen terrain. His ability to escape with his entire army and supplies from El Chipote, in the face of overpowering enemy forces, showed that the Americans would never defeat him in a guerrilla war fought on his own territory. The FSLN later took the lesson profoundly to heart: never fight the enemy on their own terms.[4]

In April 1928 Sandino captured the American mines of La Luz y Los Angeles, and saw at once the response the USA was capable of. The US air force destroyed the villages of Murra, Ojoche, Naranjo and Quiboto. Air strikes became the pillar of American strategy, and a force of six Vought Corsairs, seven Loening flying boats, and five three-engined Fokker bombers was deployed: a formidable display of aerial power for the 1920s and for such a limited theatre of operations.[5] Sandino himself gave an account of their effect: 'Our wounded are dying for the lack of medical treatment for the wounds they have received from the bombing and machine-gun attacks . . . I am talking not only of soldiers, but of civilians. Among these there are many women and children, since the enemy aircraft are doing more damage to the villages than to our trenches. Ciudad Vieja, Guanacaste and San Albino have been reduced to smouldering ruins.'[6]

Sandino's account hints at the Americans' inability to hit the Sandinista army effectively, for all the weight of military hardware. The guerrilla campaign began in the mountains and rain forests of Las Segovias, country-side which might have been designed for guerrilla warfare. Sandino employed a flexible blend of tactics, alternating attacks on military garrisons with ambushes of US columns in the mountains. As the war progressed, guerrilla action spread out from Las Segovias to cover the entire northern and central regions of Nicaragua, and the number of armed actions increased propor-tionately. By 1932, the Sandinista army registered 176 military encounters with American forces in the course of the year.

A Vietnam in Central America

United States intervention in Nicaragua shares many of the characteristics of the later war in Vietnam. In addition to the specifics of previous American involvement in Nicaragua, the arguments used to justify a full-scale military intervention cast Mexico in the role of international communist conspirator and saw the whole of Central America as vulnerable to a domino effect in a region where only US imperialist hegemony was permissible. Enormous destruction was wrought on a small country by sophisticated military techno-logy and counter-insurgency operations, and most of this was borne by the peasant population. Most important, the USA suffered defeat (and again sought to justify it as 'withdrawal with honour') at the hands of nationalism, mass popular opposition, a highly intelligent guerrilla movement rooted in the people, and the unpopularity of the war at home.[7]

Airforce bombing raids were used even before Sandino was identified as the main threat. When Liberal troops took Chinandega in February 1927, the town was retaken by Conservative forces with American air support, and much of the city was reduced to rubble. The USA subsequently brought in new Curtiss bombers because of their greater bomb capacity. In the country-side, 'neutral zones' were established, and the cruelty of both the US Marines and the new National Guard became notorious. The uncompromising methods of the Marines were consciously used by the USA as a propaganda weapon, epitomised by the widely circulated photograph of a Marine lieutenant holding the severed head of a Sandinista combatant. The most classic form of 'Vietnamisation' was a programme to create what might later have been called 'strategic hamlets'. The plan was not in fact devised by the American Government but by the National Guard commander of Ocotal. Moncada approved the idea of a forced evacuation of peasants in the *departamentos* of Nueva Segovia and Jinotega, where Sandino enjoyed massive support. Many local peasants had joined the *guerrilla*, and thousands of others were active sympathisers. Farms were burned down, crops and animals destroyed, and peasants transferred to concentration camps where, according to an American report, more than 200 died in 1929 of starvation and exposure. Anyone left in the target zones was treated as an enemy. While government propaganda spoke (as it would again in the 1960s and 1970s) of peasants fleeing from Sandinista terror, the repression was in fact the best possible recruiting drive for Sandino's army. Those peasants who did not join the EDSN flocked into the cities to tell of the National Guard's atrocities, and the image of the new military force was permanently scarred. Marine air strikes similarly only served to swell Sandino's forces, by increasing peasant hostility to the US presence and failing miserably in their military objectives. Sandino specialised in diversionary attacks which drew forth useless bombing raids — the only American response to the impotence of their ground forces, bogged down in unfamiliar country and ceaselessly undermined by the steady flow of intelligence about troop movements which Sandino received from the local population.

Sandino profited as well from the hopeless splits within the enemy over the tactics needed to defeat him, and of course each side — the USA, Nicaraguan Liberals and Conservatives — proposed options which accorded with their own longer-term plans. As the Americans stuck to their proposals for a National Guard independent of either political party, Diaz and Chamorro for the Conservatives and Moncada for the Liberals favoured a strengthened Nicaraguan force which knew the country. As the Americans knew only too well, this would mean troops dedicated to supporting the political ambitions of one party or the other in the 1928 elections. The result deepened the contradictions of United States policy. They could not accept either partisan force, and so the bulk of combat duties fell to the Marines who were visibly unable to defeat Sandino. The war became a nightmare for them: 'The well trained and elegantly uniformed *yanqui* soldiers could find only one phrase to describe it: "damned country". Rains, mosquitoes, swamps, swollen rivers, wild animals, the horror of suddenly falling into an ambush, fevers, an always invisible enemy.'[8] Having come in ostensibly 'to protect American lives and property', the Marines were often forced to destroy targets, like the American-owned San Albino mine, to prevent its falling into Sandino's hands. Marine casualties mounted.

In the USA, a powerful anti-war movement grew and Sandino assumed the stature of a romantic hero. Cecil B. DeMille even approached the State Department for permission — promptly denied — to make a film about the guerrilla leader of Las Segovias. Opposition to the war within the USA took many forms: hostility from the public to the cost of defending Wall Street's interests during the Depression; the pointless loss of American lives; the courageous work of a handful of journalists like Carleton Beals of *The Nation*; and finally open conflict within the Senate. The Democratic Party opposed intervention in its 1928 election platform and there was not even unanimity among Hoover's Republicans.[9] The new National Guard was forced even closer to the heart of American strategy: if public opinion would not allow them to dominate Nicaragua directly, then they would do so by proxy.

The People's Alternative

'Very soon we shall have our victory in Nicaragua, and with it the fuse of the "proletarian explosion" will be lit against the imperialists of the world.'
(Sandino)[10]

The brutality of American troops in a country they could not understand heightened what was already a favourable moment for the upsurge of a powerful people's struggle against oligarchical rule. Sandino's war was, however, conducted in the absence of a strong industrial proletariat. Although the initial participation of the northern miners was an important stimulus, it was essentially a peasants' war. Industrial development came very late to Nicaragua, and in the 1920s the small proletariat was based in only three sectors, each controlled by US capital. These were the miners, the banana plantation workers, and the labourers with the sawmills and lumber companies, all located in the jungles of the Atlantic Coast, with the exception of small gold mines in the western *departamento* of Leon. Their first stirrings of independent class organisation showed themselves towards the mid-1920s. Within five years their militancy increased as they suffered the worst effects of the Depression, but they remained numerically small and geographically isolated. Endemic unemployment and the problem of land were both aggravated by the economic crisis. As world coffee prices slumped in 1929, coffee production was paralysed and famine resulted among the peasants and agricultural labourers. At the same time, the Pis Pis mines and the Nicaraguan Lumber Company closed down, and a severe banana blight swept through the Nicaraguan plantations, forcing hundreds of workers into unemployment and starvation. The first working-class party in Nicaragua's history — the Partido de los Trabajadores Nicaraguenses (Nicaraguan Workers' Party: PTN) — was formed by the end of the decade, and threw its support behind Sandino. Socialist ideas circulated for the first time.

All these factors helped to swell Sandino's army and determine its class composition. His own vision of the war was crucial. Born the son of a small farmer (who had been arrested for his opposition to the Chamorro-Bryan Treaty) and a domestic servant, Sandino's experience of work in Mexico had brought him into contact with the militant trade unions of the railway and oilfield workers, and on his arrival at the San Albino mine he had devoted as much time to encouraging trade-union organisation as to recruiting miners for the armed struggle. His nationalism, however, made him reject what he perceived as 'foreign' political models, and while he welcomed the solidarity of political supporters abroad he resented any attempts they made to link his movement to international socialist or communist currents, and criticised any failure — whether from the Quakers or the Anti-Imperialist League — to understand the nationalist basis of the Nicaraguan war. Until Espino Negro he believed that the popular forces under his command could be a component part of a struggle led by the bourgeoisie, but after Moncada's betrayal he vigorously asserted the independence of working-class and peasant organisation.

Sandino employed rigorous criteria for accepting new members of the EDSN. He demanded people who would continue to fight with determination during a protracted war in difficult conditions and who had an intimate knowledge of local geography. In practice, this meant selecting *campesinos*, those who in the first place had the greatest motivation for joining the struggle. 'You see, we are not soldiers,' he would tell a Spanish journalist. 'We are of the people, we are armed citizens.'[11] The result was a flexible and disciplined force which could not be clearly distinguished from the peasant population as a whole. Because of the lack of arms, thousands of *campesino* 'irregulars' were prevented from joining the fighting except in the most important battles, but they provided a logistical support network throughout the areas which Sandino liberated. Others formed a well-structured intelligence and security service; the orphans of combatants and peasants killed in the bombing and National Guard raids formed a special guerrilla corps of 13- to 16-year-olds for missions behind American lines; numerous women joined Sandino's army, like Conchita Alday (killed by US troops in 1927), Maria Altamirano, and Sandino's wife Blanca Arauz, who took charge of communications; urban supporters in Matagalpa, Jinotega and other cities provided information about troop and aircraft movements; an international brigade was formed by volunteers from a dozen Central and South American countries. The peasant army, like the FSLN 'from the people and for the people', resisted United States aggression in this way, bound together by a strict code of military discipline, for seven years.

Anti-Imperialism and Social Organisation

'On one of those days I said to my friends that if there were a hundred men in Nicaragua who loved it as much as I, our country would restore its absolute sovereignty, placed in peril by the yanqui *empire.'* (Sandino)[12]

On 1 January 1933 the US forces withdrew, unable to win a military victory. In their place they left the National Guard, having appointed Anastasio Somoza Garcia as its first Nicaraguan commander. On 2 February Sandino accepted a ceasefire and disarmament[13] and withdrew to Wiwili in Las Segovias with a hundred soldiers to guarantee his security during the coming peace negotiations. His terms for peace, which synthesised the basic elements of his political thought, were unacceptable to Sacasa and the United States. Sandino called for an end to foreign intervention in the National Guard; the calling of a Pan-American conference to revoke the Chamorro-Bryan canal treaty; and the establishment of a large new *departamento* stretching from Las Segovias eastwards to the Atlantic Coast. It would be controlled by an independent Sandinista military force, and would allow Sandino's followers to put into effect the forms of social organisation which had crystallised in liberated zones during the war.

Sandino was no political theorist. In Sergio Ramirez's description, 'His thought was more the result of his daily experience as a military leader in the war of resistance . . . The circumstances of the struggle moulded his thinking.'[14] But practical politics made it necessary to break United States influence over Nicaraguan affairs and this led him to favour a broad alliance of progressive forces against the anti-nationalism of the two traditional parties. For a while during the 1933 peace negotiations he approved the idea of a third party (the Partido Autonomista) as a political alternative, though without ever formally breaking his own links with the Liberals. In his insistence on guaranteed national sovereignty and an end to political and economic dependency on the USA, he understood very well that the physical withdrawal of US Marines changed nothing, and his proposal for a national state based on redistribution of land in the interests of the peasantry soon found a new adversary in the National Guard.

This model of Sandino's was already taking shape. At the height of the war in 1932, the zone of his guerrilla operations covered ten of Nicaragua's sixteen *Departamentos*: Zelaya, Chontales, Matagalpa, Jinotega, Nueva Segovia, Esteli, Managua, Leon, Chinandega and Rivas. His army of 21 columns and 6,000 men actually controlled an area bounded by the Honduran border in the north, Puerto Cabezas in the east, Chichigalpa in the west and the shores of Lake Nicaragua in the south. Military columns controlled the civil organisation of each zone: the organisation of agricultural production through cooperatives, taxation and basic literacy classes for peasants and soldiers. By 1928 a kind of provisional government operated, minting its own currency from local gold mines and running an independent communications network (not purely military) with telephone and radio equipment captured from American troops. Taxes were levied on landowners who remained in the liberated areas, although many in the north left their lands and attempted to blame the collapse of local economic activity during the crisis of the 1930s on Sandinista activity. With the expulsion of the Marines, Sandino set about refining his 'state within a state' in the northern forests of Wiwili and the Rio Coco. Peasant cooperatives marketed their agricultural produce on the Atlantic Coast, harvests of tobacco were sold locally and gold panned in the Rio Coco was even sent to Managua for sale.

Above all, Sandino recognised the significance of the land question in Nicaragua. Although he never openly questioned capitalism (merely insisting that it should exist in a form which meant that 'the worker should be neither humiliated or exploited') he did favour state ownership of the land. In the north he had rich virgin farmland at his disposal on the banks of the Rio Coco, and he believed that the area might produce the meat and cereal crops which Nicaragua at that time imported. This social project, although limited in scope, came into direct conflict with the land ownership patterns of the dominant classes, who had already been antagonised by Sandino's reversal of 19th-century land laws and the redistribution of farms to peasants whose holdings had been expropriated in the expansion of the coffee bourgeoisie.

The existence of a state within a state — even in the remote north — could not be allowed to last. The instrument for his removal was the Somoza-controlled National Guard. Since the ceasefire, a confrontation between Sandino's forces and Somoza's had become inevitable and Sandino saw only too clearly the threat which the new force represented, not only to his own security but to the future of Nicaragua. 'Here there are not two states but three: one controlled by the president of the republic, one by the National Guard, and mine.'[15] By the same token, the continued existence of Sandino, with his calls for the government to arm civilians and restructure the *Guardia* on 'constitutional' lines, was a real threat to Somoza, who had been using his position as National Guard commander and his friendships in the US Embassy to pursue his own political ambitions.

The Murder of Sandino

The last year of Sandino's life was also a crucial year in the rise of Somoza, with the impending collision between *Sandinismo* and ascendant *Somocismo* relegating the first of Sandino's 'three states' — the apparatus controlled by President Sacasa — to a marginal position. Sandino had voluntarily accepted the disarmament of an intact and undefeated army, but the prestige he enjoyed and his open attacks on the National Guard presented a serious obstacle to Somoza, who now had clear designs not only on the future of the National Guard but on higher political power. The restoration to office of the Liberal bourgeoisie in the figure of Sacasa, at the same time as the withdrawal of United States Marines and the removal from the political front line of old representatives of the Conservative oligarchy, made it difficult to sustain the impetus of the popular struggle and furthered an atmosphere of conciliation to which Sandino was not immune. All the time, knowing that the peace was still fragile, the USA concentrated on building the strength of the Guard, and a State Department official expressed Washington's new realism about the capacity of old political models to meet future problems: '[It is] preferable to run the risk of revolutionary disturbances now and let the strong man emerge without further waste of time.'[16]

Somoza carefully nurtured his relationship with US officials, first as Under-Secretary of Foreign Affairs, where he was used as an intermediary in discussions between the USA and President Moncada because of his fluent English and his reputation for diplomacy, and then as *Jefe Director* of the Guard. His appointment as the Guard's first Nicaraguan commander reflected the choice of Moncada and Washington's Minister in Managua, Matthew Hanna. But it went against the wishes of the new president, Sacasa, and this prepared the way for a power conflict in the short term between a

notoriously weak president and an increasingly strong military commander
for control of Nicaragua. Somoza understood and exploited Sacasa's weakness, giving the appearance of loyalty to the Constitution while strengthening
the Guard and consolidating his personal control over it. The conventional
image of a one-dimensional tyrant is as misleading a description of the
founder of the dynasty as it was of his son. In fact, Somoza was a politician
of great and cynical intelligence; even Sandino proved vulnerable to his
apparent honesty, travelling three times to Managua for negotiations while
the National Guard committed one provocation after another against the
Sandinistas throughout 1933. His fourth visit, in February 1934, brought him
to a capital where effective control had passed from the presidency to
Somoza. The public embraces with which Sandino and Somoza had sealed
their talks the previous year were a thing of the past. Sandino had rejected
Somoza's ultimatum for the last of the EDSN to lay down their arms, and he
continued to attack the Guard as an unconstitutional force. On the 21st,
Somoza held a series of meetings with the recently appointed US minister,
Arthur Bliss Lane, and the same night, as Sandino and a group of his generals
were leaving a farewell dinner in the Presidential Palace, they were ambushed
by a Guard patrol and shot dead.

It was not sufficient to decapitate the movement: its roots had to be torn
out too. On the following day, heavy National Guard forces attacked
Sandino's base camp at Wiwili, killing 300 of his followers. A campaign of
terror, the 'Pacification of Las Segovias', began. The *Guardia* burned crops
and farms, smashed Sandinista cooperatives and restored the conditions for
the expansion of the *latifundio* system. Over the next three years, the
remnants of guerrilla resistance were wiped out, culminating in the death of
the Sandinista general Pedro Altamirano. Moncada had appreciated the need
to destroy the military strength of *Sandinismo* and its forms of social
organisation, alarmed as he had been by Sandino's talk of 'the need for the
workers to fight the rich, and other things which constitute the seeds of
communism'. Destruction of the revolutionary movement left the way open
for a certain working unity between different sectors of the country's
dominant classes, headed now by the agrarian bourgeoisie. The people's
forces lost the initiative, and it took them 25 years of repression to regain it.
The name of Sandino was banned in Nicaragua. The Partido de los Trabajadores Nicaraguenses (PTN) and other short-lived groups like the Partido
Laborista and the Partido Republicano tried unsuccessfully to fill the
vacuum, while attempts at autonomous working-class and peasant
organisation were broken up. The working class remained weak and dissident
bourgeois groups failed to seek links with the masses. Nicaragua entered a
long period of military, cultural and ideological repression.

His Legacy

What caused the annihilation of a disciplined military force 6,000 strong with widespread popular support? The implication of some historians is that Sandino was naive in accepting a ceasefire and the good faith of Somoza and Sacasa.[17] In reality, conditions in 1933 did not allow Sandino many options for transforming his anti-imperialist struggle into a prolonged popular war. Solid international support did not materialise. Internationally, anti-imperialist consciousness was weak, and although it is customary to quote the Sandino Battalion of the Kuomintang, the resonant declarations of support from the VIth World Congress of the Comintern, the First Anti-Imperialist Congress of 1928, the All-American Anti-Imperialist League and a wide range of left-wing groups, they were of no more practical use than Cecil B. DeMille's abandoned filmscript: 'not enough', in Ramirez's phrase, 'to buy a single cartridge'.[18] The support of sympathetic governments was also ambivalent — as in the case of Mexico where Sandino spent six long months in 1929 waiting for help from President Portes Gil, who ultimately decided that continuing good relations with the USA were more important. By 1933, fascism was rampant in Europe and brutal dictatorships (Ubico in Guatemala, Carrilla in Honduras, Martinez in El Salvador) were the order of the day in Central America. Farabundo Marti and 30,000 peasants were dead in El Salvador.

Internally, the Ejercito Defensor de la Soberania Nacional was exhausted and almost out of ammunition. Its peasant supporters lacked the clear understanding of Sandino himself and too easily associated the physical withdrawal of the Marines with the total victory of their cause. Petty-bourgeois support for *Sandinismo* evaporated, and a military plan to withdraw and regroup in Honduras was blocked by war in that country. Negotiated settlement genuinely seemed Sandino's best hope for further manoeuvre. He knew that negotiation with the likes of Sacasa and Somoza was a risk, but it was a risk which had to be taken.[19]

Sandino's thought and his example of anti-imperialism, class consciousness and military strategy continue to underpin the Nicaraguan Revolution. The 1960s and 1970s struggle of the FSLN against Somoza was heir to Sandino's own perception that the *Somocista* state and the National Guard were merely an instrument of continuing United States domination ('being there without being there', in Humberto Ortega's phrase[20]). It continued to recognise the urban proletariat and the peasantry as the only dependable revolutionary forces, while remaining flexible enough to accommodate progressive sectors of the bourgeoisie. And in almost twenty years of armed struggle, the FSLN inherited Sandino's conviction that the military offensive of these forces was the essential form of the political struggle. '*Sandinismo* was a force which remained alive,' noted Ortega, 'because it was the product of the specific conditions of our country. It was not a phenomenon which was imposed theoretically or pulled out of books. Through his struggle and his action, Sandino created the theory, and it is that which we have taken up.'[21]

As is natural in any revolution, there are many opportunists and small bourgeois groups in Nicaragua who — lacking a popular base — now seek to legitimise themselves and outflank the FSLN by appropriating Sandino's ideas and his resonant phrases. The red and black flags of the FSLN fly over comfortable Managua suburbs as well as over peasant huts and working-class *barrios*. Bourgeois politicians sign their declarations with Sandino's *Patria y Libertad* (Fatherland and Freedom). Sandino's nationalism provided a broad enough framework for the multi-class national unity of the Nicaraguan Revolution. The bourgeoisie, stifled in their own aspirations for national development, may find this sufficient, but they overlook Sandino's class consciousness. Since its foundation in 1961, and especially in the final critical phase of the insurrection, it has been the FSLN — not the bourgeoisie — which has defined the course of the revolution through Sandino's defence of the class interests of the masses. Sandino himself put it very simply: 'Only the workers and peasants will go on until the end; only their organised force will achieve victory.'[22]

Notes

1. Jaime Wheelock Roman, *Raices Indigenas de la Lucha Anticolonialista en Nicaragua* (Mexico City, Siglo XXI, 1974), pp. 8-12.
2. *'El Pequeno Ejercito Loco'* — 'the crazy little army': name given to the Sandinista forces by the Chilean poet Gabriela Mistral.
3. *Barricada* (newspaper of the FSLN), 3 May 1980.
4. Humberto Ortega, *50 Anos de Lucha Sandinista,* pp. 55-65.
5. *Cuadernos del Tercer Mundo,* No. 32 (August 1979), p. 19.
6. Frente Estudiantil Revolucionario (FER), *Ideario Patriotico de Sandino* (Mimeo, n.p.).
7. NACLA, *Latin America and Empire Report,* Vol. X, No. 2, February 1976, p. 7.
8. Ramirez, *El Pensamiento Vivo de Sandino,* p. xli.
9. NACLA, *loc. cit.*
10. *Augusto Cesar Sandino: Ideario Politico* (mimeo, n.p.).
11. Ramon de Belausteguigoitia: *Conversaciones con Sandino,* in Ramirez, *El Pensamiento Vivo de Sandino,* p. 290.
12. *Sandino: Ideario Politico.*
13. See the last section of this Chapter, 'His Legacy', for an analysis of the reasons for Sandino's acceptance of a ceasefire.
14. Ramirez, *op. cit.* p. lxviii.
15. Sandino, interview with *La Prensa,* February 1934.
16. Belden Bell (ed.), *Nicaragua: An Ally Under Siege* (Washington D.C., Council on American Affairs, 1978).
17. This fear was shared even by some of Sandino's own supporters. See his letter to his friend Gustavo Aleman Bolanos from Bocay, 16 March 1933; in *El Pensamiento Vivo de Sandino,* p. 301.
18. Ramirez, *op. cit.* p. lxviii.
19. Humberto Ortega, speech at the Gruta Javier, 13 December 1979; in *La Revolucion a Traves de Nuestra Direccion Nacional* (Managua, Secretaria Nacional de Propaganda y Educacion Politica del FSLN (SENAPEP), 1980).

20. *Ibid.*
21. *Ibid.*
22. *Sandino: Ideario Politico.*

3. The Somozas — Building the Family State

Somoza's Rise to Power

Divisions within the Conservative Party over its tactics in the 1932 elections left the way open for the Liberal Juan Bautista Sacasa to assume power. This initiated an inherently weak presidency, hardly a formidable obstacle to Somoza as he set about building his personal influence over Congress and the ruling Liberal Party. Whatever resistance he encountered was mobilised by Sacasa's wife, but her efforts were consistently blocked by the US Minister Arthur Bliss Lane, who shared Moncada's enthusiasm for the young Somoza.[1] Somoza realised, though, that American support could not yet be taken for granted, and with his sights fixed on the 1936 elections he proved adept at feigning democratic procedures if US favour appeared to be wavering.

Throughout Somoza's rule the Nicaraguan Constitution was a hollow sham, to be alternately flouted, rewritten or given lip service, as circumstances demanded. In the run-up to the 1936 election, Somoza first considered divorcing his wife (Sacasa's niece) to comply with a constitutional clause prohibiting the succession within six months of any relative of the incumbent president. Next, to allay criticisms of irregularities in his campaign he suddenly announced his intention to withdraw his candidacy, guarantee the neutrality of the National Guard, and support the legally elected candidate. Finally, he briefly resigned his command of the Guard once he had succeeded in forcing Sacasa out of office. This he did by launching a military drive against regional National Guard barracks, dismissing all officers loyal to the president until the entire country was controlled by pro-Somoza officers.

Somoza had demonstrated in the election year his ability to blend brute military force with a degree of populism. With some followers seeing him as a Nicaraguan answer to Hitler or Mussolini, he formed a 100-strong shock force of young Fascists, the *Camisas Azules* (Blueshirts), who were armed by the *Guardia* and allowed to mobilise in the streets without interference. They were used by Somoza to burn down an opposition newspaper and intimidate political enemies. At the same time, populism served the purpose of further undermining the authority of a frightened Sacasa as the president nervously cracked down on all signs of dissent. When a strike of drivers turned militantly anti-government, Sacasa threatened to call in the National Guard (over which he had no control), while Somoza, in a rousing speech to the strikers, promised that the Guard would take charge of petrol distribution to safeguard the drivers' interests. The prompt end to the strike was accompanied by 'spontaneous' pro-Somoza demonstrations orchestrated by the Guard.

Sacasa resigned in June and the interim president – chosen by Somoza – obligingly put the election back until December, precisely the six-month interval which Somoza needed to avoid constitutional obstacles. In December he duly came to power, backed not only by the Liberals – whom he had renamed the Partido Liberal Nacionalista (PLN) – but also by the still confused Conservatives, who had failed to come up with a more acceptable candidate. The voting, carefully supervised by the National Guard, gave 'Tacho' what he considered an adequate majority: 107,201 votes against 169 cast for his opponent Leonardo Arguello.

His intention of transforming the presidency into a dynasty became apparent in a major redrafting of the Constitution three years later. A Constituent Assembly, extension of the presidential term from four years to six, and clauses empowering the president to decree laws relating to the National Guard without consulting Congress, ensured Somoza's absolute power over the state and the military. Control over the electoral and legislative machinery gave the basis for a permanent dictatorship. Simultaneously, the opposition had to be suppressed. To achieve this, Somoza moved to exploit the weakness of the bourgeoisie, consolidate his own dominant position within the class, neutralise the Left (a task made easier by the extermination of *Sandinismo*), and maintain internal stability – of paramount importance to the USA – through the exercise of force.

The new dictatorial model faced only one period of real difficulty: the years from 1944 to 1948. Threats in that period came at Somoza from every angle[2] – from the Conservatives, Liberal dissidents, a working-class resurgence, and even US ambivalence. He faced attacks on his plans for re-election, a Liberal Party convention which produced a major split, an opposition inspired by the fall of the dictatorships in Guatemala and El Salvador, an attempted general strike of the kind which had led to the downfall of Ubico and Martinez, student demonstrations, and a new generation of intellectual critics.

Dismembering the Opposition

The so-called 'Generation of '44' is a key phenomenon in Nicaraguan history. Composed principally of middle-class intellectuals, with considerable strength in the university, it also provided an important link in the continuing legitimacy of armed action as a weapon of some sectors of the bourgeoisie. Its main expression was the formation of the Partido Liberal Independiente (PLI), a group of Liberal dissidents who broke with Somoza in March 1944

after several of its members had been placed under house arrest. The PLI
is a party which remains alive today, a committed member of the revolutionary bloc of parties headed by the FSLN. The roots of the PLI's dispute lay
in their opposition at the 1944 convention to Somoza's plans for a further
term of office and further interference with the Constitution. In the same
year one of their leaders, General Carlos Pasos, led an armed movement
– easily defeated – against the dictatorship, while younger Liberal dissidents
formed a youth movement called the Frente Juvenil Democratico (FJD:
Democratic Youth Front). The FJD acted as a breeding ground for intellectuals who later formed the *guerrilla* of El Chaparral, an immediate precursor
of the FSLN in the late 1950s. One of its members was Rigoberto Lopez
Perez, the young poet who assassinated Somoza Garcia in 1956.

Conservative dissidents too played their part in the events of 1944. Two
of them were prominent as leaders of street demonstrations in Leon and
Managua, which were brutally put down by the National Guard. They were
Pedro Joaquin Chamorro, the editor of *La Prensa* subsequently murdered
by the dictatorship in February 1978, and Rafael Cordova Rivas, a lawyer
appointed to the Junta of National Reconstruction in 1980 after the
Revolution.

A certain resurgence of the working-class movement coincided with these
signs of bourgeois opposition to the regime, and in July 1944 the Moscow-
line Partido Socialista Nicaraguense (PSN) was founded. However, 'the PSN
was born at a meeting whose aim was to declare its support for the Somoza
Government'.[3] Far from offering a militant threat to the regime, the new
party shared the conciliatory line adopted by communist parties throughout
Latin America at the end of the Second World War. In the language of Yalta,
Latin America was definitely earmarked as the United States' sphere of
influence. In Cuba, Juan Marinello, chairman of the CP, had actually entered
the Batista cabinet in 1943. The PSN similarly was at pains not to challenge
the established order. But while other communists in the region were back-
tracking from an already established base in the labour movement of their
respective countries, the PSN began its activities at the lowest point of the
Latin American CPs, under the influence of the US Communist Party leader
Earl Browder. Its founding meeting came only two months after the dissolu-
tion of the CPUSA at its May 1944 convention.[4]

Despite its conciliatory line, Somoza moved swiftly to abort the new
party. A honeymoon year of legality and the refusal to build a clandestine
network left the PSN an easy prey to Somoza's attack. As Somoza stifled a
planned general strike on the Guatemalan or Salvadorean model by threatening to confiscate the property of anyone taking part, he also gave thought
to ways of heading off radical influence among the working class. Again
populism provided the answer, and Somoza persuaded Congress to pass a
Labour Code which acceded to many of the workers' principal demands.
From here it was an easy step to installing pro-government trade unions. The
provisions of the Labour Code were set aside, and any militant organisation
of the working class was destroyed after 1945. Although intermittent strikes

continued through the 1940s and 1950s, a rudderless working class was unable to resist the repression with which they were invariably met.

In dealing with resistance, Somoza adroitly identified his opposition with the current enemy of the United States. After his flirtation with Fascism in the 1930s, he declared war on the Axis powers in December 1941, allowing the USA to install naval and airforce bases inside Nicaragua, and receiving in return large amounts of military equipment which would never be used against an external enemy. The War was used as an excuse to declare a state of siege and suspend constitutional guarantees. After 1945, he abruptly labelled all opposition as 'agents of international Communism' and continued to count on American support in his moves to eradicate it. Post-war relations with the USA were not entirely smooth, however, and the Americans added their voice to internal complaints when Somoza again declared his intention to seek re-election to the presidency in 1947. In response, Somoza found a man he thought would be a puppet: his defeated opponent of 1936, Leonardo Arguello, now old and presumably open to manipulation. Somoza knew perfectly well that the weakened Conservatives (this time supporting a joint candidate with the Independent Liberal PLI), and his own control over the National Guard and the electoral process, would guarantee victory to his chosen candidate, whether or not this bore any relation to the votes actually cast. Arguello was of course declared the winner, but once in power proved disturbingly independent and progressive. Within days of his election, a Panamanian newspaper published details of Arguello's remarkable talks with the Union Nicaraguense de Liberacion, a new ad hoc opposition group: 'Dr Leonardo Arguello guarantees the complete freedom of Nicaraguan workers to organise in trade unions and engage in political activities . . . he will give special attention to the proposals made by the Partido Socialista Nicaraguense in its campaign to improve the lot of the working class. He promises to discard the dictatorship as a form of government, and condemns the anti-working-class campaign mounted by the Conservative newspaper *La Prensa*.'[5]

Somoza allowed Arguello only 25 days of this before launching a coup, even though it meant antagonising the United States, who briefly broke off diplomatic relations.[6] This single experience of letting go of the reins of power was enough for Somoza, and after taking the presidency again he strengthened his rule still further by another rewrite of the Constitution, this time banning the PSN and adding to the powers of the *Jefe Director* of the National Guard.

It remained for him to deal with the Conservatives, who were angered by the growing identification of Somoza with the state and found it opportune to remind the dictator that he was after all exercising power on behalf of the bourgeoisie as a whole. In the face of so much adverse pressure, 'Tacho' found it necessary to restore some semblance of legitimacy to his regime. For the Conservatives of the late 1940s it was unrealistic to think in terms of regaining control of the state apparatus. What concerned them more now was their economic future. Somoza's confiscation of rich coffee and cattle farms from German *emigres* had laid the foundation for a rapid accumulation of personal wealth by means of corruption and the abuse of state power, with which other members of the bourgeoisie could not compete. These early methods of personal enrichment had brought him a fortune of several million dollars by the end of the Second World War, which increased as he made open use of state funds, including levies on cattle exports, mining and textile operations and the 5% levy on all state employees' salaries as a contribution to the PLN. More landowners were 'persuaded' to transfer their properties to Somoza for minimal prices in exchange for political patronage — little more than a crude protection racket — and the location of Somoza's new landholdings provided the rationale for national development in the form of new roads and port facilities.

An abortive military uprising led by the old *caudillo* and Conservative general Emiliano Chamorro proved the last serious Conservative challenge to *Somocismo*. Thereafter the party decided to throw in its lot with the Liberal dictatorship in exchange for certain economic safeguards, an arrangement in which the Conservatives permanently forfeited their popular support. The two parties signed pacts in 1948 and 1950, the second offering the Conservatives one-third of the seats in Congress and formal guarantees of free commercial activity and respect for their economic interests. For Somoza, the two-party state with its built-in Liberal majority meant that dictatorial control could be maintained under a veneer of political representativity and without resorting to excessive state violence. Despite repeated electoral fraud and constitutional violations, the model lasted for more than two decades owing to a degree of bourgeois consensus and the inability of a fractured popular movement to resist.

The Death of Somoza I

Around the absolute power of *Somocismo* and the passivity of the formal opposition there grew a myth that the dictatorship was indestructible. Any resumption of the revolutionary struggle depended therefore on shattering that myth. In a biography of Somoza Garcia's assassin, the poet Rigoberto Lopez Perez, the Sandinista leader Jose Benito Escobar reflected on the importance of the assassination, which took place as Somoza arrived in Leon on 21 September 1956 to accept the Liberal Party nomination for a further presidential term:

> First: an incentive which would serve as an example to the masses. It was necessary to destroy the myth of the tyrant with a successful action which could never be employed by the bourgeoisie as a demagogic weapon.
>
> Second: it put an end to the traditional methods of opposition which the bourgeoisie had imposed on our people; the bourgeoisie having been the class which had until the time of this action headed the fight against the dictatorship in its own way.

Third: it reaffirmed to the people that the forms of struggle to be employed to attain liberation should be those which correspond to the needs of the people, who should respond to the violence of exploitation with the violence of the popular masses.[7]

The death of Somoza Garcia, coinciding with a renewed economic crisis which will be discussed in Chapter 5, did not of course bring the dynasty to an end, and Lopez Perez himself saw that his action was only 'the beginning of the end.'[8] He appreciated that major historical changes were not the work of individuals, but recognised too the weakness and disorientation of the Nicaraguan masses and their need to shift their struggle on to a new plane in which the objective economic crisis battering the peasants and workers could be matched by a subjective realisation of their capacity for organisation and resistance.

For the week that Somoza lay in a coma in a Panama Canal Zone hospital, flown there on the instructions of US Ambassador Thomas Whelan, the myth lingered on, fostered by falsely optimistic medical reports in the government-controlled media, while the regime made arrangements for a smooth handover of power to the dictator's two sons, Luis and Anastasio Jr. When the team of doctors sent from the United States by President Eisenhower finally pronounced the 'good neighbour' dead, Luis was already installed in the presidency and 'Tachito' ('little Tacho') was running the National Guard. The special relationship between Washington and the Somozas (depicted in that way for domestic consumption even during the strained days which had followed Somoza's overthrow of President Arguello in 1947) was of incalculable value to the dynasty in assuring domestic control at the moment of crisis.

Whatever the personal qualms of his predecessors about the character of the Somozas, Eisenhower was to prove a solid friend to the second generation of the dictatorship. Since the 1930s Nicaragua had been considered by Washington as a useful thermometer for judging its Latin American policy, and the 'Good Neighbour Policy' announced by the incoming Franklin Roosevelt had had a good deal to do with the Marines' debacle in 1933. Nicaragua was a vital pillar of US regional control, and the close relationship brought mutual benefit — with Somoza's reliable friendship being rewarded by American support in whatever form circumstances demanded, political, economic, military and ideological. Any doubts which Somoza Garcia might have had about his own methods had been allayed as early as 1936 when Washington indicated the flexibility of its Good Neighbour Policy, particularly where Central America was concerned, by recognising the military dictatorship of Martinez in El Salvador. Previous refusal to grant recognition to *de facto* regimes was abandoned if these regimes suited US strategic interests. A government's effective control of the country now became the only criterion for diplomatic approval. In 1939, Somoza had cemented the relationship with President Roosevelt with a personal visit to Washington, where he was received with full state honours. The two presidents subsequently exchanged letters in which Roosevelt agreed, among other things, to provide an American director for the National Guard's new Military Academy, and in 1940 Somoza honoured his ally's re-election by renaming Managua's principal thoroughfare the Avenida Roosevelt. A million dollars' worth of military assistance to Nicaragua followed in 1941, and continuing aid allowed Somoza to build what was by local standards a powerful airforce. When Luis and Anastasio II inherited the state after the assassination of their father in 1956, they received with it a private army without parallel in Latin America.

The Somoza Empire

At the time of Somoza Garcia's death, his two sons also inherited a vast economic empire. Most descriptions of Somocista wealth begin with the now legendary reference to a broken-down coffee plantation near San Marcos in Carazo, the family's only property before Somoza took control of the National Guard in 1933. From then on, the Somozas' exercise of state power and their umbilical ties to United States imperialism, control of the military and Liberal Party machine, friendships with successive US ambassadors, and the exploitation of foreign aid and technical assistance, provided the framework for a spectacular accumulation of personal wealth. Somoza Garcia had already shown his penchant for irregular methods while still an accountancy student in the USA, counterfeiting dollar bills and gold coins. The method passed from father to son, with Anastasio Somoza Debayle perfecting the clan's technique. When he was overthrown in 1979 by the FSLN, estimates of the family fortune were impeded by complex financial legislation, inadequate records and extensive foreign holdings under other names. Interviewed on his arrival for exile in Miami, Somoza told reporters that he was worth only $100 million, but US government sources placed the figure at $900 million.[9]

The acquisition of the Somoza fortune, intimately associated with the overall pattern of capital accumulation by the Nicaraguan bourgeoisie, passed through a number of clearly defined stages. First, as we have seen, came the appropriation of German-owned properties in Matagalpa, Jinotega and Managua, under the pretext of anti-Nazism and taking advantage of the wartime state of seige and suspension of constitutional guarantees. This made Somoza Garcia the country's largest private landowner by 1944, with 51 cattle ranches, 46 coffee *fincas* and 8 sugar plantations, which made him the country's leading producer of sugar and associated products.[10] At the same time, he profiteered from the war economy, and came out of the Second World War with an estimated fortune of $60 million. 'Dirty business' went hand in hand with control of war exports, and Somoza Garcia cornered gambling rackets, brothels and illegal alcohol production, as well as a monopoly over contraband (electrical goods, jewellery, machine tools). His monopoly control extended, too, over the granting of import and export

licences, the centralised use of state agencies and personal influence over
transport and communications planning.

After the Second World War, Somoza moved on to meat exports and
mining concessions in the late 1940s. The latter brought him direct ownership
of some mines. The destruction of Sandino's army had already been a profitable business for Somoza. He had right at the start taken control of the San
Albino mine and extensive farmlands in the north which had belonged to
Sandinista combatants and sympathisers. From those mines — the great
majority — which remained in US hands, he extracted $400,000 a year in
exchange for tax exemption, and 2¼% of the value of gold production as a
'presidential concession'. Later, the Somoza family expanded into the
incipient industrial sector, through cement works, textile plants like 'El
Porvenir' and a monopoly of milk pasteurising. Only Somoza's plant 'La
Salud' could process milk, and the sale of non-processed milk was forbidden.
The acquisition of state transport facilities followed: the merchant shipping
line MAMENIC, the state airline LANICA, and the port installations at
Puerto Somoza on the Pacific.

After Somoza Garcia's death, industry expanded and American finance
boosted the growth of the Central American Common Market (Mercado
Comun Centroamericana: MCCA) in the early 1960s. Now the family began
to use USAID funds to extend their empire into new regional integration
industries like paper mills, fisheries and meat processing plants, all industries
which enjoyed preferential fiscal conditions. The empire continued to
diversify, and after the 1972 earthquake took on a corporate structure
analogous to that of the other big bourgeois finance groups. Somoza
Debayle's forays into property, construction, finance and insurance began to
overstep the mark which the rest of the bourgeoisie was willing to tolerate.
With the Nixon presidency in Washington, Somoza renewed his interest in
drugs, casinos, prostitution and tourism, often in partnership with Cuban
exiles and speculators from Florida and California.[11]

Each stage in this process of accumulation was reinforced by the Somozas'
handling of fiscal legislation. The techniques ranged from straightforward
tax evasion,[12] through payoffs from US companies in exchange for the free
operation of foreign capital, to the selective application of tax laws and the
use of the Central American Common Market for personal gain. In the final
years of *Somocismo*, Managua abounded with rumours and allegations of
ever more outrageous business practices.

One such story is a small but eloquent illustration of the Somocista relationship between state and economic power. Like its Central American neighbours, Nicaragua looked to its chain of active volcanoes as an alternative
energy source when oil prices rocketed in the 1970s. One such volcano,
dominating the skyline of Lake Managua, is the perfect cone of Momotombo.
Geothermal energy excited Somoza Debayle, and in 1975 he set up the
drilling company Energeticos SA and the US-based California Energy with
American business partners. The two companies were awarded government
contracts to begin exploratory drilling, and the lower slopes of Momotombo

(where Somoza owned extensive properties) were chosen as the site.. Energeticos SA proceeded to sink shafts with complete abandon in the un- likeliest spots, for the contract had specified that charges would be paid according to the area drilled, not the resources located. The next step was for Somoza to persuade Congress to pass a law granting compensation to any landowner whose property was damaged by geothermal development. The assumption was that geysers would harm farmland, but Momotombo's lower slopes are barren rock desert. To enhance his profits, Somoza insisted that compensation rates be pegged to the rise in oil prices – geothermal energy was after all a petroleum substitute. Finally the Japanese transnational Kawasaki was awarded the rights to exploit the new energy source. Somoza demanded his customary cut from foreign business, estimated by sources· working on the project at more than $1 million.[13]

The congruence of the state and Somoza's own financial interests allowed the dictatorship to guard against future setbacks in a way which has made economic life difficult initially for Nicaragua's revolutionary state sector. Large chunks of the industries and landholdings confiscated in 1979 had been mortgaged to the Banco Nacional without collateral, their revenues already salted away in untouchable bank accounts in the Netherlands Antilles, Switzerland, or the Virgin Islands.[14] Nonetheless, the wealth which the state has been able to recover is considerable. The companies administered by the *Oficina de Supervigilancia y Control de las Empresas del General Anastasio Somoza Debayle* embraced almost every economic sector: rice and meat processing plants, tobacco factories, dairies and sugar mills; seven fisheries companies; cooking oil, plastics, matches, packaging, footwear; chemical, icemaking and computing factories, recording companies, jewellers, coffee retailers and motor distributors; asbestos, cement, concrete, metalwork, furniture and building materials; extensive service industries including the state airline and merchant shipping line, port facilities and cargo handlers, hotel chains, newspapers, radio and television stations; insurance companies, banks and finance houses.[15]

Dependent Capitalism

In Nicaragua, as throughout Latin America, cultural imperialism is the most visible legacy of US economic control. The American economist Otto J. Scott, writing to encourage investors in Somoza's Nicaragua, gave an accurate enough image of pre-revolution Managua: '[An American] would hear many old, familiar US songs on the radio – in English. A trip to Managua . . . will disclose the ubiquitous McDonald's, billboards extolling the new Visa bank cards and the Diner's Club as well as BankAmericards and American movies. On the highways he will see compacts from the world's leading manufacturing centres: the United States, Japan and Germany. He can fill his tank at a Texaco, Chevron or Esso station for $1 a gallon.'[16]

The role assigned to Nicaragua by US capital, as a supplier of raw materials and a market for manufactured goods, scarred the economy with every feature of dependency. Nicaragua relies on its exports of cotton, coffee, sugar, meat, seafood — each at the mercy of world market prices. Its industry is grossly underdeveloped, unable to meet internal demand. Although the expropriation of all Somoza-owned property has given the Sandinista Revolution immediate state control of large areas of prime agricultural land and scores of factories, each sector of the bourgeoisie had its role in the framework of dependency and retains muscle through its links with Western capitalism in key areas like cotton production,[17] despite its traditionally weak political organisation and leadership.

The Nicaraguan bourgeoisie only modernised with the expansion of cotton in the 1950s. This introduced a new model of capitalism which supplanted the coffee *latifundismo* of the first half of the century. The expansion of cotton production had a triple significance: deepening dependency, sealing the predominantly agricultural character of the bourgeoisie, and dramatically widening the gulf between the dominant classes and the enlarged rural proletariat.[18] In the 1950s, the new demands of cotton production wrenched 180,000 peasants from traditional small farming into seasonal plantation labour. With no semblance of planning, the cotton crop grew 120-fold from 1949 to 1955, devouring 400,000 acres of the Pacific Coast previously devoted to cereal production. As before, the rationale was provided by the current requirements of the North American market, this time increased demand and higher prices for cotton because of the Korean War. US insistence that Nicaragua should be locked into economic dependency by primarily supplying US needs was nothing new: the pattern had been set during the Second World War. But what did change was the character of local bourgeois ownership. In the 1940s US strategy had further deformed the Nicaraguan economy by directly stimulating capital accumulation by Somoza. Old strategic interests had resurfaced with the need to protect the Panama Canal in wartime, bolstering Somoza at a time when he was consolidating his internal control and refining the techniques of personal enrichment. For the American war economy, Nicaragua became a key supplier of raw materials like rubber, minerals and timber (whose sale largely produced revenues for North American companies) and agricultural products. The US Government's development plan offered Nicaragua credits exclusively for agricultural exports, not for generating local industry.[19] The US share of Nicaraguan exports escalated. In 1938, 25% of Nicaraguan exports went to Europe and 67% to the USA: by 1944 the USA's share had risen to 91% and Europe's had fallen to only 1%.[20] Simultaneously, Nicaragua was prepared for its future role as a market for manufactured goods during the post-war recovery of the American economy.

With the cotton boom of the 1950s and the stagnation of the coffee bourgeoisie, three centres of bourgeois economic power crystallised, representing different though overlapping interest groups, each defined in its own way by dependency. They were the Somoza clan itself, the Banco Nicaraguense (BANIC), and the Banco de America (BANAMERICA). Each of the new banking groups had direct ties with US capital, BANIC with the Chase Manhattan Bank and BANAMERICA with the Wells Fargo Bank (an 18.8% stockholder) and the First National City Bank. The creation of the new finance groups also had roots in the power-sharing agreements of the late 1940s. For the Conservatives, BANAMERICA was the formalisation of the economic guarantees embodied in the 1948 and 1950 pacts, although these guarantees were rarely respected in practice if they conflicted with the interests of the Somozas. For Somoza, the pacts had brought clear economic as well as political advantage. The ensuing rationalisation of the state administration simplified management of the family economic empire. Other bourgeois sectors were caught both ways: despite the consolidation of BANIC and BANAMERICA, they could not recover the ground lost over the previous fifteen years, in which Somoza had taken full advantage of the absence of private finance institutions.

BANIC, founded at the height of the cotton boom in 1953, became the more important of the two non-Somoza finance groups, investing its cotton profits in industrialisation and the regional integration programmes dictated by US policy during the 1960s. During that 'Development Decade', it forged a close working relationship with USAID and other agencies, involving itself in social reform programmes and giving space to the younger and more dynamic bourgeois groups typified by the development institute INDE (Instituto Nicaraguense de Desarrollo), formed in 1963. At the same time, BANIC built links with US transnationals such as the Consolidated Food Corporation, Booth Fisheries, Pepsi-Cola, United Fruit, General Mills and ABC Television (the last of these owned jointly in Nicaragua by BANIC and Somoza).

BANAMERICA meanwhile originated in the same period (1952) as a modern expression of traditional Conservative interests. Its major controlling elements were the families of the old Conservative oligarchies – the Pellas and the Chamorro – and it continued to centre on antiquated sources of economic power like sugar and livestock. In contrast to the dynamic BANIC group, BANAMERICA's importance withered during the course of the 1960s as a result of BANIC's ties to USAID and Somoza's monopoly of the expanded state bureaucracy, until Conservatism again resorted to a pact at the end of the decade to secure its declining economic status. Although BANAMERICA's ties to American capital were less overt, its survival also rested on the sales of the group's agricultural products and its political dependency on Somoza.

Conventionally, BANIC is described as the *Banco Liberal* and BANAMERICA as the *Banco Conservador*. In practice the distinction was not so rigid. Shared economic interests, political convenience and the peculiarities of the Nicaraguan state made for considerable inter-penetration as well as competition, not only between the two groups but also in partnership with Somoza. Whatever the relative strengths of BANIC and BANAMERICA, the new wealth of the post-war boom was dominated by the Somoza family.[21]

Regional Integration and Industrialisation

It may seem paradoxical that an economy dominated by such faithful servants of US interests was not marked by a higher level of direct American investment. There were, however, complex historical reasons for this: the late arrival of Nicaragua's 'Liberal Reform' and its interruption by military intervention, the country's sparse population and limited internal market, the absence of significant petrochemical or mineral reserves, the restricted role of US fruit multinationals (Standard Fruit had pulled out when its plantations were attacked by Sandino in 1931).

A new opening for American investors came in 1960 with the foundation of the Central American Common Market (MCCA).[22] Nicaragua, El Salvador, Honduras and Guatemala were its original signatories, with Costa Rica joining in 1962. Indeed a legal framework for favouring the regional expansion of US monopoly capital was fundamental to Washington's strategy in proposing the MCCA. Doors opened to foreign capital throughout the isthmus, but direct investment in Nicaragua remained the lowest among the market's five member countries. But the USA's stake in Nicaraguan capitalism could not be measured in strict dollar-for-dollar terms. Even if the quantity remained small, American companies' share of all foreign investment grew until it represented 80% of the $170-million total. 'We don't have the exact figure,' said Roberto Incer, president of the Banco Central. 'We don't impose restrictions on foreign capital by keeping records of it.'

Secrecy of operations was one of the many benefits enjoyed by US companies investing in Nicaragua. They were granted exemption from foreign exchange purchase restrictions, fiscal incentives, unlimited rights of transfer of capital and profits, free importation of machinery and export of finished products, and mutually beneficial credit arrangements through Somoza's development bank INFONAC.[23] American capital increased its foothold in various ways, establishing new enterprises and buying up traditional ones, squeezing out local firms, notably in the fishing and chemical industries, by persuading competitors to reduce their level of operations, and entering into joint investment ventures with Somoza and other Nicaraguan businessmen. Eventually 63 American transnationals and 70 subsidiaries were operating in Nicaragua: 76% of all foreign-controlled enterprises.[24] The most powerful were Exxon (an oil refinery), Hercules and Pennwalt (chemicals), United Brands (a plastics subsidiary), Nabisco and General Mills (food processing), Sears Roebuck and Co. (department stores), and US Steel, who operated the METASA plant jointly with Somoza.

The MCCA was born of a crisis of capitalist development, it produced a short artificial boom, and it ended in renewed crisis. As a development strategy it was closely linked with the Alliance for Progress, seeking industrialisation rather than agrarian reform, a gradual process of import substitution for regional markets, and the relocation of foreign and domestic capital in industry as a more reliable base for capital accumulation. The MCCA was designed to rationalise the local supply of agricultural and industrial products, and the transnationals who would supervise this process were attracted by the abundance of cheap labour. But the integration plan rapidly hit structural problems inherent in the local economies. All of them relied on vulnerable agricultural exports, and their domestic markets could not expand quickly enough to keep pace with the growth of new industry. Local firms had no option but to import machinery and parts from the USA for their assembly plants. Technological dependency and foreign debt escalated, especially at the expense of the weaker member countries, Honduras and Nicaragua. At the end of the decade local markets were saturated and investment declined sharply. These contradictions were heightened first by the Honduras-El Salvador conflict of 1969 and later by regional resentment at Somoza's protectionism — designed of course to protect his own industries.[25] In 1974 he closed Nicaragua's borders to textile imports from Guatemala and El Salvador on the grounds of market saturation. Both Nicaragua's principal textile factories, El Porvenir and Vestidos SA, were Somoza-owned.

The Common Market was briefly profitable for BANIC and BANAMERICA, but the economic spurt it brought could not be sustained. For a time too, it papered over inter-bourgeois conflicts which might have been generated if agrarian reform rather than industrialisation had been the cornerstone of US strategy. Instead, 'Nicaragua's major bourgeois groups fluctuate freely across the range of commercial, industrial, financial and agroexporting activities, blurring the demarcation between these different forms of capitalism, which in other contexts might indicate class fractions within the bourgeoisie.'[26] But this only applied to the dominant groups. Integration speeded up the tendency towards monopoly capitalism at the expense of weaker bourgeois sectors. Of the 600 industrial plants employing five or more workers, 136 generated 72% of total production, and only 28 (principally in chemicals, plastics and foodstuffs) accounted for 35% of industrial output in 1971. A mere 5% of the country's industrial output came from 13,000 small enterprises whose owners derived no benefit from *Somocismo* and who turned overwhelmingly against the system. Although manufacturing accounted for one-fifth of GDP by the 1970s, its emphasis on predominantly export-oriented light industry and assembly plants did nothing to break down economic dependency. Technological dependency, as well as bringing acute balance of payments problems, also meant capital-intensive industries. The MCCA did nothing to provide work for the new legions of Nicaragua's urban unemployed.

On paper, it looked good for Somoza. Manufacturing industry brought a growth rate of almost 10%, a figure exceeded in Latin America only by Brazil. But this growth rate, boosted briefly by high export prices during the Vietnam War, largely reflected the ability of Somoza's own industries to 'grow' with the stimulus of unsecured state credits. By the turn of the decade, the MCCA was in crisis, economic growth had declined, world prices for Nicaragua's agricultural products had fallen, and private investment had also declined. Somoza tried to compensate by increasing public spending, but he only succeeded in increasing unemployment and depressing real income among the working classes.

However, a new group of investors emerged. Those who had flocked to Central America in the '60s were the traditional multinationals. Those who came now were aggressive, unscrupulous speculators based in Miami, Las Vegas and Southern California, who had made quick fortunes in electronics, aerospace and defence contracts, real estate. Their patrons were Richard Nixon and Spiro Agnew; the brightest stars in their constellation Frank Sinatra and Robert Vesco, Howard Hughes and Bebe Rebozo. Their location in the 'gateway to the south' gave them close ties with organised crime and easy access to Central America. The military bourgeoisie, headed by Somoza and President Arana of Guatemala, became their natural allies in the region; ambassadors like Turner Shelton were useful local protectors; Managua and Guatemala City were transformed into the hub of their operations. Their Cuban friends in Miami brought their experience of 'dirty business' which had made Batista's Havana the corrupt playground of the American rich. With the collapse of the Central American Common Market's planned growth, Sunbelt dollars went into quick-profit service industries: hotels, casinos and tourism. The only prerequisite for their investments was the stability which military dictatorships could provide.

Reformism and the New Militarism

The sixteen years from Somoza Garcia's death to the Managua earthquake of 1972 brought three phases in the gradual disintegration of the dictatorship. Ten years of relative reformism under Luis Somoza's 1957-63 presidency and the 1963-67 civilian facade of the Liberal lawyer Rene Schick were followed by the first two presidential terms of Anastasio Somoza Debayle's full-blown militarism (1967 and 1971). These varying models of Liberal domination reflected on one hand the dictatorship's response to the changing demands of US policy and internal patterns of economic growth, and on the other a fundamental conflict of strategies between the two Somoza brothers. Luis believed that control of the Liberal Party offered the key to power in a state whose civilian bureaucracy would grow at the expense of its military apparatus, while his more realistic brother saw that the power of the dynasty would always ultimately reside in control of the National Guard.

From the first, 'Tacho' Somoza (he had now dropped the diminutive 'Tachito') had been groomed for a military career, becoming a major on graduation from West Point, taking command of the 1st Battalion of the *Guardia* and becoming the first Nicaraguan director of the Military Academy. Luis in contrast, had followed a civilian career, in charge of negotiations for US military assistance at the end of World War Two, then a Congressman, and finally President of Congress. With the death of their father, Luis was designated presidential candidate for the 1957 elections. Anastasio meanwhile showed his concept of state power by unleashing the National Guard on opponents and arresting hundreds of dissidents including Pedro Joaquin Chamorro. His excesses led the Conservatives to boycott the elections. Throughout the early years of the Luis Somoza presidency, dissident Conservatives continued to attack the regime, resorting to arms on numerous occasions including the invasion of Olama y los Mollejones in 1959 and the seizure of the Diriamba and Jinotepe barracks in 1960. For a spell, the *Guardia's* worst excesses were held in check by Luis, and Tacho was outraged at the lenient treatment given to captured opponents.

The latter half of the presidency of Luis brought economic modernisation, a reduction of the military budget, increased foreign investment and even a degree of press freedom, despite long periods of martial law. A climate of limited democracy was in tune now with Washington's aims in Nicaragua, and it was US policy after the Cuban Revolution which brought to a head the conflicting strategies of the two brothers. As the new Castro Government made its first moves to expropriate US property on the island, first the Eisenhower and then the Kennedy administration rushed to stifle the first hint of a workers' state in the Caribbean. Kennedy inherited, and approved, a plan for direct military attack against Cuba at Playa Giron in 1961 (the Bay of Pigs invasion) and received enthusiastic support from the Somozas. But when the invasion turned to fiasco, Washington produced a strategy of permanent counter-revolution, intervention as a system. Nicaragua's history made it an ideal test case for the subtler new US policy of repression through a blend of social reform and counter-insurgency. In a matter of months in 1961 and 1962, 'developmental' agencies sprang up along with co-ordinated military programmes. First came the Alliance for Progress and the Peace Corps in 1961, then the Agency for International Development (AID) and the International Police Academy in 1962, to be followed by the Central American Common Market in 1963 and the Central American Defence Council (CONDECA) in 1964. AID appealed to Luis; CONDECA to Anastasio. It was a unique combination of all forms of US support for the dictatorship. The new programmes were designed to bring economic growth through industrial expansion and regional integration; a political and ideological clampdown on peasant radicalism through limited agrarian reform and 'civic action' schemes; military support through US-supervised counter-revolutionary terror in the countryside.

With industrial growth and economic diversification, the corresponding expansion of the state bureaucracy was at the heart of Luis's strategy to build a 'bridge to democracy' (his own phrase). The new state might provide conditions favourable to a long-lived civilian regime, since the economic interests of all sectors of the bourgeoisie now depended on their co-operation with the new state agencies like INFONAC. This was the trap which the bourgeoisie could not avoid. *Somocismo* kept them marginal, but they relied on *Somocismo* for economic survival. When Luis became the only Somoza to hand over power voluntarily, in 1963, he bequeathed an apparently healthy economy to his successor, the Liberal lawyer Rene Schick. From 1960 to 1963, Nicaragua's GDP showed an average annual growth rate of

8.4%, compared with a figure of only 1.9% for the preceding decade.[27]

Schick showed little desire for independent action, and while he held nominal executive power, real control continued to lie with Luis (through the Party) and Tacho (through the National Guard). Among Schick's few initiatives were an attempt to subordinate the National Guard to the state bureaucracy, and his government — with Luis's approval and to Tacho's fury — even took the unprecedented step of punishing abuses of power by serving military officers. As the MCCA foundered, the Schick Government proved as incapable as its Alliance for Progress counterparts elsewhere of carrying through the reforms it proposed. The reformist path which appealed so little to Tacho was already crumbling when Luis died of a heart attack in 1967, finally resolving the contradiction within the family in favour of Tacho's intransigent militarism; he had himself installed as president the same year after farcical elections.

The bourgeois opposition had been given a little breathing space to regroup during the Schick years, but any hope the Conservatives might have had of regaining political ground was obliterated by the manner in which Somoza Debayle came to power.

The 1967 Massacre

When Anastasio Somoza Debayle presented his candidacy for the 1967 elections, the opposition regrouped itself into the first of a number of coalitions which would mirror the shifting balance of bourgeois forces throughout the next decade. Conservatives, Independent Liberals and Christian Democrats formed the Union Nacional Opositora (National Union of Opposition: UNO) to support the candidacy of Dr Fernando Aguero. The Socialist Party threw itself energetically behind their campaign, insisting that the working class should stand firm behind the unity of the bourgeois opposition. At first the opposition seemed genuinely to believe that Somoza would quietly hand over power if defeated in 1967. But Tacho had never had the slightest intention of relinquishing control. Months before the election he had set about one of the family's regular purges of the National Guard and consolidation of the local power structure of their PLN. At the same time he relied on his new paramilitary shock-force AMROCS to carry out terrorist attacks against the opposition.

Sections of the opposition leadership, among them Pedro Joaquin Chamorro and others attracted by the new wave of Latin American Christian Democracy, came to realise that Somoza's control of the electoral machinery left them with no chance of coming to power through the ballot box. So they organised a mass demonstration to march on the Presidential Palace in Managua. On 22 January 1967, 60,000 people turned up, some armed. In an interview in 1978, the Sandinista leader German Pomares remembered how the episode further discredited the traditional opposition and placed the seal on the political weakness of the bourgeoisie as a force for social change:

'The Conservatives called the people to a demonstration where they said they would hand out arms to overthrow Somoza. But when the demonstration began, they didn't hand out the arms and the National Guard massacred them.'[28]

The FSLN's reading of the Conservative strategy was that they would convince the General Staff of the National Guard to mount a coup against Somoza. This in turn would provoke a popular uprising and military intervention by the Organisation of American States (OAS) along the lines of the invasion of the Dominican Republic two years earlier. The 'free' elections which would then follow would – in the fantasy of Conservative politicians – bring to power a government formed by the bourgeois opposition, under OAS supervision.[29]

What happened was very different. The National Guard opened fire on the demonstrators with machine-guns and tanks, with Somoza himself directing operations from the airforce base outside the city. Official figures put the number killed at 201, but National Guard sources privately admitted at least 600 casualties in the massacre. Opposition leaders including Chamorro were rounded up and jailed. The episode was a political catastrophe for the bourgeoisie. Its talk of an insurrection, whose only purpose was to create social chaos to justify an OAS intervention, could scarcely have been more cynical. The influence of the Conservative Party over the people fell into a sharp decline. They would never again be able to mobilise the masses in the same way. At the same time, some sectors of the bourgeoisie became radicalised by the January massacre and showed their first hints of sympathy for the revolutionary alternative of the FSLN.

The election which followed was also a predictable disaster for the disarrayed opposition parties, and Somoza was declared the winner by the traditional huge majority: this time 70% of the popular vote. In April Luis Somoza died, and the dynasty returned to state terrorism as the only effective means of prolonging family control. By now, with the breakdown of reformist government and the crisis of regional economic development, the contradictions of bourgeois rule in Nicaragua were substantially greater. The FSLN too, as we shall see, was beginning to pose its first serious threat in the mountains of the north, and the third of the Somozas moved swiftly to break both bourgeois and popular opposition. This meant asserting his regional military supremacy within CONDECA, modernising the National Guard and guaranteeing its absolute loyalty to him personally. His strategy rested on his old understanding that control of the Guard was the cornerstone of state power.

Notes

1. Millett, *Guardianes de la Dinastia,* pp. 234-5.
2. Jesus Miguel Blandon, *Entre Sandino y Fonseca Amador* (Managua,

Impresiones y Troqueles, 1980), pp.14-24.

3. Carlos Fonseca Amador, *Nicaragua — Hora Cero* (Havana, Tricontinental, 1969).
4. See Ian H. Birchall, *Workers Against the Monolith* (London, Pluto Press, 1974); especially pp.36-7, 217-18.
5. *La Estrella de Panama*, 6 March 1947.
6. For a full account of the 1947 election and the coup against Arguello, see Eduardo Crawley, *Dictators Never Die* (London, Hurst, 1979), pp.105-8.
7. Jose Benito Escobar, *El Principio del Fin* (Managua, SENAPEP, 1979), p. 25.
8. Rigoberto Lopez Perez, letter to his mother from San Salvador, 4 September 1956.
9. *New York Times*, 20 July 1979.
10. Lopez *et al., La Caida del Somocismo . . .* , p. 347.
11. Wheelock, *Imperialismo y Dictadura*, pp.158-69.
12. According to NACLA (*op. cit.*), Somoza paid only $50 in taxes in 1974.
13. Viktor Morales Henriquez, *Los Ultimos Momentos de la Dictadura Somocista* (Managua, Editorial Union, 1979), pp.35-6.
14. Based on conversations with Ministry of Planning officials, Managua, 1979.
15. For a fuller, but still incomplete list, see Lopez *et al., op. cit.,* pp. 347-9.
16. Bell (ed.), *Nicaragua: An Ally Under Siege*, pp. 114-15.
17. Adolfo Gilly, *La Nueva Nicaragua — Antimperialismo y Lucha de Clases* (Mexico City, Editorial Nueva Imagen, 1980), p. 28.
18. Ortega, *50 Anos de Lucha Sandinista,* p. 88.
19. *Comercio Exterior* (Mexico City), March 1976, p. 302.
20. *Ibid.*
21. Wheelock, *op. cit.*, Chapter 6, analyses BANIC and BANAMERICA in detail.
22. Donald Castillo, 'Crisis Generalizada', in *Cuadernos del Tercer Mundo,* No. 29 (April-May 1979), pp. 13-17.
23. INFONAC: Instituto de Fomento Nacional (National Institute for the Promotion of Development).
24. Donald Castillo, *Tres Modelos de Penetracion de las Empresas Transnacionales en Centroamerica;* Mexico City, UNAM (mimeo), 1979.
25. *Latin America Economic Report,* Vol. VII, No. 39, 6 October 1978.
26. *Pensamiento Critico,* No. 1, March-May 1978.
27. *Comercio Exterior,* March 1976, p. 303.
28. *18 Anos de Sandinismo;* interview with German Pomares Ordonez (mimeo), 1978.
29. *Analisis Historico de la Situacion de Nicaragua* (mimeo, n.p.) 1978.

4. Protecting the Dynasty

The Army of Occupation

'Nicaragua is a country invaded by its own army, by the National Guard. It reminds me of Paris under the Nazi occupation, but here it's our own army which is the invader.'[1]

This is not the place for a detailed analysis of the origins of the National Guard: that is best left to Professor Richard Millett's meticulous study. But it is vital to understand something of the nature of the Guard: how the US conception of a 'professional, apolitical force' went against the very grain of Nicaraguan history (as so often, United States imperialism was marked as much by a colossal failure to understand the target country as by malice); why the complete removal of the Guard as an institution was always a condition of any minimum programme put forward by the FSLN; and why US negotiators clung to the survival of the Guard in some form even when Somoza himself had been ditched.

The idea of a US-trained and US-commanded force on the pattern of those being created in Haiti, the Philippines and the Dominican Republic first surfaced in 1911 and was approved by the Nicaraguan Congress in 1925. Its essence was that it should be apolitical, but by the time the Marines pulled out in 1933, the future of the new army was inextricably linked to that of Somocista Liberalism. The traditional weakness of the nation-state, the almost perpetual state of civil war between Liberals and Conservatives, pronounced regionalism, and the absence of an established national army: all these factors made the US proposal a nonsense. Without the destruction of oligarchical power, in a society where neither oligarchical faction could retain power except by force of arms, any armed force would clearly be the political instrument of one or other elite. American intervention undermined the creation of a national army still further. From the induction of the Guard's first 300 recruits, the force was shaped according to US wishes without consulting the Nicaraguan Government. Among other notorious features of the *Guardia*, the combination of military and police functions was an American idea. Even some Americans had doubts about the feasibility of an apolitical force: 'Whether the president is Conservative or Liberal, he will insist that the organisation be composed of men of his own party.'[2]

It was President Moncada who directly laid the basis for Somoza's conversion of the army into a praetorian guard, by trying to place it under his direct personal control and deploying it in an overtly political way against Sandino. Again, in the mid-1930s, one of the major sources of conflict between Somoza and President Sacasa was the latter's insistence that the *Guardia* should be restructured in accordance with the Constitution. As the Marines withdrew in 1933, US politicians declared that Washington had no further responsibility for the actions of the Nicaraguan military, a cynical acceptance that the National Guard could now be left to the dictates of Washington's 'emerging strong man' who was to safeguard American interests in Nicaragua. This particular facet of the Good Neighbour Policy left a widespread belief among Nicaraguans, according to Millett, that the USA had created a monster, let it loose, and then washed its hands of the consequences, knowing very well what those consequences would be.[3]

US Military Aid to Somoza

The National Guard remained the indirect military instrument of the State Department and the Pentagon, supported by appropriate levels of assistance. Already in 1944, Military Academy cadets were sent to Fort Gulick in the Canal Zone for the final year of their training, and Somoza was able to double his military expenditure in the early 1950s because Washington, alarmed by the 'communism' of Arbenz in Guatemala, opened a military mission in Managua in 1953 and a Military Assistance Programme (MAP) the following year. By 1963, an annual grant of $1.6 million (making Nicaragua the eleventh largest recipient of military assistance in the Americas) enabled the Guard to expand and smash the FSLN's first guerrilla *foco* on the Rio Coco. With the Cuban Revolution and the failure of the Alliance for Progress, Washington updated its old theory of US-trained 'constabularies' and opened the so-called School of the Americas in the Canal Zone to train Latin American officers. As Defence Secretary Robert MacNamara put it, it was of enormous value for the USA 'to have men in positions of leadership who have first-hand knowledge of the way North Americans do things'.[4] In addition, the installation of the US Southern Command at Quarry Heights in the Canal Zone provided a major stimulus for the creation of a regional defence umbrella to play an intermediate role between the Central American armies and the Pentagon. The result was the establishment of CONDECA, with the USA having full member status through its Southern Command and taking part in all joint military operations. Nicaragua had a special place in the scheme:
* From 1946 to 1975 Nicaragua received $23.6 million in MAP and miscellaneous grants and credits.
* From 1950 to 1975 4,897 National Guardsmen passed through US military training programmes; of these, 4,089 were trained locally, the

highest figure for any Latin American country.
* From 1970 to 1975 Nicaragua put 52 graduates through the US Army Infantry and Ranger School, Army Civil Affairs School, Military Police School and Army Command and General Staff School, again the highest figure for all Latin America.
* From 1970 to 1975 303 Nicaraguan students passed through the School of the Americas.[5]

As the threat to *Somocismo* grew, so did covert assistance in counter-insurgency. An ex-National Guardsman tells this story: 'Thirty German shepherd dogs had come into the country. Each trained dog cost 5,000 dollars. They were brought in at the suggestion of the North American Gunter Wagner, who had served in Vietnam. This agent of the CIA arrived in Nicaragua at the request of Anastasio Somoza Debayle, who immediately awarded him the rank of colonel. He entered the country under AID cover, assigned as an advisor to the National Police. He restructured the security service and introduced new methods of torture. In reward for his work, Somoza made him a rich man.'[6]

Regional Control and Somoza's Side of the Bargain

As the symbiotic relationship between the USA and the National Guard deepened, *Somocismo* emerged as the staunchest ally of North American imperialism in Central America and the lynchpin of CONDECA's system of regional repression. There could be no pretence that CONDECA was designed to meet external aggression — there has been none since its inception — and CONDECA did nothing to stop the only international conflict in the region since 1964, the brief 1969 'soccer war' between Honduras and El Salvador, despite the fact that one of the organisation's founding principles was the suppression of rivalries between national armies which might weaken the strategic defence of the region. From the beginning, Guatemala and Nicaragua (having the strongest guerrilla movements) were the principal targets for CONDECA operations, and even the relatively mild Conservative incursions from Costa Rica had convinced Somoza of the need to secure his borders by destroying revolutionary groups in neighbouring countries by means of joint CONDECA manoeuvres.

The tradition of providing National Guard support to the USA had already been well established by Somoza Garcia. As early as 1950 he had offered troops to fight in Korea, and two years later was plotting with the Truman administration to overthrow the progressive Guatemalan Government, eventually allowing the overt use of Nicaraguan territory by CIA agents and Guatemalan exiles for the overthrow of President Jacobo Arbenz, who had enraged the United States by expropriating United Fruit Company lands as part of his agrarian reform programme.[7] Even before the guerrilla struggle of Fidel Castro in Cuba, Luis Somoza was selling arms to the Batista dictatorship, and strong economic and military links with Cuban exiles remained after the Revolution. Anti-Castro Cubans were allowed to organise military training camps in Nicaragua and were given economic incentives which established Managua, with Miami, as the twin poles of the Cuban mafia network. Cubans cornered the cigar industry in Esteli, and the Cuban Eddy Rodriguez, a close business associate of Somoza's, was awarded lucrative contracts for planning the rebuilding of post-earthquake Managua. The paranoia of the Somozas that Fidel was behind every Nicaraguan opposition movement even extended to the Conservative adventures of Pedro Joaquin Chamorro.

The most notorious episode in US-Nicaraguan collaboration was of course the enthusiastic offer of support for the Bay of Pigs invasion in 1961, in which the exile force put together by John F. Kennedy launched its bombing raids from a Nicaraguan air-base codenamed 'Happy Valley' and used the Atlantic Coast town of Puerto Cabezas as the departure point for its flotilla of landing craft. Four years later, when direct military intervention became an embarrassment to the USA as it did after the Marine invasion of the Dominican Republic, President Johnson resorted to a new military tactic, the creation of an 'Inter-American Peacekeeping Force' under the cover of the Organisation of American States. Again Somoza responded eagerly, despatching a National Guard contingent commanded by Julio Gutierrez, the Guard officer who 14 years later was to be proposed by the USA as an additional member of the Junta of National Reconstruction during the 1979 insurrection! Finally, inevitably, Somoza offered the USA counter-insurgency troops for use in the Vietnam War. The offer came in late 1967 after the defeat of the FSLN *guerrilla* at Pancasan and had the dual advantage of providing the USA with recently proven anti-guerrilla troops and giving the National Guard the chance of firsthand combat experience supervised by the masters of the art of counter-insurgency. To Somoza's chagrin, the offer was refused, but he continued to admire the methods of the USA in Vietnam and made extensive use of American war veterans and South Vietnamese mercenaries in the later war against the Sandinistas.

After 1964 Guatemala, El Salvador and Nicaragua joined forces for more than a dozen counter-insurgency operations by CONDECA,[8] and, although Honduras distanced itself from CONDECA after its 1969 war with El Salvador, the right-wing dictatorship of Policarpo Paz Garcia in the late 1970s brought Honduras back into the fold as FSLN actions in Nicaragua increased. For the US Southern Command, CONDECA proved an excellent instrument. It was politically more convenient for local forces to assume the old US role of regional policeman, and although Panama and Costa Rica resisted American pressure to upgrade their observer status in joint manoeuvres, anti-guerrilla strategies in Central America were in general standardised. Counter-insurgency operations were directly linked in to the CIA through US military missions in each country, and CONDECA brought the USA one further benefit: the right to use the territory of any member country as a base for future attacks on Cuba. The direct control of CONDECA by the USA was most clearly demonstrated after the 1972 Managua earthquake, when the

49

American military mission, in conjunction with the Guatemalan dictator
Carlos Arana Osorio, brought in US, Honduran and Salvadorean troops to
maintain 'stability' during the brief breakdown of National Guard control.
It was the second collaboration that year between Somoza and Arana: in
March 1972 they had personally directed military operations against
Salvadorean rebels.

Arana was a business associate as well as a military ally, and it would be
false to suppose that Somoza's use of the Guard outside Nicaragua's frontiers
was motivated exclusively by loyalty to US military interests. His father had
established a flourishing cattle-smuggling operation from Costa Rica in the
1940s – one sound reason for sending Nicaraguan troops to support the
Picado Government during the 1949 Costa Rican civil war. From these
humble beginnings Somoza investment in the region had grown to an
estimated $30 million in Guatemala alone, principally in real estate and hotels
and often in partnership with Cuban exile speculators. Furthermore, the
Somozas' regional economic power was extended by their control of regional
trade and ownership of the national airline LANICA, the shipping line
MAMENIC and the Gulf of Fonseca ferry linking Nicaragua and El Salvador.

The Military, the Family, and the State

The effective use of the *Guardia* as a defender of Somoza's economic
interests directly reflected the development of the military caste in Nicaragua,
the unique relationship between the military and state power which made
the *Guardia* capable of exceptional barbarity against its own people as the
Somocista state crumbled. There was never any danger that the FSLN would
fall into the Chilean trap of trusting in the 'professionalism' and independence of the armed forces: without the destruction of the National Guard as
an institution there could be no removal of the Somoza state.

Anastasio Somoza Garcia had converted the Guard into a personal instrument through an institutionalised blend of privilege, corruption and intimidation, and the growth of the Somoza state was determined by the consolidation of the Guard. By 1939 the model was complete, a date which coincided with the internal reorganisation of the Liberal Party. An enormous
quota of state power had been amassed by the Guard over the previous
decade: first military control of communications, then internal revenues
and the railways, and later the postal service, immigration, the health service,
liquor sales and prostitution, permits for all arms imports, including even
industrial dynamite. Loyalty to Somoza was a prerequisite for the upper
ranks, and any officer who became too popular was transferred or dismissed
before he could become a threat, a system perfected by the 1948 constitutional amendments which gave Somoza sole power over promotions and
transfers. Mass retirements, often a whole year's promotion from the Military
Academy, were commonplace, and senior officers taken off active service
received a full pension and a guaranteed job in the state bureaucracy or a

Somoza-controlled industry, with ample opportunity for tax evasion and perhaps the gift of a farm thrown in. Expertise was no criterion for Guard officers looking for work in the government: 'Over half the directors of the National Bank are retired officers whose knowledge of banking could be written on the head of a very small pin.'[9] Enforced retirements continued as a means of control until the end – after the September 1978 insurrection 30 of the Guard's 35 senior officers were pensioned off. Personnel changes were especially frequent at election time: loyalty to the ritual fraud was essential, as the *Guardia* was in charge of vote-counting.

The cultivation of family members for military leadership after spells at West Point or Sandhurst was crucial to the Somoza strategy. As well as the supreme post of *Jefe Director*, they paid special attention to the command of combat units whose loyalty had to be unquestionable. Somoza's half-brother Jose took charge of armoured columns and his son Anastasio Somoza Portocarrero was given command of the crack Escuela de Entrenamiento Basico de Infanteria (Basic Infantry Training School: EEBI) when it was set up in 1978, aggravating an already acute split between elite troops and ordinary soldiers. Although the $75 a month of a private was relatively good pay in the late 1970s, Guard salaries were traditionally kept low as an incentive for troops to supplement their income through illegal activities. The professionalisation of the military originally intended by the USA in the 1920s gave way to the purchase of loyalty. After his desertion from the Guard, Lt. Col. Guillermo Mendieta described this mentality: 'Somoza is a real godfather type. He can pass an ordinary soldier and say, "I hear your mama is sick." Then he'll reach into his pocket and peel off thousand dollar bills and say, "This is for the air-fare and this is for the clinic in Miami." You cannot talk against him, but you feel that if he likes you he'll never let you down.'[10] A local version of the American Dream ran through the Guard, the constant, pathetic hope of *campesino* recruits that they might one day rise to senior positions in an arbitrary system. But the officer ranks remained loyal because of their vested interest as a class in the Somocista state.

Military privilege and kickbacks from 'dirty business' became a way of life. Each rank carried with it a guaranteed fringe income from prostitution and extortion, with the lowest *raso* (private) making a few *cordobas* from on-the-spot fines and senior officers growing fabulously rich from appointment to the most lucrative jobs like provincial commanders, customs controllers and immigration officers. The *comandante* of an important town like Leon or Chinandega could count on $20,000 a month from bars, brothels, contraband, and traffic fines. Robbing peasant families, especially during counter-insurgency operations in the north, was considered a legitimate perk, and the robbery and rape of prostitutes were commonplace. Anti-guerrilla operations brought special rewards: not only did the Guard have the right to confiscate the homes of peasants massacred as Sandinista sympathisers during the 1974-7 state of siege, but counter-insurgency forces were virtually turned into mercenaries within their own army. Tours of duty (restricted to a maximum of six months) brought triple pay for officers, double pay for ordinary soldiers and bonuses for efficiency based on a simple head-count of those killed.

The *Guardia*'s privileged status gave them separate shops, schools and hospitals, exclusive residential areas like the suburbs of Las Colinas and Villa Fontana in the hills south of Managua, and subsidised food and clothing, including uniforms and boots produced in Somoza-owned factories. A military bourgeoisie grew rapidly, especially after the 1972 earthquake, a powerful elite which entered the war against the FSLN fighting not only for its life but for its class interests. With the destruction of Managua, members of the Guard were given priority for rehousing, and the custom was for soldiers to help themselves to whatever building materials they needed and carry them off in military trucks. Officers profited from the new state monopoly on building permits and import licences, while the lower ranks ran successful protection rackets to 'guard' damaged property. As outlying *barrios* sprung up in the wake of the earthquake, Guard officers moved in to corner the concessions for opening new bus routes to link working-class districts like Open 3 and Las Americas with the factories and commercial zones of the dismembered city.

The upsurge of FSLN activities and the spectacular new opportunities for graft among the officer class opened up serious rifts within the Guard: not threats to the loyalty of the elite, who profited hugely from the system, but a growing resentment among the lower ranks as they came to realise that upward mobility was largely a myth. Treatment of *rasos* by their superiors was appalling, and the Frente Sandinista was able to grasp and exploit this weakness in the military, demanding salary increases for common soldiers to 500 *cordobas* (then $71) a month as one of their conditions for freeing hostages taken in a successful commando attack on the house of a leading Somocista in 1974 (see below). FSLN *comandante* Tomas Borge gave his own view of the demoralisation which he had witnessed among junior Guardsmen while in prison: 'They complain bitterly about the discrimination of which they are victims, the privileges enjoyed by officers, and the way they are treated: low salaries, constant confinement to barracks, the danger of losing their lives, faced with the growing combativity of the people.'[11] Some began to desert.

By the time of the final insurrection, it was clear that Somoza's transformation of the *Guardia* into an instrument of personal power had built serious contradictions into the military machine. There were acute divisions between officers and men; the importance of a high kill-ratio as a means of securing promotion had left the National Guard adept at massacring peasants but ineffective in rooting out the FSLN. And the concentration on family-controlled elite units like the 2,000-strong EEBI made for poor combat readiness among the remaining 5,500 ordinary troops.

An Army Within an Army

The exaggerated need for elite units was a natural consequence of Somoza's failure to destroy the FSLN, as we shall see, through traditional counter-insurgency. The methods of counter-revolution are familiar from South East Asia to Latin America, and Nicaragua was a textbook case of the crude application of violence beneath a veneer of cosmetic reform projects. The road map of modern Nicaragua is like a diagram of the counter-revolution. The Americans began it, building new roads through the mountains of Las Segovias in 1929 to improve local surveillance and mop up a potentially hostile labour force by offering employment. Eisenhower continued the tradition, giving $4.5 million in aid for Nicaragua's only serviceable road to the remote eastern *departamento* of Zelaya, a stretch between Managua and the town of Rama. The Guard refined the technique in the years after the FSLN's first major guerrilla operations, linking Matagalpa with the regional command post and concentration camp of Waslala. They drove another road through to the village of Matiguas, this time passing through the zone of heaviest guerrilla activity around the mountain of Pancasan and causing a steep rise in land values which encouraged the settlement of new *latifundistas*. The *Guardia* populated the region with *jueces de mesta* — part local magistrates, part informers — and resettled peasants by force in the remote and unproductive southern region of Nueva Guinea, a US-inspired 'agrarian reform' programme which allowed for controlled colonisation and the formation of counter-revolutionary peasant recruits.[12]

The guerrilla zones also became the centre for the Somoza regime's vaccination and birth-control programmes, including the notorious 'Friends of the Americas' programme, under which US volunteers were alleged to be introducing sterilising agents in the guise of anti-polio vaccines. To Nicaraguans, such projects were widely seen as a way of implementing President Lyndon Johnson's dictum that it was cheaper to kill a guerrilla before s/he was born.[13]

A $14-million loan from the United States allowed Somoza to finance the most famous of Nicaragua's programmes of counter-revolution through reform: the so-called Institute of Peasant Welfare, INVIERNO, whose emphasis was on technical assistance, cooperatives and marketing schemes, and the creation of peasant leaders crudely bought with gifts of transistor radios and other trappings of North American civilisation. Despite the considerable sums invested, these 'civic action' programmes failed to achieve two of their key objectives: support from the local population for the armed forces, and the backing of the bourgeoisie. In Nicaragua, hatred for the Guard was too deeply rooted, and the bourgeoisie too fragmented to commit itself decisively to US reform plans. It was impossible for an army like the National Guard to pretend to work among the people. Its whole history and formation had driven it in the opposite direction.

Somoza's only answer, in the face of a revolutionary challenge which continued to grow, was to create elite units indoctrinated with an anti-popular, anti-national mentality. The doctrine of national security took firm root in Nicaragua, showing itself as an extraordinary paranoia among the soldiers at any sign of opposition activity, no matter how peaceful.

Nicaraguans came to fear for their lives from the nervousness of troops who were always liable to open fire without reason. To anyone visiting Nicaragua after the Revolution, this is the most obvious change. The hatred and fear, which existed before, of an army whose only logical response was massive and indiscriminate violence: all this has gone, replaced by a new trust between the people and the forces of the FSLN.

It was common for officers in charge of peasant massacres in the north of the country to have the nicknames of wild animals – *'El Chacal'* ('the Jackal') or *'El Tigre'* ('the Tiger'). Elite units like *'Los Cascabeles'* ('the Rattlesnakes') travelled around in army jeeps stencilled with a skull and crossbones. Somoza revived the shock-force of the 1930s in the shape of the paramilitary group AMROCS,[14] and the new state terrorism was underwritten with doubled expenditure on the Servicio de Inteligencia Militar (SIM) and the Oficina de Seguridad Nacional (OSN) between 1970 and 1975. The orange jeeps of the hated BECAT (Brigadas Especiales Contra Actos de Terrorismo) swarmed in the streets of every city, accompanied by 400 plain-clothes *orejas* (informers: literally 'ears') in Managua alone.

In June 1978 the FSLN's magazine *Lucha Sandinista* reported the formation of the *Guardia*'s supreme elite force, the EEBI, with an initial budget of $2.3 million: an army within an army, which was to serve as the vehicle for the ascent to absolute power of Anastasio Somoza Portocarrero, son of the dictator, and like his father nicknamed 'Tachito', or *'El Chiguin'* – a Nicaraguan word meaning 'tough little kid'. The autonomous control which Somoza Portocarrero, while still in his twenties, was granted over the new corps alarmed even senior officers of the Guard. He cultivated an intense personal loyalty among EEBI recruits, who enjoyed the Guard's best living conditions and most modern weapons. They had cinemas, new recreation facilities and air-conditioned quarters against the intense Managua heat. They were armed with M-16s and Israeli Uzi sub-machineguns, instead of the ubiquitous Garand rifles of the other troops. Combat skill was particularly rewarded in the EEBI, to such an extent that soldiers were rumoured to fight over Sandinista corpses for the bonuses handed out by Somoza's son to his favourite soldiers, who could aspire to the highest honour of becoming *boinas negras* (black berets). Hatred of the people was a matter of systematic propaganda, from the EEBI's magazine *El Infante* (The Infantryman), with its pictures of Nazi troops and swastikas, to the call-and-response drills which Managuans claimed could be heard a full kilometre away. Under the direction of the American mercenary Michael 'Mike the Merc' Echannis and his assistant, the South Vietnamese Nguyen Van Nguyen, two of these became especially notorious as training routines:

'Quien es el enemigo de la Guardia?' ('Who is the enemy of the Guard?')
'El pueblo!' ('The people!')
'Quien es el padre de la Guardia?' ('Who is the father of the Guard?')
'Somoza!'
'La Guardia arriba!' ('Up with the Guard!')

'El pueblo abajo!' ('Down with the people!');
and
'Quienes somos?' ('Who are we?')
'Somos tigres!' ('We are tigers!')
'Que comen los tigres?' ('What do tigers eat?')
'Sangre!' ('Blood!')
'Sangre de quien?' ('Whose blood?')
'Sangre del pueblo! ('The blood of the people!')

The unpredictable, elitist violence of the EEBI led to its being an object of fear even among other National Guard divisions. When EEBI units were sent in to relieve beleaguered Guard posts during the 1979 Managua insurrection, a resident picked up this message on short-wave radio: 'Attention all mobile units in Monsenor Lezcano and Las Americas [two -Managua *barrios*]. The Combat Battalion and the EEBI are headed in your direction. Take cover immediately in your vehicles so they don't mistake you for the enemy, because these people are coming through like a cyclone and killing anything that moves.'

Israeli Arms for the Military Elite

When it became an embarrassment for the United States to continue direct arms supplies to Nicaragua, a surrogate rapidly emerged, and from his position as commander of the EEBI Somoza Portocarrero was instrumental in getting the family's reward for 30 years of loyalty to Zionism in the United Nations and other international forums. The expanding Israeli armaments industry found an ideal market in Nicaragua. From Mexico, the solidarity publication *Gaceta Sandinista* reported that in the second half of October 1978 the Somoza regime received large consignments of war materiel from Israel. The Israeli Government delivered anti-aircraft artillery and rockets, 500 Uzi sub-machineguns, 500 Galil assault rifles, bullet-proof vests, ammunition, mortars, military vehicles and four naval patrol boats. The consignment was received by Anastasio Somoza Portocarrero at the dictator's private airport on his estate at Montelimar.[15]

It was entirely appropriate that 'El Chiguin' should have taken delivery. By now he had acquired a reputation for managing arms deals independently, not only with Israel but with Spain and Argentina. The first Galil assault rifles to be sent to the EEBI had arrived without the knowledge of either his father or the General Staff of the National Guard.[16] The Israeli connection continued to the end. As late as April 1979, Israeli military technicians arrived to instal a mobile air-defence system, and in May Israeli ships landed a further consignment of light artillery, armoured cars, missile launchers, helicopters and transport vehicles as the Guard was dying on its feet.

Israel has been interested since the 1960s in penetrating the attractive Latin American arms market, signing successive arms supply contracts with the dictatorships of Chile, Argentina, Bolivia and Paraguay. According to the Stockholm International Peace Research Institute (SIPRI), Israel in the 1970s accounted for 81% of arms imported into El Salvador, and a staggering 98% of all those received by Nicaragua. Israel itself accounted for almost half of the $2.5 billion which the US extended in military aid during 1978, and took up observer status with the Inter-American Development Bank (IDB) and the Organisation of American States. Despite the ostensible pressure from the Carter administration that other Western governments should discontinue arms sales to Somoza, it was not difficult for the FSLN to conclude that United States imperialism continued to underpin the National Guard until the moment of its final collapse.[17]

Notes

1. Interview with Fernando Cardenal SJ in San Jose, Costa Rica, July 1978.
2. US Minister Eberhardt, 1926. See Richard Millett, *Guardianes de la Dinastia*, p. 69.
3. Millett op. cit., p. 234.
4. Quoted in *Cuadernos del Tercer Mundo*, No. 29, April-May 1979, p. 21.
5. NACLA: 'The Pentagon's Proteges: US Training Programmes for Foreign Military Personnel', *Latin America and Empire Report*, Vol. X, No. 1, January 1976.
6. J.A. Robleto Siles, *Yo Deserte de la Guardia Nacional de Nicaragua* (San Jose, EDUCA, 1979), p. 155.
7. Susanne Jonas, 'Anatomy of an Intervention', in NACLA, *Guatemala* (New York, 1974), pp. 57-73.
8. The most important of these CONDECA joint operations were code-named 'Fraternidad' (1964), 'Falconview' and 'Aguila I' (1965), 'Nicarao' (1966), 'Aguila II' (1970), 'Pina' (1971), in which militant Honduran peasant organisations were destroyed, and 'Aguila VI' (1976), in which South Vietnamese counter-insurgency advisors were used.
9. Richard Millett, quoted in *Newsweek*, 16 July 1979.
10. *Newsweek*, 16 July 1979.
11. Interviewed in *El Dia*, Mexico City, 8 September 1978.
12. On Somoza's agrarian reform programme, see *La Prensa*, Managua, 30 December 1977, article entitled 'La Reforma Agraria: Farsa y Gran Pinata.'
13. Doris Tijerino, *Inside the Nicaraguan Revolution* (translated by Margaret Randall), (Vancouver, New Star Books, 1978), pp. 137-9.
14. AMROCS: Asociacion de Militares Retirados, Obreros y Campesinos Somocistas (Association of Somocista Retired Soldiers, Workers and Peasants).
15. *Gaceta Sandinista* (Organo del Comite Mexicano de Solidaridad con el Pueblo de Nicaragua), Year III, No. 3, September-December 1978.
16. *Ibid.*
17. For an extensive article on Israeli arms sales to Latin America, see *Latin America Weekly Report*, WR-80-19, 16 May 1980.

5. The 1972 Earthquake and After: *Somocismo* in Crisis

Somocismo in the 1970s

'There are very few unchanging principles governing the relations between nations. Some however do exist, and for the Americans the Monroe Doctrine is one of the most enduring of them all.' (James Theberge, US Ambassador to Nicaragua from 1975 to 1977).

If the 1960s was the period of the Somoza dictatorship's greatest strength, the next decade brought its progressive decomposition. The story of *Somocismo* in the 1970s is at least in part the story of two American ambassadors. Anastasio Somoza Debayle's first presidential term already faced mounting difficulties: the rising influence of the FSLN and the establishment of its first urban bases; economic difficulties; the memory of the massacre of hundreds of opponents in the 1967 election campaign; and even hints of discontent among younger officers of the Guard who turned their eyes south to the nationalist experiments of the Peruvian generals.

The election of Richard Nixon to the White House was a great boost for Somoza. Nixon remembered Nicaragua as the rare Latin American country which had given a friendly reception to his vice-presidential tour in 1958, and in 1970 he appointed an ambassador, Turner Shelton, who became an overt propagandist for *Somocismo* and a close personal friend of the dictator. Shelton too was influential in opening a new model of direct US investment in Nicaragua. NACLA described him in these terms: 'Turner Shelton, a personal friend and campaign contributor to President Nixon, was about to be retired from the foreign service when Nixon appointed him ambassador to Nicaragua in 1970. From 1966 to 1970 he had been consul-general in Nassau where he had ties with Bebe Rebozo and Howard Hughes: in fact, it was Shelton who arranged a personal meeting between Hughes and Somoza when Hughes first came to Nicaragua in 1972.'[1] Shelton, whose portrait still graces the Nicaraguan 20-*cordoba* bill, followed in the tradition of Thomas Whelan (ambassador from 1951 to 1961): he spoke not a word of Spanish. But Shelton did little to impress the State Department, and he failed to survive the downfall of the Nixon administration despite Somoza's strenuous efforts to keep him in the job. Even for the Ford presidency,

Shelton's total identification with a corrupt regime was an embarrassment. The State Department needed a change of image, a more subtle touch in its relations with Managua. Washington's choice was James Theberge, not a career diplomat but a right-wing academic, author of *Russia in the Caribbean* and *The Soviet Presence in Latin America*. Theberge continued to encourage cooperativism in the north of the country (it was during his ambassadorship that INVIERNO was created) while the *Guardia* unleashed counter-revolutionary terror on an unprecedented scale during the first two years of his service, massacring as many as 3,000 peasants in suspected guerrilla zones. Back in Managua, Theberge looked for ways of tranquillising the newly active 'civic' opposition, hoping in particular that his track record would allow him to prise the Moscow-line Socialist Party and its trade unions away from Pedro Joaquin Chamorro's recently founded UDEL (Union Democratica de Liberacion) coalition. The new ambassador implied no change of policy, merely a modification of the tactics required to keep Somoza in power. Although Shelton's personal inclinations might have encouraged the regime to survive through brute force, there was a logical continuity in the policies of the two ambassadors. Washington recognised major structural weaknesses in the dictatorship: the strategy to strengthen it was twofold. First unite the Liberals and the Conservatives to consolidate bourgeois rule; then split the opposition by drawing the bourgeoisie away from the left, giving Chamorro and his like room to breathe and a sympathetic ear. The first part of the strategy fell to Shelton, the second to Theberge.[2]

Somoza's re-election in 1971 had not run smoothly, but Shelton stepped in to help. As so often before, a pact was the answer, this time with the Conservative leader Fernando Aguero. It was the final breakdown of legitimacy of the two-party system, and the opposition which agreed to be bought off in this way was now no more than a rump, known dismissively to Nicaraguans as the *'zancudo'* (mosquito) Conservatives. The Shelton-inspired deal raised Conservative participation in the legislature to 40% and installed a Constituent Assembly which was to reform the Constitution yet again and pave the way for Somoza's re-election in 1974. Its most novel feature was the appointment of a triumvirate to govern from May 1972 to December 1974. Aguero took one seat as his reward, with the other two going to Somoza nominees. The dictator, needless to say, kept control of the National Guard and continued to exercise real power, representing Nicaragua as before as head of state in international forums. Bourgeois dissidence was unable to prevent the pact, but there was nothing the government or the USA could do to stem mounting political mobilisation among workers and students.

The Earthquake

A little after midnight on 23 December 1972, with the triumvirate only seven months old, the centre of Managua was torn apart by a massive earthquake. Up to 20,000 died, 75% of the city's housing and 90% of its commercial capacity was destroyed beyond repair, and damage was conservatively estimated by the United Nations at $772 million. Every contradiction of the Somoza regime was immediately heightened. Overnight, patterns of economic control and Somoza's relationship with the bourgeoisie were transformed. A boom in the construction industry brought new opportunities for speculation as well as an explosion in the size and militancy of the urban working class. In the aftermath of the earthquake, National Guard corruption was seen at its ugliest. The importance of the earthquake as a pivotal moment in the disintegration of *Somocismo* can hardly be overstated.

The true nature of the *Guardia* stood exposed. Officers led their men in systematic looting of the ruined capital and a complete breakdown of discipline meant that Somoza was unable to guarantee public order without the prompt arrival of 600 US soldiers and other Central American troops. Any remaining public respect for the military evaporated. Until the *Guardia* recovered its discipline, Managua residents described the city as under virtual American occupation, leaving an indelible impression of US troops storming through the devastated streets, shouting orders in English to a bewildered population and incinerating corpses with flamethrowers.[3] In its rush to get rich, the *Guardia* forgot all about guerrillas. A thriving black market sprang up, filled with stolen property and medical and food aid from overseas. One observer described the sale of goods donated by Catholic relief agencies and foreign governments in hastily opened shops staffed by the National Guard: 'Tinned food, clothing . . . you can even buy anything from a small electric generator to a water purifier, electric torches, pickaxes and spades, complete factory-sealed blood transfusion equipment. There are also shops selling goods from looted warehouses; in Chichigalpa, for example, where the military commander's wife looks after marketing goods stolen from the *Casa Mantica* in Managua.' *Guardia* demolition crews directed by Anastasio Somoza Portocarrero made off with anything they could shift: toilet fittings, furniture, street-lights, electric wiring. And unemployed rural labourers of Carazo and the north were pressganged to help in the so-called 'Civil Reconstruction Corps'.

Somoza described the earthquake as a 'revolution of possibilities', and certainly for members of the ruling elite the phrase was accurate enough. Paradoxically, the earthquake was a means of pulling the country out of its stagnation and inducing immediate economic growth, but at the cost of new economic distortion and an insoluble political crisis which went to the heart of bourgeois rule. The loans contracted for reconstruction projects brought an escalating foreign debt, and Somoza's increased tendency to stave off economic disaster by resorting to foreign loans was reflected in an external debt which shot up from $255 million in 1972 to more than $1 billion by 1978, half of it at interest rates above 8%.[4]

Somoza himself cornered the reconstruction of Managua. His company ESPESA took charge of demolition work; Inmuebles SA of real estate speculation; a host of other companies, generally with a monopoly, took on contracts for concrete, building materials, metal structures, roofing, asbestos, and plastics. Fifty new construction companies mushroomed, the most prominent controlled by the Somoza clan, and speculative property corporations threw together cheap housing (11,132 temporary homes in 1973 and 4,033 permanent ones),[5] which they resold at four or five times their original value. The streets were no longer paved with the traditional asphalt but with paving-stones (*adoquines*) from a Somoza factory using Somoza-produced cement. The quality of new housing was scarcely better than what had gone before. 'Our climate lends itself to good living without our needing to make massive investments in housing,' Somoza was later to tell *Le Monde* in a cynical 1978 interview.

Politicians like Alfonso Lovo Cordero of the ruling triumvirate were awarded building contracts even when lower tenders were submitted, and speculation with prime housing land became a national scandal. In one incident, Cornelio Hueck – President of the Constituent Assembly – bought up empty land earmarked for temporary housing for the homeless. Having paid $17,000, he resold the land two days later to the state housing bank for $1.2 million – the funds having been received from USAID.[6] But whatever private doubts the USA may have had, it was no time for niceties. Above all, the strong man had to be pulled out of the chaos. Although some of the aid which arrived was disinterested – like a Cuban hospital in Managua – the purpose of the vast American aid effort was clear: to shore up the dictatorship, and there was evidence that a large part of ostensibly humanitarian funds was placed at the disposal of the Pentagon. Even AID money not expressly designed to prop up the dictatorship ended up in Somoza's pockets because of the monopoly control he exercised over the reconstruction projects which that money paid for. The sums were large: $78 million from AID ($12.7 million in emergency grant assistance and a further $65.3 million in reconstruction loans) plus $54 million from the Inter-American Development Bank (IDB) – a striking contrast to the USA's later meagre initial response to the devastation of the 1979 war.

The earthquake accelerated the class struggle in Nicaragua. It came in the middle of a two-year drought which wrecked the production of staple food crops, bringing hunger to the countryside and a wave of peasant migration to the capital. The rapid growth in construction and related industries absorbed many of Managua's unemployed, causing a dramatic rise in numbers of the the urban proletariat. Rampant government corruption, coupled with longer working hours, lower wages, a generalised attack on working-class living standards, and the agitational work of the FSLN, all brought a corresponding rise in class consciousness. Organised working-class activity was on the increase, highlighted by *campesino* land invasions in the north and the big 1973 construction workers' strike led by the CGT, the trade union federation of the Socialist Party. The aftermath of the earthquake also introduced a new phrase into the vocabulary of the bourgeois opposition: *competencia desleal,* unfair or disloyal competition. The rules of the capitalist game, and with it the fragile consensus which held the dictatorial state together, had been broken.

A new phase of absolute power opened. The triumvirate survived in name but Somoza ruled by decree from the newly invented position of President of the National Emergency Committee. To comply with the new constitutional ruling that no serving military officer could stand for the presidency, Somoza gave up the title of *Jefe Director* of the National Guard and instead took the title of *Jefe Supremo* of the Armed Forces. The September 1974 election, which Somoza won with the traditional overwhelming majority over the traditional hand-picked Conservative opponent, was boycotted by a number of dissident bourgeois politicians including Pedro Joaquin Chamorro, who by now had organised an opposition coalition, UDEL. For their pains, 27 leaders of the boycott were arrested and deprived of their political rights until March the following year. But they did not give up. They filed charges with the Supreme Electoral Tribunal, a body composed of one representative of Somoza's Supreme Court, two of the Liberal Party and the guaranteed 40% minority of two Conservatives. The charge of fraud, bribery and coercion was dismissed out of hand, but the Tribunal's replies to the two charges of constitutional violation were remarkable for their candour. The accusation that Somoza's rule had been continuous, thereby infringing the Constitution, was quashed by citing the two-year rule of the figurehead triumvirate, and the Tribunal ruled that Somoza's new post as *Jefe Supremo* of the *Guardia* was purely administrative, and did not disqualify him from the presidency on the grounds of active military service. The Tribunal even admitted that the *Junta*'s February decree creating the post of *Jefe Supremo* had been specifically designed to allow Somoza's candidacy in September. It was a bizarre attempt to provide a legal fiction for a wholly discredited regime.

The Frente Sandinista had other more impressive ways of registering its disgust with *Somocismo*. On 27 December 1974 it launched a spectacular commando raid in Managua (described in Chapter 6). This was the catalyst for a new chapter of institutionalised repression. Within hours, Somoza decreed a state of siege, martial law, permanent military courts and press censorship, just as much to smash trade union militancy as to drive the FSLN into clandestinity and prevent the raid from having its desired impact on class consciousness and perhaps fusing two hitherto unconnected facets of the popular struggle – the guerrilla war and the open trade-union work of the PSN. The new repressive legislation might also allow all Nicaraguan capitalists to increase their profits by permitting super-exploitation of the workforce, a calculated move by Somoza to woo back some of the bourgeois support forfeited after the earthquake.

The emergency press laws were draconian. All newspaper copy had to be submitted to the National Guard before publication, and was sent back with all offending articles blocked out in red ink. An offending article was any which made reference to trade unions, labour disputes, allegations of defective public services, including transport, roads and housing conditions – precisely the issues which the mass movement was beginning to mobilise around in the *barrios*. The Church, whose acceptance of Somoza was fast waning, protested vigorously about the peasant massacres which were taking place under the blanket of press censorship: Somoza's only response was to extend censorship to include Church publications and radio broadcasts. Even US Ambassador Theberge acknowledged the scale of human rights violations, and with the election of Jimmy Carter in November 1976 and the ensuing 'Human Rights' policy of the US Government, Somoza's attempts to dismember the popular opposition led to grave doubts in Washington about the future viability of the dictatorship.

Somoza's repression of the mass movement was designed in part to restore favourable conditions for the capitalist class as a whole, but the result was the opposite. Within the bourgeoisie, contradictions merely deepened, and institutionalised terror frightened off every bourgeois group which preferred government by consensus. At the same time, the reign of terror of the mid-1970s failed to root out the popular movement led by the FSLN, and the basis for mass radicalisation grew. New possibilities for economic growth, by contrast, contracted. By the end of 1977, the combination of these three factors threw *Somocismo* into its acute final crisis.

From Class Dictatorship to Family Monopoly: The Crisis of Bourgeois Rule

Greed, theft, corruption and repression may have been the style of *Somocismo*. But until the 1972 earthquake the dynasty was not merely the arbitrary exercise of power by a single family. It would not have survived for so long without recognition from Washington and from Somoza's fellow Nicaraguan capitalists that the dictatorship was the most appropriate instrument for sustaining the power of private enterprise as a whole. Certainly there were contradictions within the bourgeoisie. BANIC, BANAMERICA and especially the smaller capitalists may have found the style at times unpalatable; but these bourgeois groups depended on *Somocismo* to destroy working-class organisation, to maintain the militarily imposed order within which they could go about their business of making profits. Until the post-earthquake period, divisions within the bourgeoisie were always secondary to class unity. At each critical stage of development the bourgeoisie relied on the Somozas: in the 1950s to profit from the cotton boom, in the 1960s to receive state finance for industrial development. They benefited directly from Somoza's relationship with the USA through the sales of their exports, and in specific instances the special friendship between Managua and Washington brought them rich pickings. With the US blockade of Cuba, for example, the businessmen of BANAMERICA joined Somoza in supplying the USA with Cuba's former sugar quota.

From its earliest days, Somoza power had rested on the family's ability to achieve dominance within the ruling class and then reach mutually beneficial agreements — political pacts on one hand, commercial alliances on the other

— with the remaining bourgeois sectors. Accepting these rules, the bourgeoisie grouped itself into BANIC and BANAMERICA, and flourished. With their consolidation, their need for Somoza grew. Agribusiness, commerce and industry were allotted, with each group enjoying certain preserves,[7] and the crude monopolistic control they exercised over the mass of the Nicaraguan people produced an increasingly violent class conflict which a unified bourgeoisie relied upon Somoza to suppress.

When the first serious cracks appeared in this consensus, the earthquake was the most visible cause, as Somoza's inroads into the construction industry trampled on traditional BANIC and BANAMERICA concerns. But the roots lay much deeper. The generalised economic decline of the 1970s reflected the inability of a dictatorial regime to sustain economic growth. The inevitable consequence was more acute capitalist competition, a revision of the rules of the game, and it was a competition which only one group had the power to win. Corruption of state power reached unacceptable levels, so that the Somoza clan was the only bourgeois group which could go on benefiting from the system. That is not to say that BANIC and BANAMERICA were put out of business: they remained extremely rich, but their possibilities of further growth were stifled. Only Somoza's share of the cake increased. Government credits increasingly favoured Somoza interests and foreign investors, while taxation only affected non-Somoza sectors. The bourgeoisie found itself in a profound contradiction: their most reliable power base was also cutting back its potential for expansion. Their dilemma was summed up by Comandante Jaime Wheelock of the FSLN, today Nicaragua's Minister of Agricultural Development: 'The crisis of the Nicaraguan bourgeoisie is summarised in its inability to resolve the contradictions of aggressive United States intervention in the economic sphere — since that intervention is indispensable and beneficial in the political and military sphere — and at the same time in its ineptitude at releasing the brake on its "free" business development represented by the enormous weight of investments of the Somoza clan, whose presence in political power, although dynastic, is its safest guarantee of maintaining the stability of the bourgeois regime.'[8]

The monopoly of power by one class was turning, inevitably, into monopoly by a single fraction of that class. The disintegration of economic interests in turn produced a break-up of party political interests. Both the main parties split,[9] and bourgeois groups began to seek alternative political formations such as the Union Democratica de Liberacion (UDEL). The fragmentation of the bourgeois consensus gave rise to pronounced nationalism among certain groups, making it possible for the Sandinistas later to take extensive bourgeois sectors with them — especially the most defenceless petty bourgeoisie — on a revolutionary path whose basis was nationalist and anti-imperialist. The FSLN knew, as did the more perceptive bourgeois dissidents, that a divided class could never lead the revolution, much less turn it into a bourgeois democratic one. Their flight from *Somocismo* accelerated in the three years of state of siege from 1974 to 1977, as peasant massacres and indiscriminate National Guard atrocities opened many eyes to the brutality of the regime. But many of the bourgeoisie's most vocal leaders made demands which would not have been out of place in the French Revolution, without appearing to realise that the national crisis could only be solved by transforming the entire bourgeois order. If they did realise, the prospect terrified them, for they could see that all their strikes and peaceful protests would never unseat Somoza. The force which would overthrow *Somocismo* – the organised working class and peasantry – potentially threatened the future of the bourgeoisie as a class. When they formulated their demands into the semblance of a political programme, it was not BANIC or BANAMERICA who led the attack, but groups like the development institute INDE, which represented the sectors worst hit by Somocista corruption and monopoly. Their aims were clear: the restoration of a state which would once again represent the whole of their class, based on the elimination of corruption in the administration, respect for the Constitution, and a 'professionalisation' of the National Guard under non-Somocista commanding officers. One INDE spokesman made a typical comment after the September 1978 insurrection: 'The problem is the man. He's taking over our market. We have no quarrel with anyone else or the system. Just get rid of him.'[11]

Disloyal Competition and Bourgeois Realignment

After the 1972 earthquake, the phrase on every businessman's lips was *'competencia desleal'*. Somoza was attacked not as a capitalist but as a dictator; not for exercising power against the interests of the Nicaraguan people, but for refusing to spread a little of it around among other capitalists. The most influential voice of this bourgeois discontent was the private enterprise group COSEP,[12] of which INDE was a member. COSEP was a federation of more than a dozen employers' groups representing almost all middle-class industrial and commercial interests. It was, and remains, a more effective spearhead of bourgeois interests than any of the centre or right-wing parties, although originally designed as a pressure group to give its members some of the economic privileges monopolised by the Somoza clan.[13]

In the decade after the 1967 election fraud and massacre, an enormous number of miniature political groupings of the Right and Centre emerged, made up in many cases of small nuclei of business associates with common economic interests and a very restricted constituency. For the most part, Somoza left them well alone, aware that they presented no real threat to his rule and complacent at the evidence they offered of the fragmentation of bourgeois hostility to his government. The private enterprise lobby held a national conference in March 1974, at which its limitations as a credible political opposition were made painfully clear. Although the conflicts of interest with Somoza required little discussion, these contradictions failed to produce any decisive action which the dictatorship would take seriously.

The old complaints of *competencia desleal* and demands for 'the removal of corruption and inefficiency from the public administration' were tossed back and forth, but no hard proposals emerged for an opposition strategy. The representatives of the private sector were just not politicians, although several of them — like INDE president Alfonso Robelo — were later turned into politicians by force of circumstance. In a country where the only political traditions were an institutionalised and discredited two-party system and militant popular resistance, the bourgeoisie lacked both a power base and a political background to guide their actions. Until the final crisis of the Somoza regime, their lack of political experience brought only indecision and disunity.

Some private enterprise groups were radicalised by the final economic collapse of the system after 1977 and were willing to join a concerted battle against Somoza, although not of course against the capitalist system as a whole. But while they added their numbers to the organised popular opposition, they did so far too late to assume any kind of dominance within that movement. These sectors, who bore the brunt of the effect of the economic crisis on the bourgeoisie, were above all small businessmen and not the representatives of large-scale finance capital, despite having commercial links in some cases with the big bourgeoisie of BANIC and BANAMERICA. They were small factory- and shop-owners, minor cotton producers of the northwest, entrepreneurs who had achieved some economic status with the post-earthquake building boom and now saw the bottom falling out of the construction market.

Some form of political coalition was the only answer for the bourgeois opposition, which had for once to take a firm political initiative even at the risk of any new organisation's fragility and contradictory composition. The response came in 1974 from a jumble of political and trade-union groups without a clear political programme. It brought together Conservative and Liberal Party dissidents, the old Independent Liberals of the PLI, the Social Christian Party and the Moscow-line PSN, the last two bringing with them their respective trade-union federations. Any effectiveness which the new UDEL coalition had was due as much as anything to the force of personality of its founder and leader Pedro Joaquin Chamorro, editor of *La Prensa* and a figure who commanded genuine popular appeal in the country.

The timing of UDEL's foundation was no accident. In the final days of 1974, the FSLN had carried out a spectacular commando raid on the home of a senior Somocista, and the bourgeoisie as well as Somoza were alarmed by the overwhelming demonstrations of popular support for the FSLN as the successful commando unit made its way through crowds lining the road to Managua's Las Mercedes airport. Bourgeois leaders, constantly looking over their shoulder for Washington's approval, felt an urgent need to convince the United States that there was a viable 'democratic' alternative to both Somoza and the FSLN, which would merit State Department backing. Chamorro and other UDEL leaders, with their eyes on US-endorsed success in the 1981 elections, aggravated the organisation's lack of political clarity by concentrating on a purely electoral strategy at the expense of developing its skeletal programme of government.[14] UDEL frankly admitted that it had no internal consensus on what might follow Somoza. Right-wing members wanted little more than cosmetic reforms, while the PSN at least converged with the Sandinistas on demands for the nationalisation of all Somoza's property. Chamorro himself confessed in a 1975 speech to UDEL's youth section that 'UDEL has no design for a new society'.

Although Chamorro was attractive to many Liberals in Washington, UDEL's dominant force remained the disenchanted petty bourgeoisie, and it failed to enlist the support of the country's major economic groups who, while still to some degree unhappy with Somoza, were prepared to bide their time in the mistaken hope that the National Guard would wipe out mass discontent by destroying the FSLN. UDEL never came out openly on its own relationship with the Frente, a relationship which was very complex. Many UDEL leaders made little secret of their sympathy for the FSLN, often because wealthy families grew confused between their economic interests and family loyalties to sons and daughters from middle-class Managua suburbs like Los Robles and Altamira who flocked to join the Frente in the late 1970s. Nevertheless, both the right and left wings of UDEL were afraid of the political stature of the FSLN: afraid of its seizure of the political initiative in the face of their own vacillations, and afraid that any overt contacts between the two organisations might expose UDEL to more direct repression at the hands of the National Guard.

Economic Crisis

The stability sought by the big financiers of BANIC and BANAMERICA and foreign investors of the Sunbelt corporations could not last. When the FSLN launched its final offensive against Somoza in 1979, it had to be sure that all the necessary revolutionary conditions had been fulfilled, not only the correct balance of military forces and the readiness of popular organisation, but the culmination of a deep-rooted economic crisis.

Most economic analysts have pointed to 5-to-6-year cycles of growth and slump in the Nicaraguan economy: growth from 1950 to 1956 and 1962 to 1967, decline from 1956 to 1962 and 1967 to 1972. No single spell of growth was capable of resolving the structural crisis of the economy under Somoza, and the brief respites of 1973-74 (the false post-earthquake boom) and 1976-77 (with the worldwide rise in coffee prices) were only interludes in an irreversible decline. After 1974, the construction boom petered out, and periods of renewed growth could be bought only at the cost of an astronomical foreign debt. Nicaragua's relative weakness in the Central American Common Market had already brought a regional debt of $24 million by 1967, although the following year the Nicaraguan Government proudly placed an advertisement in the *New York Times* proclaiming its $49-million total external debt as the lowest of any Central American country. Somoza had traditionally been considered creditworthy as much for strategic as for strictly economic reasons, but the low level of local investment, among other factors, made it impossible for MCCA-induced industrialisation to be financed except through increased foreign borrowing.

The early cyclical crises of the 19th century, the 1920s, and the 1930s were repeated, with each new slump highlighting the problems of a heavily export-oriented dependent economy. In 1977, exports accounted for 32% of Nicaragua's GDP. Four agricultural products made up 60% of export earnings. Cotton led the way with 24.5%, coffee accounted for 18.1%, sugar 10.2% and meat 7.3%. Until the introduction of cotton in the 1950s, Nicaragua's economy had rested squarely on coffee, with predictable results during the Great Depression. The difficulties of *Somocismo* in the years following the assassination of its founder were due less to a revolutionary upsurge than to the collapse of cotton and coffee prices. Again in 1975, a four-year drought combined with the decreasing value of cotton, sugar and meat exports to produce a slump mitigated only by the buoyancy of coffee prices over the next two years. The cycle of economic crisis became more rapid.[15]

By 1979 external debt servicing had grown to 22% of the value of Nicaraguan exports. Investment showed negative growth in 1975 and 1976, rallied briefly in 1977, and then plunged to – $42.8 million in 1978. In the same year, GDP fell by 5%, and the foreign debt reached $1 billion for the first time, a fourfold rise over six years. US and multilateral agencies began to ask themselves questions about Somoza's credit rating. The willingness of USAID to prop up the dictatorship for strategic reasons was understandable, but the eagerness of the private banks to leap into the crisis with lifelines for the crippled dictator was harder to grasp. Once the Interamerican Development Bank and the World Bank began to question soft loans to Somoza, he had no alternative but to turn to assistance on harsher terms, appealing to 133 US private banks.[16] Domestic measures to ease the balance of payments crisis only weakened Somoza's political situation. In 1978 his congress introduced a bill to end tax exemption on industrial profits. The move gave the government an extra $17 million in revenue but antagonised yet another sector of the bourgeoisie. All-out war against the FSLN doubled military expenditure, which could only be financed by printing money: 60% more than planned in 1978 alone. Taxes on consumer goods and cuts in real wages brought militant opposition from the working class, and the punitive terms of private bank loans ate away most of the cash raised through taxation. The $41 million in private loans raised after the September 1978 insurrection came on punitive terms – repayment in two years and 8.75% interest.

From the Banco Central, Bank President Roberto Incer asserted that the government would reject further approaches to the International Monetary Fund, after the Fund had rebuffed a credit request at the end of 1978. Incer denounced the IMF's 'political bias' against Nicaragua, but by March 1979 it was hard to see where else the lifeline would come from. The result – a

$66 million loan granted on 15 May — was accompanied by the customary IMF medicine of austerity.[17] The enforced devaluation of the *cordoba* put the seal on the bankruptcy of *Somocismo*. This time the economic crisis could not be held back by means of pacts with the opposition. Instead, Somoza made wild populist promises: exports would expand, renewed foreign investment would bring jobs to thousands, prices would be controlled. But the Nicaraguan people knew that price controls would not work unless they were monitored by popular committees (a valuable lesson), and they saw that their newly decreed wage rises lagged far behind the 60% inflation rate. Nor was there any escape from the crisis within the bourgeoisie. The world capitalist recession added its own dimension of chaos to the inherently weak Nicaraguan economy, hitting small and medium-sized enterprises hardest. Hundreds of them were driven into bankruptcy by the devaluation. Class polarisation and the fragmentation of bourgeois unity were now irreversible.

The Working Class: Engine of the Revolution

'National unity,' FSLN Comandante Jaime Wheelock reminded journalists after the resignation in April 1980 of businessman Alfonso Robelo from the Junta of National Reconstruction, 'revolves around the two great forces of this country: the workers of the town and the workers of the countryside.' Today, Robelo and others like him are outraged by the FSLN's insistence on equating *el pueblo*, the people, with the masses who suffered abject poverty and oppression under *Somocismo*. But a simple glance at statistics indicates that the fragmentation of the bourgeoisie, for all its gravity, was the crisis of a tiny elite. Somoza's Nicaragua brought 80% of the population a per capita income of less than $805 a year. For two-thirds of these, it was a mere $286.[18]

One of the extraordinary features of the Nicaraguan Revolution is that it took place with one of the smallest and traditionally worst-organised urban proletariats in the Latin American continent. The fragmentation of the working-class movement, and the consequently economistic nature of its demands, born of misery, disorganisation and crises of leadership, were for decades a powerful weapon for Somoza. The Nicaraguan working class was first created when peasant farmers, violently deprived of their means of subsistence, were left with no option but to sell their labour. In time the expansion of cotton planting brought explosive growth to the population centres of the Pacific Coast, and industrialisation and urbanisation in the 1960s increased the size of the urban working class, brought mass unemployment, and extended the proletarianisation of the rural poor. At the height of industrial growth, from 1963 to 1973, 15,000 agricultural jobs were lost but only 13,000 new ones appeared in the modern, capital-intensive factories. The original growth of the proletariat, then, was not linked to manufacturing industry but to plantation labour and the mechanisation of agriculture. At first the people found work in the banana fields and coffee *fincas,* later in the sugar refineries, cotton gins, oil processing plants. The miners of the north, although combative in the time of Sandino, were for the most part Miskito Indians from the jungles of the interior, and they remained both culturally and geographically remote from the development of the proletariat as a whole.

Nicaragua is a country of great geographical distortions. Its working class is centred in the western *departamentos* of Managua, Leon, Chinandega and Carazo. The capital alone is the home of a quarter of the population, containing 85% of Nicaragua's industry, 90% of government and 60% of commercial activity. From 1960 onwards there has been a steady rise in urban population, from only 41% to its current 52%. In 1979, 343,000 people were employed in agriculture, 90,000 in industry and construction, and 228,000 in commerce and services.[19] 231,000 or 28% of the economically active population were unemployed. In a capital city of 600,000, the industrial working class is disproportionately small. The main reasons for rapid urban growth lay elsewhere, in the expropriation of farmlands, the expulsion of peasants from the countryside, and the migration of thousands to the cities. The industrial expansion of the '60s quite simply failed to keep pace with the growth of the urban population. This dynamic was also largely due to the explosion of service industries, commerce and a wide, desperate range of marginal activities.

Behind this pattern of urban growth, as in any Central American country, is the crucial struggle for land, which dates back to the earliest 19th-century expulsions of indigenous communities by Liberal and Conservative landowners. *Latifundismo* produced a perpetual crisis of domestic food production and an army of dispossessed peasants who found work, if they found it at all, in the harvesting and processing of Nicaragua's main export crops, cotton, coffee and sugar. Official figures of the economically active population are deceptively low. They do not take into account the thousands of spouses and children who added their labour to that of the family's main wage earner in a desperate attempt to ward off starvation. In coffee picking alone, 40% of workers were women and perhaps another 15% young children. It was invariably piece-work, forcing labourers into 12- or 14-hour days in the scorching sun, beginning at 5.30 a.m., six days a week. Those lucky enough to find semi-skilled jobs processing the crop would commonly work up to 18 hours. Their pitiful wages went on basic foodstuffs sold at inflated prices in the landowner's store, the *comisariato,* so that cotton pickers or cane cutters would often return home at the end of the season locked into an endless cycle of debt to their employer. Outside the season, there was nothing. In 1973, cotton employed only 25,035 permanent workers but 202,295 labourers for the three-month picking season. At night, they slept in *galerones,* each serving as a dormitory for up to 150 workers, sordid huts of unfinished planking in which each labourer occupied a coffin-like wooden box, two metres long by one metre high, without light, water, furniture or sanitation.

Seasonal agricultural labour like this and the constant migration from home to place of work made class organisation and solidarity difficult. For three months of the year, the rural poor were thrown up against the brutalities of Nicaraguan capitalism, with a brief opportunity to organise and share experiences. For the other nine, they dispersed once more to their homes to scratch out a living through subsistence farming. The few who found year-round work in cotton gins or sugar refineries worked in isolated locations, easily divided and repressed. Their revolutionary potential as a class came not from their tradition of organisation, but from the objective facts of their misery.

In the cities too, the slow consolidation of the proletariat as a unified class had a great deal to do with built-in high levels of unemployment and underemployment. There was a clear and damaging division between the active and the reserve proletariat, a vast unproductive army whose existence kept wage levels low and class consciousness undeveloped. For the unemployed, any work could mean survival. In the sprawling urban slums of Acahualinca by the lakeside, hundreds of women gathered each morning around the sewage outlets from the Managua slaughterhouse. Breaking holes in the concrete pipes, they waited to fish out rotting offal which might be sold in the market for a few *centavos* to be made into sausages. Their children, whom the Sandinistas call *los Quinchos* (after Quincho Barrilete, child hero of a revolutionary song), swarmed in the streets of Managua to sell newspapers or chewing-gum, to mind cars or clean shoes. Their husbands rarely worked. Their families lived in shacks of cardboard, tin and car tyres with earth latrines and stand-pipes half a mile apart. They are the urban *marginados* of Nicaragua.

Organising the Labour Movement

The first stirrings of working-class organisation came at the turn of the century with the founding of small mutual aid societies. The first socialist unions followed in 1920 when workers in Leon founded the Federacion de Trabajadores Liberada (Free Federation of Workers) and celebrated May Day for the first time in Nicaragua. But after the miners' and agricultural workers' strikes against American rule, the murder of Sandino and the outlawing of the Socialist Party neutralised the labour movement for two decades. Government-controlled unions held sway during the late 1940s and early 1950s.[20] Trade-union membership increased only in 1958, when electricians, building workers and stevedores swelled the number of unions to eighteen. But even with this jump, only 16,000 Nicaraguan workers were unionised, just 3.4% of the economically active population. Unionisation had reached less than 1% of rural workers.[21] The formation of these new unions coincided with a wave of strikes by teachers, railway workers, miners, hospital workers, and shoemakers, who demanded full implementation of the 1944 Labour Code and an extension of social security benefits, but the strikes lacked clear political direction.

The issue of working-class leadership was posed more starkly by contrasting strikes in the 1970s. After the earthquake, construction workers became a key political group. In 1973 the booming construction industry offered favourable employment conditions, high wage rates and the opportunity for workers to organise coherently. In the same year, building workers who were grouped together in the Confederacion General de Trabajadores — Independiente (CGT-I), loyal to the Socialist Party, went on strike, but their negotiators settled after four weeks for a 10% wage hike and defused union activism. The strike was a valuable exercise in mobilisation, but failed to transcend economistic demands, and when the construction boom collapsed the following year, building workers lost much of their momentum.

A strike involving very different workers in the same period took place at the country's largest sugar refinery, the Ingenio San Antonio, where 5,000 came out, most of them *paileros* (cane cutters). In a series of stages, the San Antonio workers learned at first hand the whole gamut of strike-breaking tactics that could be brought against them. Their first unions were dismantled by the Conservative Pellas family, owners of the refinery, by means of the expulsion and victimisation of union activists. Next the National Guard was deployed against the strikers, and finally the management attempted to buy off unrest by granting minor wage concessions. The *paileros* remained unimpressed. In their own struggle, the land invasions of peasants nearby in Subtiava and Chinandega, and the formation of the first Rural Workers' Committees (Comites de Trabajadores del Campo: CTCs), where the germ of a worker-peasant alliance.

Now, in 1975 and 1976, the question of the leadership of the working class was being resolved in favour of the FSLN. Earlier it had been in doubt. Any serious claim to leadership by the old Conservative opposition had begun to crumble after the death of Somoza Garcia. The economic crisis of the late 1950s, and the still-fresh memory of the latest Liberal-Conservative pacts, had begun to open the eyes of many in the small workers' movement to the true nature of the Conservative option. The PSN, *faute de mieux*, established control of important urban groups, but its inability to provide revolutionary leadership recalled its origins. This suggests not only the prevailing conciliatory line of Latin American communist parties at the time of its formation in 1944, but also the specific class structure of wartime Nicaragua. With an agriculturally based economy and industrialisation blocked by American development strategy, the human material available to the Socialist Party was not an urban proletariat but an artisan class which was later swallowed up as manufacturing industry took root.[22] The first Socialist Party leaders were artisans too, and their ideological level was low. The FSLN's founder, Carlos Fonseca Amador, analysed the early mistakes of the PSN: 'It is necessary to explain their grave errors not simply as a product of the leadership's bad faith . . .; they did not remain sufficiently composed in the face of Conservative hegemony over the anti-Somoza movement; they were unable to distinguish between the correctness of opposing Somoza and the manoeuvres of the Conservatives.'[23]

These early difficulties which the PSN experienced, and the ease with which Somoza took it apart three years after its foundation, offer another reason for the historic weakness of Nicaraguan working-class organisation. PSN Secretary-General Luis Sanchez reflected on his party's history in a 1977 interview: 'Somoza managed to dismantle its incipient organisational structure, sweeping away trade-union cells and jailing or exiling leading cadres. Nicaraguan Communists were unable to resist these attacks and went into hiding, so that in fact the PSN ceased to function for several years.'[24] After the Cuban Revolution it looked everywhere for alliances with the bourgeoisie, but without success. According to Sanchez, 'the reason was that anti-Communist prejudices were still very pronounced among sectors of the opposition bourgeoisie and petty bourgeoisie.'[25]

As the influence of the FSLN grew in the 1960s, the PSN found itself bitterly divided over its relationship to the armed struggle. The crisis reached a head in 1967, and most of the original leadership were expelled over their intransigent opposition to any cooperation with the growing guerrilla movement. Three years later, those expelled set themselves up as the Partido Comunista de Nicaragua (PC de N) still vociferously anti-Sandinista and still claiming unconditional allegiance to Moscow, though in practice disowned by the USSR which continued to relate to the PSN.[26] The PSN continued to have its doubts about the FSLN, and to criticise actions which they saw as extremist or adventurist: 'they tried traditional *foquismo,* at other times putschism, suffering Maoist, almost Trotskyist influences.'[27] It came as no surprise, then, when the Socialist Party joined the bourgeois-led UDEL coalition in 1974, although in fairness the presence of the PSN and its labour federation, the CGT-I, accounted for many of UDEL's most progressive demands for labour reform. As the crisis of *Somocismo* mounted, the PSN began to look for a rapprochement with the Sandinistas, and in 1977, when major sectors of the FSLN pointed to the critical weakness of the bourgeoisie as grounds for a rapid insurrectional strategy, active steps were taken to heal the rift.

It was no easy matter for the FSLN to unite the trade union movement and present a solid working-class front. The Socialist CGT-I was only one of four labour *centrales* in Nicaragua. Of the others, the CUS was Nicaragua's docile ICFTU-ORIT affiliate, the CTN was loyal to the small Social Christian Party, and the CAUS to the sectarian Partido Comunista. As well as the established *centrales,* new workplace organisations sprang up as the crisis of *Somocismo* approached. Among these, the FSLN attached special importance to what they saw as incipient factory councils, the Comites de Lucha de los Trabajadores (Workers' Fighting Committees: CLTs) which cut across party affiliations. An urgent need arose for the FSLN to discuss and reassess its strategy, to look for ways of channelling the revolutionary energy of the urban proletariat, perhaps even to set up a new party of the proletariat, in the face of the growing economic importance of the urban working class in the 1970s at the expense of the peasantry, which latter class had given *Sandinismo* its historic base of support in the northern mountains. The debate within the FSLN was bitter but indispensable. In the three years from 1975 to 1978, a traditionally weak and divided working-class movement, newly dynamised by economic collapse, repression and the visible decomposition of the dictatorship, had to be transformed into the second pillar of the Nicaraguan Revolution. The transformation had to be achieved by a revolutionary vanguard with a clear and intimate understanding of Nicaraguan history. That vanguard is the subject of the following chapter.

Notes

1. NACLA, *Latin America and Empire Report* Vol. X, No. 2, February 1976, p. 22.
2. *Ibid.*
3. Doris Tijerino, *Inside the Nicaraguan Revolution*, pp. 128-9.
4. Banco Central de Nicaragua, *Informe Anual*, 1973-1978 editions.
5. Wheelock, *Imperialismo y Dictadura*, pp. 174-5.
6. NACLA, *op. cit.*, p. 23.
7. Wheelock, *op. cit.*, Chapter 6 *passim.*
8. *Ibid.*, p. 189.
9. In addition to the existing PLI, Liberal dissidents formed the Movimiento Liberal Constitucionalista (MLC). The Conservatives divided into four factions. The congressional opposition was known as the Partido Conservador Oficialista. Dissident groups were the Partido Conservador Autentico (PCA); the Partido Conservador Aguerista, loyal to Fernando Aguero; and the Accion Nacional Conservadora (ANC). The last three came together in 1979 to form the Partido Conservador Democrata (PCD). See Lopez *et al., La caida del Somocismo*, pp. 354-5.
10. See documents of UDEL, 1974-7, especially *El Programa de UDEL* (1974) and *Pronunciamiento* (24 August 1977).
11. *Latin America Economic Report*, Vol. VI, No. 39, 6 October 1978.
12. COSEP: Consejo Superior de la Empresa Privada, formerly known as COSIP: Consejo Superior de la Iniciativa Privada.
13. See Lopez *et al., op. cit.*, pp. 89-90 and 298-9. Also Wheelock, *op. cit.*, p. 183.
14. See interview with Pedro Joaquin Chamorro in *El Dia*, 24 November 1977.
15. Lopez *et al., op. cit.*, pp. 274-5.
16. 'Desangre de la Economia,' in *Nicaragua en Lucha*, COSOCAN ' (Barcelona)., No. 1, July-August 1979, p. 15.
17. *International Herald Tribune*, 22 May 1979.
18. Figures for 1977. Source: United Nations Economic Commission for Latin America (ECLA), 1979 report on Nicaragua.
19. *Datos Basicos sobre Nicaragua* (Managua, SENAPEP, Coleccion Juan de Dios Munoz, 1979), p. 10.
20. See also James Dunkerley and Chris Whitehouse, *Unity is Strength: Trade Unions in Latin America, a Case for Solidarity* (London, Latin

America Bureau, 1980), pp. 112-13.

21. Torres, *Interpretacion del Desarrollo Social Centroamericano*, p. 305.
22. *Estructura Agraria, Dinamica de Poblacion y Desarrollo Capitalista en Centroamerica* (San Jose, CSUCA, 1978), pp. 236-41.
23. Carlos Fonseca Amador, *Nicaragua-Hora Cero*,
24. Interview in *El Dia*, 26th November 1977.
25. *Ibid.*
26. *Intercontinental Press*, New York, 7 July 1980, p. 710.
27. Sanchez interview, *loc. cit.*
28. See Chapter 13 for fuller details on the trade-union movement in Nicaragua.

PART 2
Overthrowing the Dictatorship

6. Guerrilla War – People's War

'A guerrilla war is a people's war, and it is a mass struggle. To attempt to conduct this kind of war without the support of the populace is a prelude to inevitable disaster. The guerrilla force is the people's fighting vanguard.'
(Che Guevara)[1]

Reviving the Broken Thread

'You can never map out a strategy from A to Z. You must have enough flexibility to change course, to accommodate the line of action to changing historical circumstances, without ever losing sight of the strategic objective. That is the great lesson of the FSLN.' (Comandante Henry Ruiz, 'Modesto')[2]

In July 1961, three men gathered in Tegucigalpa, capital of Honduras. They were Carlos Fonseca Amador, Tomas Borge and Silvio Mayorga, all former university students. The question before them was the foundation of a revolutionary movement, a national liberation front. The spectacular assassination of Anastasio Somoza Garcia in 1956 and the slump in cotton prices had given the stimulus for the greatest political mobilisations since the 1930s. With the cotton slump came increased rural unemployment. Simultaneously, capitalist expansion in the countryside expelled more peasants from desirable lands, and their migratory influence was felt in the cities. The generalised protests which took place throughout the country were specific demands as yet unlinked to a firm political programme, protests against the increased cost of living, poor housing conditions and the lack of public services. They marked a clear upsurge in class consciousness but without a clear revolutionary leadership. For more than two decades, popular discontent had gravitated towards the Conservative Party, not because it offered a particularly attractive alternative to *Somocismo*, but because no other option was available. In their way, too, the Conservatives responded to the crisis of the late 1950s, mounting the Olama y los Mollejones invasion in 1959 and the seizures of the Diriamba and Jinotepe barracks a year later. But the operations lacked popular support and strategic vision,[3] and while they proved that the bourgeoisie was still willing to take up arms against

Somoza, their failure also wrecked the myth of *cuartelazo* politics, the attempted seizure of power from above through intrigues and isolated military adventures. From now on, opposition had to be built from the bottom, not imposed from the top.

Between 1958 and 1960, there were more than 60 armed actions against the dictatorship. Many were old-style military adventures, but others sought a new way. From his earliest student days, Carlos Fonseca had insisted that this way was to recover the tradition of Sandino. Survivors of an older generation shared Fonseca's conviction, and in 1958 twenty-two men crossed into Nicaragua under cover of darkness from the Honduran border town of Danli, under the command of General Ramon Raudales. Raudales and four other members of the guerrilla unit were veterans of Sandino's war. The other seventeen were for the most part university students. Their weapons were relics from the 1930s. Gathering support from local peasants, Raudales's group went into combat with the National Guard, and although Somoza's detachment was badly mauled the guerrillas lost their leader, the old general.

The young students began voraciously to read Sandino's own writings and every available biography and memoir. In the middle of their political preparation came the triumph of Fidel Castro's revolution against Batista in Cuba. 'For us', wrote Tomas Borge, 'Fidel was the resurrection of Sandino . . . the justification of our dreams.'[4] Within months, the 'Rigoberto Lopez Perez' guerrilla column, named after Somoza's assassin, had been formed with strong moral support from Che Guevara. But the column was ambushed by the National Guard in the northern mountains of El Chaparral. Several Nicaraguans and Cubans died, and Fonseca himself was seriously wounded. Nonetheless, El Chaparral showed the way forward, and in other guerrilla actions of the period names like Manuel Diaz y Sotelo, Chale Haslam and Francisco Buitrago were added to the list of early revolutionary martyrs. The Cuban experience was by now the subject of intense debate within the future nucleus of the FSLN. Although there were few ideological lessons to be drawn from the Cuban Revolution as it stood in 1959, it reconfirmed to Fonseca, Borge, Mayorga and others the essential teachings which they had already taken from Sandino: the central importance of the armed struggle in the mountains and the need to build sympathetic support among the local peasant population. Over and above this, the example of Sandino provided a national thread which embodied every feature of Nicaragua's 20th-century history – intervention, the striving for independence, the bankruptcy of two-party oligarchical rule, the class basis of resistance. When Fonseca, Borge and Mayorga emerged from their Tegucigalpa meeting, a new revolutionary movement had been born, and on Fonseca's insistence it would be known not as the Frente de Liberacion Nacional, but the Frente Sandinista de Liberacion Nacional (FSLN).

Internally, the new current of revolutionary *Sandinismo* remained weak, and its first military actions were launched from neighbouring Honduras, caused by – and of course aggravating – the lack of real contact between the small vanguard group and the masses whose demands it sought to project.

The point was not lost on the Moscow-line Socialists, who were swift to
criticise what they considered the 'adventurism' of the actions of 1963.
'From 1959 to 1962', noted Fonseca, 'we still maintained the illusion that it
was possible to bring about change through the peaceful means proposed
by the PSN leadership.'[5] But as the guerrilla force consolidated, its leaders
had harsher words for the PSN's own efforts. 'The traditional parties of
the left gave the struggle a strictly defensive dimension . . . economistic,
centred on immediate demands. Our working class in general is not spontaneously revolutionary – neither here nor anywhere else – but must be
given leadership towards its role as the vanguard of the revolutionary
process.'[6]

In 1963, the FSLN gathered together 60 combatants on the banks of
the Rio Patuca in Honduras, still not on Nicaraguan soil. The group this time
included both Fonseca and the Sandinista veteran Santos Lopez, so uniting
two generations of revolutionary fighters under the single banner of
Sandinismo. The group faced the prospect of military defeat, but this was in
Borge's words 'only the loss of an arm. The FSLN did not disappear.'[7]
This was because the nascent movement had never seen military action as an
end in itself, but as the expression of a political struggle. The first workers'
and students' cells had sprung up at the end of the previous decade in the
cities of Managua and Leon, while rural workers were organising for the first
time in the sugar and cotton mills of Chinandega and among the coffee-
pickers and seasonal labourers of Matagalpa, Esteli, Somoto and Ocotal, the
very areas controlled by Sandino's army in the 1930s. In the universities,
small groups of Marxist students began to put working-class demands into a
political framework, and many of these student militants and theorists went
on to form part of the FSLN. After his visit to Moscow in 1957 to attend the
VIth Congress of the World Federation of Democratic Youth, and his subsequent imprisonment and torture, Fonseca used written propaganda[8] and
public meetings to present the case for revolutionary politics and to show
the relevance of Sandino's thinking to contemporary conditions in Nicaragua.
For the first time in a quarter of a century the name of Sandino began to
circulate clandestinely among the people. Although a strong mass movement
remained a distant project, Fonseca linked his intellectual arguments through
the magazine *Nueva Nicaragua* with direct political action and was instrumental in organising popular committees in Leon, giving immediate local
barrio demands a more clearly political dimension. The ideological silence
stifling Nicaragua was broken.

The young FSLN went out in search of support among the working class
from the start, concentrating its efforts not on the unemployed or the
artisan class but on workers tied to important productive centres. In a token
of the same internationalism which had sustained Sandino, the Mexican
Victor Tirado Lopez was placed in charge of this work, seeking out not
only urban factory workers but the rural proletariat of the west and workers'
nuclei in the northern towns of Esteli, El Viejo and Wiwili. The problem of
financing the new organisation was a grave one. Foreign solidarity with the

FSLN was non-existent, and the organisation had to rely on its own resources inside the country. A unit led by the student Jorge Navarro carried out the Frente's first bank raid, recovering 35,000 cordobas ($5,000) which were despatched to the mountains, but bank raids were dangerous and costly. A single death in such a raid could break down an entire urban support network at a time when the FSLN's urban presence was still fragile. Contributions from sympathetic factory workers and students — 5 *cordobas* here, 10 there — brought barely enough to feed the guerrilla force, let alone buy arms, ammunition or transport, and Victor Tirado's group was rumoured to have lived in the mountains for nine months with only 5 *cordobas* in their pockets.[9]

Conditions of life for the FSLN were appalling. The guerrilla force established its base on the Rio Coco on the Honduras-Nicaragua border. 'There was nothing to eat, not even animals to hunt. There was no salt. It wasn't just hunger that was terrible, but constant cold 24 hours a day, because we spent all our time in the river. We were always wet through with the clinging rain of that part of the country, the cold a kind of unrelieved torture, mosquitos, wild jungle animals and insects. No shelter, no change of clothes, no food.'[10] So the FSLN relied on support from the local peasants, keeping morale high with the help of Sandinista veterans like Santos Lopez who had been through the torture of the mountains before.

Choosing the Terrain

The inhabitants of Nicaragua's north-eastern border with Honduras are for the most part Miskito Indians. Almost all are illiterate, few can speak Spanish. In 1963, even fewer could have named the president of the country. To the Miskitos, the difference between the FSLN and Somoza's Guard was hazy. Both wore olive green uniforms and carried guns; neither could communicate with the sparse local population. When the incipient guerrilla *foco* clashed in 1963 with the National Guard at Bocay and Rio Coco, there seemed little on paper to distinguish it from earlier armed invasions. The military encounters brought heavy loss of life to the Sandinistas, and coming at the height of Alliance for Progress reformism they succeeded in calling forth only a limited political response. But in one essential the guerrilla detachment offered something new, and its importance was recalled by the FSLN eleven years later: 'The guerrilla movements of Rio Coco and Bocay were our armed response at that time. It should be emphasised that the 1963 *guerrilla* represents the emergence of the first armed organisation with a consistent ideological character and the proposal of a revolutionary programme for the construction of a socialist society.'[11]

After these defeats, the Frente went into a prolonged withdrawal from armed action, having neither the arms, the numbers nor the organisation to confront the National Guard again. The main political thrust now was to build unbreakable links with the people, an urban network capable of financing the organisation and projecting its demands in the heart of the working class, and a rural support system which would sustain FSLN guerrilla units.

The choice of terrain for the armed struggle was effectively dictated by a mixture of geography, class structure and history. The need to operate in clandestinity, the central economic importance of the peasantry, and the legacy of Sandino's war of liberation all pointed to the mountains of the north and especially to the *departamento* of Matagalpa. Matagalpa was one of the more heavily populated regions of a sparsely settled country. Its population in 1961 was about 160,000, and its landscape offered the FSLN clandestinity without isolation from the people. The mountains of Matagalpa are thickly forested and merge into the impenetrable jungles of Eastern Jinotega, Boaco and Zelaya. It is broken and difficult terrain, with a rainy season which lasts for nine or ten months of the year. Among the peasants, for all their poverty and marginalisation from national politics, there was widespread hostility to Somoza and a lingering loyalty to Sandino. Many older people had fought or collaborated with Sandino's army, and stories of the 1926-33 war continued to circulate in the northern villages. Some of its survivors had fought on alone for three decades in the jungle, unconnected to any political movement but carrying on their own private struggle against the National Guard. From 1967 onwards, the Guard found itself facing a landscape ideally suited to guerrilla struggle but impossible for conventional warfare, with a local population who increasingly identified with the *muchachos* (kids) of the FSLN.

However, winning this sympathy was no easy matter. Hardship and isolation had made the Nicaraguan peasant withdrawn and uncommunicative, reluctant to trust strangers. Old sympathies for Sandino did not prevent a percentage of peasants from being convinced Somocistas, while many others were at least superficially under the sway of the dictatorship's ideological control. For the FSLN, the key was to distinguish between the two and avoid the constant risk of exposure and betrayal. Family relationships are the backbone of Nicaraguan peasant communities, and acceptance meant not only shared political convictions but the integration of guerrilla fighters into family life until they were accepted as virtual blood relatives.[12] After the mid-1960s, no recruit entered the FSLN without a commitment to live as the *campesinos* did, sharing all their privations and so gaining their confidence. For most of the *guerrilleros,* urban middle-class youth, it meant abandoning the class of their birth, with no turning back. Support from the *campesinos* came in a slow chain-reaction. In each new village or hamlet, a single slowly built friendship brought the sympathy of an entire family; every political contact brought three or four more. Gradually, the network of support swelled, an infinitely patient and arduous process guided by every combatant's belief in ultimate victory. The guerrillas came and went, getting to know the lie of the land, establishing arms caches, teaching the peasants a political understanding of their situation. Recruitment of peasants became easier. Many of the peasants captured by the National Guard admitted to cooperating with the Frente because the guerrillas had taught them to sow their crops better, taught them to read and write, given them medicine or clothing.[13] And National Guard repression in turn only increased peasant sympathy for the *muchachos*.

In the cities, the task of building an urban base was equally difficult, and after the military reverses of 1963 the Frente turned to two years of semi-legal work among the urban masses, but with little success in building the movement. This work was directed mainly at the working-class *barrios* of Managua and other major cities, and the FSLN later admitted that its entire conception of mass organisational work had been mistaken.[14] In an ill-starred political alliance called Movilizacion Republicana, the Sandinistas worked together with the Socialist Party, but in a context where they had no hope of establishing leadership within the coalition. Key militants came down from the mountains, and their dispersion in the cities left little room for continuous political organising among the peasants of the north. Some peasants too were sent down to Managua for political instruction in the Frente's urban cells; others were sent in delegations to departmental capitals to protest against working conditions and land seizures; a few scattered peasant assemblies were held in northern villages, and in isolated cases small farmers physically resisted attempts by capitalists to evict them from their lands. But both urban and rural work proceeded with little rhythm or co-ordination for four painful years. The concentration on clarifying a political programme, the lack of money and arms, the slow work of a handful of militants in the mountains — all this made it difficult for the FSLN to project itself as a real political force to the masses. 'You joined the Frente because you believed in its political line,' remembered Omar Cabezas, later to become a guerrilla *commandante*. 'You believed that the Frente was capable of over-throwing Somoza and the *Guardia* . . . we went up into the mountains with the idea that this was where the power lay, that myth of the *companeros* in the mountain, mystery, the unknown, "Modesto"[15] . . . arms, the best men, indestructible power. And when you get to the mountains, you find that there's "Modesto" and fifteen others split up into small groups. You almost reach the point of saying, My God, I've made the worst decision of my life. You feel as if you've set off on something which has no future . . . In the whole of Leon, the Frente consisted of Leonel [Rugama], JJ [Juan Jose Quezada] and Edgardo Munguia, then me. That was the FSLN in Leon.'[16] As 1967 opened, the organisation was alive, but it was a small and frail thread.

Pancasan 1967: The Peasants Take Up Arms

As that year began, the 22 January massacre of demonstrators changed the context of political opposition overnight. The tranquil elections which followed led Somoza to believe that he had successfully neutralised opposi-tion to his regime, but popular hatred of the dictatorship was at its height and the discredited manoeuvres of the Conservatives left an acute vacuum which the FSLN moved swiftly to fill. It was time, the leadership decided, to resume the armed offensive. Accordingly, the Frente made careful preparations to consolidate the *guerrilla* in the area around the mountain of Pancasan, thirty miles or so east of Matagalpa. To support it, they launched a new wave of bank raids, and gathered considerable assistance from local peasants. 'They took on the job of wiping out our tracks where the column had passed; the *companeras* hung out coloured cloths to warn us of any danger; they invented signals for us with different sounds . . . We had a whole team of *campesino* brothers and sisters who knew the area like the back of their hand.'[17] The money which came in from bank raids served to stock food, clothing and medical caches in the forest, to break the absolute dependence of the rural *guerrilla* on its urban support network.

Around Pancasan, the Frente's peasant sympathisers were organised into cells, each with different responsibilities: to act as informers of National Guard movements, as mountain guides, cooks, suppliers of food and accommodation, purchasers of equipment. Many began to fight in small-scale harassment operations against the Guard, returning their weapons afterwards and going back to their farms. There were still problems in the integration of peasant recruits into the regular guerrilla columns, and although the Sandinistas received active support from the local population, peasant combatants tended to become demoralised easily by rumours of enemy troop movements (the National Guard by now was mounting sophisticated counter-insurgency operations), and by the physical hardship of forced marches at night, food shortages and obsessive security precautions. Many peasants deserted or had to be dismissed, and a number even turned informers. The urban or student cadre by contrast had greater staying power, having made the decision to move into the mountains with all that that entailed, and usually having a clearer political understanding of the need for the armed struggle.

Nonetheless, the preparation of the Pancasan *guerrilla* marked a vital step forward. 'It was no longer the habitual preparation of an armed movement from a neighbouring country, far from the main enemy's sight, but an armed movement rooted in the mountains in the very heart of our country.'[18] In addition to the numerous peasants who were now fighting, the FSLN had brought its entire leadership into the Pancasan area, a huge but unavoidable risk if the new *guerrilla* was to be successful. But at the end of August 1967, Somoza's troops located the Pancasan columns and forced them into combat. With limited firepower, the outcome for the FSLN was inevitable. Thirteen senior members of the organisation died, including Silvio Mayorga, of its founder members: a severe military blow and the loss of years of accumulated political experience.

Somoza too, however, was forced to admit that his troops had suffered serious casualties. Guard units were drafted into the mountains on a systematic and unprecedented campaign against peasant sympathisers, and the government newspaper *Novedades* screamed from its headlines for the

guerrilla movement to be exterminated. The earlier forays against the
National Guard at Bocay and Rio Coco had passed almost unnoticed among
the population at large, but this was different. Workers and students staged
solidarity actions with Pancasan, and the name of the FSLN took on a new
political authority in Nicaragua. Word spread of National Guard brutality
in the countryside, and the legitimacy of the armed struggle was reaffirmed
at the very time when the bourgeois opposition found itself in disarray. The
FSLN may not yet have signified a real or immediate alternative to the
dictatorship or to the 'formal' opposition, but August 1967 proved that,
unlike guerrilla movements annihilated throughout Latin America in the
disastrous years of *foquismo*, the Frente was very much alive.

The surviving leadership of the organisation sought to give immediate
political continuity to the military action, in order to reinforce the point
that Pancasan was merely the military expression of a coherent mass struggle.
Rejecting the failed option of political alliances with the Socialist Party and
other groups on the Left, which were merely a barrier to effective communication with the masses, the FSLN instead set about strengthening its direct
links with the people. The method was to create 'intermediate organisations'
connected to the FSLN but not bearing its name. In the universities, the
Frente Estudiantil Revolucionario (Revolutionary Student Front: FER)
became a major force after Pancasan. And in the working-class *barrios*, the
Frente encouraged the formation of the *Comites Civicos Populares*. The
FSLN now had a visible presence among the masses, and organisations which
could identify with the Sandinista political programme. Clandestine FSLN
documents began to circulate widely, denouncing Conservative electoralism
and National Guard repression of peasants. Years of intensive mass organisational work still lay ahead, but the importance of Pancasan as a turning point
in the development of the Nicaraguan Revolution remains incalculable.

Accumulation of Forces

'After Pancasan,' remembered Tomas Borge, 'we began the silent accumulation of forces which gradually formed an organic structure in the *barrios*.'[19]
An urban base was a critical necessity for the Frente, and although small
Marxist cells in Managua and Leon dated back to the late 1950s, the FSLN's
urban actions had been designed mainly as a means of economic support for
the rural *guerrilla*. The 1967 bank raids, coming in the midst of electoral
scandal and a blanket of repression, had a certain impact among the urban
working class, but they were no substitute for coherent organisational work
in the factories and *barrios*. The late '60s also saw a reassessment of the need
for guerrilla movements throughout the continent to establish themselves in
the cities, with the failure of Che Guevara's rural *foco* at Nancahuazu in
Bolivia and the emergence of urban-based movements like Carlos Marighela's
in Brazil and the MLN (or Tupamaros) in Uruguay. As usual in reassessing
its tactics and strategy, the FSLN looked for lessons to Vietnam, China and

Algeria as well as to other Latin American struggles. The experiences of a predominantly urban country like Uruguay were certainly not transferable to Nicaragua. The mountains were still seen, in Ruiz's phrase, as 'the crucible of the revolution', and it was difficult to develop the same qualities in urban militants as in the rural *guerrilleros*. In Managua especially, the nerve centre of Somoza's military machine, cadres had little space or time in which to develop. As the most exposed members of the organisation, they required particular qualities of courage and commitment, yet for security reasons they could not be privy to detailed information about the location and movements of the rural *guerrilla*. A single captured urban cadre cracking under torture might reveal an entire rural network.[20]

Urban cells in Nicaragua were peculiarly vulnerable to the insidious intelligence network which Somoza had built, not only through the Office of Security (OSN) but through the hundreds of *orejas* ('ears') painstakingly recruited by the dictator's father to give him advance warning of political opposition. The dilemma for the Frente was to keep the Guard off balance by building small centres of resistance throughout Managua, but at the same time ensuring that the discovery of a single safe house would not mean the decapitation of the whole urban movement. Even so, the *Guardia* did pick up information on one such house in the Delicias del Volga, a few blocks west of the old city centre of Managua. On July 15 1969 they attacked, and as usual Somoza's response was military overkill: a 2½-hour attack supervised by Samuel Genie, director of the OSN, in which regular troops carrying heavy machineguns and teargas were backed up by aircraft and a Sherman tank. Five FSLN militants died in the raid, including Julio Buitrago of the national leadership, and two others were captured alive. In the weeks that followed, Sandinista suspects were rounded up throughout Managua.

It was a time of great introspection and self-criticism. Not only was the Frente's overall strategy unclear, but the documents circulating within the organisation at the end of the 1960s catalogued a whole series of errors – inadequate recruitment methods, insufficient membership, cases of individualism within the leadership and a poor understanding of the relationship between urban mass organisation and rural warfare. The last complaint was eventually instrumental in dividing the FSLN in 1975. For the time being, however, the leadership remained unified, if in some instances chastened.

The Frente evaluated the lessons of the previous decade, and in doing so faced the classic contradiction of any guerrilla organisation in its early years, analysed in Debray's *A Critique of Arms,* between the military need for mobility to avoid pursuit and encirclement, and the political need for a base from which to organise civilian support and create an embryonic local power structure.[21] Pancasan had partially answered this question as far as the rural areas were concerned, but the urban dilemma remained unresolved. Fonseca and other leaders had already identified the danger of allowing the battle front to develop only in a localised theatre of operations easily isolated from the rest of the country, but the absence of fixed guerrilla camps would in turn impede the training of local cadres able to go off and organise the revolutionary struggle in other parts of the country. The proof given by the Delicias del Volga attack of the Frente's vulnerability in urban areas imposed even greater secrecy on the organisation. This combination of factors led to a painful decision: the national leadership ordered in 1970 that the organisation should go completely underground and only go into combat as a last resort.

The last major rural guerrilla action of the period came just before this decision – in the early months of 1970; again it took place in the *departamento* of Matagalpa in the mountains of Zinica and El Bijao. But this was no simple re-run of Pancasan. The FSLN had agreed to forsake the galvanising effect of dramatic military action, and was now talking of a strategy of 'prolonged popular war in the mountains. The Zinica battle with the National Guard formed part of this conception. The composition of what was by now a small guerrilla army was different too: the peasant support for Pancasan had now come to fruition, and the Zinica *guerrilla* was almost exclusively made up of peasants. The group had gained combat experience in a series of minor skirmishes throughout 1969, and at Zinica for the first time a guerrilla column was not destroyed. Somoza threw a military cordon around the area, but the combatants succeeded in piercing it. Nor could the dictator hide his own losses, which included a helicopter gunship.[22] Peasant fighters gained new confidence in their military abilities as a result of Zinica.

Many members of the original leadership were absent from Zinica. They were now directing their efforts towards defining the Frente's ideological programme more clearly. Fonseca had left for a protracted stay in Cuba, where he set about consolidating old friendships and writing extensive studies of Nicaraguan history, having now been named General Secretary of the FSLN. The Frente published its minimum programme and internal statutes and the leadership was restructured in a move away from centralised to collective authority. With the FSLN underground, the need to project itself through intermediate organisations became more urgent than ever. Work began in earnest in the factories and working-class *barrios,* and the FSLN gained support at the expense of the PSN, with former Socialist militants flocking to join the organisation after the 1967 election debacle in which the Socialist Party had supported the presidential ticket of the Conservative Aguero. The new FSLN recruits were almost all factory workers,[23] and the groundwork was laid for later advances in Sandinista trade union organisation.

In the universities, it was the same story. Although the FSLN remained invisible, middle-class parents began to notice their student sons and daughters disappearing at weekends and returning home from meetings in the middle of the night. The student organisation FER was again active. Pedro Joaquin Chamorro's assessment of the student movement in Managua was this: '70% of them are Marxists, about 25% are *social-cristianos,* and the remaining 5% are nothing at all. For these youngsters, to be a Conservative or a Liberal is like going out into the tropical sun wearing a bowler hat.'[24]

Somoza, despite forming a Liberal Party student federation, the FEL, had never made any inroads into the universities, and the FER came to control the Student Council of the National University (Consejo Universitario de la Universidad Nacional: CUUN), with CUUN statutes formally prohibiting affiliation by any member to Somoza's Partido Liberal Nacionalista.

The FER and other intermediate organisations presented FSLN demands at a local level and in the workplace, putting across – as far as conditions permitted – the political line of the underground leadership. An unstoppable spiral began: National Guard terrorism on one hand, popular mobilisation and protest on the other. The maltreatment of political prisoners, with the torture, solitary confinement and threatened killing of those held in the *Carcel Modelo* prison in Tipitapa, formed part of an aggressive strategy by the Guard and the Office of Security to flush the Frente out into the open. But only a handful of combatants died in armed confrontations between 1970 and 1972, and the Sandinistas managed to avoid any ill-considered frontal response to Somoza's provocations. All long-time FSLN militants admit that the task of building the organisation's mass credibility while remaining hidden was one of the hardest periods in a decade of struggle. But it worked. Nicaraguans began to lose their fear. Mobilisation increased, and the FSLN was its focus. In May and June 1970, mothers and students carried out a hunger strike in solidarity with political prisoners, and in September a massive national protest swept through all major cities. In January 1971, students and workers in Leon mobilised against increases in transport costs. More hunger strikes followed in April, and peasant groups demonstrated against National Guard savagery in the north, with Somoza sending in helicopter gunships to put down protests in Matagalpa in May. 1972 continued in the same vein: more hunger strikes in April, student and worker protests against gasoline and milk price rises in May, marches in Managua to demand freedom for Sandinista prisoners in November.

In the southern *departamentos* of Masaya, Granada, Carazo and Rivas, the most heavily populated areas outside the capital, the Sandinistas had been trying to open up a new front for revolutionary work under the direction of Tomas Borge. The village of Nandaime, which stands at the intersection of the Panamerican highway and the main road to Granada, was a key point in this effort, controlling communications between the four *departamentos*. Here the Frente had installed a safe house known as 'La Ermita', and again, disastrously, Somoza's intelligence managed to locate it. Juan Jose Quezada, who had become an important figure in organising peasant support for the *guerrilla* in the northern mountains of Waslala and Cerro Grande, was on guard outside La Ermita on 17 September 1973 when a National Guard patrol attacked, leaving Quezada and three other Sandinistas dead. Two of them, Oscar Turcios and Ricardo Morales, had been members of the FSLN's national leadership.

The severity of this blow to the FSLN's clandestine structure coincided with an economic situation which restored some initiative to the PSN in the face of increased working-class discontent after the earthquake. Through its

CGT-I trade union federation, the Socialists led the successful building workers' strikes of 1973, and the FSLN was not yet able to provide leadership for a strike on this scale. Nevertheless, the FER gave vocal backing to the construction workers' action and tried to project its significance beyond the narrow economism of the PSN strike call. The FER also threw itself behind 1973 and 1974 strikes by hospital workers, protests by banana workers on Standard Fruit Company plantations in Chinandega, and demands by market traders and other groups affected by the economic crisis. But this was support, not leadership, and 1974 was a difficult year. More than four years had passed since the last major military action, and with PSN control over the strike movement, a fresh bourgeois alternative being presented under the banner of Pedro Joaquin Chamorro's UDEL, and Somoza going through the motions of re-election in preparation for a new presidential term on 1 December 1974, the FSLN had to break its silence. A renewed offensive was necessary for the Frente to confirm its ascendancy within the opposition movement.[25] Equally important, the guerrilla forces in the north, now swarming with counter-insurgency forces, were imploring the leadership to move on to an urban offensive to disperse the National Guard and take the heat off what had become an essentially defensive rural struggle. The form of the new offensive was unclear, but the objective need for it was overwhelming.

Breaking the Silence

Los Robles, which borders the main road out to Masaya in the south, is one of the elegant new residential developments which ring the old city centre of Managua since the 1972 earthquake. It is an area of quiet, winding streets lined with single-storey mansions in the colonial style, with inner courtyards full of palms and flowering plants and swimming pools at the back. The streets are quiet except for the sound of sprinklers on the lawns during the dry season, songbirds in the trees and the occasional Mercedes or Chevrolet gliding into the kerb.

The Frente had waited over the Christmas holiday of 1974 for a suitable time and place to stage their new offensive. On the morning of 27 December, one of the Sandinista commanders, German Pomares, picked up an announcement on the radio by Laszlo Pataky, a former Foreign Legionnaire and now a journalist and close friend of Somoza's, giving details of a reception which would be given that night at a house in Los Robles for the United States Ambassador Turner B. Shelton. The host was Jose Maria ('Chema') Castillo Quant, formerly linked with Somoza's Office of Security and then Minister of Agriculture. Castillo was also a rich cotton exporter and a close political confidant of the dictator.

The target was perfect. As well as Castillo, the party would include Guillermo Sevilla Sacasa, who was Nicaragua's ambassador to the United States as well as dean of the Washington diplomatic corps and the man who had done more than any other to promote the Somoza image of 'loyal friend' to every US line in international affairs. Other guests would be Alejandro Montiel, Minister of Foreign Affairs; Guillermo Lang, Nicaraguan consul in New York; Noel Pallais Debayle, Somoza's first cousin and president of INFONAC, the state institution responsible for managing 90% of foreign credits and all agricultural and industrial development programmes; Alfonso Deneken, recently appointed ambassador of the Chilean junta; and half a dozen other prominent politicians and industrialists.

Once Pomares had picked up the news, the plan went into action swiftly. 'Marcos', one of the members of the commando unit, gave this account: 'At eleven in the morning, the order was given for the commando unit to prepare for action. The M-1 carbines were checked, along with the .22 hunting rifles, one R-18, a .45, several small arms and six hand-grenades. In a woven cotton bag, each member of the group carried a large plastic bag to store water in case the supply was cut off, torches, bicarbonate, vitamins, medicine, glucose, serum, nylon ropes, aspirins and notebooks. The mark of identification was to be a red and black handkerchief — the colours of the Sandinista National Liberation Front — and as a disguise we were to wear stocking-masks.'[26]

The raid had to be delayed until a few minutes after Ambassador Shelton had left, but at 10.50 p.m. the commando of 13, including three women, was given the order to attack. As they burst in, their first words were 'This is a political operation. Hands on your heads and against the wall. This is the Sandinista National Liberation Front. VIVA SANDINO!'

The attack took the dictatorship utterly by surprise. Somoza was in his favourite haunt of Miami at the time and had to be summoned back to Managua by his half-brother Jose to direct operations. He threw a cordon of 500 soldiers of the 'General Somoza' combat battalion around the area, and within hours declared a state of siege, martial law, press censorship, and a dusk to dawn curfew. The state of siege was to last for 33 months. The Frente requested Archbishop Miguel Obando y Bravo of Managua, a figure now firmly opposed to the regime, as mediator, and held firm to their demands. The central demand was the release of a number of political prisoners whose presence was essential for the new phase of the war, among them Daniel Ortega Saavedra of the national leadership and the leading trade union organiser Jose Benito Escobar. This new phase would begin with the Chema Castillo attack, the opening of a general offensive in which broad sectors of the Nicaraguan people would participate, by dealing a debilitating blow to the morale of the regime. Clearly the attack, a dramatic surprise raid planned in absolute secrecy, could not be accompanied by organised mass action. But the masses, though unprepared, showed solidarity with the action and were inspired by this proof of the regime's vulnerability. In the days which followed, there was a striking if as yet incoherent upsurge in working-class combativity.[27]

Somoza had no alternative but to meet the Frente's political objectives. The prisoners were released, a $2-million ransom paid, and long communiques published in *La Prensa, El Centroamericano* and the government paper *Novedades;* they were also broadcast on two TV channels and six radio stations. In its second communique, the 'Juan Jose Quezada' combat unit, named after one of the Nandaime killed the previous September, spelt out the Frente's demands for the Nicaraguan working class. These were for immediate across-the-board wage rises for all industrial and agricultural workers, special provisions for domestic workers, a one-month bonus for hospital, construction, textile, and sugar workers, and a wage increase for enlisted men of the National Guard to 500 *cordobas* ($71) a month. This last demand particularly infuriated Somoza, although he had no option but to pay. When the commando flew out to Cuba after the 60-hour siege, accompanied by 18 prisoners and applauded all along the airport road by crowds shouting 'Viva el Frente! Viva Sandino! ', they left behind a humiliated dictator. Arriving at Jose Marti International Airport in Havana, one of the group told the waiting press: 'We are not supermen, we are mothers of children, nurses, workers, peasants, students, humble people whose lives sum up all the exploitation of our people.'

As well as humiliating Somoza, and publicising that humiliation through the world's press, 27 December 1974 aggravated the political crisis of the Nicaraguan bourgeoisie. It delineated more clearly than ever before those sectors of finance capital who would ultimately stick by the dictatorship and those other bourgeois groups whose opposition would now grow more outspoken. 'After the action,' remarked Borge sardonically, 'they became the most ardent revolutionaries in the world.' And after taking a brief initiative in 1973 and 1974, the PSN could hardly deny that the Chema Castillo operation had done more to radicalise the working class, by directly linking major wage increases to a political document denouncing the crimes of the dictatorship, than any number of strikes and peaceful forms of 'civic action'.

Somoza's Offensive: The State of Siege

'If Somoza was unable to pull the fish out of the water', wrote a Nicaraguan author describing the 33 months of repression which followed, 'he would try to empty the pond or poison it.'[28] Although the Chema Castillo operation opened up a new phase in the struggle, the Frente was driven back on to the defensive by Somoza's frenzied response. While the FSLN managed to make some inroads into labour movement organising, helping to radicalise the hospital workers and construction unions, the dictatorship moved on to the attack as soon as the 'Juan Jose Quezada' commando and the liberated prisoners were on the aircraft to Cuba. Moving to smash factory and *barrio* militancy in the cities, the dictator took the military war to where the vanguard was, in the mountains of Matagalpa, taking full advantage of the state of siege and press blackout to grant extraordinary military powers and cover up the atrocities committed by the Guard against the northern peasant population. In throwing the Guard's crack troops into the north, he stifled one of the major aims of the December attack: to relieve pressure on the beleaguered rural *guerrilla*. The remaining weaknesses of the FSLN's urban network, meanwhile, left it unable to sustain an offensive designed to keep the National Guard simultaneously engaged on two fronts, or to develop fully the new potential for resistance among the urban masses.

Somoza ordered the *Guardia's* best counter-insurgency troops to comb every inch of the mountains where the guerrillas operated most freely. To accompany these 'search and destroy' missions, aircraft of the Nicaraguan Air Force bombed the area, resorting in many cases to the use of napalm and defoliants.[29] Peasant huts were burned out and their crops destroyed, women raped. Half a dozen concentration camps were set up in Matagalpa and Zelaya, and another in Chinandega. In April 1976, 100 peasant families disappeared from three northern hamlets, and in November 1977 Nicaraguan and American church sources listed a further 350 peasant disappearances. The number of those who died in the 33 months of the state of siege can never be calculated, but 3,000 is a frequent estimate.[30]

It was a repeat of course of the 1930s. All Somoza's counter-insurgency failed to inflict real damage on the guerrillas: those who suffered were the local peasant population, and a few FSLN combatants who died in action. By now, the guerrilla columns had a familiarity with the terrain which rivalled Sandino's own. 'We grew to know the ground inch by inch, so that we could pull the enemy's beard . . . We had discovered that if the *campesinos* gave their support, if you master the terrain, then you can prod the enemy in the back and he won't notice.'[31] Military activity during this period was necessarily limited. In March 1975, Sandinistas briefly seized the small National Guard barracks at Rio Blanco in the Pancasan area. The resulting militarisation of the settlement of Rio Blanco, a blend of colonisation and repression, was characteristic of Somoza's methods in trying to smash the rural guerrilla. The hamlet, a collection of a few poor peasant huts with a small military outpost, was rapidly transformed into a thriving small town of several hundred people, and the news that the government was to drive a strategic new road through the zone brought speculative landowners into Rio Blanco at the expense of the local *campesinos*. The small guard post was turned into a regional counter-insurgency centre and concentration camp, where captured peasants were held in infested mud pits, interrogated, tortured and killed. 'About 75 *campesinos* were brought to Rio Blanco on one occasion for execution,' recalled a National Guard deserter who had served there. 'They came from El Sauce and El Viejo [villages near Esteli and Chinandega], where the intelligence service had detected Sandinista training schools where peasants received instruction before going to fight on the northern guerrilla front.'[32]

The ferocity of Somocista repression kept the FSLN pinned down in its rural strongholds, and it seemed momentarily as if the movement might have been destroyed. Certainly, admitted Henry Ruiz, 1977 was the year of the rural *guerrilla*'s greatest weakness. Neighbouring countries, especially Costa Rica to the south, were suddenly full of FSLN combatants and militants.

After dealing the organisation its severest blow, Somoza boasted that the FSLN was finished, and began to think in terms of pacifying the newly active bourgeois opposition by giving his regime the appearance of returning to normality, and offering minimal reforms such as lifting the state of siege. The worst blow to the FSLN came on 7 November 1976. For several days, counter-insurgency patrols had been mounting night ambushes in the mountains near Zinica, after receiving information from a peasant collaborator. On the night of the 7th, a patrol surprised a small guerrilla group, and opened fire. The second body they found was that of Carlos Fonseca Amador.

On Revolution Square in Managua, there are nowadays two huge portraits flanking the entrance to the National Palace. One is of Sandino, the other of Fonseca. Nearby, an eternal flame burns next to a simple mausoleum, where Fonseca — the 'Supreme Commander' of the Nicaraguan Revolution — lies buried. In November 1979, a crowd of 100,000 gathered in the square to mark the third anniversary of his death. Of all the casualties suffered by the FSLN leadership in the mid-1970s (fortunately not repeated during the final insurrection), none hit the Frente harder than the death of Fonseca. It robbed them of their General Secretary and their clearest political thinker, who had been convinced for twenty years that the armed struggle was the only path to achieve a very unique kind of revolution in Nicaragua. Unlike many who continued to believe throughout the insurrection that Somoza was the only obstacle to democracy, Fonseca had stated clearly from the first that: 'The question is not only to bring about a change of the man in power, but to transform the system, to overthrow the exploiting classes and achieve the victory of the exploited.'[33] He had foreseen too that the Nicaraguan Revolution would be achieved by a heterogeneous mix of different ideologies, and in 1964 — at a time when he disclaimed the title of 'Marxist-Leninist' he had written that: 'I believe the Nicaraguan revolutionary should embrace a doctrine which can lead the Nicaraguan people victoriously to liberation. In my own thought, I welcome the popular substance of different ideologies: Marxism, Liberalism and Christian Socialism.'[34] In this letter from prison, his arguments anticipate the need for class alliances more than a decade before the strategy of the final insurrection put them into practice, recognising that no ideology could be rigidly applied to the revolutionary struggle in Nicaragua without encompassing the peculiarities of the country's class structure and history of nationalist resistance. Like many later Nicaraguan radicals, he believed that Sandino's teachings provided a sufficient frame of reference for revolutionary opposition to Somoza.

Since his death Fonseca has become part of the best tradition of Nicaragua's revolutionary myth-making. When a jubilant National Guard officer brought a copy of the government newspaper *Novedades* to Tomas Borge's prison cell in the *Carcel Modelo* with the news of Fonseca's death, Borge paused for a moment before replying: 'No, colonel, you're wrong. Carlos Fonseca is one of the dead who never die.' The officer answered: 'You people really are incredible.'[35]

The FSLN Splits

Fonseca's death came at a moment when the question of class alliances and insurrectional strategy had become a major polemic within the FSLN. For another major consequence of the state of siege had been a serious division within the Frente, and sadly Fonseca did not survive to see it healed. Certainly the split horrified him, for he had always paid obsessive attention to the need for discipline and unity within the organisation and the meticulous selection of militants. There had been differences of opinion between leadership and the rank and file before, as well as within the leadership itself, but this time they ran much deeper. The loss of Ricardo Morales and Oscar Turcios – killed in Nandaime in 1973 – had been a serious one for the leadership, and to this could be added criticisms of excessive centralism and a self-confessed immaturity at the highest levels of the FSLN.[36]

The enforced clandestinity and suffocating repression of 1974-77 brought a physical disarticulation of the Frente, its rural guerrilla forces cut off from its urban cadres, and much of the leadership in exile or in hiding. The crucial historic interdependency between the mountains and the city was broken. The Frente's crisis came in the midst of a generalised rethinking by all opposition forces of the strategy and ideology needed to overthrow the dictatorship. Opposition restructuring took into account a new factor, the urban working class, paying less attention to the qualitative increase in its size than to the explosion of its militancy. Political consciousness and mobilisation among the industrial workers of Managua continued to grow even under the state of siege, with the FSLN's intermediate organisations providing a thread of continuity. Demonstrations were organised throughout the city in protest against the harassment of trade unionists, the poor quality and escalating cost of National Guard-controlled public transport, the lack of a good water supply, street lighting and adequate housing in the *barrios*. They grew to such a pitch that large groups within the formal opposition, the Catholic Church and the daily *La Prensa,* voice of the bourgeois opposition, began to sit up and take notice of the new urban militancy. In both town and countryside, there was a convergence between FSLN and Church groups organising workers and peasants around their new demands.

At the very time when the objective conditions of the war suggested a variety of strategic options, sectors of the FSLN were operating in different locations, with different class groups and different modes of military struggle. They were unable to make contact with each other, and rational unified discussions on future strategy became impossible. Was the battle against Somoza to be a protracted one, to be won by adhering to the established forms of rural guerrilla warfare? Did the upsurge in working-class militancy mean that the formation of a mass Marxist party was on the cards to lead the the struggle of the proletariat? Or were the decomposition of the regime, its growing international unpopularity, and the revulsion of ever greater sections of the bourgeoisie and the Church, sufficient grounds for believing that the war could be won in the short term by explosive insurrectional actions and broad class alliances? These in synthesis were the three options, each a legitimate one with many supporting arguments and the potential for all three to complement one another. But there was no climate in which the discussion could take place, and by 1975 an open rift developed. During the critical period of the state of siege, the bourgeois opposition had far more room to manoeuvre than the Sandinistas. The Frente had to rethink its relationship to the bourgeoisie or risk being outflanked by it. Clashes broke out between the older military leaders of the rural *guerrilla* and younger urban recruits. Clashes over the relative merits of military and political work, the way in which the FSLN was to consolidate its vanguard role, the timing and strategy of the final push against Somoza.

The arguments crystallised into three separate tendencies. They were the urban *Tendencia Proletaria* (Proletarian Tendency: TP); the rural *Guerra Popular Prolongada* (Prolonged Popular War: GPP); and a third group, the protagonists of broad class alliances and a rapid overthrow of Somoza, the *Tendencia Insurreccional* (Insurrectional Tendency, commonly known as 'Terceristas'.). When the world's press began to pay attention to the Nicaraguan crisis in 1978, it became conventional to describe the FSLN as 'two parts Marxist, one part moderate'. Like most media labels, the description is simplistic and grossly misleading.

For A Marxist Party: The Proletarian Tendency
The critiques and independent actions of a small urban-based section of the FSLN became incompatible with the continuing unity of the organisation in the harsh conditions of the state of siege. In October 1975, the leadership accused the group of sowing sectarianism among the rank and file and undermining their authority. They felt that disciplinary action against individuals, expulsion or suspension, was the only solution to the problem. In response, a section of the Frente's membership including both factory workers and intellectuals, split off, and called itself the *FSLN-Proletario* or *Tendencia Proletaria* (TP) believing that the key strategic role of the proletariat should now be reflected directly in the name of the vanguard. The overall dominance of agriculture in the Nicaraguan economy had obscured to many analysts the new revolutionary potential of the urban workers and the steady proletarianisation since the 1950s of their rural counterparts in important agroexporting enterprises. It was a trend which some Marxist intellectuals had touched on persuasively, and not least among these was Jaime Wheelock Roman, whose important piece *Imperialismo y Dictadura* had been completed the previous year, 1974.[37] Wheelock emerged now as one of the leaders of the new tendency, together with Roberto Huembes – later killed in combat – and Luis Carrion, today second in command of the Sandinista People's Army.

The Proletarians saw major contradictions between the dominant role of the working class and over-concentration on a rural guerrilla war depending on peasant support, a strategy which the Frente had used, with modifications, for fourteen years. Nor could the proletariat be left to go its own way. The certain outcome of that would be to hand it on a plate to the Socialist Party

and the bourgeois opposition group UDEL. The TP saw only one answer:
the creation of a Marxist-Leninist party of the proletariat. Like the national
leadership, it also claimed to be the vanguard of the Nicaraguan Revolution.
Not only, however, 'the vanguard detachment of the proletariat and the
Nicaraguan people', but also 'the embryo of the future revolutionary party
of the working-class.'[38] The TP therefore concentrated its energies on political, educational and agitational work with urban working-class cadres, among
the marginal *barrio*-dwellers of Managua's outlying slums and the prole-
tarianised agricultural workers of the Pacific Coast, in the sugar refineries
and cotton-processing plants of the *departamentos* of Leon and Chinandega.

They launched two publications, the ideological *Causa Sandinista* and the
military *El Combatiente Popular*. In the second number of *Causa Sandinista*,
the Proletarians argued their case: 'We must promote the formation of
unions, peasant leagues, professional associations, democratic organisations
of workers, women and youth; every kind of legal, illegal, open or clandestine
organisation. Without mass organisations, the revolutionary struggle against
the dictatorship has no effective underpinning.'[39] Each of these organisations,
the TP stressed, must maintain its class independence from the bourgeoisie.

Because of the problems of communication, TP activity was forcibly
divorced from the activities of the rest of the FSLN. Autonomously, they
created the Comites Obreros Revolucionarios (Revolutionary Workers'
Committees: COR) in factories and *barrios*. Nor did they neglect the military
aspects of the struggle. Although the Proletarians' resources were limited,
they proposed armed detachments of the working class around the notion of
'popular violence', arming their members in Comandos Revolucionarios del
Pueblo (Revolutionary People's Commandos: CRP). These managed to
sustain a certain level of harassment of the National Guard and armed propaganda in Managua, Masaya, Granada and the north-west.

By the last months of 1977, when the majority tendency of the FSLN was
attempting to channel popular anger through rapid insurrectional strikes, the
Proletarians stuck to their work of building these popular committees and
other class-based organisations. In addition to the COR, five other groups
loyal to the TP came together to produce an agitational publication called
Libertad. They were the FER-Marxista Leninista, which had split from the
main body of the student federation; the Movimiento Cristiano Revolucionario (Revolutionary Christian Movement: MCR); the Movimiento Estudiantil de Secundarios (Secondary School Student Movement: MES); the
Federacion de Movimientos Juveniles de Barrios de Managua (Federation
of Managua *barrio* Youth Movements: FMJBM); and the Comite
Universitario de Solidaridad con el Pueblo (University Committee of
Solidarity with the People: CUSOP). The backing for *Libertad* suggested
strongly the groups from which the TP drew its support – above all the
youth and student Left. But the tendency also tried to project itself at a
national level, and put together a minimum programme of government. The
document, outlined in a 1978 communique, went much further in its
demands than the parallel minimum programme of the FSLN's national

leadership at the time, especially on the central issues of agrarian reform and nationalisation. While the majority tendency was demanding the confiscation of all Somoza-owned property, the Proletarians called for 'liquidation of the *latifundio* pattern of land ownership and lands left idle by their owners; their reorganisation into collective modes of production and individual ownership which benefits poor and landless *campesinos*. [And] nationalisation of the banks; control of foreign trade by the state; nationalisation of foreign-owned industries and basic industry.'[40]

The Frente's national leadership came down hard on the TP, accusing it of misusing the name FSLN. Internal documents of the time admitted that the group was maintaining a certain level of activity among popular sectors and the student movement, while attacking it for placing greater emphasis on propaganda (circulars, wall-paintings, etc.) than on more sustained organisational work. It is true that the TP's achievements were restricted by its size and the conditions in which it worked. Nevertheless, its work made a long-term impact (at least at the theoretical level) out of all proportion to its small number of militants. Its impact was also manifested in the embryonic formation of class-based organisations which have powerfully represented the Nicaraguan masses through the first year of their revolution. Despite the predominance of middle-class intellectuals in the *Tendencia Proletaria*, it is not uncommon to come across workers and slum-dwellers in post-insurrectional Managua who trace their first identification with the vanguard back to the agitational work of the Proletarians in the *barrios* and factories.

Prolonged Popular War

Much of the original guerrilla nucleus of the FSLN, claiming that they faithfully represented the founding principles of the organisation, remained in the mountainous north to build up its forces. The name of this tendency came from its strategy of a 'prolonged popular war' – *Guerra Popular Prolongada,* or GPP. This in no sense meant that the GPP was exclusively concerned with the rural struggle. Like the Proletarians, it believed in the necessity of building up socialist consciousness among the urban masses. But since its main military force was pinned down in the north among the peasants, it suffered more than other sectors of the FSLN from the urban-rural dislocation of the state of siege. The GPP was headed by Henry Ruiz ('Modesto'), now Nicaragua's Minister of Planning and acknowledged as one of the organisation's finest strategists of guerrilla warfare. For long periods during the state of siege, the GPP's other most prominent leader – Tomas Borge – was languishing in Somoza's prisons, while a third, Pedro Arauz, was killed in action.

The term *guerra popular prolongada* had been in current use to describe mainstream FSLN strategy in the period before the split became apparent, and had been defined in a message from the Juan Jose Quezada commando unit as 'the political and military confrontation of the organised people against their foreign and local enemies during the time required for careful preparation and development before the final battle.'[41] In other words, the GPP still believed that a decisive insurrection against Somoza was a relatively distant project, and that the dictatorship would crumble slowly in the face of organised mass action. The level of consciousness of a working class coming to power was also a source of great concern to the GPP. Seeing the political backwardness in which four decades of *Somocismo* had submerged the people, they believed that only a lengthy struggle could allow socialist consciousness to develop adequately.[42]

But the military pressure on the GPP, and the physical isolation of their best militants, made it difficult for them to break out of a defensive posture and sustain the level of military action which would have significant repercussions in the country. While the Proletarians worked in the cities and a new majority tendency around the FSLN national leadership began to talk of the likelihood of a successful insurrection in the short term, the GPP was forced into keeping a low profile in the northern mountains, carrying out brief occupations of villages and harassing National Guard detachments to wear down the morale of the troops and slowly build up stocks of arms. The repression which left the GPP cut off as a tendency also affected its internal organisation. Columns were unable to contact each other directly, even when operating only a few kilometres apart, and had to rely on *campesino* intermediaries to retain any semblance of concerted military operations.

When the GPP talked of accumulating forces, what they had in mind was a gradual build-up of material, human and ideological resources, a solid and patient process. But others in the FSLN believed that the term could have a different significance, one which depended on a less defensive reading of the political situation of the country: 'We measured accumulation not merely in material terms but also in terms of the dynamics of the enemy's decomposition.'[43] It was an analysis which the GPP was badly placed to exploit. Only towards the end of 1977 did spectacular military actions by the majority tendency, discussed in the following chapter, ease the pressure on the GPP a little. Until then, their isolation had been almost total, and the disputes between rank and file militants and local leaders in some towns had become worse. The GPP saw its urban base stagnant, if not eroded, and it relied for its mass impact on the student FER, though this too had split in the wake of the Proletarian Tendency schism. It was a vicious circle for the GPP: little military vanguard action to stimulate the urban support network, and a limited base of support outside the combat zone, further weakening its military capacity. Finally, GPP leader Henry Ruiz – a firm believer in eventual FSLN reunification, and who might have been expected to adopt a conciliatory position on the organisation's internal crisis – had been interned for months at the head of the 'Pablo Ubeda' guerrilla column in a remote mountain area and was effectively out of touch with his fellow members of the FSLN national leadership.

Third Alternative: Insurrection
Members of the FSLN leadership in exile tried to find a way through the

dispute racking the Frente. Emerging as mediators, they came to represent a 'third force' within the FSLN, and this led to their being popularly known – especially outside Nicaragua – as the *Terceristas*. The two who came back to Nicaragua to heal the rift were Carlos Fonseca, founder of the Frente and its undisputed leader, and Eduardo Contreras. But the split had run too deep for any immediate reconciliation. The new strategic line which emerged from the talks put insurrection on the agenda as a complement to the war of attrition being waged by the GPP and the urban organisation of the Proletarians, and rapidly the new analysis was supported by a majority of the national leadership.

Those who put forward the new approach were staking their hopes on two factors: the immediate capacity of the people to be galvanised into mass insurrection by decisive military action from the vanguard, and the increasing rapprochement between sectors of the opposition bourgeoisie and the Left. They based their analysis on the 'floating' nature of many of Nicaragua's middle sectors, and saw that the petty bourgeoisie, professionals and many Church groups could be won over to an insurrectional struggle, without this tactical alliance placing the FSLN under bourgeois leadership. Rapid recruitment to the new *Terceristas* (or *Tendencia Insurreccional*) followed from Church and lay workers, lawyers, academics and some *lumpen* elements. To some, it seemed an over-hasty sacrifice of ideological purity, not to mention a security risk, but by 1977 the Insurrectionals found themselves making preparations for a swift push against a weakened dictator in the face of open criticisms from the other two tendencies. Using their middle-class contacts to build a powerful movement of international solidarity in Latin America, North America and Western Europe, the Insurrectionals quickly became by far the majority tendency within the FSLN.

The split was by now public knowledge, and the Insurrectionals became impatient at the other tendencies' refusal to admit the logic behind a prompt uprising from broad sectors of the population. They were stung too by the harsh public attacks on the new strategy, attacks which they believed could only benefit Somoza and the bourgeois opposition by projecting the image of a bitterly divided vanguard. In the three-way split, each of the tendencies took corresponding sectors of the established student movement with it, and it was here that the *Terceristas* were arguably weakest. The bulk of the old Frente Estudiantil Revolucionario remained loyal to the GPP; the Proletarians took the FER-Marxista-Leninista and the new Juventud Revolucionaria Nicaraguense (Nicaraguan Revolutionary Youth: JRN); while the Insurrectionals gained the support of the Juventud Revolucionaria Sandinista (JRS).

The severe blows which the Frente had suffered during the state of siege also had serious repercussions on the stability of the leadership. Depleted by imprisonment and by deaths in combat, notably that of Fonseca, it was forced to restructure more than once. With the release of Daniel Ortega and Jose Benito Escobar from jail after the Chema Castillo operation in December 1974, the leadership had expanded to twelve members in the early part of 1975, but losses in battle cut it again to seven. By 1977, the effective leadership was further reduced to six, with the renewed imprisonment of the GPP *comandante* Tomas Borge. The losses brought a salutary lesson: that no member of the leadership could be considered indispensable. Accordingly, deputies were named to assume leadership functions in the event of further deaths, and the leadership became more flexible and less centralised.[45] Of those who remained in 1977, a definite majority favoured the insurrectional strategy. In this belief the Ortega brothers, Daniel and Humberto, were joined by two men who were an eloquent indication of the Central American internationalist tradition, the Mexican Victor Tirado Lopez (already referred to) and the Costa Rican Plutarco Hernandez. Henry Ruiz and Jose Benito Escobar (killed in combat near Esteli in June 1978) were clearly aligned with the GPP, while the Proletarians had no voice on the national leadership.

With the death of Hernandez and the isolation of 'Modesto', the Ortega brothers and Victor Tirado Lopez became the joint signatories of all FSLN leadership declarations. The identification of the *Direccion Nacional* with the Insurrectional Tendency was now manifest, though the tendency's name never appeared in documents. In mid-1978, one such communique synthesised the aims of the national leadership: 'The armed insurrection of the masses is a means to achieve the revolutionary overthrow of the Somoza dynasty and open up a process of popular democracy, which will allow our people to enjoy democratic liberties, a more favourable framework in which to accumulate the revolutionary energies required for the march towards full national liberation and socialism.'[46]

The question which would be posed to the Insurrectionals was whether their military actions were mere spontaneism, divorced from the masses, or whether their encouragement of alliances with other anti-Somoza forces was in itself a legitimate step towards creating a mass base. It remained now for the Insurrectionals to mount the spectacular armed offensive which would bring the masses on to the streets and assure the FSLN of a dominant role in the overthrow of *somocismo*.

Notes

1. J. Gerassi (ed.), *Venceremos – The Speeches and Writings of Ernesto 'Che' Guevara* (London, Weidenfeld and Nicolson, 1968), p. 267.
2. Henry Ruiz, 'La Montana Era Como un Crisol Donde se Forjaban los Mejores Cuadros', in *Nicarauac*, No. 1 (Managua, Ministerio de Cultura; May-June 1980), p. 24.
3. Blandon, *Entre Sandino y Fonseca Amador*, pp. 91-6, 142-7.
4. Tomas Borge, *Carlos, El Amanecer Ya No Es una Tentacion* (Managua, SENAPEP, 1979), p. 23.
5. Fonseca, *Nicaragua – Hora Cero*.
6. Tomas Borge, 'La formacion del FSLN', in *La Revolucion A Traves de Nuestra Direccion Nacional* (Managua, SENAPEP, 1980) pp. 27-8.
7. *Ibid.*, p. 30.

8. See Carlos Fonseca, *Un Nicaraguense en Moscu* (Managua, SENAPEP reprint, 1980).
9. Henry Ruiz, *loc. cit.*, p. 16.
10. Borge, 'La Formacion del FSLN', p. 31.
11. Unidad de Combate 'Juan Jose Quezada', *Mensaje no. 2 al Pueblo de Nicaragua;* communique, 27 December 1974
12. Henry Ruiz, *loc. cit.*, p. 16.
13. Robleto Siles, *Yo Deserte de la Guardia . . .*', p. 21.
14. Humberto Ortega, *50 Anos de Lucha Sandinista*, p. 107.
15. 'Modesto' was the *nom de guerre* of Comandante Henry Ruiz.
16. Omar Cabezas, 'Por el Duro Camino de Nuestra Revolucion', in *Nicarauac*, No. 2, July-August 1980, pp. 28-9.
17. Gladys Baez, *Pancasan* (Leon, Editorial Universitaria de la UNAN, 1979), p. 17.
18. Tomas Borge, *Carlos, El Amanecer Ya No Es una Tentacion*, pp. 46-7.
19. *Ibid.*, p. 51.
20. See Henry Ruiz, *loc. cit.*
21. Regis Debray, *A Critique of Arms*, (Harmondsworth, Penguin, 1977), p. 145.
22. Doris Tijerino, *Inside the Nicaraguan Revolution*, p. 173. The chronology contained in this book, pp. 168-76, is a useful guide to FSLN political and military action, and Somocista repression, in the period from 1961 to 1974.
23. Borge, *Carlos, El Amanecer Ya No Es una Tentacion*, p. 57.
24. Quoted in Crawley, *Dictators Never Die*, p. 150.
25. Humberto Ortega, *op. cit.*, p. 121.
26. Jaime Wheelock, *Diciembre Victorioso* (Managua, SENAPEP, 1979), p. 9.
27. *Barricada*, 27 December 1979.
28. Lopez *et al.*, *La caida del Somocismo*, p. 167.
29. Ernesto Cardenal, interview with *Excelsior*, March 1977.
30. See Fernando Cardenal, testimony before the International Organisations Sub-Committee of the House Foreign Relations Committee, Washington D.C., 8-9 June 1976. Major parts of this testimony are reproduced in *Nicaragua: El Pueblo Frente A La Dinastia* (Madrid, Instituto de Estudios Politicos para America Latina y Africa, 1978), pp. 96-104..
31. Henry Ruiz, *loc. cit.*, p. 21.
32. Robleto Siles, *op. cit.*, p. 151.
33. Carlos Fonseca, *Nicaragua – Hora Cero*.
34. Carlos Fonseca, *Desde la Carcel Yo Acuso A La Dictadura*, Managua, Carcel de la Aviacion, 8 July 1964.
35. Borge, *Carlos, El Amanacer Ya No Es una Tentacion*, p. 80.
36. Humberto Ortega, interview with Marta Harnecker, originally published in *Bohemia*, Havana; English version, 'The Strategy of Victory', reprinted in the English-language edition of *Granma*, Havana, 27 January 1980.
37. Wheelock, *Imperialismo y Dictadura*, especially pp. 18-19, 82. Wheelock deals most extensively with the break-up of the old peasantry and the introduction of wage labour in relation to coffee, rather than sugar or cotton production.
38. *Causa Sandinista*, No. 2, January-February 1978, p. 5.

39. *Ibid.,* p. 4.
40. FSLN-Proletario communique, somewhere in Nicaragua, 1978.
41. Unidad de Combate 'Juan Jose Quezada', *Mensaje no. 2 Al Pueblo de Nicaragua.*
42. See particularly broadsheets and communiques of the Frente Estudiantil Revolucionario during this period.
43. Daniel Ortega, interviewed in *Alternativa,* No. 189, Bogota, Colombia, 20 November 1978.
44. Lopez, *et al., op. cit.,* p. 115.
45. Henry Ruiz, *loc. cit.,* pp. 18-19.
46. FSLN circular, signed by Humberto Ortega, Daniel Ortega and Victor Tirado, somewhere in Nicaragua, July 1978.

7. The FSLN Takes the Lead, 1977–78

'Practical revolutionary politics means tracing a line of demarcation between the revolutionary camp and the reactionary camp, between the forces for the revolution and those against it. That demarcation line will of course shift with the movement of events, varying from one stage of the revolution to the next . . . The way the nature of the revolution is defined at any given stage of its development determines the identification of the prime enemy, and of the goals, the moving forces and the leadership of the revolution. It also governs the policy of alliances which must be pursued. It is the business of every political vanguard to draw the line of demarcation as it is now in their country.' Regis Debray[1]

End to the State of Siege

The state of siege had failed to have the effect Somoza had so often boasted of. The revolutionary opposition, though largely invisible, was still very much alive. The consensus of tacit support from the bourgeoisie was crumbling before Somoza's eyes. Thirty-three months of martial law and press censorship from 1974 to 1977 had left the dictatorship with a crippling contradiction: bourgeois opposition was mounting, but any partial democratisation of the kind demanded could only bring to light the extent of the crimes committed under cover of the press blackout, thus further exposing the corruption and moral disintegration of the regime.

Conflicts within the bourgeoisie were by now acute. Private sector groups like the *Consejo Superior de la Empresa Privada* (Higher Council of Private Enterprise: COSEP) and the development institute INDE were making ever more vocal demands for a more equitable set of rules of the capitalist game. They campaigned against state corruption, and their demands for a clean-up of the public service now found an echo in the United States Embassy. The foreign debt was out of control, and small businesses began to go to the wall. *La Prensa,* the main channel for bourgeois discontent, had been silenced by press censorship, and it was left to church groups and independent journalists to speak out in whatever way possible against the peasant massacres in Zelaya and Matagalpa.

In August 1977, the very core of the family dictatorship itself was shown to be vulnerable. Somoza suffered a massive heart attack, his second in a year, and was flown off to a Miami clinic. Within the ruling Nationalist Liberal Party cracks began to show. There were those who thought that Somoza's prolonged illness, and the real chance that he might not recover, meant laying plans for a change of command. But when Somoza returned to his desk, under doctor's orders to reduce his workload but still bearing something of his father's myth of indestructibility, those who had dared to question his permanence swiftly found themselves out of favour. Cornelio Hueck, the 'Lord of Masaya' and President of the Chamber of Deputies, was the most prominent casualty. Faced with a crisis which touched even his own party, the only effective power base remaining to Somoza was the National Guard. Even the support of the United States was in doubt: with the Carter Administration's 'human rights' policy in its first year — and Somoza's Nicaragua one of its prime targets — there was an insistent pressure from the US Embassy to lift the state of siege. Sensing that the dictatorship was faltering, wide sectors of the Carter State Department began to cast around for a suitable mid-term replacement, perhaps Pedro Joaquin Chamorro's UDEL coalition. In that case *La Prensa* could not be silenced. The bourgeoisie must be given space to breathe and organise, or the initiative was likely to pass to the Left.

Faced with this pressure, Somoza lifted the state of siege on 5 September 1977. But he thereby produced of course the very response he had most sought to avoid — an explosion of popular protest. If the private sector found it convenient to use the new situation to press for an extension of democratic freedoms (and first on their list was the free exercise of capitalist competition), the initiative passed rapidly to the working class. In the middle months of 1977, there had been apparent convergence between popular and business demands. Mass demonstrations had called for an immediate restoration of minimum constitutional guarantees. But working-class protests after September 1977 received unprecedented publicity, even in *La Prensa*, and with this came spectacular new opportunities for previously uncoordinated struggles to be channelled into new forms of mass organisation. Resistance in the *barrios* took many forms: demonstrations, mass meetings, seizure of churches and schools, destruction of Somoza-owned properties, armed confrontations with the National Guard, the first small-scale use of barricades, roadblocks and bus-burnings in the working-class districts. The first radical political fronts sprang up. Some, like the women's organisation AMPRONAC, were formed spontaneously with a marked input from middle-class women, and only later acquired an openly Sandinista character. Others, like the organisation of the rural proletariat in the *Asociacion de Trabajadores del Campo* (Rural Workers Association: ATC) were tied from the beginning to the agitational efforts of the FSLN, particularly the Proletarian Tendency.

To the Insurrectionals, or Terceristas, organising the people now also meant arming them. As early as April 1977, they had begun to distribute arms and give clandestine military training for an armed uprising which they now saw as inevitable within a matter of months. And 80% of those who took part in the new secret military training schools were workers. The Insurrectionals felt the need to break the military silence, as the FSLN had done in December 1974, with a spectacular armed action, even if in relative isolation from the organised masses. Popular resistance to Somoza had to be ignited, the majority tendency argued, behind an insurrectional strategy. Otherwise the bourgeoisie, for all its divisions, might take advantage of the removal of the stifling restrictions of the state of siege.

In October 1977 the Insurrectionals risked everything: the antagonism of the GPP and the Proletarians, military annihilation and the sympathy of the masses. Taking all these dangers into account, the Insurrectional leadership ordered coordinated attacks on three National Guard targets in different parts of the country. The plan also rested on the bourgeoisie's notorious inability to master a crisis, and in this the Terceristas could claim complete success. The events of October, and their galvanising effect on the people, threw UDEL into further disarray.

October Offensive: Propaganda for Insurrection

Although the remote southern barracks of San Carlos, on the southern edge of Lake Nicaragua, was the first step in a planned strategy of attack, few outside the Tercerista leadership knew what the plan was. 'The leadership of the Frente, the Tercerista tendency, planned the operation. I imagine that it obeyed an overall plan, because later the departmental command-post of Masaya was attacked as well. We didn't know the reasons why the leadership had chosen San Carlos as its target. The combatants were merely following the instructions of the leadership.'[2] Certainly the proximity of San Carlos to the Costa Rican border, and the sanctuary offered to the Terceristas by that country, had something to do with it. The small group of combatants left the contemplative community run by Ernesto Cardenal on the archipelago of Solentiname on the night of 12 October. For weeks the community had been practically converted into a military training school. There had been divisions within the community over the decision to take up arms against Somoza, but for the eighteen or twenty members who joined the Frente in 1977, it was the logical expression of their Christian faith, and one which was increasingly shared by large sectors of the Nicaraguan church.

> In Solentiname, we tried to resolve problems, the problems of the whole community, using the Sunday mass . . . if one person was ill, or another had no money, or another's son had been imprisoned by the National Guard. And in these Sunday assemblies we talked about the justification of revolutionary violence for a Christian . . . the image in the gospels of Christ as a proletarian revolutionary. The Nicaraguan people were involved in a fight against injustice, and to use violence was to be willing to give your life for the liberation of Nicaragua; it

was a violence of love. And so, many decided to take up arms. To go into combat as a group. And that group left Solentiname on October 12 1977 to attack the National Guard barracks at San Carlos, which was the nearest town to the island.[3]

Maybe our plan was a little naive: we thought that we would take the barracks of San Carlos, move on from there to Masaya, and then to Granada, leaving a few people in charge of each barracks in turn. But the Granada attack never happened. Three of us who took part in the assault on San Carlos were women, and when the news broke I think it inspired other women to believe that they could join in the revolutionary struggle. We were also Christians, which had a great impact on Nicaraguans. It added a fresh dimension to people's idea of the Frente Sandinista.[4]

The San Carlos combatants were poorly armed, and although the new training school at Solentiname had given some basic instruction in the use of arms, the group took only one Garand rifle, an M-3 sub-machinegun, an M-4 carbine, a shotgun and a .22 rifle.[5] On the same day, another Sandinista commando unit attacked the National Guard post at Ocotal near the Honduran border, and ambushed Guard troops on the road between Ocotal and Dipilto. And four days later the Frente hit their most ambitious target: the heavily fortified command-post in the main square of Masaya, a strategically important town only 18 miles south-east of the capital. Even Managua was no longer secure, as the Frente attacked military targets in the city centre and ambushed patrols on the main highway into the city. On a military level, the Insurrectional Tendency had learned the art of striking the enemy on several fronts simultaneously.

But the gulf between military action and political work had still to be bridged. There could be no immediate mass response — beyond an emotional one — to the October attacks, for the people had not been involved or consulted. But the example of direct combat, the proof that even a few poorly armed fighters could dent the regime's image of impregnable military strength, filtered through to the Nicaraguan people, and there was overwhelming sympathy for the courage of the combatants. As people lost their fear of openly confronting the Guard on unequal terms in the early months of 1978, the galvanising effect of October became clear. Sandinista units briefly occupied the towns of Rivas and Granada in February 1978, and in both cases found growing popular support in towns not previously known for their militancy.

In a later interview, Daniel Ortega of the FSLN leadership stressed the historical importance of the October offensive: 'Without October, there could have been no February, no National Palace in August 1978, no September 1978 insurrection.'[6] At the time, though, October 1977 was hard for many to understand, and to the Proletarians and GPP it looked like old-style military politics, unconnected to the mass struggle. Both tendencies

responded sharply to the attacks. From Honduras, the GPP declared on
24 October that only a *prolonged* war would oust Somoza.[7] And a Proletarian communique in early November was phrased in even stronger terms:
'The Tendencia Proletaria of the FSLN expresses its disagreements with the
actions of Masaya, San Carlos and Ocotal, which constitute *golpista* adventures which have not counted on the organised support of the working
masses; they form part of the purest tradition of bourgeois *cuartelazos*.
We direct our disapproval not at the heroic combatants who took up arms
. . . but at the Tercerista leadership.'[8]

But the fighting strength of the FSLN was no longer to be taken lightly.
In late October 1977, in the midst of a rash of UDEL and private sector
declarations on the crisis, *La Prensa* carried a bold headline: '50 TRAINING
SCHOOLS IN OPERATION, SAYS ORTEGA.' Accompanying this
announcement of the FSLN's new military and organisational capacity was a
photograph of Humberto Ortega, one of the Tercerista leaders. The headline
coincided with the appearance of a new group who were central to the
Frente's policy of class alliances and gave the Sandinistas a new legitimacy
among much of the disaffected bourgeoisie.

The Group of Twelve

La Prensa's front page the previous day had carried an explosive political
document which at a stroke shattered Nicaraguans' assumptions about the
alleged gulf separating the Frente from the 'formal' opposition. It was signed
by a group of twelve prominent professionals all known for the strength
of their opposition to Somoza but not for any prior political activity.
Fernando Cardenal, a Jesuit priest and member of the group, admitted in an
interview in Costa Rica: 'This group of twelve is an unusual one. None of us
is a politician. None of us has ever been involved in politics. None of us is
interested in power.'[9] But the time had come, they felt, to speak out in
favour of the FSLN. The signatories of the document — 'Los Doce', as they
came to be known — were two lawyers (Ernesto Castillo and Joaquin
Cuadra); two businessmen (Emilio Baltodano and Felipe Mantica); two priests
(Fernando Cardenal and Miguel D'Escoto); an academic (Carlos Tunnermann);
a writer (Sergio Ramirez); an agronomist (Ricardo Coronel); an architect
(Casimiro Sotelo); a banker (Arturo Cruz) and a dental surgeon (Carlos
Gutierrez). It was precisely their lack of a specific political constituency and
their impeccable professional credentials which gave the Los Doce group such
influence at a time when the bourgeois opposition and the FSLN were
following separate, and apparently mutually exclusive, paths in their fight
against Somoza. The main impact of Los Doce's declaration was their
insistence that no solution could be found to the country's political crisis
without the full participation of the FSLN. 'For more than a decade,' said the
document, 'the FSLN and the blood spilt by so many young people are the
best testimony to the permanence and presence of this struggle, carried out

with an ever greater degree of political maturity.'

For a group of prominent citizens of purely bourgeois extraction to praise the Frente for its political maturity shook a confused opposition bourgeoisie even further out of its stride. The UDEL leadership promptly went into closed session to decide on their response, but failed to find one. The development institute INDE attempted, but without success, to distort the Los Doce document and portray it as endorsing their own concept of dialogue with Somoza. As for the FSLN, it reacted enthusiastically. Within a week of the document's publication, the national leadership — in a communique signed not only by Tercerista leaders but by Henry Ruiz of the GPP — formally asked Los Doce to represent the Sandinistas in any search for a political solution.

The close relationship between the Frente and Los Doce was enduring. In the construction of a broad anti-Somoza front under revolutionary leadership — an essential part of the FSLN's insurrectional strategy — Los Doce provided a bridge for programmatic agreements between the Sandinistas and the more progressive sectors of the bourgeois opposition. Eventually, after eight months of mounting insurrectional activity, and a rapprochement between the Frente's three tendencies, Los Doce returned from exile in defiance of Somoza's threats to have them imprisoned as a threat to public security. The FSLN judged the moment right for a broad opposition movement to be built on the Frente's own terms, with Los Doce playing a central role in the realignment of class forces. An FSLN document of July 1978 put their position:

> We consider Los Doce a unifying force in that the minimum programme to which they have put their names coincides with the democratising demands of the bourgeois opposition, while in no way conflicting with the popular democratic proposals sketched out in the minimum programme of the popular and revolutionary forces. With the entry of Los Doce on to the scene it is genuinely the honest and progressive forces of Nicaragua which now occupy the pivotal position which makes unity possible.

Later, when the September 1978 insurrection was launched, the FSLN called on Los Doce to head a provisional government whose programme would be based on the confiscation of all Somoza-owned property and the formation of a new army to replace the National Guard. And in mid-1980 (a year after the Revolution), two members of the original group of twelve were in the Junta of Government of National Reconstruction, with a further seven occupying senior government posts.

The Terceristas held firm to the insurrectional strategy of the October 1977 offensive, although upset that the criticisms of the Proletarians and the GPP should have been made so publicly, in a way which might only benefit UDEL and the private sector. There might have been a stalemate at this point over the leadership of the opposition movement, but the intervention of

105

Los Doce in the final months of 1977 tipped the scales. They were helped by the impotence of the bourgeois opposition in the face of the crisis.

Response of the Private Sector: National Dialogue

After the October offensive, the pages of *La Prensa* were suddenly full of proposals to defuse the crisis, from UDEL, from COSEP, from INDE, from the Catholic hierarchy. Almost overnight, the watchword of the private sector was a 'national dialogue'. In December, Pedro Joaquin Chamorro handed the leadership of UDEL over to Rafael Cordova Rivas, a Managua lawyer from the most progressive wing of the Conservative Party, but the change of leadership did nothing to improve UDEL's ability to channel business discontent into a coherent political strategy. From the start, the new dialogue was less a vehicle for confrontation with the dictatorship than a means of allowing accommodation in order to neutralise the crisis until the 1981 elections. The pages of *La Prensa* during the last three months of 1977 make monotonous reading: the same complaints repeated, if infused with a new panic as businessmen took stock of the popular impact of the Frente's October actions. In the absence of any other medium of mass communication but the government's own *Novedades,* the use of the Chamorro family columns was also a useful way of legitimising UDEL in people's minds as the major voice of anti-Somoza feeling, thereby channelling mass discontent towards UDEL's reformist intentions.

UDEL also tried, with some success, to use the Catholic hierarchy as a mouthpiece for its policies. An eight-column *La Prensa* headline on 21 October announced: 'PRIVATE ENTERPRISE UNITED FOR CHANGE! INDE resolves to visit archbishop to ask him to initiate dialogue.' Similar announcements made it clear that the private sector saw the state of incipient civil war primarily as another obstacle to the free pursuit of bourgeois economic development: 'worried by the situation of violence which blocks business activity' (INDE Granada, 29 October 1977); 'the national situation is affecting the normal development of economic activities' (INDE Matagalpa, 24 October 1977).' INDE, although representing the sector of private enterprise worst hit by government corruption, was wholly unable to grasp the real nature of a crumbling dictatorship. The Granada communique concluded lamely: 'We appeal to the government to respect the constitution.'

At the end of October, the private sector named its 'National Dialogue Commission' to talk to Somoza. It consisted of Archbishop Obando y Bravo of Managua, two other bishops, a church lawyer and a young businessman who found himself thrust into a new political career which ultimately lasted through the first year of revolutionary government: the INDE president and cooking-oil manufacturer Alfonso Robelo Callejas. Somoza, to nobody's surprise, scornfully rejected the call for a dialogue. It was, he said, 'unconstitutional'.

As 1977 ended, Somoza was weakened but intransigent. The private sector appeared to be at an impasse. Popular resistance was growing, but the FSLN remained divided. It took a single unexpected event in January 1978 to spark off the final crisis which would determine clearly whether the bourgeoisie or the popular forces were to guide the push against *Somocismo*. It was an event which neither side could have anticipated as part of its strategy.

Chamorro Assassinated

Pedro Joaquin Chamorro, despite the open antagonism of the Somoza regime towards him, always travelled to his offices at *La Prensa* without a bodyguard. As he was driving through the earthquake-ruined centre of Managua on 10 January, a burst of gunfire hit him in the chest and face, killing him. Despite Somoza's protestations that he had had ample previous opportunities to kill the editor of *La Prensa* if he had chosen to, the whole of Nicaragua blamed the dictator for the crime.

As a political phenomenon, the Chamorro assassination followed the usual Latin American pattern of the Right eliminating troublesome progressives and moderate politicians. Examples abound: General Carlos Prats, assassinated by the Chilean junta in Buenos Aires; the Uruguayan politicians, Zelmar Michelini and Hector Gutierrez, who had shown dangerous sympathies with the Tupamaros; Bolivian nationalist, General Juan Jose Torres; the assassination of Orlando Letellier by agents of the Chilean DINA in Washington. All the murders had similar motives. Each man represented a political position which might have united divergent forces of the Centre and Left in their own countries. Chamorro was the most dangerous of them: in no other country was the political situation so critical for the ruling dictatorship, and Chamorro was the most plausible figure to head a short-term civilian alternative to the regime.

Although there were those in Washington who could seriously say 'Pedro Joaquin Chamorro may or may not have been a Marxist',[10] the UDEL leader's politics could best be described as those of a traditional Nicaraguan Conservative *caudillo* increasingly influenced by the Latin American version of Christian Democracy. His family had a long-standing political feud with the Somozas, and Chamorro himself had taken part in the disastrous Conservative armed invasion of Olama y los Mollejones in 1959 as well as writing a powerful attack on the regime in his book *Estirpe Sangrienta: los Somoza* ('Bloody Lineage: the Somozas'), which reflected his imprisonment by the regime in the 1950s.

Though Chamorro had relinquished the leadership of UDEL to Cordoba Rivas the previous month, his political ambitions for the 1981 elections had not diminished. His role in the National Dialogue had been to pave the way for peaceful elections in 1981 and presumably for his own candidacy – by defusing current social tensions. In addition to this political threat, the end of press censorship had seen an onslaught by the Chamorro newspaper *La Prensa* against the regime: denunciations of human rights violations and peasant massacres during the period 1974 to 1977; enormous space devoted to the activities of the bourgeois opposition — and latterly even to the FSLN; and an uncomfortable investigation into the blood plasma processing firm *Plasmaferesis* which exported the blood of Nicaraguans to the United States under the management of Cuban *gusano*[11] exiles who received generous tax concessions from Somoza.[12]

Among those arrested in connection with the murder was the Cuban director of the firm, Pedro Ramos, who offered some vague hints about the real authors of the crime and fled to the USA before he could be arraigned as an accessory. But if Somoza himself still thought that Chamorro's opposition could be controlled, his son Anastasio Somoza Portocarrero, with his own ambitions for the 1981 presidency, may well have thought otherwise. 'We got rid of Tacho,' said a middle-class Managua woman shortly after the July 1979 victory, 'Thank God we never had to put up with "El Chiguin".[13] He would have been a hundred times worse.' Somoza Portocarrero, who controlled the elite force of the National Guard, the Basic Infantry Training School (EEBI), had early on achieved a reputation for brutality and arrogance even among those sectors of the Managua bourgeoisie most closely identified with the regime. While still a teenager, he used to slap the faces of cabinet ministers who displeased him! Among the Guard, too, he had made enemies for the same reason, and he was one of the few members of the ruling elite who dared to challenge the regime's unwritten law. 'No-one could make a move in Nicaragua without consulting Somoza,' as Carlos Fernando Chamorro put it when speaking of his father's assassination.[14]

Although it is not impossible that Somoza Debayle himself was involved in the discussions of the Chamorro assassination, it is rather more likely that it was Somoza Portocarrero who saw the editor and former UDEL leader as an obstacle to his own presidential aspirations. And those were ambitions which his father clearly shared, having given his son control over the key unit of the National Guard — an invariable step in the Somoza pattern of succession. Whether or not 'Tacho' was involved directly in the planning, neither father nor son could have predicted the consequences of the crime — an unprecedented wave of riots and mass mobilisations which the Sandinistas' October offensive alone could never have unleashed, and a flurry of international condemnation. The remarkable mass actions of January and February 1978 even caused the GPP to reconsider their position and move closer to the Terceristas. The aftermath of the Chamorro murder showed that conditions might, after all, favour a rapid move towards popular insurrection.

The January Riots

The massive scale of popular anger which followed the Chamorro assassination presented a new problem for the Insurrectionals. Here was a new form of largely spontaneous popular violence which refused to obey the time-scale of Tercerista strategy, and the vanguard was faced with the urgent task of putting itself at the head of a new upsurge in mass hostility to the regime.[15] The nature of the protests showed an anti-Somocista feeling qualitatively different from the anti-*Somocismo* of UDEL and the bourgeoisie, who also found themselves with a dilemma: how to damp down this new violence which was rapidly leaping out of their control. The roots of the new violence were much more in line with the militant popular actions of the final months of the state of siege, when peasants had carried out militant land take-overs in the northern *departamentos* of Leon and Chinandega.

Even as Chamorro's body was receiving the tribute of the crowd, the first fires started, and the first building to go on the Carretera Norte, near the installations of *La Prensa*, was the infamous Plasmaferesis, known to Nicaraguans as the 'House of Dracula'. From here, each litre of blood extracted from Managua drunks and *marginados* was sold abroad for 40 cordobas (at that time around 5.50 dollars). Next in line was Somoza's textile factory El Porvenir, which as well as producing textiles was notorious as a storehouse for contraband destined for Somoza interests: radio sets, televisions, stereo equipment and refrigerators, packaged as industrial equipment free of import duties. The targets were carefully chosen by the crowd. On 11 January, demonstrators burned down fifteen buildings, among them banks and finance houses, some factories, building firms, ironmongeries and commercial establishments. Each of them represented a symbol of Somoza, foreign capital or particularly voracious members of the Nicaraguan bourgeoisie. One thousand demonstrators blocked access to the burning Plasmaferesis to prevent the fire brigade reaching the scene. They were only part of a total crowd of 10,000 who congregated in three groups on the Carretera Norte, less a demonstration than a small-scale popular uprising. A second group of 5,000 gathered outside *La Prensa* itself. A worker in the crowd shouted that the protesters should attack the nearby branches of Francofin, a French banking consortium, and the First National City Bank of New York, and within minutes both buildings were in flames.

But the partial insurrection lacked clear organisation and arms. Many of the workers who confronted the National Guard complained bitterly, and *Libertad*, the paper of those people's organisations linked to the Proletarios, protested in its editorial: 'When we fought the Guard, there were many of us who said "we need arms" . . . If we were armed, then you'd see.'

On the third day, when Chamorro was buried, another 50,000 assembled on the way to the cemetery, even though the UDEL leadership had persuaded the Chamorro family to change the time of the ceremony to prevent it becoming the focus of another militant working-class demonstration. The dictatorship, too, tried to minimise the effect of the funeral, with the National Guard turning back hundreds of vehicles arriving from all over Nicaragua.

With the January riots over, the Frente moved on to the offensive in the northern part of the country, again attacking economic targets, destroying large consignments of baled cotton waiting for export in Managua, Leon and

the northern port of Corinto. Simultaneously, combat increased between
FSLN forces and the National Guard in the *departamentos* of Nueva Segovia,
Jinotega and Matagalpa.

The January Strike

The Sandinista poet, Gioconda Belli, wrote in 1978 of 'a strike where silence
is born . . . to hear the footsteps of the tyrant leaving.' But what materialised
after the January riots in Managua was something quite different: Nicaragua's
first bosses' strike, a desperate attempt by the bourgeoisie to control an
explosive situation through peaceful means. Its aim was to force Somoza's
resignation, but the private sector overestimated its members' capacity to
bring about change.[16]

The unprecedented flight of capital from Nicaragua since the summer
of 1977, large amounts of which belonged to the opposition bourgeoisie,
had aggravated the financial problems of small businessmen and traders. The
subsequent credit restrictions bankrupted many small and medium-sized
enterprises and further increased unemployment. With these economic
pressures bearing on previously docile bodies such as the Chamber of
Commerce and the Chamber of Industry (CADIN), a strike committee was
formed by the non-Somoza bourgeoisie and a national general strike called
on 23 January, thirteen days after the Chamorro murder. But Nicaragua's
most prominent capitalists, grouped around the BANIC and BANAMERICA
finance houses, would have nothing to do with it. From the start it was a
strike organised and financed by the economically less powerful groups
attached to the reformist project of UDEL.

Although employers were soon able to claim an 80-90% success rate for
the strike, they made vigorous attempts to dissuade their workers from
involvement in more militant action for as long as the lock-out lasted. Many
firms laid off their workforce on full pay. The slogans emanating from
UDEL at the end of January were eloquent testimony of the employers'
vision of the strike: 'Civic work stoppage', 'Peaceful resistance', 'Don't leave
your homes'. The message was clear: don't take to the streets, don't organise,
leave it to us. But the workers were now in no mood to treat the strike as a
paid holiday, and the employers' strike committee soon realised their
mistake. For the first time, the working class was liberated from the factories
en masse, free to organise a resistance to the dictatorship, and this terrified
their employers. After barely a week, the businessmen started to lose their
grip on events, and both the FSLN and Los Doce called for the strike to be
transformed into active popular resistance. The first week of February made
it clear that the fragile UDEL coalition had run its course. Within its ranks,
undisguised conflict broke out between the Socialist and CGT-I labour union
representatives, who wanted the strike to continue and intensify, and the
right-wing leadership who wanted it called off before further damage could
be done to their credibility.[17] A sign of the timidity of UDEL's right-wing

was that even the Archbishop of Managua, Miguel Obando y Bravo, chose this moment to justify the people's right to collective armed resistance.

As an alternative to the strike committee, a Committee of Popular Resistance was formed, encouraging people to refuse to pay taxes, to withdraw any savings from the banks and to buy only such food and other basic goods as were strictly necessary. It was an important moment, too, for several of the newly formed popular organisations: the women's movement AMPRONAC, the Comite de Lucha de Empleados Publicos (Public Employees Fighting Committee) and others rapidly radicalised their demands. UDEL's discipline over the strike collapsed as more and more businesses reopened their doors; it became an open secret in Managua that many had done so in response to mounting pressure from the US Embassy.[18] The Embassy, alarmed that the strike was moving rapidly from a business protest to the beginnings of popular insurrection, called in their allies in UDEL to recommend new tactics designed to stop the strike movement falling into the hands of the popular organisations. In doing so, the Embassy also appealed to the economic self-interest of the businessmen. What was the point, they argued, of prolonging a ruinous strike which had already cost the industrial and commercial community 50 million dollars and which was not going to get rid of Somoza anyway? While the US spoke of non-intervention, the choice seemed to them increasingly polarised between Somoza and the Left. And as always when faced with this choice, Washington placed itself reluctantly but squarely, once again, behind the dictator. For six months, the rhetoric of human rights all but disappeared from the USA's Nicaragua policy.

Faced with Somoza's intransigence in the face of demands for peaceful reform, unable to mobilise mass support and unwilling to see it mobilised by others, the failure of the strike exhausted UDEL's peaceful repertoire for unseating Somoza. Equally important, the strike showed where real economic power lay in Nicaragua. The leaders of BANIC and BANAMERICA continued to conduct business as usual with Somoza; deprived of their support, the strike committee led by the remaining employers lacked the economic muscle to force political change. Somoza realised that he had won a reprieve from UDEL and Washington pressure alike and he returned to his customary confidence, denouncing the strike leaders with a cynicism remarkably close to the truth: 'This was a strike of millionaires who have forgotten that my government assured them the social peace necessary to build up their fortunes.'[19]

To the people of Nicaragua, the strike committee's failure of nerve looked depressingly like a re-run of Espino Negro and the long tradition of Somoza-Conservative pacts. And the businessmen made the important discovery that their economic interests were ultimately better served by the dictatorship than by a militant popular opposition which threatened to sweep them away along with Somoza. UDEL, INDE and the various other associations of businessmen were thus robbed of their last shreds of prestige as political leaders of the masses. On 5 February the strike committee called for the action to end. The strike was twelve days old. On the same day, Somoza's municipal elections were massively boycotted, with a voter turnout of only 20%, and 52 out of 132 Conservative candidates withdrawing from the contest.

As the strike committee's resolve faltered, the FSLN's Insurrectional Tendency launched its February offensive. Tercerista columns moved into Nicaragua across the Costa Rican border, taking on the National Guard at the important southern road junction of La Virgen and moving on to the command-post at Rivas, where they succeeded in holding the city for several hours. At the same time, other columns of the 'Benjamin Zeledon' Southern Front attacked the barracks of La Polvora in the lakeside city of Granada, again controlling the city for five hours, holding a popular assembly and withdrawing in perfect order with only minimal casualties. In the north, GPP units showed their new willingness to ally themselves with the insurrectional strategy and struck at the counter-insurgency camp of Santa Clara. Within hours control over the strike, which still continued, had passed firmly to the FSLN and popular resistance. When a UDEL leader was murdered by Somocista paramilitaries at the northern sugar refinery of San Antonio, his body was wrapped for burial in the red and black flag of the FSLN. UDEL was dead.

Chamorro's death and the collapse of the UDEL-backed strike left a vacuum for an ambitious new political leader to take charge of a revised version of bourgeois opposition. Although almost bereft of popular support within Nicaragua, this opposition could still hope to gain the ear of Washington. Alfonso Robelo, from his strategic position as president of INDE, rapidly made his presence felt, and many capitalists began to see the cooking-oil millionaire as a likely future presidential candidate. 'It's an interesting challenge, and one which I accept,' said Robelo in an interview published by the Buenos Aires newspaper *La Nacion* on 5 March. 'I'm not a candidate, because we are not in an election period. I'm not a politician anyway, but an organiser . . . but I'm looking for a civilised opposition movement. If Somoza continues in power, giving the people no option but armed insurrection, the country will be in danger of falling under communist rule.'

In the wake of the strike, Somoza reshuffled his government, but the changes took back with one hand what Somoza appeared to concede with the other. He removed a number of key figures associated with the regime's corruption — his uncle Luis Manuel Debayle, who had made a spectacular fortune through embezzlement from his position as director of the state energy agency ENALUF, and his Finance Minister General Gustavo Montiel, a former head of the National Guard's Office of Security. But at the same time he appointed to the government members of the shock-force AMROCS, the Somocista Liberal Youth and other paramilitary groups of the extreme Right.

But it was too late for either changes in the state apparatus or new capitalist opposition figures to interrupt the momentum of the growing mass movement. And nowhere had the new insurrectional mood taken deeper root than in the city of Masaya.

Monimbo: The People Without The Vanguard

When Los Doce defied Somoza and returned to Nicaragua from exile in July 1978, their first visit was to Masaya, to the Indian *barrio* of Monimbo, whose name had become synonymous with popular resistance to the dictatorship. Masaya is a beautiful old town of 50,000 people, laid out around a tree-shaded square with a massive colonial church and a thriving market now destroyed after Somoza's bombing. As well as its beauty, Masaya has special traditions of political struggle and local craftsmanship. General Benjamin Zeledon, 'El Indio', died there, at the hands of US troops in 1912, in the hill-top fortress of Coyotepe which overlooks the city. And a few kilometres from Monimbo, along a road which is dusty or muddy according to the season, is Niquinohomo, the birthplace of Sandino himself. The Indians of Monimbo have also made the city the craft centre of Nicaragua. The livelihood of the *barrio* rests on the production of embroidered clothes, *marimbas* and other musical instruments, wooden toys and carved hand-painted gourds. The *barrio* also has a highly developed sense of community and a unique geography. Between fifteen and twenty thousand people live in an area which contains a number of smaller sectors: Las Cuatro Esquinas, La Escuelita, Don Bosco, Padre Emilio Bottari. Earth yards are a common feature of poor houses throughout Nicaragua, but nowhere else do they all interconnect as they do in Monimbo. To the stranger – as it was to the National Guard – Monimbo is a confusing warren of narrow earth streets and wooden or adobe houses. But to the *monimbosenos,* every inch is familiar territory which, when the insurrection came, allowed easy communication as well as easy escape for the combatants.

When these local conditions were added to the generalised militancy resulting from the Frente's October and February offensives, the Chamorro assassination and the frustrations of the general strike, Nicaragua experienced the first stage in its popular insurrection. The people of Monimbo organised a series of masses and demonstrations in memory of Pedro Joaquin Chamorro, after whom the main square of the *barrio* was named. They also brought thousands on to the streets to mark the anniversary of Sandino's murder on 21 February.

First, the National Guard violently dispersed a peaceful demonstration leaving a mass for Chamorro. On the 21st, they launched their first aerial attacks on a crowd winding its way up to the Masaya cemetery on the hill above Monimbo. And then they shot down a young boy, Lorenzo Lopez, from the Masaya *barrio* of Pochotillo at the very doors of the San Sebastian church. When Lorenzo was buried on the 25th, days of skirmishing with the Guard erupted into full-scale insurrection and the people of Monimbo took over the city. At once the streets were filled with barricades and fires; burning car tyres and broken bottles were strewn over the roads to block a National Guard attack; Monimbo became a sea of red and black Sandinista flags. The same creative skills which the Indians normally showed in their handicrafts were now turned to making barricades and the famous

113

home-made Monimbo 'contact bombs', for use against Somoza's Guard.
'We improvised bombs from black aluminium, sulphur, chemicals, string . . .
bombs with just rolled-up newspapers and petrol, nail bombs, bombs filled
with pebbles.'[20] The *bomba de contacto* passed into the popular myth of the
Nicaraguan Revolution.

After several days of relative restraint by the local military commander,
Colonel Gonzalo Martinez, who according to local residents kept most of his
troops massed in the command-post on Masaya's main square, the prolonged
resistance of Monimbo became too much for Somoza. The dictator sent his
son, El Chiguin, into Masaya with instructions to regain control of the situation by whatever military means necessary. With Somoza Portocarrero came
a battalion of crack troops and a collection of the most hated generals on the
Guard's general staff: Fernandez, Gutierrez, Alegrett and Perez Vega. El
Chiguin, though outranked by Martinez, promptly dismissed him as
commanding officer. The isolation of Monimbo, a single *barrio* rising up
against the massed weight of the armed forces, made it possible for Somoza
to concentrate all his military strength with the most brutal results. An Indian
from Monimbo described the Guard's military response:

> The *Guardia* entered the *barrio* and attacked us with tanks, armoured
> cars, helicopters and heavy machine-guns. People defended themselves
> with machetes, contact bombs, sticks and whatever else they could lay
> their hands on. Some boys who were carrying flags of the Frente
> Sandinista had their hands cut off with bayonets . . . other children and
> adults who shouted 'Viva el Frente Sandinista' had their tongues cut
> out . . . The Guard attacked with brand-new rifles, those ones they say
> were sent by the *gringos* . . . I think they call them M-16s. But people
> here are prepared to go on fighting until the dictatorship falls. I believe
> they killed more than 200 people, without even respecting the lives of
> children. The people improvised popular prisons where they held
> captured soldiers of the armoured battalion . . . Some Guards and
> agents of Somoza deserted and crossed over to the side of the people
> with their arms, so that we could defend ourselves . . . But what we
> need in Monimbo are not .22 rifles or .38 pistols. We've got those.[21]

The Monimbo insurrection proved to the FSLN that the war between the
people and the dictatorship would not always follow the timetable set by the
revolutionary vanguard. The insurrection had begun spontaneously with
barricades, but was quickly taken over with more systematic organisation
by the people themselves, block by block and house by house throughout
the *barrio*. But the vanguard was absent. In Humberto Ortega's words: 'They
began to work as a Sandinista unit when they still lacked the organised leadership of the Sandinista movement.'[22] To try and remedy the situation, the
Frente sent in some of its most outstanding militants, including Ortega's
brother Camilo, who was killed in combat on 26 February. But the Frente's
response was inadequate: its organisation still lacked the necessary cadres

who might have taken control of the situation in Monimbo.

But Monimbo did show the FSLN the way forward. It placed the actions of the masses themselves in the forefront of the armed struggle. Mass violence previously had taken place irregularly and in the context of other political action. Here for the first time it was organised by the entire community. Those who took up arms against the dictatorship were no longer the isolated groups of FSLN guerrillas who had struck at small southern towns in the dead of night. The heart of the insurrection would in future be the people themselves, organised at the level of each *barrio*. Monimbo also dispelled illusions about the participation of women at every level of the armed struggle: the women of Monimbo had taken up arms, made contact bombs, built barricades. And Monimbo showed what the National Guard was capable of in its military defence of the regime.

Within days, another indigenous *barrio* rose up in arms. This time the location was Subtiava, a district of Leon populated by Indians ethnically unrelated to the *monimbosenos*. Supported this time by regular FSLN guerrillas, the Subtiavas attacked National Guard patrols, burned a score of buses and the house of a National Guard officer, and took to the streets of the city in mass demonstrations accompanied by Indian flutes and drums.

Alfonso Robelo: The Organiser as Politician

As the Indians of Subtiava took to the streets, UDEL, with what little energy it had left, called a further strike. It was impossible to see what UDEL hoped to achieve. This time the strike was a token one-day affair, badly organised and called for 1 March with less than a day's notice. Its success was very limited, and most businessmen simply ignored the call. Alfonso Robelo, from his new position of political prominence, was sceptical about the idea and refused to encourage businessmen to join in, saying that the new strike call should be left to the conscience of each individual.

Within days, Robelo had founded his own party, the Movimiento Democratico Nicaraguense (MDN), estimating its initial membership at around 3,000. In the political spectrum of the Right and Centre, the MDN did not replace UDEL but was complementary to the coalition. Its limited power base was mainly among the cotton producers of the north-west, and it called for social reforms which certainly went beyond those of the right-wing sectors of UDEL. The MDN gave a political voice to those middle-level capitalists who saw their economic growth most directly stifled by the regime and who therefore required more profound structural changes in the fabric of Nicaraguan capitalism. In terms of a strategy to bring down the dictatorship, however, it had nothing to offer which UDEL had not already tried unsuccessfully. The MDN shared the same crisis as the rest of the opposition bourgeoisie: by itself it had neither the economic muscle to threaten the dictatorship nor the political authority to assure National Guard loyalty (in the event of a right-wing solution) or to control any movement of the Left which included the Sandinistas. The weakness of the bourgeois opposition during the two months of January and February had shown that ultimately this class would not be capable of controlling its own destiny. It either had to face a new model of *Somocismo,* without the dictator itself at its head, or an alternative which included the FSLN, as Los Doce had proposed.

At every stage of Robelo's political evolution over the next two years until his resignation from the Junta of the Government of National Reconstruction, it is tempting to remember the man's own assessment of himself: 'I am not a politician.' His lack of political vision was soon demonstrated, alongside the opportunist rhetoric of his new party. 'This is our moment,' the MDN announced in a declaration on 1 April 1978. Sensing which way the wind was blowing, the MDN spoke in the language of nationalism and social democracy, even of liberation struggles. Robelo envisaged his role as a catalyst in the new broadening of the opposition coalition, and the MDN was in fact instrumental in bringing together a new coalition in May, the Frente Amplio Opositor (Broad Opposition Front: FAO), which offered a point of contact with the FSLN through the presence of Los Doce in addition to the old constituency of UDEL.

In the face of all the evidence, Robelo asserted that Somoza would be brought down before the end of 1978 without the use of violence, somehow imagining that the dictator could be persuaded to leave office on the strength of a guarantee of personal safety and his right to take the family fortune with him. Still Robelo remained a figure for whom the Frente could find a role in their scheme of things. The formation of tactical class alliances, which had been a tacit element of the Insurrectional strategy since the formation of Los Doce, now moved into the foreground, and the economic changes required by the MDN's own bourgeois power base placed it to the left of the 'demarcation line between friends and foes'. Nevertheless, the FSLN retained a healthy scepticism about Robelo's ultimate loyalties, not least because of his ties with the finance capital of BANIC, and they kept a watchful eye over the new party's activities. When rumours broke of an impending military coup against Somoza a year later in March 1979, the MDN were among those accused by the Frente of trying to instal a system of '*Somocismo* without Somoza.' And Robelo himself argued, in an April 1979 interview, that a Sandinista-led victory would lead to an equally 'totalitarian regime'.[23]

The Practical Politics of Class Alliance

The Frente's encouragement of temporary and tactical class alliances, so widely misunderstood at the time, must be seen against this background of a disintegrating bourgeois opposition and an ascendant mass movement. The labyrinthine sets of initials of the non-revolutionary opposition parties and coalitions in themselves spoke volumes about the bourgeois crisis: a Liberal Party which had split into three groups opposed to Somoza; a Conservative Party divided into four factions; two-way splits within both the Social

Christians and Socialists/Communists; the disintegration of UDEL, its ;
replacement by the FAO, and the emergence of the MDN. And in the case of
almost every one of these groups, the FSLN was confident that tactical
alliances might mature into strategic unity.

Like Fidel Castro's calculation in Cuba twenty years before, the Sandinista
art of making revolution was the art of increasing one's forces and aiming,
at every stage of the struggle, for the highest degree of unity within the
popular movement, without sectarianism and without ever sacrificing
hegemony over these new alliances. Los Doce of course offered much of the
cement which made such alliances possible, giving the Sandinistas some
legitimacy for the first time among the more progressive sectors of the formal
bourgeois opposition, and at the same time making that opposition less
unpalatable to the masses because of Los Doce's entry into the Broad Opposition Front (FAO).

The maturing of this new strategy of alliances also coincided with renewed
attempts to heal the rifts within the FSLN, and to coordinate the traditional
guerrilla war in the mountainous rural areas with the new phenomenon of
popular insurrection in the cities. The danger was that the GPP, working with
only a single battle-front in the north of the country and a relatively limited
back-up in the Pacific Coast heartland, would become isolated from the mass
activity in the towns.[24] Although the GPP was moving towards convergence
with the Insurrectionals, or Terceristas, on important points of strategy, its
leaders were still concerned that Tercerista action was substituting spectacle
for dialectics. GPP *Comandante*, Henry Ruiz, analysed the problem in this
way: 'For some sectors of the FSLN, an offensive means creating a beach-
head with a certain amount of arms and men, starting from the assumption
that the army is already in retreat . . . that the failure to destroy the army is
a technical military problem and not a problem of the dialectical development of the war, which is how we understand it.'[25]

The Proletarian Tendency proved for the moment more intractable, and
had grave misgivings about the wisdom of class alliances, similarly
condemning military action as a substitute for mass organisational work.
Their doubts were shared by the only two organisations of the revolutionary
Left who remained outside the FSLN: the small Peking-oriented
Movimiento de Accion Popular and the even tinier Trotskyist Liga Marxista
Revolucionaria.

But the Insurrectionals were confident that the radical basis of their
political platform was sufficient to maintain the unity of working-class,
peasant and certain progressive bourgeois forces, while avoiding dangers of a
traditional popular front in which the bourgeoisie might gain control. Within
its ranks, the Frente manifested ample evidence of the peculiarities of
Nicaraguan society and the measure of flexibility which was a natural result
of the country's class structure and history. To Nicaraguans, it was no contradiction that widely respected FSLN leaders such as Eden Pastora
(*Comandante* Cero) and German Pomares should have begun their political
careers as Conservative Party activists in the late 1950s and early 1960s.

117

To the Insurrectionals, the strategy of alliance also meant casting the Sandinista net wide enough to embrace radical Christians sympathetic to the armed struggle, and even those disaffected members of Somoza's National Guard now deserting in significant numbers.

The majority of the FSLN grasped that now the Nicaraguan bourgeoisie could be drawn in only two directions – towards the Left or towards United States imperialism. For the revolutionary movement it would have been suicidal to abandon the bourgeoisie to Washington.[26] At the same time, the Socialist Party with its working-class base had to be attracted to the insurrection. The gap between the two organisations began to narrow, albeit gradually, without the Sandinistas submerging themselves in any bourgeois-led coalition as the PSN had done. No agreements were entered into, no programmatic concessions made: there was simply unity of action on convergent points. At the same time, tactical demands led the majority tendency of the FSLN to drop overt references to Marxism from its vocabulary, their sensitivity to the peculiarities of Nicaraguan history as always their guiding principle: 'We had to avoid intellectualising the revolution, as had happened in other countries . . . we had to look for ways of applying Marxist-Leninist principles in accordance with our national conditions. The Nicaraguan bourgeoisie is not the same as in other countries, it has very particular characteristics.'

This was the context for class alliances: precisely to head off the danger of the non-Somoza bourgeoisie being granted renewed authority with the support of Washington. The move neatly undermined US strategy. Frustrated by the incoherence of the Broad Opposition Front and the absence of a convincing pro-Washington leader, one State Department official recalled the United States 'solution' to the Dominican Republic crisis twelve years earlier: 'Of course we must avoid another Cuba . . . We've been looking for another Balaguer, but we can't seem to locate him.'[27]

Notes

1. Regis Debray, *A Critique of Arms* (Harmondsworth, Penguin, 1977) pp. 32-33.
2. Ricardo Coronel, of the group of Los Doce, interviewed in Roger Mendieta Alfaro, *El Ultimo Marine* (Managua, Editorial Union, 1979), p. 114.
3. Interview with former members of the Solentiname community, Managua, March 1980.
4. Interview with Miriam Guevara, FSLN combatant at San Carlos, Managua, March 1980.
5. Alejandro Guevara, 'El Asalto al Cuartel de San Carlos' in *Nicaragua – Patria Libre* (Havana, Casa de las Americas No. 117, November-December, 1979), p. 173.
6. Daniel Ortega Saavedra, interviewed in *Alternativa* (Bogota) No. 189/

78, 20 November 1978.
7. Lopez et al., *La caida del Somocismo,* p. 159.
8. Ibid, p. 158.
9. *Nicaragua: Combate de un Pueblo, Presencia de los Cristianos* (Lima, Centro de Estudios y Publicaciones, 1978), p. 96.
10. *Nicaragua: An Ally Under Siege* (Washington D.C., Council on American Affairs, 1978), p. 41.
11. *Gusano:* 'worm', term applied to anti-Castro Cuban exiles.
12. See 'Somoza's Trade in Blood', *The Guardian,* 16 January 1978, and 'Le President Somoza s'efforce de conserver le soutien de Washington', *Le Monde,* 18 January 1978.
13. 'El Chiguin': nickname applied to Anastasio Somoza Portocarrero, a Nicaraguan word meaning 'tough little kid'.
14. Interview with Carlos Fernando Chamorro, editor of the FSLN newspaper *Barricada,* Managua, February 1980.
15. Humberto Ortega, *La Estrategia de la Victoria,* interview with Marta Harnecker.
16. 'Crisis in Nicaragua' in NACLA, *Report on the Americas* (New York) Vol. XII, No. 6, November-December, 1978, p. 16.
17. Harald Jung, 'Behind the Nicaraguan Revolution', *New Left Review,* No. 117, September-October, 1978, p. 82.
18. *El Dia* (Mexico) 12 February 1978.
19. 'Revoltes contre une Dictature en Sursis', *Le Monde Diplomatique,* March 1978.
20. Interview with Monimbo combatant, July 1979.
21. FLSN, *Boletin Informativo,* No. 3, January-February 1978.
22. Humberto Ortega, loc. cit.
23. *Latin America Political Report,* Vol. XIII, No. 17, 4 May 1979.
24. Interview with Bayardo Arce, GPP Comandante, undated mimeo, mid-1978.
25. Henry Ruiz, interviewed in *Alternativa* (Bogota) No. 190/78, 27 November 1978.
26. Daniel Ortega, interviewed in *Alternativa,* No. 189/78, 20 November 1978.
27. The reference is to Joaquin Balaguer, President of the Dominican Republic in 1960 and again after the US Marine invasion of 1965. A key figure in US plans for the 'democratisation' of that country. Quoted in 'Nicaragua Update', *Contemporary Archive on Latin America,* (London) October 1978, p. 17.

8. Insurrection, 1978

The People United

'*Nobody in Nicaragua now is talking or thinking about anything but politics. Everyone knows what is going on, everyone is conscious. Somoza says "there is nothing wrong in Nicaragua, the situation is under control", while he goes down to his finca at Montelimar on the coast with his mistress, or goes out jogging in the morning. But we can see the whole structure crumbling around him. Everyone is saying the same thing: "Somoza must go" – the business- men, the people here in the barrios. This is the people united. In the shops here we're selling T-shirts with "Nicaragua Libre" printed on them, and out- side the National Guard are patrolling the streets constantly, six of them in each jeep with their machine-guns trained on the people. Yes, we're afraid, because we know our task won't be easy . . . but we're confident. Look at the walls here in the city. All of them are covered .with pro-FSLN slogans. The people paint them, the Guard come along and wipe them off, next day they're back again. We're going to be all right, we're organising. It's only a matter of time.*' (Women in Masaya, July 1978).

Within nine months of the attacks on San Carlos, Ocotal and Masaya, the FSLN had developed a national political organisation capable of projecting its demands throughout Nicaragua. This was the Movimiento Pueblo Unido (United People's Movement: MPU), born in the early summer of 1978. The FSLN had emerged from the January and February riots with unquestioned vanguard status, the only political force capable of directing the nation's revulsion against *Somocismo*. In the MPU, it saw the fruit of long years of work by the Frente's intermediate organisations, a unifying force which would give the people strength to overcome their fear of National Guard terror and the hard battles to come. The three tendencies of the FSLN, who had at the same time reached broad agreements on operational unity, all gave their full support to the MPU. The composition of the new move- ment – political parties, trade union federations and grass-roots organisations – made it a cross between a left-wing political coalition and a mass insurrect- ional front. Its minimum political programme was signed by fourteen groups, half of them youth or student bodies. These were joined by working-class organisations loyal to the FSLN, breaking away from the sectarian positions of the existing trade union *centrales*. The factories were suddenly alive with Comites de Lucha de los Trabajadores (Workers' Fighting Committees: CLT) and cells of the Movimiento Sindical Pueblo Trabajador (Working People's Trade Union Movement: MSPT). Both joined the United People's Movement, as did the national organisation of white-collar workers. Other left parties also now accepted the vanguard role of the Sandinistas. The Communist Party of Nicaragua threw its labour federation, the CAUS, behind the MPU and, most important of all, the Socialist Party and its trade union *central*, the CGT-I, were soon won over to the new unity of the Left. From the influential women's movement AMPRONAC to tiny groups of the extreme Left, the MPU offered a programme which finally attracted a total of twenty-three organisations.

The programme to which they put their name was in essence the political manifesto of the FSLN. But while the Sandinistas had put forward a twenty-five-point fighting programme,[1] the MPU went further and talked in detail about the specific structures of a post-Somoza government. The Movement's 'Immediate Programme' contained these fifteen points:

1. The unity of all anti-Somoza forces within a flexible policy of alliances, 'without renouncing our political independence or that of our allies.'
2. A 'Government of Democratic Unity' in which there would be room for all political forces which had fought responsibly against the dictatorship.
3. A full programme of democratic liberties: freedom of thought and expression; freedom of the press; freedom of assembly and trade union organisation; freedom of religious practice; freedom for all political prisoners; the establishment of a Constituent Assembly with representatives of all parties and organisations opposed to the dictatorship.
4. A reform of the judicial system, with an independent judiciary and the elimination of judicial corruption.
5. Removal of the National Guard and its replacement with a popular and democratic army.
6. A non-aligned foreign policy.
7. An economic policy based on: confiscation and nationalisation of all Somoza-owned property; nationalisation of all natural resources; nationalisation of airlines, shipping lines and public transport; price controls on basic goods; reform of state agencies; a development and integration programme for the Atlantic Coast region; a National Economic Plan incorporating guarantees for the private sector; economic and trade relationships with all countries on the basis of respect for national sovereignty.
8. An agrarian reform based on lands confiscated from the dictatorship.
9. An industrial development programme within a mixed economy.
10. A reform of commercial activity directed at breaking monopolies.
11. A revision of the fiscal system and a restructuring of repayments on loans contracted by the Somoza regime.
12. A new Labour Code embodying a 48-hour working week, job creation

programmes, equal pay for equal work, and an end to child labour and sex discrimination in the workplace.

13. A universal, free and compulsory education system, an increased state education budget and a national adult literacy campaign.

14. Creation of a National Health Service with particular emphasis on preventive medicine.

15. A housing programme designed to remove the *barrios marginales,* regulate rents and break the power of big landlords.[2]

For the Sandinistas, the new MPU had three purposes: '(1) To develop organisational work within the mass movement, among both workers and peasants; (2) To consolidate the unity of all democratic and revolutionary sectors against the Somoza dictatorship; (3) To push forward with the armed popular insurrection.'[3]

As well as offering an alternative political bloc to the Somoza Government at a national level, the MPU evolved a network of underground local cells which gave the people a parallel structure of local power whose forms were drawn from the experiences of the February 1978 Monimbo insurrection and previous efforts by the FSLN to organise the masses. This would be a *barrio*-based organisation fusing political work and military preparation, both defensive and aggressive. Within weeks, hundreds of such local committees were working: the Comites de Defensa Civil (CDCs). Inside the United People's Movement and its local cells, there were clear signs that the FSLN had overcome the worst of its internal crisis as the insurrectional mood of the country quickened. Militants from different tendencies worked hand in hand. The Terceristas applauded the creation of the MPU and hailed it as the nucleus of a future government based on the organised power of the people, while five grass-roots groups loyal to the Tendencia Proletaria could now happily put their names to a document which called for flexible class alliances.

In the first mass actions of January 1978, the bourgeoisie's indecisiveness and lack of clear political judgment had left the way open for the popular movement to gain an initiative which as yet lacked clear organisation. But by August, when sections of the bourgeois opposition repeated their earlier strike tactics, there was no danger of the situation being repeated. The masses had found a new coherence and an organisation which could coordinate their struggle politically. In February, the response to bourgeois timidity had been an ad-hoc Committee of Popular Resistance, stepping into the vacuum left by the failure of the UDEL strike. Now, in August 1978, the MPU was able to project itself onto a larger plane: no longer just a strike committee, but a genuinely national mass organisation which could afford to keep its options open as far as its relationship with the Broad Opposition Front (FAO) was concerned. 'The MPU is a product of the current period of transition. It offers an alternative for the Left, but was not formed to oppose the FAO'.[4]

Within the MPU, previously defensive organisations such as the Committee for the Freedom of Political Prisoners were able to make their stance more combative. In every area, people went on the offensive. The MPU's work in organising was crucial, forming strike committees in every *barrio* of Nicaragua's cities, structuring CDCs on every street and every block, and linking them with People's Combat Brigades to harass the National Guard and defend the neighbourhoods against attack. At a higher level of the pyramid, coordinating committees were built up for each district, each factory and workplace, each college and university. There were clandestine schools for political education, and military and civilian preparation for insurrection, and an instrument for political unity at national level.

In April and May 1978 the country's students, organised now even in the primary schools, threw themselves into a national strike to demand the removal of *Somocista* teachers and school administrators and freedom for imprisoned students, and Somoza was forced to accede to their principal demands. In July they were joined by the hospital workers, who met more intransigent opposition from the Junta Nacional de Asistencia Social (National Council of Social Assistance), the state agency headed by Somoza's North American-born wife Hope Portocarrero de Somoza. Rapidly, the hospital workers transformed their original economic demands into part of the generalised political struggle against the dictatorship. There had been a qualitative change in political conditions: Nicaragua was now in a pre-revolutionary situation, and whereas the regime's earlier repression had been able to make open mass organisational work very difficult, that work was now being done under conditions in which it was impossible for the Guard to decapitate it or even dent it seriously. The mobilisations of local communities — Managua *barrios* like OPEN 3, Bella Cruz, Riguero and Schick — were no longer spasmodic events, but a complete way of life. In the countryside too, the people were on a war footing. At the end of May 1978, 400 peasant families at Tonala in the northern *departamento* of Chinandega had sparked off a wave of land seizures which could now count on political and armed support. 'We can't go on in these conditions,' said one of the Tonala peasants.

> This land is ours and we've taken it . . . so that we can work, so that we can live. The poison dust from the fumigation of the cotton fields is killing our pigs and our chickens. At night, the place is alive with mosquitoes from the Standard Fruit Company's banana plantations. It's years since we've seen a single bird near Tonala because of the pollution. And the people don't escape either. Every year in the cotton season, the crop-dusting planes poison the land with chemicals, and they poison us . . . women, children, old people. Either God will save Tonala or we'll save it ourselves. Tonala will be Nicaragua's second Monimbo.

With the militancy of the *barrios* and the countryside growing every day, and the political demands of the FSLN known nationally through the work of the United People's Movement, the Sandinistas decided that it was time to ignite a national insurrection.

The National Palace Attacked: Striking at the Heart of the System

As in the attack four years previously on the house of Chema Castillo, the Frente had to select a target of massive political importance. Another San Carlos, an isolated barracks attack, would not correspond to the now dramatic polarisation of the country. 'The plan seemed too simple to be sane,' wrote Gabriel Garcia Marquez. 'Take the National Palace in Managua in broad daylight with a force of only twenty-six, and hold the members of the House of Deputies hostage in exchange for the release of all political prisoners.'[5]

The timing of the assault was also influenced by a new factor: the need for the Frente to give an urgent political response to rumours of a US-backed coup which would install a military-civilian junta in an attempt to neutralise radical opposition to Somoza. In addition, the FAO had published a statement outlining their plans for a transitional government to succeed the dictator. The FSLN attack on the National Palace had three principal purposes: to give immediate publicity throughout Nicaragua and abroad to the FSLN's political demands, complementing the political work of the Frente and the MPU; to inspire a national insurrection; and to secure the release of key militants able to direct it.[6]

The need to bring prisoners, including senior militants, back into the organisation was not new. On 8 March the Frente had kidnapped General Reynaldo Perez Vega, the soldier who had directed the Monimbo massacre and the National Guard's 'Operacion Veloz' against the FSLN in the north of Nicaragua. The Sandinistas had given Somoza four conditions for the release of Perez Vega: 'Freedom for Sandinista prisoners, at that time numbering more than 60; safe-conducts for those who had taken refuge in the embassies of Mexico, Costa Rica and Venezuela; a large sum of money for the orphans of Monimbo and the withdrawal of troops carrying out counter-insurgency operations in the north.'[7] These conditions were not met, and Perez Vega was killed, the only occasion in the FSLN's history that a hostage had been executed.

Five months later, the Frente moved against the National Palace. The code-name for the assault was 'Operation Pigsty'. It had been meticulously planned, and only the three militants in charge knew what the target was to be. The three were Eden Pastora (*Comandante* Cero), who had been toying with the idea of such a raid since 1970, Hugo Torres (Uno) and Dora Maria Tellez (Dos). The remaining twentythree combatants had been assembled only three days earlier, selected from among the best and most experienced fighters on each front. Even so, their average age was only eighteen or nineteen.[8]

The Palace covers an entire city block, surrounded by the empty lots of post-earthquake Managua and facing the open concrete of the main square, now the Plaza Carlos Fonseca. Heavily and easily defended, the palace presented a target which could only be taken by audacity and surprise. The

plan depended on the fear with which the building's politicians, bureaucrats and even guards would greet the arrival of a National Guard elite unit
accompanying the dictator. Accordingly, the members of the FSLN
commando drew up on either side of the Palace in army trucks, their beards
and hair shaved, carrying rifles and automatic weapons captured from
Somoza's troops and wearing the olive-green uniforms of the EEBI. At
Pastora's screamed order 'The boss is coming! ', crowds in the Palace
corridors melted away in panic, while the guards on the door surrendered
their weapons to the disguised Sandinistas without a word. In the *Salon
Azul* (Blue Room), where the deputies were in the middle of a debate on the
budget, the Sandinistas' impersonation of the Guard again ensured the
success of the operation. Pastora burst into the chamber at the head of the
commando, firing at the ceiling and yelling 'This is the Guard! ' All forty-
nine deputies flung themselves to the ground. 'I thought it was a military
coup. I couldn't understand what kind of coup . . . the attackers looked like
members of the Basic Infantry Training School commanded by the young
Anastasio Somoza Portocarrero.'[9]

The 'Rigoberto Lopez Perez' commando, named after the man who had
taken the first step towards the elimination of the dictatorship in 1956,
immediately issued a communique stating its demands. It was the afternoon
of 22 August. As in the Perez Vega kidnap, the sum of money demanded —
this time 10 million dollars — was the least important of the Frente's
objectives. Eighty-five militants were named in the list of prisoners to be
released, and they included vital figures from each of the three tendencies:
Tomas Borge, Charlotte Baltodano, Edgard Lang, Martha Cranshaw, Rene
Nunez and Doris Tijerino. Twenty-seven of those listed never appeared,
already murdered in Somoza's jails.

Although only Terceristas took part in the operation, all sectors of the
organisation were aware of the plan and had been actively discussing unity.
The political document which accompanied the demands not only called
for the installation of a popular and democratic government with the removal
of the entire Somocista state apparatus and denounced US attempts to block
a democratic solution; it also insisted that 'The hour of unity of the revolutionary forces must not be delayed; the path to be taken by the popular
democratic process depends on Sandinista unity.'[10]

For each member of the Sandinista unit, there were a hundred hostages,
many of whom openly expressed their support and admiration for the FSLN.
But the key prizes were in the Salon Azul, and as in 1974 Somoza proved
vulnerable to threats to members of his family. This time the hostages
included Jose Somoza Abrego, son of General Jose Somoza, half-brother to
the dictator and Inspector-General of the National Guard; and Luis Pallais
Debayle, Somoza's cousin, Vice-President of the House of Deputies and
director of *Novedades*, the government newspaper. When Somoza learned
who the hostages were, he called off the military siege of the Palace,
withdrawing a National Guard helicopter which had been firing on the
building. And in successive rounds of negotiations, relayed to Somoza by

Dora Maria Tellez through the Archbishop of Managua and the Bishops of Leon and Granada, the dictator's attitude shifted from insolence through evasiveness to furious impotence. The status of the Liberal and Conservative deputies in the Salon Azul, visibly enraged by the dictator's delaying tactics, coupled with the equally visible response of people throughout the country to the new call from their vanguard, convinced Somoza that he had no alternative but to yield to the FSLN's demands. Even before negotiations were completed, prisoners were being transferred to Managua airport from the Carcel Modelo at Tipitapa, the police stations of the capital and the distant prisons of Esteli and Zelaya.

The impact of the operation exceeded even the Frente's expectations. As a result, talks on internal unity were greatly strengthened, with many of the GPP and Proletarios now increasingly convinced of the imminent viability of the insurrectional strategy. With the text of their communiques published and read as demanded in the press, on radio stations and television channels, the members of the 'Rigoberto Lopez Perez' commando left the Palace on the morning of 24 August, after a forty-five-hour siege. With them, they took the most important of the hostages: Somoza Abrego, Pallais Debayle, the Somocista minister Antonio Mora and the prominent Conservative deputy Eduardo Chamorro. And although Somoza broke the final agreement that no National Guardsman should be visible anywhere on the twelve-kilometre drive to the airport, the troops could do nothing to prevent the massive demonstration of popular support as thousands of Nicaraguans lined the Carretera Norte while others formed a motorcade of cars, trucks and motorcycles to accompany the school bus carrying the Sandinistas and their hostages. At Las Mercedes airport, two planes were waiting to take the *guerrilleros* and the fifty-eight freed prisoners out of Nicaragua. The aircraft had been provided by the sympathetic governments of Carlos Andres Perez in Venezuela and Omar Torrijos in Panama, both by this time powerful foreign allies of the Sandinista cause.

Within a matter of hours, there were two entirely different responses to the seizure of the National Palace, one from the Broad Opposition Front (FAO) and the other from the people of Matagalpa. While Matagalpa erupted in a spontaneous insurrection leaping ahead of even the most ambitious FSLN timetable, the bourgeoisie again played the strike card. A bosses' strike can rarely have cost its organisers so little. August and September are months when many Nicaraguan workers take their holidays, and the employers simply told their entire workforce to stay at home. But while the FAO still had considerable difficulty in organising effective mass support around its model of anti-Somocismo, the lessons of earlier strikes had not been entirely lost. The wide coverage given to the FAO's political programme by *La Prensa* had enabled the coalition to manoeuvre shrewdly, within its limitations, during the summer months. Two things were favourable to the FAO project: the growing opposition to Somoza among even the most reactionary sectors of the bourgeoisie, and the overwhelming popular reception given to the eminently respectable figures of Los Doce as they returned to Nicaragua on 5 July.

The businessmen's original strike in January had been followed soon afterwards by a token one-day stoppage. Now, in August, the all-out strike came a month after another one-day gesture. On 19 July, with the impact of Los Doce's return at its highest, the FAO staged a one-day strike, 75% effective in Managua and other major cities, to protest against National Guard repression of demonstrations supporting Los Doce. Inevitably, however, despite the call from the strike leaders for the workers to keep off the streets, the demonstrators had ideas of their own and fighting broke out in the streets of Esteli and Masaya. The new strike call came on 25 August, and the US Embassy was delighted at 'moderate' attempts to regain the political initiative from the Frente. Within two days, the call was taken up by the Federation of Chambers of Commerce, with INDE joining in on the 29th. Somoza's answer was to strip INDE of its charter and suspend credits to businessmen participating in anti-government activity: 'It's time to crack some heads,' was his comment on the new decrees.[11] At the same time, he sent 300 troops in to patrol the commercial areas of Managua and to 'make sure businesses have the necessary protection to re-open'. Pro-Somoza vigilante groups also tried unsuccessfully to intimidate businessmen favourable to the FAO's call.

The chaotic geography of post-earthquake Managua was again a problem for both the Sandinistas and the middle-class opposition. Although the strike grew rapidly, and FAO leaders were claiming an 80% shutdown by the end of the first week, it was almost impossible to organise the capital coherently. Individual businessmen and shopkeepers were isolated from any sense of a unified political strategy. Managua has no central commercial area, but instead a series of modern precincts — the Centro Comercial Managua, Metrocentro, Plaza de Compras — scattered along the ring-roads which now skirt the old (pre-earthquake) city centre. The same problem affected the FSLN's plans for an urban insurrection in Managua, with vast open areas of earthquake rubble and scrubland impeding easy guerrilla movement. Except in the eastern sector of the city, where fifteen or twenty *barrios* interconnect, working-class neighbourhoods straggle over a wide area, cut off from each other by fields. Inside each *barrio,* small-scale attacks could be launched against the Guard, but for the moment the city was not ready for mass insurrection. The signal came instead from the northern mountain town of Matagalpa.

The September Insurrection

By 26 August, the strike had shut down 90% of all commercial establishments in Matagalpa, the birthplace of many of the FSLN's leaders and centre of the guerrillas' traditional stronghold area. Women took to the streets to demonstrate against new rises in taxation; and the harassment of young people and students by the National Guard during the previous months had reached intolerable levels, finally exhausting caution and patience. The moment was not yet right for mass military action, but the revolutionary leadership was unable to hold the people back. The yough of Matagalpa threw themselves into spontaneous street fighting, albeit with no hope of success against an enemy with vastly superior fire-power. Barricades sprang up on every street corner; snipers were posted on strategic rooftops; trenches were dug and road communications with the city cut. The GPP began to circulate leaflets to inspire the population with stories of the 1967 guerrilla movement in Pancasan.

By the following day, the working-class *barrios* of El Chorizo, La Chispa and others were in the hands of the people. On the 29th, after only low-level resistance from the local National Guard garrison, the EEBI moved in and established the pattern for Guard counter-offensives in each of the cities involved in the September insurrection. With aircraft and Sherman tanks, the Guard rocketed and shelled the city; Matagalpa's churches were transformed into military headquarters. Two-thirds of the population streamed out of the city into the surrounding hills, leaving behind their dead, estimated by the Red Cross as at least eighty. When the Guard finally regained control of Matagalpa on 3 September four hundred of Somoza's crack troops had been held at bay for four days by the *muchachos*, armed pitifully with a handful of 30-30 rifles, .22 carbines and handguns.[12]

The Frente had not chosen the timing of the insurrection, but once the masses began to act autonomously as they had in Matagalpa, the Sandinistas faced a stark choice: either to block the insurrection or to support it and put themselves at its head, to give it a political direction which might avoid further crushing defeats like that inflicted on the people of Monimbo.[13] Even so, for several days the call to insurrection did not materialise. Many expected the word to come at the end of August, with Matagalpa in arms and the strike at its height. Instead, with Somoza boasting that the Matagalpa insurgents had been 'neutralised', the strike dragged to the end of its second week. On 9 September, the FSLN leadership decided it could no longer ignore the pressure from below. The communique on that day began: 'The hour of the Sandinista popular insurrection has come. Everyone on to the streets! The Sandinista army, the Sandinista militias and the Sandinista people must take up arms against the National Guard of Somoza. Everyone to organise around the provisional government headed by Los Doce.' The three-man leadership chosen for the provisional government was remarkable for its moderation: Sergio Ramirez of Los Doce, Alfonso Robelo of the MDN, and the Conservative lawyer Rafael Cordova Rivas, who had acted as Tomas Borge's defence counsel. It was a historic decision, the meshing of the guerrilla war and the organisation of the urban masses, the fusion of the military and the political. For the first time, the Nicaraguan people and their political and :ary military vanguard fought together on the barricades.

The call to insurrection came unilaterally from the Terceristas, although the other tendencies soon gave their full military support to the people. The remaining geographical imbalance of the three meant that they complemented each other on a national level, each fighting in the zone where it had greatest strength. The GPP fought in its stronghold of the north, coming down from the mountains to play the leading role in Esteli and Leon; the Proletarios in the urban centres of Managua and Carazo; the Terceristas on the southern front, the immortal Frente Sur. The FSLN's own estimate of their fighting strength at the time still numbered no more than a few hundred, but from September onwards it became meaningless to gauge the strength of the organisation by the number of fully trained military cadres. On the battlefield, any effective distinction between regular and irregular forces became blurred, and the true sense of a phrase from the FSLN's political platform became clear: 'The Sandinista National Liberation Front fights from the people and with the people.'[14]

Within twenty-four hours of the 9 September communique, there was war on all fronts. One early victory was profoundly symbolic – the destruction of the National Guard command post in Monimbo. Elsewhere, ten Managua police stations were attacked and there was partial insurrection in half a dozen *barrios* of the capital. Militias struck at the small northern town of Chichigalpa; there were battles in Diriamba and Jinotepe, in the verdant coffee-growing area of Carazo; assaults on National Guard posts at Ocotal in the north and San Rafael del Sur in the south; a raid on the frontier post of Penas Blancas by columns driving in across the Costa Rican border. But the main focus of combat remained the departmental capitals. There was total war in Leon, Esteli, Masaya and Chinandega, the four towns which after September would collectively be known as the 'Guernicas' of Nicaragua. It was no accident that the insurrection should be concentrated here. During the workless months between harvests, the marginal *barrios* of these towns attract rural workers expelled from the cotton, coffee and sugar fields who live in enforced idleness from April to October. The insurrection was not restricted to the urban poor, but embraced rural labourers and 'in the final stages, peasants [who] came down to join the struggle in the cities'.[15]

In strict military terms, however, the balance of forces was still far from equal. The dominant image of the September insurrection was of the *muchachos* holding back the National Guard with any weapon that came to hand: hunting rifles, small calibre firearms collected house to house, sticks, stones, bottles and knives. The regular guerrilla forces had rifles and machine-guns captured from the Guard, but as yet they lacked the heavy arms – field artillery, 50mm machineguns and anti-tank weapons – which might have allowed them to immobilise the aircraft and armoured vehicles which gave Somoza such massive military superiority. It was only on the southern front that the FSLN used mortars, bazookas and heavy machine-guns, in evidence for the first time during the 17 September attack on Penas Blancas.

But despite the inevitability of military defeat in this September insurrection, the leadership of the Nicaraguan Revolution was no longer in question. Everyone fought under the banner of *Sandinismo*. 'With the September insurrection, thousands of us came to realise that in the FSLN we had both a military instrument capable of overthrowing the dictatorship, and a political organisation whose programme synthesised all the deeply felt history of the

Nicaraguan people,' said one middle-class resident of Leon the following year. 'It's crazy looking back to imagine that we ever realistically thought we could defeat the Guard in September, but our morale was so high that we thought anything was possible.' Nor did the terrible suffering inflicted on the masses (in contrast to the regular forces of the FSLN, who suffered only minor casualties) do anything to dent their faith in Frente leadership. In September, with the vanguard still numbering only a few hundred adequately trained combatants, a military victory had never been on the cards. But the people had taken the decision en masse to launch the insurrection, and the Frente's decision to join and lead their fight meant that the people would not be left alone to face inevitable slaughter. The popular decision had been taken consciously, in full knowledge of the human cost it would imply. Brutal repression was the only possible response from a decomposing regime, and air and artillery strikes against densely populated towns were bound to result in indiscriminate massacres. 'Liberation movements must learn,' said Humberto Ortega, 'that the cost of their struggle will be even greater than ours. If there had been a less costly path to victory, we would have taken it. I can conceive of no triumph in any part of Latin America without this massive participation of the people . . . Our guerrilla columns were not the axis, but merely part of a larger axis, which was the armed struggle of the masses.'[16] By launching the September insurrection, the Nicaraguan people served notice that they had reached this understanding. As each city in turn fell to the National Guard, the FSLN's guerrilla columns slipped away largely intact, taking with them thousands of new recruits. Those who remained faced the reprisals of the Guard, the savage 'mopping-up operations' in which repression turned to mass murder.

In spite of the press censorship imposed by Somoza on the sixth day of the insurrection, eye-witness reports began to filter out of the besieged cities. Here are some examples of what people saw:

Matagalpa
'On 30 August a number of young combatants of Matagalpa took refuge in the Hotel Soza to hide and escape from the National Guard. When they learned of this a few hours later, the Guard smashed their way into the hotel. But meanwhile, the *muchachos* had had time to leave the building, no-one knew where. When the Guard entered, the only people they found were the owner's family: the father, mother, two children and a friend of the family, the engineer Roger Miranda. People outside the hotel heard a tremendous burst of machine-gun fire. A young inhabitant of Matagalpa who entered the hotel once the National Guard had left found that everyone inside had been killed, ripped to pieces by machine-gun fire. The father had been castrated and the woman raped.'

Masaya
'The people of the town feel an enormous resentment and hatred against the National Guard. At three in the afternoon (on 19 September) they began to

hide so that the Guard would not pick them up on the street. People told of seeing foreign Guardsmen, perhaps [South] Vietnamese or [Nationalist] Chinese from the description. Disposable syringes were found wherever the Guard had been, which suggests that they were acting under the influence of drugs. Down by the station people are beginning to rebuild the market to try and earn some sort of subsistence income. They are telling stories of entire families massacred by the Guard.'

Leon

'Two out of every three houses show the marks of military attack. Material losses are conservatively estimated at 500 million cordobas. Since Thursday the 14th, the main commercial centres have been raked by gunfire, and the destruction caused by aerial machine-gunning, incendiary bombs, cannon fire from armoured vehicles, shelling, rockets launched from the fortress and white phosphorus bombs has left nightmarish scenes amongst the civilian population. Adjacent to the ring-road, a common grave was dug to bury the corpses of twenty-two young people from the Barrio Nuevo de Guadalupe. That day, Friday, the Guard took control of the streets yelling at people to evacuate the area because they had orders to burn down every inch of it. A Red Cross volunteer managed to evacuate one group from the *barrio* but others were detained by the Guard. Two *muchachos* told what they had seen: "Apparently they found one kid with a gun. At that point they stopped checking people and let the women, children and old people leave. But they made all the young men lie down on the ground: 'We'll put these sons of bitches to work pulling down the barricades,' shouted one Guard. We stayed behind because we had three brothers among the prisoners. They made them kneel in two lines. Another Guard told us to look the other way, and the firing started. Thousands of shots maybe. Then they drove a tractor over the bodies, smashed them to pieces, poured petrol over them and set fire to them. While they were still burning, two Guards came over to us. 'Now fuck off out of here,' said one, 'and make sure you don't shoot your mouth off about this'."

Chinandega

'Chinandega is totally destroyed, there are a tremendous number dead, the Guard have bombed and wrecked the city and have made entire families disappear. Only the slightly wounded are being taken to hospital; anyone more seriously wounded is finished off by the Guard on the spot. People are traumatised . . . You could see dogs gnawing at decomposing bodies in the streets; mass burials in the streets and courtyards; burning corpses in the streets. From the 20th onwards you could say the Guard had effectively regained control of the city.'

Esteli

'They're bombing my town . . . For us, the Guard are monsters, they terrify us, the children are crying all the time. The Guard are bombing everything in

Esteli. Esteli is in flames. We haven't got water or light. We've got nothing in Esteli. We're dying of hunger . . . I saw four *muchachos* killed about 50 yards from my house, they dragged four kids outside, one twelve year old, the others fourteen or fifteen, kids who were with their mothers, and they shot them with those Garand rifles that they carry.'

While the first outsiders to enter the ruined cities began to piece together the stories of National Guard atrocities, which had left 5,000 dead, others told how the civilian population had responded to the FSLN's call for insurrection:

> On 9 September, around 1 o'clock in the morning, a group of FSLN guerrillas dressed in olive-green and their faces covered with the red and black handerkerchief of the Frente, knocked on the door of my house. I got up and saw them . . . two men about twenty-three years old, armed with machine-guns. One of them told me that this was the day for the big battle against the Guard, and that the Frente needed support from the people. The other asked if I had any weapons: if so, could I give them to the Frente, or could we come out ourselves to help in the fighting. He told me that, if we didn't want to fight, we should make barricades inside the house to protect the family against flying bullets. I went back inside, told my wife to hide the children safely, grabbed a 30-30 rifle, a pistol and some rounds of ammunition and went off to help the *muchachos*. By two in the morning, it was like the middle of the day in the streets of Esteli: thousands and thousands of men, women and children working together to put up the barricades. By six, there were barricades along every street; on every corner, houses had been turned into command posts with one or two *muchachos* of the Frente. By six in the morning, we had managed to arm around 1,500 people, maybe more, men for the most part but many women too . . . If we had only had more weapons, we could have armed a fighting force of five or six thousand. Every time a Guard or a combatant was killed, someone else was there to pick up the gun and go on fighting.[17]

War of Positions and War of Movement

Esteli did not fall to Somoza's troops for two full weeks. This prolonged resistance was due in large measure to the heroism of the combatants and the new strength of local MPU organisation, but it was also made possible by the strategy of the National Guard. This was to use the mobile elite forces of the 2,000-strong EEBI, backed up by air-strikes from the Nicaraguan Air Force against each city in turn. These were in fact the only sections of the 7,500-man army seriously deployed in the September insurrection. Esteli, isolated in the north, was the last town to be retaken. 'It was as if Somoza was storing up a special kind of vengeance for us,' said one woman there. 'Somoza had a particular hatred for two places . . . Leon, because his father – the first "Tacho" – had been assassinated there by Rigoberto Lopez Perez, and Esteli because we held out for so long, and because the people here were so united against the dictatorship. We all used to say that it looked as if Somoza had decided to remove Esteli from the map of Nicaragua.' Even when the insurrection had been crushed, the people of Esteli refused to accept emergency food supplies offered by the government, preferring to rely on aid from the Nicaraguan Red Cross.

The reimposition of martial law, the state of siege and a news blackout enabled the National Guard to carry out its mopping-up operations undisturbed. As each city in turn fell, the EEBI swung into action, sealing off the area and denying access to journalists and even Red Cross officials. The EEBI swept through the towns, torturing and killing anyone suspected of collaborating or sympathising with the Sandinistas.[18] The widespread public suspicion that Guardsmen were drugged for these operations was confirmed by a military doctor who admitted that 'the troops were injected with Demerol and given stimulants to keep them awake and alert.'

With the Frente's military strategy limited at this stage to a war of positions, in which towns were seized and held, the Guard was given a breathing space in which to reorganise and force the insurgents on to the defensive once the initial factor of surprise had been lost. There was no dynamic relationship yet between rural guerrilla units and the urban insurrection, or between one town and another. Although the fighting capacity of local barracks was weak, the efficient elite units of the Guard waited to gauge the strength of resistance in each town before launching its counter-offensive, and did not fall into the trap of dispersing its forces. With Managua under control, the Guard allowed the FSLN to hold on to Leon, Chinandega and Esteli, and turned its firepower first on Masaya. Located only 31 kilometres from the capital, close to the population centres of Jinotepe, Diriamba and San Marcos and the coffee fields of Carazo, and controlling communications with the southern part of the country, Masaya presented the most direct threat to Somoza and was rapidly retaken by the Guard. Leon was next in line, then Chinandega, and finally Esteli. The Guard's tactics were similar on each occasion in their brutal simplicity. Town after town was softened up with maximum firepower before the EEBI moved in to clean up. The scale of the slaughter which resulted grew as each new town was recovered, culminating in Esteli.[19]

Somoza's genocidal response to the insurrection was not simply a sign of psychopathic cruelty, but an absolute military necessity for survival. September represented a united frontal attack on the very basis of his regime, the accumulation of a year of strikes, ambushes, attacks on barracks, demonstrations, hunger strikes and local *barrio* uprisings. Somoza was no longer fighting against isolated *guerrilla* groups but against an entire people. The slogan of the insurrection was *'Cada casa un cuartel sandinista'* ('Every house a Sandinista barracks'), and the air-force had to destroy whole city blocks houses, schools, hospitals and refugee centres to reimpose the order of

Somocismo.

The Frente had failed to capture its primary military targets in the departmental capitals. Each National Guard garrison, unable to deal with the insurrection until reinforcements arrived from Managua, simply withdrew to barracks to sit out the siege, leaving the streets in the hands of the people and allowing the urban militias and *barrio* committees to run the towns. Only smaller barracks like Monimbo were ever captured by the FSLN; elsewhere days dragged by without control of the streets by the people turning into full-scale military takeovers. The insurrection was forced into a second week, much longer than anticipated, without being converted into the essential war of movement which might have kept the enemy engaged on several fronts at once. The core of the insurrection in each town was in the *barrios* of the working class and the migrant rural proletariat, and the Frente was not yet able to combine fluidly the urban and rural forms of the military struggle as they would in the final offensive of May 1979.

Nonetheless, the Sandinistas' original strategy had been careful and disciplined. The opening shots of the insurrection were fired almost simultaneously in Managua, Masaya, Leon, Chinandega and Esteli, in the space of a few minutes between 6 and 6.30 on the evening of 9 September. The basic plan of action had been for a synchronised offensive on these five key regional centres, with the aim of forcing the dispersal of the National Guard. At the same time, the most experienced combatants and the heaviest weaponry would cross the Costa Rican border and move on to take Rivas and Granada. With control of the principal cities on the Pacific seaboard, the FSLN would then install its provisional government in liberated territory — Rivas was a likely candidate — and look to Venezuela, Panama and Costa Rica for diplomatic recognition to forestall any military intervention by the forces of the Central American Defence Council, CONDECA.[20]

But two early defeats weakened the plan. First, the Frente had not yet mastered the complexities of an insurrection in the sprawl of Managua, and after early skirmishes over the weekend of 9-10 September, the rising petered out in the capital. Second, the squadrons of the Frente Sur failed to make decisive headway, with the Guard repelling a powerful invasion force on 12 September. Both in September and in the 1979 final offensive, the Southerr Front presented massive difficulties. Although the force was led by some of the FSLN's most experienced military commanders, such as Eden Pastora, the landscape of Southern Nicaragua is not ready made for guerrilla warfare. The ribbon of flatland where the chain of volcanoes falls away to the sea calls instead for conventional artillery warfare and a painfully slow advance from one row of trenches to the next. The Panamerican Highway to Costa Rica runs straight along a narrow strip hemmed in by Lake Nicaragua and the Pacific Ocean, at times a mere twenty kilometres across and with little vegetation to provide cover. A handful of small hills, heavily fortified by the Guard, provided military strongholds which controlled broad tracts of countryside. When the Sandinista forces which had been driven back on the 12th launched a second assault on Penas Blancas five days later, the National

Guard had already dealt with much of the north and could afford to release some of its elite troops to repel this renewed FSLN incursion.

The Frente took the lesson to heart: if the *guerrilla* and the urban insurrection were not transformed into a war of movement, the revolution was doomed. In May 1979, they would not repeat the error.

Learning from September

The temporary military defeat forced the FSLN to make a tactical withdrawal, regroup its forces in the mountains where the Guard could not root them out, and draw the necessary conclusions from September. Within a year, the organisation had grown from a small guerrilla force of a few hundred men and women into a national mass movement embracing countless thousands of Nicaraguan peasants, workers and students as well as sympathisers from the middle classes and the Catholic Church. In September, the new 'irregular' military forces had come into their own, the teenagers grouped in militias, people's combat brigades and urban commandos. Some of these were the product of painstaking work by the Frente in the urban centres in the early months of the year but the majority comprised disenchanted, angry and unemployed youth, most without any clear picture of what would come after the dictatorship. Even young children took part, competing with each other to see who could build barricades the fastest; amongst them were those with extraordinary political maturity, like the nine-year-old Luis Alfonso Velasquez, who led the primary school children's Movimiento de Educacion Primaria (he distributed FSLN propaganda, raised money to support strikers and finally covered Sandinista combatants by hurling contact bombs at the Guard, until shot dead by paramilitaries in May 1979).[21] In the words of Humberto Ortega:

> We could not stop the insurrection. The mass movement went beyond the vanguard's capacity to take the lead . . . and aware of its limitations, it decided to adopt the general decision taken by the masses. In other words, the vanguard set the example in October [1977], the masses followed suit for the first time in an organised fashion in Mobimbo; the vanguard created the conditions on the basis of that example and the masses moved faster than the vanguard because a whole series of objective conditions existed . . . The decision to call for the uprising in September [1978] made it possible to harness the avalanche, to organise the uprising for the victory that was to follow.[22]

For the Frente, harnessing the avalanche meant three things: military leadership, grassroots organisation and political education. The training given to combatants and the many new recruits in the months after September was both political and military, as the FSLN set up schools of political education side by side with military training schools. To rectify the critical shortages of September, international solidarity began to guarantee the flow of heavy arms, and street-fighting weapons were improvised ingeniously in clandestine workshops. One weapon designed in the working-class *barrios* of Managua to fire .22 bullets was constructed from a section of metal tubing one-inch in diameter, and a firing mechanism built around a rubber band. It was christened 'La Proletaria'. Clandestine editions of the writings of Sandino were studied, together with FSLN internal circulars and the theoretical journal *Pensamiento Critico*. The false distinction between military and political work disappeared with the September insurrection, and with it the damaging splits within the Frente. The original division had occurred at a time when it was possible – and arguably necessary – to talk of different strategic options. That time had now passed. With the intensification of the struggle in the months following the death of Pedro Joaquin Chamorro, there was only one possible direction for the revolutionary movement to take: a popular insurrection whose political and military vanguard was the FSLN and not any one of its tendencies. With strategic debate now irrelevant, it became clear that the ideological divisions betwen the tendencies had been largely illusory. The work put in by the three of them in different areas – rural and urban, military and political, superstructural and grassroots – could now be seen for what it had always in essence been: complementary, not conflicting.

With many lessons learned from September, and the masses preparing actively for another offensive, the political formation of new cadres became a task of paramount importance. No longer Proletario, or GPP, or Tercerista/ Insurrectional cadres, but FSLN cadres. Commander German Pomares, writing in his diary in the early months of 1979, shortly before his death, noted:

> There is one thing which worries me, and that is that not everyone has political clarity even though they want to fight against the tyrant. The danger will come afterwards, in the process of reconstruction, that's when we may have problems. The *compas* are the finest people and they ask interesting questions about what a revolution really means, the fact that it will continue after we have buried Somoza; that makes me happy, because it helps me in my own development, to explain what a revolution is. I like to sit and talk with these *compas,* because they have that interest and because there's the hope that they will become the cadres of the future. With their youth, they could turn into good cadres.[23]

Many of the Frente's new recruits were remarkably young, due to the 'Herod policy' pursued by Somoza after the insurrection when any young male was automatically supposed to be a potential *guerrillero.*' Unfortunately, it's a crime to be young in Nicaragua today. The young are being persecuted mercilessly, from 13 or 14 upwards . . . or even 12, depending on their size.'[24] And so thousands of teenagers poured out of the devastated cities to join the FSLN. The savagery of the National Guard's mopping-up operations was the best recruiting drive possible.

Many of the new cadres had already received a rich education in practical revolutionary politics through the Civil Defence Committees. The long months of work at the heart of the mass movement and the creation of the United People's Movement had allowed the CDCs to play a major role in the running of the briefly liberated cities, developing most strongly in the strategic towns of Masaya, Leon and Managua and active in the strike in the *departamento* of Carazo. Although their level of organisation was not yet uniform throughout the country, all were ready when the final call for insurrection came. During 1978, the CDCs had become organs of great political prestige among the people. Converting specific community demands into mass agitation and mobilisation, they came to represent the nucleus of future popular power as victory, and the transition to a new kind of state, approached. In the urban *barrios,* their tasks had multiplied since their creation. In the less politically developed areas, people's committees concentrated during the insurrection on defensive tasks – building air-raid shelters, organising food distribution and medical care. In Leon, there was the most advanced blend of this kind of activity with both military preparation – weapons training, lessons in strategy, barricade building – and the growth of a real parallel power structure, evolved through a year of intensive political work at the community level. The CDCs here had mobilised people around transport problems, the escalating cost of living, and the scarcity of land and public services; they had operated clandestine propaganda and information networks, and proved themselves to be bodies capable of acting as popular assemblies, distribution centres for food and medical supplies, and price control watchdogs.

While the influence of the CDCs continued to grow, the Movimiento Pueblo Unido to which they were intimately linked moved on to a new level as the insurrectional struggle entered its final and highest phase and the last remnants of the bourgeois plan collapsed. The MPU, together with the FSLN leadership, judged that the time was finally right to create the broad anti-Somoza front which Carlos Fonseca had written about fifteen years earlier, the *'frente unico'* proposed by Sandino.

Parallel Power

All sides saw September 1978 as a clear watershed for Somoza and for the revolutionary movement. The anti-*Somocismo* of the masses now projected itself clearly as *Sandinismo,* with far-reaching consequences not only for the dictatorship but for the future of the opposition bourgeoisie. Both the USA and right-wing groups within the Broad Opposition Front (FAO) fell over themselves to find a negotiated solution to the conflict. The initiative came from Washington as the September fighting was still raging, and by the beginning of October the Organisation of American States had approved the Carter Administration's proposal for a 'Tri-national Commission for Friendly Cooperation'. The FAO, whose rhetoric only a month earlier had been of strikes and militant opposition, leapt at the chance on 5 October. The composition of the mediation mission was briefly disputed, with Somoza rejecting the Colombian Government of Julio Cesar Turbay Ayala and the FAO turning down the military junta of El Salvador. The three representatives finally chosen — from the USA, the Dominican Republic and Guatemala — suited Washington nicely and were unlikely to upset either Somoza or the reactionary sectors of the FAO.

The FAO's political commission was made up of the Conservative, Rafael Cordova Rivas, the Movimiento Democratico Nicaraguense leader, Alfonso Robelo, and Sergio Ramirez of Los Doce. A year after their foundation, Los Doce continued to insist that no solution was possible without the presence of the Sandinistas. Their participation in the FAO political commission certainly did not endorse the FAO platform as the basis of a post-Somoza government, and Sergio Ramirez was under no illusions about the direction some groups within the FAO would have liked to take: 'The strongest force in the new Nicaragua will be a Sandinista Party, and a Social Democratic Party may find some support among the middle classes. Marxist parties will also have a future . . . Other parties within the Broad Opposition Front are corpses, and must be buried along with the dictatorship.'[25] Participation by Los Doce in the FAO political commission was to be, rather, an instrument for bringing the Sandinista message to the attention of the American Government: 'We must tell the United States that no solution exists to this crisis unless the Somoza system is dismantled, unless the Somoza family is separated from power, and unless the Sandinista National Liberation Front participates in any future stage of national life . . . We felt the duty to confront the USA directly.'[26]

As the mediation talks began, right-wing sectors of the FAO tried to appropriate the radical language of *Sandinismo* as their own, a crude populist attempt to win back some of their waning support and a tactic which was to continue during the first year of the Revolution. But this opportunism soon reached its limits when it came to direct opposition to the US negotiators. The talks began by showing great deference to Somoza, so the FAO denounced them as an interference and the columns of *La Prensa* were filled with learned studies of North American intervention in Nicaraguan affairs. But as Somoza became more intransigent, the bourgeois leadership frantically asserted that 'intervention' and 'mediation' were two different matters. In truth, the mission suited both Somoza and the FAO. The dictator was well pleased by the ease with which the negotiators yielded to his intransigence, the FAO by the mission's determination to exclude the FSLN from any solution.

On 25 October, as soon as the USA announced its plans for a provisional government including Somoza's Partido Liberal Nacionalista and the National Guard, Los Doce pulled out of the talks. It was logical that only those sectors of the FAO closest to the big non-Somoza finance groups should retain further interest in the mediation talks, and prominent among them was Alfonso Robelo, with his links to BANIC. The FAO disintegrated, with the

Moscow-line Socialist Party following Los Doce out of the talks. The attitude of the smaller centre-right parties was more ambiguous, in keeping with
their traditional relationship to the Left. The FSLN had never considered
these groups, such as the Social Christian Party (PSC), to be very dependable:

> This party has some social base within the petty bourgeoisie. Until
> 1969 its ranks had young people who took leadership roles within the
> student movement. These young people have been gradually abando -
> ning its ranks, mainly because of the duality of the group's political
> position. There are even some comrades within our organisation who
> some years ago were working with the PSC. You have to be very care-
> ful with the PSC, as it is not a very staunch ally.[27]

But with the departure of Los Doce, a number of other groups not clearly
aligned with the Left decided that their future no longer lay with the bourgeois opposition movement. The PPSC (a small progressive breakaway group
from the Social Christians) and the Independent Liberal Party (PLI) left the
FAO out of clear political conviction; others like the Social Christian trade
union federation merely pulled out because they recognised which way the
wind was blowing.[28] It now remained for the mass movement to attract these
groups towards the umbrella of the Movimiento Pueblo Unido (MPU).
Although ferocious repression by the National Guard had driven the MPU
further underground in the weeks since the insurrection, the time had been
devoted to work whose value was tested precisely by the conditions of
extreme secrecy: perfecting the national chain of Civil Defence Committees,
improving their insurrectional capacity by building networks of escape
passages, tunnels and communications routes, passing on guidance from the
most highly developed committees to the least experienced ones, integrating
the CDCs more closely with local community conscientisation groups built
up by the Church, the Christian *comites de base,* and refining their democratic structures of neighbourhood and regional steering committees
composed of elected representatives from each city block. Under MPU
supervision, the mass movement had become a well-oiled and genuinely
democratic machine.[29]

Discussions began on 11 January 1979 between the leadership of the MPU
and representatives of those groups which had broken with the FAO.
Although obstacles remained, the smaller parties found themselves in a
dilemma. Having rejected the discredited FAO, they had no power base
strong enough to build a third alternative to bourgeois leadership or the
revolutionary front. Finally convinced that their future lay with a unified
and ascendant mass movement, the PPSC and PLI agreed to join forces with
three representatives of the MPU and one of Los Doce in a six-person
National Secretariat. Events of the previous week may well have helped to
speed their decision. On 6 January, Somoza had banned a proposed march to
commemorate the death of Pedro Joaquin Chamorro, only to reverse his
decision three days later. Thirty thousand marched through Managua, and the

MPU was quick to capitalise on this new sign of Somoza's weakening grip on events. Thousands more gathered in the Managua baseball diamond on 1 February for the announcement of the new coalition. Twenty constituent organisations of the United People's Movement, Los Doce, the Popular Social Christians, Independent Liberals, Social Christian trade unionists and the small Frente Obrero (which had recently transferred its loyalties from Peking to Albania) put their names to the founding document. The Frente Patriotico Nacional (National Patriotic Front: FPN) was born, and its first declaration announced: 'This situation, now more than ever, calls for the highest degree of unity among the democratic and patriotic forces of Nicaragua.'[30]

The FPN united around a twenty-two-point statement of principles with three pillars: national sovereighty, effective democracy, justice and social progress. As a precondition for 'effective democracy', the document insisted on 'the overthrow of the Somoza dictatorship and eradication of all its vestiges, rejecting all manoeuvres that imply the continuation of the system of *Somocismo* without Somoza.' In the six-person National Secretariat of the Frente Patriotico Nacional, Los Doce were given the key portfolio of international relations, so continuing fifteen months of attempts to isolate the dictatorship diplomatically.

Notes

1. FSLN Direccion Nacional, *Por Que Lucha el Frente Sandinista Junto al Pueblo,* mimeo, somewhere in Nicaragua, 1978.
2. Movimiento Pueblo Unido, *Programa Inmediato* (1978). The full text of the MPU programme is reprinted in Lopez et al., *La Caida del Somocismo,* pp. 360-72.
3. FSLN, *El Frente Sandinista de Liberacion Nacional Presenta a Movimiento Pueblo Unido',* mimeo, somewhere in Nicaragua, November 1978.
4. GPP Comandante Bayardo Arce, undated interview (mimeo), late 1978.
5. Gabriel Garcia Marquez, 'Sandinistas Seize the National Palace', *New Left Review,* No. 111, September-October 1978.
6. The remainder of the account of the seizure of the National Palace is drawn from testimonies in the FSLN magazine *Lucha Sandinista,* Costa Rican press coverage, and interviews with Comandantes Humberto Ortega, Eden Pastora, Hugo Torres and Dora Maria Tellez in *Muerte Al Somocismo,* Managua, Publicaciones del Consejo de Estado, No. 2, 1980.
7. Anonymous FSLN leader interviewed in *Alternativa* (Bogota) No. 156/78.
8. According to Dora Maria Tellez in *Lucha Sandinista,* October, 1978.
9. Conservative Deputy Roger Mendieta Alfaro, in his account *Cero y Van Dos* (Managua, Editorial Tiposa, 1978).
10. FSLN Direccion Nacional, *La Consigna es 'Muerte al Somocismo',*

communique, August 1978.
11. Quoted in *The Guardian,* 29 August 1978.
12. *Algunos Datos sobre los Acontecimientos Recientes de Nicaragua,* Managua, anonymous mimeo 22 September 1978.
13. Humberto Ortega, 'The Strategy of Victory', interview with Marta Harnecker.
14. FSLN, *Por Que Lucha el Frente Sandinista Junto al Pueblo.*
15. Humberto Ortega, *loc. cit.*
16. *Ibid.*
17. The source for eye-witness accounts in this section are censored editions of *La Prensa,* September 1978; *Algunos Datos sobre los Acontecimientos Recientes de Nicaragua; Lucha Sandinista,* October-November 1978; and human rights reports published by the Centro Victor Sanabria, San Jose, Costa Rica.
18. *Report on the Situation of Human Rights in Nicaragua:* findings of the Inter-American Commission on Human Rights of the Organisation of American States (OAS), October 1978.
19. Ibid.
20. Humberto Ortega, *loc cit.*
21. *Luis Alfonso Velasquez, Datos Biograficos* (Managua, FSLN Secretaria Nacional de Propaganda y Educacion Politica, 1980).
22. Humberto Ortega, *loc. cit.*
23. German Pomares Ordonez, *Diario,* reprinted in *Barricada,* August 1979.
24. Sergio Martinez Valerio, former head of Somoza's death squad, after capture by the FSLN, interviewed in the Costa Rican film *Patria Libre O Morir,* Istmo Film, 1979.
25. Interview with Sergio Ramirez: 'Die Grosse Macht der Zukunft ist der Sandinismus'. in Informationsburo Nicaragua, *Ein Volk im Familienbesitz* (Hamburg, Rowohlt, 1979).
26. *Los Doce* communiques, 14 and 27 October 1978.
27. Doris Tijerino, *Inside the Nicaraguan Revolution,* p. 160.
28. Lopez, et al., *op. cit.,* pp. 259-60.
29. See press interviews in numerous Western European newspapers with Moises Hassan, Julio Lopez and other members of the MPU political commission, May-June 1979.
30. Frente Patriotico Nacional, *Acto Constitutivo* (Managua, February 1979).

9. The Favourable Moment: Preparing the Final Offensive

FSLN Unity

There is more than a subtle semantic distinction between 'unity' and 're-unification'. When the FSLN finally reached internal agreement early in 1979, they did not speak of reunifying; rather they reaffirmed their unity. A favourite question of foreign journalists and even many observers on the Left after the fall of Somoza was 'will this unity last or will the three tendencies fall apart again?' To a Sandinista, the question made no sense.

These same observers had viewed the convergence of the three tendencies in the months after the military defeat of September as primarily a response to immediate military necessity as a sinking of ideological and strategic differences. But that is to dismiss the organic relationship between the FSLN and the Nicaraguan people and to forget the history of Sandinismo. No member of the Frente questioned that the organisation had eventually to be unified, although in the difficult years of the mid-1970s the divergences had at times appeared irreconcilable. A vanguard organisation is the highest political expression of the people's struggle, and as such it is subject to constant recall by the people. Failure to achieve unity in early 1979 would have been the gravest act of desertion of the will of the Nicaraguan people. In 1975, the Frente had split at a time of accelerating social crisis, and state brutality which had left the small organisation physically dispersed, unable to communicate internally and threatened with extinction, and when the class structure of the country was undergoing dynamic change and the options for a revolutionary strategy were genuinely open to debate. 'We needed to split in order to survive' was the view of one FSLN militant. A few days after the July 1979 victory, another prominent Sandinista talked of unity in these terms:

> Of course many people thought that the unity achieved by the Frente prior to the overthrow of the dictatorship was merely a tactical exercise. Before this process of unity began, we declared that it was irreversible. Within the Frente Sandinista there had been contradictions which naturally had been most acute when the repression was at its toughest. But we always had in common our political tradition, *Sandinismo*, our experiences of struggle, our willingness to fight for a

democratic society, our people. We said that we were in a process of internal discussion: a process in which the three tendencies had to be reintegrated into a single united FSLN. We don't deny that in all the conversations leading to unity there were differences of opinion about specific measures taken, but the fundamental and decisive point is that the unity of the FSLN is solid and strong, confirmed by the fact that the sense of [separate] identity of the three tendencies has effectively dissolved. Now you cannot find any unit in any part of the country which would claim allegiance to one or other tendency. The three have fused.[1]

With the forging of an alternative power bloc (the Frente Patriotico Nacional), the existence of parallel popular power — Sandinista power — at the grassroots level, and an insuperable political crisis at the heart of the dictatorship, it was impossible for the FSLN to remain divided any longer. Nevertheless, the history of three difficult years of divisions, the gap between the political maturity of the leadership and some of the Sandinistas' rank and file, and the tremendous security problems and enforced clandestinity of the final months of 1978, did mean that it took several months before the necessary unity could be cemented.

As early as 1977 there had been informal agreements between the three tendencies, a tacit acceptance of broadly demarcated areas of work. A crude division of labour assigned the countryside to the GPP, the urban working class to the Proletarios and military work to the Insurreccionales. At the time, however, the division did little to enhance the long-term prospects for unity or to multiply the impact of the FSLN's work nationally. It was only later that the Sandinistas saw clearly that the efforts of this period had been complementary and not competitive. Humberto Ortega described it in this way:

> Different areas of work had been determined by the Movement. The fact that we all sprang from common roots helped us a great deal. It made for mutual respect for the work of other tendencies. For example, the Insurrectional Tendency did not fight to create another revolutionary students' front. It left the control of that organisation, which played such an important role in Nicaragua, with the other tendencies. Neither was there any interference with the work being carried out by the Proletarian comrades in a number of factories. And this attitude was reciprocated. They did not attempt to set up another Northern Front or Southern Front, which was the most important military work carried out by the Insurrectionals. On the contrary, the work was complementary and coordinated.[2]

The history of three years of independent work by the tendencies proved that it was no longer relevant to debate whether one area of work or another should be given greater prominence, considered 'more important' or 'more correct'. In the light of the events of 1978 and the extension of the struggle into every part of Nicaraguan society, it was clear to the FSLN that any talk of the supremacy of any one tendency was now a thing of the past. The new conviction was expressed by Henry Ruiz in an interview with the Costa Rican newspaper *El Trabajador:* 'The guarantee of the democratisation of our country lies in Sandinista unity. No fraction of our organisation can assume the leadership of the whole revolutionary movement.'

In June 1978 the first *acuerdos* were written down: agreements on immediate action. A national Sandinista coordinating committee was set up, and although the emphasis was more on tactics than on strategy, the leadership of all three tendencies clearly understood them as the first step in a continuing debate which could only have one conclusion. The June agreements were based on the recognition by all three that formal unification was still a thorny problem, and so a long way off, while joint proposals for immediate action were an absolute necessity, easier to reach, and would in themselves create many of the conditions for eventual unity. The major debate until now had been on the desirability of a rapid insurrection but, as had happened before, all sections of the vanguard now recognised that their responsibility was to respond to the actions of the masses and provide clear leadership. And mass action in mid-1978 was moving irreversibly towards insurrection. With this argument disposed of, the agreements centred on three points: (1) a propaganda drive against sectarianism in the rank and file of each tendency and every mass and popular organisation regardless of its affiliation, an end to personal attacks, and increased personal discipline; (2) joint planning and consultation on all political and military action to ensure the success of the coming mass insurrection; (3) agreed tactics to present a united front against any manoeuvres by Somoza, the US Government and the Nicaraguan bourgeoisie. This point was especially critical: a disunited FSLN would be vulnerable to any concerted right-wing 'solution' to the Nicaraguan crisis.

The upsurge in the mass movement during 1978 necessarily brought with it more favourable and more compelling reasons for a degree of operational unity. Under conditions of relative weakness, during which the Frente had tried to build its strength in different sectors of the population while being prevented from communicating easily, it was only logical that differences should have been exaggerated and strategies uncoordinated. But with tens of thousands now seeking the revolutionary leadership of the FSLN, it was natural that there should be a growing overlap between assigned areas of activity, no longer under the threat of duplication and competition, but with the aim of strengthening the national influence of the movement. Increasingly convinced of the need for insurrection, the GPP set about strengthening its urban base, while the Proletarios complemented their work among the urban proletariat with a new drive to enlist the support of the peasantry and rural proletariat in the major production centres of the Pacific Coast. The fruits of this effort were already visible as early as 25 March 1978, with the founding meeting in Diriamba of the ATC (Asociacion de Trabajadores del

Campo: Rural Workers' Association), which brought together the dozens of newly formed Comites de Trabajadores del Campo. And through the Revolutionary People's Commandos, the Proletarios also ended any remaining isolation on their part from military aspects of the struggle.

Discussions between the three tendencies were speeded on by unified FSLN opposition to the manoeuvres of the Trinational Commission for Friendly Cooperation, whose efforts to bring about a negotiated solution after the September insurrection ended by rapidly conceding ground to an intransigent dictator. By mid-December the basic elements of an agreement had been worked out, sufficient to allow the three to put their names — though still as distinct tendencies — to a major public document in the following months. It was already an open secret that unity was close at hand. The document, entitled *Del FSLN a los Pueblos del Mundo*, received massive international distribution. It analysed the history and disintegration of the dictatorship and the current state of the mass movement, and condemned imperialist attempts to snatch victory from the Nicaraguan people. It was also one of the final public documents in which the Frente made explicit their commitment to the overthrow of the dictatorship as a first step in achieving socialism in Nicaragua.[3]

The development of unity within the FSLN was also closely linked with the creation of left-wing unity with other groups. Above all, this produced agreement with the Moscow-line PSN, which now broke years of hostility to the armed struggle by putting its voice — and the important sectors of the urban working class which it represented — behind the insurrectional strategy. In accepting the cooperation of the PSN, the Sandinistas also welcomed unity around a common programme with any other left-wing group, no matter how small. Given the importance which all sectors of the FSLN now placed on the creation of a broad anti-Somoza front, the internal unity of *Sandinismo* was additionally important in order to ensure that the revolutionary forces did not surrender their hegemony within the MPU, and later the FPN, in the face of bourgeois threats.

While the agreements were firm at the level of the leadership, there remained residual problems of sectarianism among the rank and file. But from mid-1978 this was largely overcome. Increased discipline within the organisation meant that all debate about the future now took place internally, and no longer publicly and damagingly as had happened after the October 1977 Tercerista offensive. In addition, large-scale recruitment into the ranks of the FSLN over the last year of the offensive brought in hundreds of new militants unmarked by the damaging sectarianism of the past.

Not surprisingly, the FSLN also had to contend with political problems within the new FPN in the first months of 1979, although they came from the Left and not the Right. The small, ultra-Stalinist Nicaraguan Communist Party (PCN) and the trade union federation which it controlled (CAUS) began to criticise the vanguard role of the Frente, attempting to wean popular support away from the armed struggle. The initial problems with this group, which was led by Eli Altamirano, were but a foretaste of the obstructive

145

policies it was to follow during the first year of the Revolution. Although the PCN was an irritant, its criticisms in fact only served to strengthen what was an established fact: that the FSLN was overwhelmingly recognised by the people as the only legitimate leadership of the Nicaraguan Revolution. In the months after the September insurrection, there was a critical need to strengthen and re-structure grass-roots organisation and improve military action. Battered at the hands of the National Guard and outraged at the way in which the bourgeois opposition bent to Somoza and the USA during the mediation talks, the people were more than receptive to FSLN leadership. With National Guard repression continuing unabated through the early months of 1979, assassinations running at 280 a month, and five or six disappearances daily,[4] it was difficult for the FSLN to keep up a sustained offensive against the dictatorship. Nonetheless, they believed that a series of conditions still had to be fulfilled before a second insurrection could be contemplated. The FPN had to be consolidated, with the MPU playing the determining role within the new front. The international isola-tion of Somoza (apart from the support he could continue to count on from other Central American dictatorships) had to be assured, together with sufficient international recognition for a provisional government of the FSLN's choosing. The combativity of the masses had to be intensified to a point where all forms of popular organisation were on a war footing. And the National Guard had to be unceasingly harassed and weakened.[5]

On the military level, the Frente had to mesh together different forms of guerrilla warfare and urban insurrection. This meant strengthening the regular forces on the regional fronts, and improving the capacity of the irregulars: the militias, people's brigades and urban commandos. Although all this involved a number of difficulties — demanding, for example, radically changed tactics from the FSLN's regular combat units — there could be no question of allowing the necessary military restructuring to break the rhythm of sustained attack which would keep the Guard on the defensive and chip away at the morale of Somoza's troops. On more than one occasion, the Sandinistas invoked the lessons of the Vietnamese struggle. At the same time, the Frente devoted considerable energy to forming the nucleus of a regular army. The purpose was not simply to diversify the military resources and tactics available for the coming offensive, but also to provide a ready trained people's army which could supplant the defeated National Guard.[6]

Throughout the first four months of 1979, the Frente stepped up operations of every kind in all parts of the country. Economic targets were carefully selected to inflict maximum damage on the dictatorship's major sources of foreign currency earnings. Armed attacks were launched against coffee warehouses, cotton processing plants, tobacco stores and sugar refiner-ies, destroying valuable exports. In the words of Carlos Nunez, the TP coman-dante in charge of the Frente Interno, and as such responsible for organising the central *departamentos* of Managua, Carazo, Granada and Masaya:

> So many efforts and so many sacrifices made by our cadres and mili-
> tants, leaders and combatants, had the desired results. In Managua,

Leon, Chinandega, Carazo and Masaya, armed combat became general, we attacked military convoys with effective ambushes, intensified strikes against agents of the regime, increased the recovery of funds. Militia activity was stepped up in every *barrio,* the ability of the enemy to patrol at night was restricted, with the *barrios* controlled by the Sandinistas at night. New arms were obtained for combat, frantic training was given to hundreds of fighters in every possible place, we began to inflict significant losses on the elite troops of the Somocista Guard, the Basic Infantry Training School (EEBI), we strengthened clandestine structures, and at the same time systematically built new guerrilla fronts where there were none or consolidated those which already existed. In the streets, at certain times, the only people who moved were either Sandinistas or Somocistas. The Frente Patriotico Nacional, whose axis was the Movimiento Pueblo Unido, continued its work of denunciation to the masses, demonstrating in the streets the people's rejection of the regime, preparing urban services for the final battle, organising the masses for the general strike and the necessary structures to sustain the war effort: hospitals, secret clinics, basic food provisions, stockpiling of war material, training the population in first aid, preparing shelter for combatants. All these were the daily tasks of the mass organisations, who were aware of the imminence of the final struggle.[7]

And as these preparations advanced, a secretly made film was released showing an announcement by six Sandinista leaders. The brief prepared statement read by Henry Ruiz proclaimed the long anticipated unity of the three tendencies, 'the irreversible and unbreakable unity of the FSLN'. It was 7 March. The Frente appointed a nine-person Joint National Directorate, with three representatives of each tendency. For the Insurrectionals, Daniel Ortega, Humberto Ortega and the Mexican Victor Tirado Lopez; for the Proletarios, Luis Carrion, Carlos Nunez and Jaime Wheelock; and for the GPP, Bayardo Arce, Tomas Borge and Henry Ruiz. Interviewed after the declaration, Borge announced that: 'FSLN unity is not a sum but rather a multiplication, a geometric progression in the development of Nicaragua's revolutionary forces.'[8]

Within days of the announcement, a small group of journalists were taken to a secret press conference, conducted in dramatic circumstances. They were briefly abducted by an FSLN squadron and taken to the house of a UPI correspondent in Managua to hear details of a plot uncovered by Sandinista intelligence — a coup which was to be carried out by a section of the National Guard with Washington's blessing. While the release of the story was a major victory for the Frente on the international plane, they also moved rapidly to mobilise the mass organisations within Nicaragua in condemnation of this fresh US attempt to block a revolutionary victory. Although the national leadership of the FSLN did not yet consider all the conditions ripe for the final offensive, they had prepared contingency plans for an insurrection in the event of a military coup. But with the coup aborted, the Frente moved instead to a series of local and diversionary attacks by guerrilla columns which prefigured the final offensive.

Fulfilling the Conditions

The attacks described by Nunez were by now an almost daily occurrence. On 21 February, the forty-fifth anniversary of Sandino's assassination, simultaneous assaults were launched against National Guard positions in Diriamba, Granada, Leon, Masaya and some *barrios* of the capital. Within days a Sandinista column fifty-strong took over Yali, a small town of 8,000 people in the mountains north of Jinotega, holding it for eight hours. As March wore on, other columns staged hit-and-run attacks throughout the north: in Chichigalpa, El Viejo, Leon, Chinandega and the sugar refinery of San Antonio. The aim was always the same: to recover arms, to wear down the Guard and disperse its forces, and to draw reserve troops into the northern mountains where they would be vulnerable to the mobile forces of the Sandinistas' Frente Norte. In desperation, the Guard resorted once again to aerial bombing of peasant villages throughout the area.

In the new wave of Sandinista attacks, one stood out. On 27 March, under the command of German Pomares, a unified column of eighty guerrillas briefly occupied the mountain town of El Jicaro, the first major operation involving combatants of all three tendencies under a single joint command. It was the first step in the general insurrectional plan drawn up by the newly formed National Directorate. The unification of the Frente alarmed Somoza. Leaving his son Anastasio Somoza Portocarrero in charge of military operations, he took advantage of Nicaragua's traditional Easter Week holiday to fly out of the country, ostensibly for a family holiday at his Miami mansion. But as well as relaxing, he took the opportunity to lobby right-wing US politicians, claiming that the unity of the FSLN marked a decisive swing to the left, and hoping that he might simultaneously alarm sectors of the Nicaraguan bourgeoisie who continued to waver. 'Let's look at the nature of whom we're talking about,' he said at a press conference on arrival in Kansas. 'We're talking about Communist, Marxist-Leninist guerrillas who have no real popular backing in Nicaragua and who would never make a dent in the electorate of Nicaragua. So they insist on overthrowing the government by force and establishing a Marxist-Leninist state in Nicaragua.' Of equal importance for Somoza was the need to drum up support for his recent application to the International Monetary Fund for an economic lifeline of $66 million, two-thirds of it in new stand-by credits. But while the IMF delegation considered its response, the first precondition imposed by their negotiators – an immediate devaluation of the *cordoba,* the first for forty years – only galvanised working-class hostility to the regime by producing an overnight 40% price rise on basic foodstuffs.

As Somoza departed for the USA and anger at the devaluation exploded, the Sandinistas made their next important military move, this time a guerrilla column assault on Esteli, commanded by Francisco Rivera. Although the column was much larger than before – some 200 – the aim was still one of harassment and diversion. What had not been sufficiently anticipated was the response of the local people. Here is an account of the April fighting in Esteli given by a local combatant:

> We knew there had to be another offensive, a big one, but we thought Leon would explode, along with Chinandega, Esteli and the rest of the country . . . everything together. But we didn't know that Esteli would end up alone holding out for more than a week, facing the strongest troops that *el hombre* could send in against us. With Israeli arms and Guatemalan mercenaries. In April they must have killed a thousand people here. It was the same as in September, dragging people out of their beds at 4 a.m. and shooting them, after the Frente had moved out. It was those memories of the torture, the massacre in September, that made us so committed to fight again when the Frente came back, although that obviously hadn't figured in the plans for the assault on Esteli. Our main concern was that we needed arms, everyone was crying out for arms . . . we weren't going to let ourselves be massacred again defencelessly.
>
> We saw the Sandinista column, over 100 *muchachos* moving into the city in the morning. We just saw them coming, but we didn't know the plan, what form the offensive was going to take. They came in fighting and took the school, hitting the Guard directly, and the Guard pulled back. All over Easter weekend they held their positions. They came in without knowing what the strength of popular resistance would be . . . if it was strong, they would stay. And God, it was strong. In September, the *muchachos* hadn't been heavily armed, but this time it was different . . . the same arms as the Guard. Then they sent in 1,000 soldiers, or more, commanded by El Chiguin, with aircraft of the FAN, those Israeli Push-Pulls, and rocketed and bombed us, just like before. The support which the people gave the Frente was extraordinary . . . And one thing had changed: No-one asked themselves 'which tendency is behind this?' All we cared about was how to arm ourselves. We weren't thinking about tendencies.
>
> There were two squadrons of the Frente trapped in the countryside around here, and that was one of the purposes of April . . . to force the Guard to move their forces around, to relieve the pressure. There was no attempt to turn Esteli into a nationwide insurrection. When it became clear that the Frente were going to have to pull out, they asked the people to leave with them, everyone to take to the mountains. But even now, there were some people who couldn't believe that the Guard would take the repressive measures it did, in spite of all the evidence; so they stayed behind, and of course the Sandinistas couldn't force the them to leave. There was a big problem, though. The Guard had the town completely surrounded, encircled. But the Frente broke the circle

with a brilliant move. They had foreseen this situation and left a couple of squadrons outside the city limit, in the district known as San Roque, and there they carried out a swift diversionary operation, to distract the Guard. That left a gap, and hundreds of people – the attack unit plus hundreds of new recruits – poured out along the track called El Terrero. After that came another of the Guard's famous 'Cleaning-Up Operations', and that was important for the consciousness of the people here. We were the only city that went through three separate uprisings and three waves of National Guard barbarity. April meant that there was no-one at all left in Esteli who didn't support the Frente. When the call came for the final insurrection in June, everyone was ready.[9]

Humiliated by the inability of their elite troops to crush a relatively small number of FSLN combatants, the Guard sealed off the town to Red Cross personnel and reporters and prevented civilians from leaving the area. The Guard were thus left undisturbed to carry out atrocities equal to those committed in September. In one incident, National Guard patrols invaded the San Juan de Dios hospital, dragging two doctors from the operating theatre and rounding up forty patients, many still unconscious, suspected of collaboration with the Frente. All were bundled into the yard and machine-gunned.[10] The *Guardia* appeared determined to fulfil its promise of *Semana Santa Sin Sandinistas* ('Holy Week Without Sandinistas').

The mistakes of Esteli were severely criticised within the FSLN for, although the capture and holding of a single town had not been planned, the exercise had again shown the dangers of a war of fixed positions. But at least the organisation had avoided any temptation to call an ill-prepared national insurrection according to a timetable dictated by the National Guard. More positively, operations in this critical theatre of the war had given proof of the Sandinistas' newly acquired firepower – heavy machineguns, anti-aircraft weapons, mortars. Two government aircraft had been shot down in the nearby town of El Sauce, and another further north in Condega on the main highway. Within a fortnight, Somoza was once again compelled to deploy armoured cars, Sherman tanks and air-power to dislodge FSLN units from Leon, this time leaving a further 100 dead.

And despite his April tour of the USA, Somoza came under increasing pressure from Washington the following month. The FSLN, too, had stepped up its diplomatic initiatives in the US, sending two members of Los Doce to seek support from sympathetic Democrats. In early May, more than 40 of them, including Senator Edward Kennedy, wrote to President Carter, Secretary of State Cyrus Vance and Treasury Secretary Michael Blumenthal, insisting that, if the IMF loan were granted, this would amount to an international vote of confidence in the regime, as well as being economic folly. Their arguments were unpersuasive, and US representatives 'did not dissent' from the IMF decision, announced on 14 May, to approve a $66 million package. US protestations that the loan did not constitute a 'political' decision were the purest hypocrisy from a government which, seven months earlier, had blocked IMF credits to Somoza as a means of forcing him to the negotiating table after the September insurrection. But for Somoza the decision provided only a brief respite. While remaining quiet about the Esteli and Leon massacres of April, the US State Department vehemently condemned the arrest of five FAO leaders, including Alfonso Robelo and the Conservative Rafael Cordova Rivas. Within days of the IMF announcement, Somoza's international standing took a further toss when President Lopez Portillo of Mexico declared his country's decision to break off diplomatic relations because of the 'horrendous acts of genocide' committed by the National Guard, and urging other Latin American governments to follow suit. Lopez Portillo's announcement came at a meeting with the recently elected Costa Rican leader Rodrigo Carazo Odio, whose government had taken the same step the previous year in response to National Guard air and land incursions into Costa Rican territory in pursuit of Frente Sur combatants encamped across the border.

In spite of long-standing Costa Rican hostility to Somoza, the new Carazo Odio presidency was an ambiguous ally for the Frente. Costa Rica had been one of the countries pressured by the USA to acquiesce in the planned coup in March; and irritated by the open use which the FSLN was making of the Costa Rican provinces of Liberia, Guanacaste and Alajuela as rearguard territory, Carazo Odio ordered the Civil Guard to tighten their vigilance in the border area, as a result of which thirteen Sandinistas were arrested. This unaccustomed harassment of bases inside Costa Rica may have partly explained the FSLN's decision to take the pressure off the narrow border strip between Lake Nicaragua and the Pacific, by opening up a completely new area of military activity in the remote southern part of the *departamento* of Zelaya, around the town of Nueva Guinea where they had little history of local peasant support. From a purely military point of view, the Nueva Guinea front was one of the FSLN's new major disasters. Humberto Ortega explained the relationship between the Nueva Guinea operation and the insurrectional plan:

> The plan was correct, but our comrades were unable to deal with certain tactical situations and they were hit hard by the enemy . . . [The plan was] to infiltrate a column there, to bog down the enemy, to mount a guerrilla attack. This would create conditions in the rest of the country to carry out political and military work in the cities, once the *Guardia* had been dispersed. So the repression would be felt less severely because the *Guardia* would be tied down in Nueva Guinea. But instead of following guerrilla tactics our *companeros* operated on the flat plains, where they were an easy target for the enemy.[11]

The *Guardia* detected the Sandinista column, this time composed of 140 combatants, after it had crossed the Nicaraguan border at Los Sabalos on 18 May. One thousand troops with air support were diverted to the region (to this extent the operation achieved its purpose) and almost the entire column was wiped out in open country. The Frente's losses were 128, including Ivan Montenegro, one of the senior leaders of the Frente Sur, and for once the *Guardia*'s claim to have received local peasant support was probably correct. Elsewhere in the country, however, the military failure of Nueva Guinea was compensated for by its political impact. In difficult terrain, the FSLN had pulled one-third of the *Guardia*'s southern divisions out of position, and the heavy Sandinista losses increased public sympathy still further.[12] Additionally, the propaganda impact of events in Nueva Guinea and elsewhere in May was enhanced by a new FSLN weapon – the clandestine Radio Sandino, capable of broadcasting up-to-date news throughout Nicaragua.

In the unanimous view of the FSLN National Directorate, all the necessary objective and subjective conditions had been fulfilled for the launching of the final offensive. It was the third week in May. The economic contradictions of the IMF loan were immediately apparent, with large compensatory wage rises for government employees and an empty May Day promise of 15% increases for the working class. Mexico's severing of diplomatic relations with Somoza provided the crucial precedent for future international support for a new government. Guerrilla columns were in position in all areas, and the Frente Interno provided a political and military leadership supple enough to combine the three pillars of the struggle in the central cities of the Pacific: a general strike, mass insurrection and military action. In the future organs of popular power, the Comites de Defensa Civil and the MPU, there was an adequate combination of ideological and practical readiness. Mass consciousness had reached the same level as mass organisation. Within the FPN, bourgeois influence was entirely secondary, and the revolutionary thrust of the Front, provided by the MPU, was oriented correctly towards each element of the coming insurrection: combat efficiency, civilian rearguard support and political agitation.

The Nicaraguan bourgeoisie had suffered the political effects of its traditional weakness as a class. That weakness left large sectors of the middle classes exposed, with no real alternative but to ally themselves with the revolutionary leadership. Some gravitated towards the FSLN because their only very slight relationship with the Somoza clan and the powerful finance groups left them open to genuine radicalisation, (a radicalisation that was sustained during the first year of the Revolution), while others only did so from political expediency which did not imply any surrender of class interests. This acceptance of the class alliances proposed by the Frente was their only path to a share in future power, albeit as part of a bloc which they could never hope to dominate. Thus, the FSLN knew that it could rely on the necessary tacit acceptance by many employers of a fresh call for a general strike, which this time would be under Sandinista and MPU leadership. The economic collapse brought about by the IMF-imposed devaluation had drastic effects on those employers who had previously vacillated. At the same time, the most reactionary sectors of the bourgeoisie turned in panic to a defence of their class position, more alarmed by the FSLN than by a slightly modified version of *Somocismo*. In mid-March, the Conservative opposition in Congress proposed a series of constitutional amendments, while the three dissident factions of the Conservative Party joined forces on the 18th to form the Partido Conservador Democrata (PCD). As the people of Esteli showed the direction which the majority of Nicaraguan people chose to follow, the Conservatives set up a so-called Comite de Reflexion to intercede between Somoza and the opposition. The suggestion that Nicaragua should return to the politics of mediation at this stage was predictably ridiculed by every other opposition group.

As well as the consensus on the timing of the final offensive, the FSLN National Directorate was also agreed on where it should begin, with an attack on Jinotega by forces of the Frente Norte, a military action which technically was the last of the pre-offensive period. The attack had a number of consequences, the worst of which was the irreparable loss of its commander, German Pomares, one of the FSLN's most respected leaders. But Jinotega did prove a humiliating blow for the National Guard, who took five days to regain control of the city. As the Frente had calculated, the *Guardia* were thus compelled to deplete their forces on the southern frontier, transferring elite units of the EEBI to the north. But the very success of the operation brought its own problems: the need to reorder the dislocated columns of the Frente Norte, and to give instant training and military discipline to the hundreds of new combatants from the Jinotega area who flocked to join the Frente. This made it difficult for the Frente Norte to assume the leading military role assigned to it. The combatants of Jinotega regrouped in the hills around the town, waiting like the rest of Nicaragua for the call to the final offensive.

Notes

1. Interview with Enrique Schmidt, Director General of the Ministry of the Interior and later Comandante of the Managua Police, Managua, July 1979.
2. Humberto Ortega, 'The Strategy of Victory', interview with Marta Harnecker.
3. *Del FSLN a los Pueblos del Mundo: Informe sobre la Coyuntura*, Tendencias Guerra Popular Prolongada, Proletaria, Insurreccional, (Ediciones Conosur, reprint, Barcelona, 1979), p. 34.
4. *Report on Human Rights in Nicaragua* (Centro Victor Sanabria, San Jose, Costa Rica, March 1979).
5. Lopez, et al., *La Caida del Somocismo*, pp. 326-28.
6. *Del FSLN a los Pueblos del Mundo*, pp. 36-8.
7. Carlos Nunez, *Un Pueblo en Armas* (Managua, FSLN Secretaria Nacional de Propaganda y Educacion Politica, 1980), pp. 8-9.
8. Interview with Tomas Borge (mimeo), April 1979.

9. Interview with FSLN combatant, Esteli, February 1980.
10. Interview with Dr. Raul Rivera, director of the Hospital San Juan de Dios, Esteli February 1980. For details of earlier repression against medical personnel in Esteli, see testimony of Dr. Alejandro Davila Bolanos (one of those killed in the April 1979 massacre) in *El Interrogatorio* (Nindiri, Herrera Impresores, 1979).
11. Humberto Ortega, *loc. cit.*
12. *Ibid.*

10. The Triumph of Sandinismo

The Battle for Nicaragua: A Chronology

The following chronology of Nicaragua's war of liberation shows the military, insurrectional and diplomatic flow of the fifty-two-day struggle in three broad phases. The first, from 29 May to about 8 June, was a period of co-ordinated military attack on all fronts; the second, until 26 June, brought the Managua insurrection, the FSLN's major diplomatic initiatives and US attempts to head off a Sandinista victory through the OAS; the third and final phase saw the consolidation of FSLN control over Central Nicaragua and the major cities, and the collapse of Somoza.

29 May: A 300-strong column of the Frente Sur crosses the border from Costa Rica.
30 May: The National Guard seals off the south and Las Mercedes airport in Managua is closed.
31 May: 'Heroic people of Nicaragua, the hour of the overthrow of the infamous dictatorship has come . . . ' The FSLN calls for a national insurrection and general strike. Combat around Leon, Chinandega and Chichigalpa, and in the north-eastern goldfields of Siuna, Bonanza and La Rosita.
2 June: FSLN enters Leon.
4 June: Leon falls. The general strike begins.
7 June: Somoza declares martial law, curfew and state of siege.
8 June: Insurrection in Carazo. By now, the FSLN controls twenty-five towns and villages throughout the north.
9 June: The Managua insurrection begins. Somoza confiscates his cabinet members' passports.
10 June: The Frente Sur withdraws from its positions south of Rivas.
11 June: The vital Sierra 13 police station in Managua falls.
12 June: Evacuation of US citizens.
13 June: National Guard shell and burn the offices of *La Prensa*.
15 June: The Frente Sur launches its second offensive.
16 June: The provisional Government Junta of National Reconstruction is named in Costa Rica. Andean Pact countries grant the FSLN

belligerent status. The Frente Sur takes Sapoa.

17 June: The National Guard barracks at Leon falls. The Managua insurrection controls two dozen *barrios,* mainly in the east of the capital.

18 June: First proclamation of the new Junta. In the south, battle for the strategic road junction of La Virgen, with the plan of setting up a provisional capital in Rivas. Ecuador breaks diplomatic relations with Somoza.

20 June: Local revolutionary *junta* set up in Leon.

21 June: American television reporter, Bill Stewart, murdered by National Guard in the *barrios orientales.*

22 June: US intervention plan presented by Secretary of State Vance, proposing an OAS peace-keeping force, rejected.

23 June: Counter-proposal by Venezuela, demanding Somoza's resignation, approved by the OAS. Intense helicopter bombing of Managua.

24 June: Masaya barracks taken.

26 June: Brazil breaks diplomatic relations.

27 June: 6,000 combatants begin strategic withdrawal from Managua towards Masaya. New US Ambassador, Pezzullo, arrives in Managua without presenting credentials. The FAO and the private sector organisation, COSEP, endorse the Junta.

28 June: US special envoy, William Bowdler, meets Junta members in San Jose, Costa Rica.

29 June: Rivas National Guard post under siege. Thirty National Guard officers defect. Emergency session of Congress boycotted by the Conservative Party.

2 July: Matagalpa falls to the FSLN.

3 July: The strategic town of Sebaco is liberated, giving the Frente control of the whole northern half of the country.

5 July: Effective control of Esteli. Offensive in Jinotepe. Bowdler's proposals for additional Junta members are rejected.

6 July: Jinotepe and San Marcos fall, cutting Guard supply lines to the Frente Sur and liberating the *departamento* of Carazo.

8 July: Somoza offers the USA his resignation on condition that a future role for the Partido Liberal Nacionalista and the National Guard is guaranteed.

9 July: US helicopters land in the Costa Rican province of Guanacaste. The Costa Rican Government demands their immediate withdrawal.

10 July: Managua surrounded by Sandinista forces.

12 July: The FSLN announces proposals for a ceasefire.

13 July: Advance units re-enter Managua. Somoza seeks military support from Guatemala and El Salvador.

14 July: Twelve members of an eighteen-strong Cabinet are named by the Junta.

16 July: Esteli barracks fall, the last important military installation outside Managua. An all-out attack on Managua is held back because of the

imminence of Somoza's resignation.

17 July: Somoza resigns and leaves for Miami at 4.30 a.m. Congress names Francisco Urcuyo Malianos as interim President, whose only function is to hand over power to the incoming Junta. But Urcuyo announces his intention to serve out Somoza's term until 1981 and orders the National Guard to fight on. Granada offensive.

18 July: Disintegration of the *Guardia.* Ambassador Pezzullo recalled by Washington in protest at Urcuyo's announcement. Junta members Ramirez, Chamorro and Robelo fly into Leon.

19 July: Urcuyo leaves the country for Guatemala and the National Guard surrenders.

War on All Fronts

After the massacres of September, the Nicaraguan people realised the implications of mounting a full-scale war against the dictatorship. The Frente looked to Lenin: 'To hide from the masses the need for a hard-fought and bloody war as an immediate necessity to be borne in the coming action is to fool oneself and fool the people.' Early in the final offensive Eden Pastora, now commander of the Sandinista army on the Frente Sur, estimated that liberation would cost 30,000 lives. In fact it cost more, but Nicaraguans were not deterred. They applied this consciousness to the general strike called for 4 June, having learned the impotence of the old peaceful stoppages led by UDEL and the FAO. The strike was the immediate precondition for insurrection, preparing the ground for mass mobilisation and participation in every city, which would in turn create optimum conditions for the action of guerrilla forces and combat units. On its first day it was 90% effective, and the insurrection took off with such speed and impetus that it overtook the Frente's original calculations. Somoza's need to deploy 2,000 troops to 'protect' those wishing to work further undermined the mobility of an army already stretched on several battlefronts simultaneously. When insurrection reached Managua, a resident of the eastern *barrio* of Bello Horizonte described the paralysis of the capital: 'The strike was in its sixth day. It was completely effective, not a single shop was open, not a bank, not an office. No petrol stations, no public transport, no buses out of the city. No supermarkets, no grocers. Everything shut. Nothing working . . . absolutely nothing.'[1] In the silent streets, the anti-terrorist units of the BECAT and foot patrols of the *Guardia* waited for the inevitable explosion.

Each action carried out between March and May − El Jicaro, Esteli, Jinotega, Nueva Guinea − had had a complementary function, each new attack relieving pressure on other fronts and increasing military flexibility. In each area, the unification of the FSLN command was translated into the integration of military forces previously loyal to one or other tendency. The twin poles of the FSLN's military strength were troop concentrations in the north and the south whose actions dislocated the National Guard and allowed the urban masses to rise up. To support the principal theatres of combat, the

157

structure of the Frente Nor-Occidental in Leon and Chinandega was refined and new fronts brought into play in Zelaya and Chontales (see map). Between them, four fronts in the east, north-east, north and north-west interlocked to squeeze the National Guard and drive on towards Managua once each area was secured. The Frente made a clear distinction between strategic forces, which were heavily armed troop concentrations capable of sustaining prolonged battles against the Guard's principal combat forces, and tactical forces designed to bog down Somoza's reinforcements with constant ambushes and hit-and-run raids. But 'the basic weight of the armed struggle was carried by the people: the armed detachments of the vanguard were designed as no more than an instrument to develop a strategy based on the decision and capacity of the masses to rise up and launch the insurrection.'[2]

With an infinitely flexible combination of conventional field warfare, tactical combat units, urban militias and commandos and the organised violence of the people, the war made itself felt in every corner of Nicaragua, even in parts of the Atlantic Coast untouched by the September 1978 insurrection. The war of movement in the north recovered hundreds of vital weapons from defeated National Guard positions and, with each new village taken, freshly armed combat brigades were formed from newly recruited local youngsters who kept up permanent harassment operations throughout the interior. Somoza no longer dictated the timetable as he had in September. In the new offensive, the FSLN held the military initiative from the outset. There were still intermittent crises of armaments: no amount of weapons recovered could keep pace with the numbers who flocked from the local population to join the Sandinistas. Occasionally there was no alternative but to abandon local positions or leave them defended by handfuls of pitifully armed youths who fought a superior enemy with extraordinary courage.[3]

That courage was nowhere more evident than on the Frente Sur, and nowhere did Sandinista forces confront worse conditions, as they inched their way up the Panamerican Highway from Costa Rica. For the first week of the offensive the Frente Sur was the main theatre of war, a vital holding operation to pin down the best of Somoza's troops. Six hundred guerrillas commanded by Pastora crossed from Costa Rica, the main column hitting the frontier hamlets of El Naranjo and El Ostional and others fanning out to strike at a dozen targets south of Rivas. Even after President Carazo's halfhearted Operation Checkmate against the Frente Sur, the sanctuary of Costa Rica continued to play a decisive role. The border was almost impossible to secure and the Sandinistas poured across it in both directions, carrying their wounded back to Red Cross posts and holding impromptu press conferences for foreign journalists in the Costa Rican village of La Cruz.[4] The success of the El Naranjo operation was essential for the war to unfold on other fronts, and although villages and strategic hilltops changed hands frequently and Somoza claimed a major victory when the FSLN pulled back into Costa Rica on June 10, the Frente Sur only retreated when its purpose had been achieved and large sectors of Managua were in the hands of the people. In all this, the improved communications of the FSLN through

Radio Sandino were notable, both to communicate news instantly from one battlefront to another and to maintain the morale of the people with reports of fresh victories. With the first successful raids on the south, the order was given for the Rigoberto Lopez Perez Front in the north-west to launch attacks on Chinandega and Leon on two consecutive days, so as to keep Guard forces on the run between the two towns. The Frente took the small town of Chichigalpa and the sugar refinery of San Antonio, although for the moment Chinandega proved intractable.

An essential part of the Frente Sur plan to pin down the elite troops of the EEBI under the notorious Pablo Emilio Salazar ('Comandante Bravo') was the formation of a new kind of armed force, the nucleus of the future Ejercito Popular Sandinista, which would be able to confront Somoza's forces on relatively equal terms. 'In the south of the country, an irregular army was waging a regular war. I say it was an irregular army because it did not have a conventional formation, but it was not a guerrilla army either. It came to be a force of 1,200 people, with large-scale logistical support, against the same number of National Guardsmen.'[5] As plans advanced for the formation of a provisional government, the Southern Front became a more sophisticated form of the embryonic plan of September 1978, to open up a liberated stretch of territory in which Rivas could act as provisional capital for the new Junta. Somoza realised the significance of the Frente Sur, and in the early days of the war made one of his rare sorties from his air-conditioned bunker in Managua, dressed in full military fatigues, to rally his troops at Sapoa. Rivas, not a traditionally militant town, was pulled into the war · because of its strategic importance. The FSLN did not take Rivas until the end of the war. Instead it became a military and propaganda centre for the Guard, the only Nicaraguan city whose walls carried slogans like 'long live the National Guard' and 'Death to international terrorism and the Sandinista Communists'. In the ruins of the Rivas command-post at the end of the war, hundreds of these anti-FSLN propaganda leaflets fluttered in the rain:

> **Happy We Nicaraguans Would Be, Were It Not For That Satanic Force Of So-called National Liberation**
> Nicaraguans: do not allow this land, made for the freedom of strength and glory, to be used for the installation of a Communist government, which is what the Frente Sandinista wants. Those who run up the red and black flag murder people indiscriminately, like born killers. They burn and destroy private property . . . Like bandits, they use children to carry out acts of terrorism. They execute anyone who will not cooperate, their terror leaves widows and orphans. They destroy the workplaces of the honest citizen. They keep a free and hardworking people in perpetual fear. They uncaringly bring misery, suffering and unhappiness to the homes of all poor Nicaraguans, who resign themselves to the will of God like good, faithful Christians.

Comandante Bravo concentrated his forces along the lakeside, in Rivas,

San Juan del Sur, Penas Blancas and Sapoa, fighting the FSLN for control of every strategic hilltop in this inhospitable landscape so unsuited to guerrilla warfare. Sapoa, one of the most vital, is no more than a small mound, a few concrete buildings with a mounted machine-gun, where the land drops away sharply from the highway to the lake, but it became the focus for a series of ferocious battles. The rest of the narrow ribbon separating Lake Nicaragua from the ocean is mainly unprotected flat scrubland. The FSLN edged its way northwards from one slit trench to the next in tropical rain-storms as Somoza's air force made daily rocket and machinegun attacks on Sandinista positions, wheeling in from the east over the line of volcanoes. The advance was made even more painful by the *Guardia* blowing the small bridges dotted along the Panamericana Highway. Nonetheless, the morale of the Frente Sur became legendary. As in Sandino's war, local children carried' out important intelligence missions behind enemy lines, and dozens of Latin American internationalists came to fight alongside the FSLN, headed by the Panamanian Brigada Victorino Lorenzo, named after a hero of Panamanian independence and commanded by the country's deputy Health Minister, Hugo Spadafora.

As the Frente Sur dug in, the plan in Leon and Chinandega was to draw large *Guardia* forces into zones which could be easily defended with small numbers. The timetable had to be flexible. 'The rhythm of the war definitely began to vary, not as a result of the Frente Sandinista's plans, but from the demoralisation of the Guard.'[6] In the north especially, the reliance on elite units became notorious. Badly trained local garrisons, in most rural villages no more than a wooden hut with a handful of *campesino* recruits and a few sandbags, were overrun. Soldiers simply refused to fight. 'This was the change of plan – that if the enemy weren't going to come looking for us, then we would go looking for the enemy. The way of doing this was to launch our-selves on the cities.'[7] As in September, Somoza's basic strategy was to allow the cities to remain occupied and then turn maximum firepower on each in turn. But the new blend of movement and positional warfare, urban in-surrection and rural harassment, with a war front which shifted unpredictably from one day to the next, made this impossible.

The densely populated central area organised by the Frente Interno called for different tactics. Here, tactical combat brigades struck incessantly at the National Guard and neutralised its advantages in troop concentration, superior weaponry and central communications. Bringing the war to the *departamentos* of Carazo and Masaya was critical, on the one hand because the area contained the heart of the urban insurrection, on the other because control of Carazo meant cutting Somoza's supply lines to the Rivas area and isolating the EEBI in the south. The Frente Interno was to take Diriamba, lay siege to Jinotepe and coordinate the Managua insurrection. Under its leadership, the Popular Action Commandos, People's Brigades and Sandinista Militias carried out their 'armed propaganda' fluently, sabotaging public services, attacking Somocista *orejas* (informers, literally 'ears') and linking the urban *barrios* and outlying districts of Managua to give some coherence to the chaotic geography of the capital, in which particular *barrio* insurrections might easily become isolated. The heart of the Managua strategy was the eastern sector of the city, a compact network of some seventeen *barrios*.

The Final Offensive: May–July 1979

Battle Fronts:

1 Northern Front 'Carlos Fonseca Amador'
2 Southern Front 'Benjamin Zeledon'
3 North-Western Front 'Rigoberto Lopez Perez'
4 Central Front 'Camilo Ortega Saavedra'
5 North-Eastern Front 'Pablo Ubeda'
6 Eastern Front 'Roberto Huembes'
7 Nueva Guinea Front

All this urban activity, by pinning down the National Guard, was to enable regional fronts to consolidate local control in preparation for an advance on the capital. Managua could not be risked before combat in the provinces had reached its peak. It was the final piece in the jigsaw. The Frente knew that Managua presented special difficulties, and to combat possible demoralisation there it brought the United People's Movement into its own. The political commission of the MPU carried out a crucial propaganda function through the Civil Defence Committees, bringing news of advances in the north, reminding the civilian population of the September insurrection and the consequences of defeat. In the nineteen days of the Managua insurrection, Somoza's troops were bogged down, any positions they gained in the liberated zones being promptly lost again, until Somoza could only resort to saturation bombing of the eastern *barrios* of his own capital to try and dislodge Sandinista positions.

Insurrection in Managua

As insurrection came to the capital, there were tactical setbacks on the Frente Sur and around Chinandega and Chichigalpa. The Frente Interno's order was to hold the city for three days and wait for reinforcements.[8] As in September, the will of the people to fight, whether or not a formal call for insurrection was made, determined the timing. The FSLN had three instruments to lead the Managua insurrection: the three-person directorate of the Frente Interno; a joint military command formed by three *comandantes;* and a five-person political commission. Between them, they selected the eastern *barrios* as the natural focus. Every positive feature of Managua's difficult layout had to be turned to military advantage, and the complex of storm drains in the *barrios orientales* provided a natural obstacle to the National Guard's advance. The western sector was also to play a part, but the east presented the best conditions. They were compact, they were the home of poor workers, and in the pre-insurrectional build-up they had shown their militant resistance to Somoza. Within the eastern *barrios,* lower-middle-class districts like Bello Horizonte and El Dorado, with their key locations, more solid buildings and better communications, were to serve as the Frente Interno's strategic control centres.

By noon on Sunday the 10th, the insurrection had taken firm hold. Regular Sandinista troops had slipped into the city and hit-and-run attacks had given way to barricades, trenches and well-defended positions. The morning broadcast of Radio Sandino gave the order: 'Open ditches! Build barricades! Immobilise the enemy in the streets.' The barricades appeared overnight as if by magic. The streets filled with tree-trunks, rocks, overturned cars and broken bottles. Along the ring-roads which cut through Southern Managua, the paving stones from which Somoza had made a fortune in 1973 were turned into barricades against him, a symbol which escaped nobody. Children broke through the initial reluctance and fear of middle-class neighbourhoods and were the first to run out and build the barricades; rapidly their families joined them. Within two days the whole eastern sector was controlled by the people, a stretch of twenty-five *barrios* bounded by the Carretera Norte, the pista suburbana and the pista de enlace (see map). Control of the main highway and its industrial zone cut access to the airport, which was declared a military target. When the eventual order to abandon Managua temporarily was given, the Frente still controlled eighteen of its original twenty-five neighbourhoods. The insurrection was divided into hundreds of small interlocking areas each under the command of an FSLN militant responsible for a given number of barricades and roadblocks and for civil authority in conjunction with the local CDCs. In the first days of the war for Managua, the fall of the Sierra 13 police station in the eastern market was an important barometer of the plummetting morale of Somoza's troops and the effectiveness of the Sandinistas' urban forces. Being the centre of operations of 'Macho Negro', one of Somoza's most notorious murderers, the fall of the police station was a profoundly symbolic victory.

Of the countless testimonies of the insurrection in the *barrios orientales,* this one from an MPU activist in the Barrio Blandon is typical:

> On the third day, the enemy, in desperation because of the failure of National Guard infantry to dislodge us from our positions, showed no hesitation in throwing the airforce against the people. For sixteen days, air raids became a daily routine for us. We all knew that at 11 o'clock the plane would come to launch at least forty rockets, and then in the afternoon 'the tortoise' would arrive (that was the name we gave to an old Lanica plane which used to machine-gun us indiscriminately)'. What worried us most was that the main targets for the Somocista air force were places where women and children took refuge . . . in the very first attack a lot of children were killed in the Santa Faz Church.
>
> For the whole time that the *barrio* was liberated, the Civil Defence Committees stepped up their work. Food distribution centres were opened to share out food among the civilian population. The militias prevented neighbours from looting luxury goods. Expensive stereo systems, colour TVs, electric fans, all sorts of household goods were destroyed by those in charge of keeping order. Lookout squads were posted to stop snipers infiltrating our lines. In Bello Horizonte we got the loudspeakers working in a playground and from there gave instructions and political talks to the people.[9]

The international importance of the Managua insurrection was critical. It became a frontline war for the world press. Holed up in the Hotel Intercontinental with most of Somoza's Congress (who spent the war in an alcoholic haze and fled to Miami leaving unpaid bills to the tune of 1½ million *cordobas*), foreign journalists witnessed the decomposition of the government and the full ferocity of Somoza's reply to the insurrection.

The Managua Insurrection and the Retreat to Masaya: June 1979

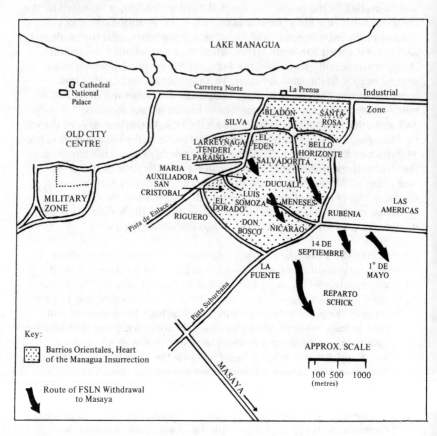

LAKE MANAGUA

Carretera Norte · La Prensa · Industrial Zone

Cathedral
National Palace

OLD CITY CENTRE

SILVA

BLADÓN · SANTA ROSA

LARREYNAGA · EL EDEN · BELLO HORIZONTE
TENDERI
EL PARAÍSO · SALVADORITA

MARIA AUXILIADORA
SAN CRISTOBAL

MILITARY ZONE

Pista de Enlace

RIGUERO

DUCUALI

LUIS SOMOZA · MENESES
EL DORADO

DON BOSCO · NICARAO

RUBENIA

LAS AMERICAS

14 DE SEPTIEMBRE

1° DE MAYO

LA FUENTE

REPARTO SCHICK

Pista Suburbana

MASAYA

Key:

Barrios Orientales, Heart of the Managua Insurrection

Route of FSLN Withdrawal to Masaya

APPROX. SCALE

100 500 1000
(metres)

Anastasio Somoza Debayle, using his military code name Alfa Sierra Delta, conducted operations personally and ordered aerial attacks on his capital with T-33 jets, Israeli 'push-pulls', Cessna light planes fitted with rockets, C-47 transports equipped with 50mm machineguns and helicopter gunships. The twin-tailed 'push-pulls' first appeared in the skies over Eastern Managua on the 11th. To the people, the scale of destruction, for all the suffering it brought them, was a tacit admission of Somoza's defeat. After all, they asked, who could want to rule over a country in ruins? The full counter-offensive began on the 12th. It fell into two phases, the first to clean up the weakest outlying points of resistance, the second an all-out military push against entrenched positions. Infantry assaults backed up with mortars and armoured vehicles began in the west of the city, in districts like San Judas, Altagracia and Monsenor Lezcano, where the scale of the uprising had not been as great as hoped. In the east, Somoza's aim was to drive the people out of their homes by terror, isolate the zone from the rest of the city, and deprive the Sandinistas of the basis of their support. Linked with this was a parallel attack on the *Carretera Norte.* It began with the shelling and burning of *La Prensa* — the first non-military target hit — and developed into a systematic, and highly selective, series of bombing raids against opposition-owned factories. One resident of Bello Horizonte estimated that three to five factories were bombed out each day along a six-kilometre stretch of road. The bourgeois opposition suffered in other ways too, as the scale of National Guard looting exceeded anything seen in 1972. At the entrance to the Casa Pellas — a Conservative-owned commercial centre — a National Guard major charged an entrance fee to any civilians wishing to join the military in the looting; at the La Colonia supermarket, the military's special offer was a full trolleyload of goods on payment of 1,000 *cordobas.*

Despite thirteen days of continuous bombing, Somoza made little progress. The Frente had responded to his elite infantry troops with its customary ingenuity, forming a highly mobile combat unit of hand-picked fighters armed with the best machineguns, bazookas and mortars. It was called 'The Hare' and was modelled on the Vietnamese's famous Invincible Battalion. But on the 23rd, a government radio broadcast ordering people to evacuate their homes heralded a new and devastating form of war. Helicopters, hovering at 1,000 metres out of range of machinegun fire, dropped an endless stream of 250- and 500-pound bombs. From that height there could be no pretence of precise targeting and, with what one local woman called 'the hell of the helicopters', the stream of refugees became a flood.

It was time for a major decision from the Frente Interno. The Managua insurrection, planned to last three days, had sustained itself into its third week, and still it had not been possible to launch a direct attack on Somoza's centres of power, nor had field column reinforcements arrived. Having been encouraged by the decomposition of the *Guardia* in the countryside, the Frente admitted they had miscalculated the strength of resistance they would encounter in the capital. Even by the end of the first week, the leadership had become concerned. The western *barrios* were caving in, and the momentum of the east could not be maintained indefinitely. Disturbingly, there were problems in the military balance between 'regular' and 'irregular' combatants: 'The militias assimilated the notion of regular combat, became confused about their street-fighting role and began to demand automatic weapons. There was competition between the FAL rifle and the .22, and the militias felt jealous and marginalised. This was even more serious when the Guard, with its massive firepower, began to make inroads, and militia forces were compelled to abandon their trenches, often in disorder.'[10] By the 18th, the militias' lower calibre arms were out of ammunition. What was being recovered from the Guard now was largely modern Israeli ammunition, and it did not fit their weapons. With the militias reduced to secondary guard duties, a crisis of discipline arose. In the western sector, *barrios* had been abandoned for lack of weapons; now in the east, people were arming themselves with *machetes*. A brief respite came the following dawn when a planeload of ammunition was airlifted in. Its arrival, like the bombing of Somoza's military installations in Central Managua by light planes of the FSLN's Carlos Ulloa squadron — named in memory of a Nicaraguan airman killed defending the Cuban Revolution — had a great impact on morale. Comandante Carlos Nunez recalled how one old man, watching the aircraft drop its cargo over the *barrios orientales*, looked up with a smile and said 'Look — we've even got an air force now'.

The days following the OAS meeting were dangerous ones. Middle-class Nicaraguans began to despair of a rapid solution. 'At times we wanted to change Somoza for anything, whatever the cost,' admitted one bourgeois politician. 'Even the intervention of a peacekeeping force.'[11] FSLN with-drawal from Managua had always been a tactical option. Now, its timing became critical. The idea disturbed many, who feared the inevitable 'cleaning-up operation' which would be launched against the undefended *barrios* if the Sandinistas withdrew, but the directorate of the Frente Interno saw no alter-native. After holding the eastern sector of the city for nineteen days, the night of 27 June was agreed as the date, and Masaya to the south-east was to be the destination. It was close, strategically situated, and its combativity was unquestioned. Once there, FSLN forces could regroup and operate over a wide area. Outside Managua there was military stalemate and the Managua combatants themselves were exhausted, but over and above these essentially defensive reasons, the withdrawal of Masaya would allow the Sandinistas to pull out voluntarily from positions which they might later be forced to leave, and would preserve the unity of combat forces with a rich and varied experience of the urban struggle. The retreat was a major political decision at a critical moment in the war, a decision requiring objectivity, realism and courage. When the FSLN pulled out of Managua on the night of 27 June, the retreat — far from being the admission of defeat depicted by Somoza and the world's press — was a tactical masterstroke. Leaving only snipers behind, the Sandinistas moved thousands of combatants the 31 kilometres to Masaya in a two-day trek across open country, which consisted largely of exposed stretches of volcanic rock. The audacity and success of the *repliegue estrategico* had awesome propaganda value, and allayed any fears that the FSLN might yet lose the war.

The plan was to take all the regular and militia forces, with any civilians who wanted to leave, to evacuate all the wounded, and to reach Masaya in twelve hours on foot. All this to be done without revealing the plan in advance to those who would participate — the risk of discovery was too terrible to contemplate. When the *Guardia* launched its habitual morning attack on the 28th, they were met with sporadic gunfire from isolated snipers left to cover the retreat. As it died down, Somoza's men took stock of the situation. The eastern *barrios* were deserted. Under cover of night three columns — containing 6,000 people instead of the 1,500 originally planned — had left Managua in single file. In the darkness they had become hopelessly lost, but despite taking 30 hours to cover the distance and being sighted on the volcanic flatlands of Piedras Negras by six aircraft, the columns reached Masaya with only six dead and sixteen wounded. 'If we can do that,' said one man, 'we can do anything.'

Popular Power in Action

The 6,000 who arrived exhausted in Masaya in the early morning of 29 June found a buoyant town, with all public services operating efficiently under popular control. The Nicaraguan people came to power on 19 July with the experience behind them of exercising popular power in the liberated cities. The long and close relationship between the masses and their vanguard, the twelve years of patient work since Pancasan, building intermediary organisations, bore its fruit in the block and neighbourhood committees, organs of local power whose form was not preconceived but moulded with pragmatism according to the demands of the war and the needs of the people.

On 2 June the Frente had distributed its new *Manual of Civil Defence* to the population of the combat zones. The information it contained on building barricades and trenches, selecting safe houses and refuges, and dealing with air raids, was essential to any Civil Defence Committee, but the committees' functions went much further. Correspondents entering Leon the following week found how agile and efficient liberated community organisation could be, as the use of money was abolished, resources collectivised and Sandinista jeeps sped around assuring rapid food distribution. Leon was the first city where revolutionary committees took charge of essential public services, and their *comites de limpieza* (street cleaning committees) drew up strict duty rotas. The FSLN's regional general staff appointed the country's first local revolutionary government which provided an effective system of local legislation and security. Although some barter went on, food supplies were mainly organised centrally by the MPU. Production restarted in three of the city's largest food-processing plants, turning out cornmeal, flour and cooking oil.[12] Within days, the picture was similar throughout the liberated north.

Once the retreat to Masaya was completed, the Frente Interno began to look critically at how to organise the central cities. There were various issues: the practical education and discipline needed to defend the towns from attack; the creation of local *juntas* (councils) and tribunals; the administration of property confiscated from Somoza (something which did not need to wait for a government decree); the reactivation of commerce and industry wherever possible; steps to deal with speculators and profiteers; and policing and public order. Again, the work of the MPU's political commission was fundamental. In Masaya, too, new Junta member Moises Hassan swore in the first city council to be established by central authority. The block committees held regular daily meetings with the military *responsables* of their area, and communicated their decisions to everyone in the neighbourhood.

'Clandestine journalism' put out broadsheets with up-to-date news and instructions at the *barrio* and city level. At night, even without electric light, the committees organised solidarity marches with the FSLN, with hundreds walking through the liberated *barrios* in the darkness, singing, banging saucepans and chanting the FSLN slogan *'Patria Libre O Morir'* ('Free Country or Death'). They dug air raid shelters under their houses to hold entire families, set up medical units and first-aid centres, improved their propaganda and information networks and extended the defensive cordons around their cities. One function of the popular committees, in particular, marked the relationship between the people and the Frente: the committees were charged with identifying any abuse of power, any failure by a Sandinista to show respect for the civilian population.

In Masaya more than anywhere, the need for defence and vigilance was enormous. When the *Guardia* evacuated the town, they had withdrawn to the hilltop fortress of El Coyotepe from where they began to bombard the town indiscriminately. Somoza desperately wanted to retake Masaya after 27 June and sent his air force in with napalm. In response, the FSLN intensified its military training, setting up new schools in the gardens of large houses confiscated from Somocistas, while the committees ripped down drainpipes and collected tin cans to fabricate home-made arms and bombs. And there was a need to defend the liberated cities not only against the air raids and artillery offensives, but also against the more sinister weapons of *Somocismo*, the ever-present threat of *Guardia* infiltrators. A knock on the door at dead of night and the whisper of 'Help me, *compa*, the *Guardia* are after me' might be a trap. The shout of *'Patria Libre . . .'* from a stranger might mean death to anyone who answered ' . . . *O Morir!*' To deal with Somocistas, the people set up revolutionary tribunals. Francisco, who began by working with Radio Sandino was a lawyer.

> I was a kind of revolutionary legal adviser for the people's trials against Somocistas. This meant murderers, thieves, anyone who had committed proven crimes against the people. As a lawyer, respecting legal procedures, my interest was to ensure that these courts functioned in a legal context, within the universally accepted norms of jurisprudence. The popular tribunals were formed, and carried out their deliberations, in the same city or village where the crime had been committed.[13]

In Masaya, the CDCs first evolved into what they are today — Comites de Defensa Sandinista (CDSs), and their most advanced expression was in Monimbo. In Masaya too, one of the Revolution's key slogans first emerged: 'Raise Production!' The people of Masaya looked to the examples of Leon and Managua, where the La Perfecta pasteurising plant had been seized, production resumed and the local committees had organised milk distribution. Throughout the country, people knew what the Revolution was achieving in other regions. Their medium was the radio. In Matagalpa, Radio

Insurreccion went on the air after the city's liberation, and in Leon Radio Venceremos began to broadcast. But above all, people listened to Radio Sandino, the official voice of the Frente Sandinista.

The idea was not a new one. Radio communication was a long-standing plan of the National Directorate, who saw it as an essential medium for creating and accelerating revolutionary conditions. The handset which combatants had used in the mountains was replaced by a small mobile transmitter, with a T-shaped wire as an antenna which could be hoisted on any tree. Three militants, none with previous broadcasting experience, were enlisted to operate it, and Radio Sandino began transmissions on the Frente Sur in March 1978. It started with programmes of news and information, but rapidly became a key strategic element, and Somoza detailed Guard patrols to locate and destroy the transmitter, forcing it to shift locations several times. By mid-1979, 'Radio Sandino was the principal means of propaganda for the uprising and the strike.'[14] The National Directorate had elaborated on its purpose the previous summer in a circular: 'To prepare the Nicaraguan people for the coming insurrectional tasks . . . to carry out a role of conscientisation . . . a vehicle for agitation . . . its slogans are the expression of the people's desires, and being recognised as such, are converted into popular action . . . It is a counterpart to the propaganda which *Somocismo* tries to drum into the people.'

In addition to its role in mobilising the masses, the National Directorate used Radio Sandino as a vehicle for coded messages to the leadership of the regional fronts and columns, and broadcast theoretical instruction programmes on the thought of Sandino for the formation of new cadres and local organisers. In addition the FSLN in Costa Rica and its newly appointed Government Junta of National Reconstruction could count on permanent access to the sympathetic broadcasters of Radio Reloj, whose transmissions also reached Nicaragua.

Radio Sandino was at the heart of an essential facet of any revolution: the development of an authentic parallel culture. It was essential to head off the "mediating" propaganda of the bourgeoisie, who enjoyed easier access to the media, and to break down bourgeois – and specifically *Somocista* – cultural hegemony. The slogans were crucial, carefully selected to bind the vanguard and the people more closely together. The most famous, *'Patria Libre O Morir'*, synthesised the nationalism of the Revolution and provided a unifying rallying-cry for all the differing class forces involved, just as *'Cuba Si! Yanquis No!'* had done twenty years before.

The new Nicaragua has a rich revolutionary culture which first flourished in the insurrectional phase. The music of the Meija Godoy brothers and the Pancasan group drew together Nicaragua's traditional musical forms, revived its folk culture, and used both to convey a revolutionary message. Carlos Mejia Godoy's *Misa Campesina* (Peasant Mass) had long been used as a means of consciousness-raising in the countryside and the *barrios,* and Somoza – fearing its explosive contribution to the growing 'Marxist-Christian dialogue' – sent in the BECAT to break up any meetings where the participants sang:

> I believe in you, companero
> . . . the worker Christ.
> You are reborn
> in every arm which is raised
> to defend the people
> against domination and exploitation.[15]

At the height of the war, Radio Sandino brought a new and eminently practical set of songs from the Mejia brothers:

> 'Of all the rifles
> this Garand calls the tune . . .
> If you want to dismantle it
> follow these instructions to the letter.[16]

In the same way, people rescued poetry and theatre and placed it at the service of the Revolution. They mingled with the clandestine wall newspapers, the broadsheets and pamphlets of the FSLN, the slogans painted on every house. Street theatre swept through the *barrios,* poems were painted on the walls of liberated zones. It was simultaneously agitprop, a reassertion of long-repressed cultural traditions, and a practical expression of solidarity. People recognised the significance of popular culture as another weapon in their struggle, a direct challenge to the deformations of television programmes made in the USA, of the regime's appropriation of ethnic art-forms, and the *Somocismo* propaganda machine.

The New Political Superstructure

In the third week of the war, the FSLN decided to name its provisional government. The revolutionary forces now held wide stretches of the country outside the capital, although the Managua insurrection was bogged down, unable to take decisive control of the city as rapidly as planned. The USA meanwhile was manoeuvring furiously to abort a Sandinista victory through intervention, and the FAO — or what was left of it after its rump had been isolated by the FPN — had already offered the United States its own option on 2 June. This was a seven-member *junta* to include Somoza's Nationalist Liberal Party, the National Guard, the FAO, the private sector, the liberal professions, the trade unions, and precisely one FSLN-FPN representative. (a joint one at that). The FSLN therefore judged it necessary to move on to the diplomatic offensive, naming a provisional government Junta and Cabinet, and combating US initiatives in international forums such as the Organisation of American States. The executive power to replace Somoza would be a synthesis of the different class forces at play within the Revolution. A formidable challenge would await it: presiding over the transitional period of national reconstruction, rebuilding the country's shattered economic base and maintaining the unity of divergent political forces during this initial phase, while laying the foundations of a radically new state.

Despite the continued ambiguity of Venezuela, whose Foreign Minister had again arrived in Managua for talks with Somoza, and the perpetual danger that the USA might look to the Andean Pact countries (Colombia, Venezuela, Ecuador, Peru and Bolivia) as a diplomatic surrogate, indications that the Pact's member countries were ready to acknowledge a 'state of belligerence' gave the signal that the Frente could take the diplomatic initiative. Naturally, each of these regimes had its own ideas for the future of Nicaragua after Somoza, as did Costa Rica, Panama, Mexico and European Social Democracy, but they represented the first sign that Western Europe and the Latin American democracies were capable of foreign policy initiatives in Central America independent of the dictates of Washington. The flexibility of the FSLN's foreign policy and the strenuous efforts of Los Doce in the international arena since 1978 had mobilised an intensive solidarity effort from social democrats, some of whom saw the FSLN tactics of class alliances and national unity as an opportunity to put their weight behind a bourgeois democratic revolution, which — although going further than the USA's 'Somocismo without Somoza' — would seek an essentially reformist outcome. They had overlooked Tomas Borge's dry comment that: 'What we are aiming for in Nicaragua is not social democracy. We're after something rather more than that.'[17]

The five-person Junta named by the FSLN was the instrument they had outlined in April: 'A Provisional Government of National Unity in which there will be real effective participation of all the political and social forces who consciously maintain a position of unequivocal struggle against the dictatorship.'[18] The five appointed were Comandante Daniel Ortega for the FSLN, member of the Sandinista National Directorate and leader of the former Tercerista tendency; Moises Hassan of the leadership of the United People's Movement and National Patriotic Front; Sergio Ramirez of Los Doce; the industrialist Alfonso Robelo of the Nicaraguan Democratic Movement; and Violeta Barrios de Chamorro, widow of the murdered editor of *La Prensa*.

The Junta was conceived of, and continues to be, the executive instrument of FSLN policy. In a telling gesture which alarmed the Right and eluded much of the Left, Junta members were introduced on their arrival in Leon on 18 July by Tomas Borge, thereby underlining the fact that the National Directorate of the FSLN was the ultimate authority of the Revolution. Borge himself, however, named as Minister of the Interior, was the only member of the Sandinista leadership to hold a post in the first Cabinet, which lasted until December 1979. Before the naming of the full Cabinet, the Maryknoll priest Miguel D'Escoto Brockman had been named as interim ambassador to the OAS, where he had eloquently presented Nicaragua's case to the June meeting of foreign ministers. Otherwise, the eighteen-

member Cabinet was composed predominantly of figures drawn from the
bourgeoisie. This applied particularly to the economic team, faced with the
task of renegotiating on friendly terms the highest *per capita* foreign debt
in Latin America and ensuring a flow of foreign aid for the programmes of
national reconstruction. In this team, Arturo Cruz, a former economist with
the Inter-American Development Bank (IDB) in Washington, became
president of the Banco Central; Roberto Mayorga, once a secretary of the
Central American Common Market, was appointed Minister of Planning;
and Joaquin Cuadra, with BANAMERICA connections, took on the Finance
portfolio. Colonel Bernardino Larios, a deserter from Somoza's National
Guard, became Minister of Defence.

Many Marxist critics leapt to accuse the Frente of selling out the
Revolution to the bourgeoisie. Their mistake was to measure revolutionary
power and the configuration of the new state by a head-count of the new
government's *executive* arm, thus failing to grasp the relationship between
that executive and the political authority of the FSLN's National
Directorate. Nor did they attach sufficient importance to the new forms of
Sandinista power crystallising in the Sandinista Defence Committees, the
Workers' Fighting Committees, the Association of Rural Workers and the
other emerging mass organisations. These mass organisations would not be
demobilised by a government executive of largely bourgeois extraction, but
rather were spurred on to a dominant role in the revolutionary process by the
FSLN. James Petras's sceptical article 'Whither the Nicaraguan Revolution?'
typified the response of Marxist critics. 'This regime,' he stated, 'will be
unable to solve any of the fundamental problems of the masses. On the
contrary . . . it will demobilise the masses . . . while restructuring the old
class society . . . In effect, this will be a transitional regime facilitating a drift
to the right.'[19] Such commentators who foresaw a Portuguese-style outcome
to deeply rooted class conflict in Nicaragua based their conclusions on a
misreading of the process of the FSLN's unification, envisaging the GPP and
Proletarians as 'a loyal opposition'.[20] It was the old trap of seeing the
Terceristas/Insurrectionals as social democrats. To seek social democratic
support as part of a defined revolutionary strategy agreed by each tendency,
and under unquestioned revolutionary hegemony, is a very different matter
from promoting a social democratic project. Left-wing critics of the new
government programme focussed particularly on the planned creation of a
thirty-three member Council of State which was to guarantee 'broad representativity to all political, economic and social forces who have contributed
to the overthrow of the Somoza dictatorship'[21] — forces, that is to say,
formally constituted as of June 1979. As it stood, it gave a clear majority
to bourgeois groups. But within a short time of coming to power, the FSLN
gave their critics the answer and engaged the bourgeoisie in a major battle
over future state power. The inauguration of the Council of State, conceived
of as the highest form of Sandinista democracy, would be delayed and its
membership expanded and altered to take account of the disappearance,
on the one hand, of small bourgeois parties and the emergence, on the other,

of the organs of popular power, the CDSs and the mass organisations. The bourgeoisie was enraged.

On 13 July, a press statement from the new Junta set the terms for Somoza's departure:

> Somoza must present his resignation to Congress. From there we must proceed to the installation of the Government of National Reconstruction; member countries of the Organisation of American States will recognise it as soon as it is installed. The new government will then abolish the Somocista Constitution; a Basic Statute will come into force as the Junta's provisional law; the order will be given to the National Guard to remain in barracks where its lives and human rights will be respected. Members of the National Guard may be integrated into the new army or incorporated into civilian life; a ceasefire will take effect on the part of the Sandinista army; an Organic Law will be decreed regulating the functioning of state institutions; the Programme of National Reconstruction will be put into effect; and guarantees will be provided to all those military personnel and state functionaries who wish to leave the country, if they have committed no crimes against the people and their institutions.

It was the authoritative document of a government on the point of taking power, but which still faced difficulties in supplanting the entire state apparatus of *Somocismo*. Some of the FSLN's key aims had yet to be won. Above all, the press statement's clauses relating to the National Guard reflected the fact that Somoza's army, though defeated and demoralised, remained intact as an institution. Somoza remained in control of the power centres of Managua, if nothing else. And as for the USA, it still retained hopes in the last week of the war of salvaging some of its influence from the wreckage of Nicaragua.

Ditching the Loyal Friend

Imperialism does not surrender its prizes lightly. But in its attempts to salvage *Somocismo* while shedding Somoza, the United States had the unfailing knack of being one step behind events. It was the victim of its own contradictions, the foreign policy vacillations and divisions of the Carter presidency and the weakness of the bourgeois centre it desperately sought, a weakness which US policy had been instrumental in creating. The Carter Administration was not unique in its ostensible hostility to Somoza. An American government had been cold to the dictatorship before, when Somoza Garcia had ousted President Arguello in 1947, but this time that coldness coincided with the internal crisis in Nicaragua. Somoza had reacted rapidly to the Carter election, securing State Department approval for a consignment of 6,000 M-16 automatic rifles before the new president was inaugurated,

173

and thereby re-equipping his National Guard with light arms. And midway through 1977, with help from Somoza's Washington friends, the House of Representatives overturned an earlier decision to suspend military assistance to the country.[22]

Nicaragua was one of the major Latin American test cases for Carter's 'Human Rights' policy, but for all the noise surrounding Carter's ratification of the Inter-American Convention on Human Rights, State Department reports and OAS declarations, military aid to Nicaragua was not cut off until 1979. In April 1977, human rights hearings before a House of Representatives sub-committee were given damning reports on Nicaragua which repeated accusations made a year earlier by Father Fernando Cardenal (a Jesuit priest who was to direct Nicaragua's Literacy Crusade in 1980) citing National Guard atrocities during the state of siege.[23] But the State Department promptly accused Cardenal of a dozen 'errors of fact' and Judge Irwin Stolz of Georgia – interestingly enough a Carter appointment to the state judiciary – declared that 'Father Cardenal is not intellectually honest and is a tool, wittingly or unwittingly, of a Marxist movement seeking to undermine and then take over the government of the Republic of Nicaragua.'[24] In September 1977, the new Washington Ambassador, Mauricio Solaun, arrived in Managua. He was to last only eighteen months, resigning in April 1979 due to his inability to influence Somoza to accept the recommendations of the Carter Administration in the wake of the September insurrection. The state of siege was promptly lifted and the State Department agreed to $2.5 million worth of new arms credits. Splits in the State Department over Nicaragua, and human rights in general, were now evident, and April 1978 had already seen the removal of Terence Todman, the right-wing Assistant Secretary of State for Latin America, after his criticisms that human rights policies were undermining traditional friendships.[25] By July 1978 the rift was gaping. The Washington Somoza lobby pressurised Carter into sending the dictator a letter praising him for human rights improvements while at the same time Washington's Ambassador to the OAS was expressing his government's grave concern at the serious violations of human rights in Nicaragua.

Above all, it was the FSLN's leadership of the mass opposition after the Chamorro assassination which forced the United States back on to an inevitable 1970s version of the Roosevelt Administration's original 1940s dictum: 'son of a bitch, but our son of a bitch'. A wave of government and private bank credits, totalling $162 million, flowed into Managua. Somoza was still Washington's best man, at least until the 1981 elections. Somoza's friends in Washington, some of them old West Point classmates, others more recent business associates from the Nixon era, had another powerful weapon: their ability to withhold support from Carter's Panama Canal negotiations. The lobby's two most influential members, Democratic Representative Charles Wilson (Texas) and Democratic Representative John Murphy (New York), were on the House Appropriations Committee and Merchant Marine and Fisheries Committee respectively, both crucial for the Canal legislation.

Their support for Somoza continued to the end. 'Those two have been unbelievably disruptive,' complained one Washington official in June 1979. 'They are on the phone to Somoza constantly, advising him on how to evade our strategy, which was designed to push middle-class Nicaraguan businessmen forward.'[26]

Throughout the Carter presidency, Washington's nightmare was the lack of viable pro-US alternatives. There was no strong national bourgeoisie, for any possibility of political and economic consolidation had been undermined by intervention and the free hand given to Somocista rule. The more perceptive US politicians grasped the central contradiction of American policy: the American administration had long seen that Somoza was unable to contain the class struggle in Nicaragua and thus had pressured him to extend the dictatorship's social base, but in crisis there was simply no available suitable bourgeois option. But these same US politicians drew back into acceptance of Somoza's own *apres moi le deluge* rhetoric. Indeed by the rules of American foreign policy it was logical. Somoza portrayed all opposition to his regime as anti-American, and it could hardly be otherwise since the mass of the Nicaraguan people now identified Somoza as a servant of US imperialism.

The September 1978 insurrection had shown American policy in its true light. In the weeks of National Guard massacres, Nicaraguans waited in vain for White House condemnations of these gross human rights violations. Instead they saw a mediating mission between Somoza and the FAO, a strategy aiming – in line with State Department thinking at the time – to influence the bourgeois opposition while there was still time. In the active search for '*Somocismo* without Somoza' (and above all without an FSLN presence) the FAO was eager to cooperate, and demanded as its preconditions for negotiating only the release of political prisoners and an end to censorship. Among FAO leaders, Alfonso Robelo was particularly keen on direct negotiations with Somoza which would marginalise the Sandinistas. '*Somocismo* without Somoza' meant an agreement between the FAO and the dictatorship. Somoza himself would be persuaded to leave, thus removing the clearest reason for the regime's stigma, administrative corruption would be cleaned up, and the state would again become an efficient apparatus. The executive would be a so-called Government of National Unity comprising the Liberal Party, the National Guard and the FAO. During the protracted talks, however, Washington's thinking changed. The uncomfortable choice between Somoza and the revolutionary Left was heightened by Somoza's intransigent dismembering of the bourgeois opposition. The dream of coherent middle ground became even more elusive. At this stage in the mediation, Pentagon and National Security Council thinking took over. If Somoza would not budge, then the USA would leave him there long enough to destroy the FSLN, and only then worry about democratisation. The American negotiator William Bowdler, a former member of the National Security Council and the State Department Office of Intelligence, who had worked on Cuba (1956-61) and the Dominican Republic invasion of 1965, made one concession after another to Somoza, finally proposing a domestically supervised plebiscite. The plebiscite plan suited the new US mood well. If Somoza lost, he would resign and give way to a government of Washington's choosing. If he won, he would stay on, but the debilitated FAO would have guaranteed US support, electoral experience and three more years to prepare for the 1981 elections.

In the months between the mediation and the final insurrection, US pressure on Somoza lifted and Washington appeared seriously to misjudge the capacity of the FSLN to launch another, decisive drive against the dictatorship. By the time they reacted decisively to the insurrection and realised the imminence of a Sandinista victory, they revealed the full impotence and confusion which Carter policies to Nicaragua had brought. Military intervention was now the only realistic option for the United States to secure its position. Zbigniew Brzezinski, Chairman of the National Security Council, his assistant Robert Pastor and Defence Secretary Harold Brown lined up in favour of intervention. The State Department remained paralysed by what it saw as the consequences of its Human Rights pressure on Somoza, and Sergio Ramirez of the new Junta described William Bowdler – again nominated as Washington's chief negotiator – as 'one more dupe in the whole tremendous State Department indecision over applying a coherent policy'.[27] It was a US National Security Council meeting which generated the first request for the OAS to intervene in the Nicaraguan crisis. In the middle of preparations for the seventeenth consultative meeting of OAS foreign ministers, a single unforeseeable tragedy outraged the United States Government and American public opinion: the cold-blooded murder by a National Guardsman of ABC television reporter Bill Stewart in the *barrios orientales* of Managua, an event captured on film and networked throughout the USA within hours. Yet the very next day, 21 June, Secretary of State Cyrus Vance presented in Washington his US intervention plan, one of whose principal aims was the preservation of the National Guard, Bill Stewart's murderers.

With insufficient domestic support for direct intervention by US troops, Vance proposed an OAS 'Peacekeeping Force' as the appropriate instrument for a military adventure which, far from stopping bloodshed as the USA claimed to want, would have merely intensified the war. The American proposal was doomed from the outset. The foreign ministers of Panama, Mexico and the Andean Pact flatly rejected any use of outside force to resolve the Nicaraguan conflict. The Panamanians, in a remarkable gesture of solidarity, allowed Miguel D'Escoto to present Nicaragua's case as a member of the Panamanian delegation, and used the OAS meeting to recognise the FSLN's new Junta, the first country to do so. The military dictatorships of the region, of whom some – like Brazil and Chile – had been helped to power by American intervention, also rejected the Vance Plan because of the precedent it might set for future intervention against their own regimes.[28]

On 22 June the Andean Pact countries presented their counter-proposal. This scrupulously respected the principle of non-intervention and insisted on the immediate resignation of Somoza and the installation of the Junta named the previous week by the FSLN. It was a historic break in the traditional role of the OAS as the USA's 'Colonial Ministry'. Most member states, for whatever differing reasons, were outraged by the Americans' blatant use of the Organisation as a means of furthering their own political designs. Washington was further humiliated by the refusal of the counter-proposal's sponsors to acknowledge any common ground between the two alternative plans, and was left with no option but to vote against itself. The Andean Pact resolution was adopted by 17 votes to 2 (Nicaragua and Paraguay) with 5 abstentions (Guatemala, Honduras, El Salvador, Uruguay and Chile).[29]

In the wake of Washington's humiliations, the policy splits continued. The State Department declared that unilateral intervention was unthinkable, but Defence Secretary Brown stated that it was 'not inconceivable' and the Pentagon reviewed its contingency plans for an invasion force. The 82nd Airborne Division (used in the 1965 Dominican Republic invasion) was placed on alert.[30] The FSLN's evacuation of Managua clearly deceived much of Washington into hoping that Somoza might yet win an outright military victory and that the Marines might not be necessary. When the new US Ambassador, Lawrence Pezzullo, arrived in Managua on 27 June to insist on Somoza's resignation, he found the dictator encouraged by the Frente's withdrawal and ordering renewed bombing raids on Masaya. Preparing the recall of Congress, Somoza told the Costa Rican newspaper *La Republica*: 'I shall not resign. If Congress asks me to, I shall dissolve it.' While Pezzullo put pressure on Somoza in Managua, Bowdler, who was now in Costa Rica, demanded the expansion of the Junta. He put forward five names: the National Guard General Julio Gutierrez, who had commanded the Nicaraguan contingent in the Dominican Republic invasion; the Conservative politician Emilio Alvarez Montalvan; Jaime Chamorro of *La Prensa;* Mariano Fiallos, rector of the National Autonomous University (UNAN) – the most progressive of the five candidates; and banker Ernesto Fernandez. Acceptance of any four of these five would give right-wing dominance on the Junta. At the same time, the Social Christian politician, Jose Esteban Gonzalez, tried to mobilise sectors of the FAO to back his own candidacy for the Junta. The Frente and the Junta of National Reconstruction promptly rejected any such plan.

With the rejection of the Bowdler proposals, the Americans lost what had perhaps been their most cynical negotiating tactic: Ambassador Pezzullo had privately received Somoza's resignation on 8 July, which the dictator had made conditional on the survival of his Partido Liberal Nacionalista and the National Guard. Washington held up the resignation formally taking effect in order to play for time and gain bargaining strength for its insistence that US nominees be incorporated into the Junta. The threat was that reconstruction aid to the war-shattered country would be blocked if the composition of the Junta was not to Washington's liking.

There was little now that the USA could do to influence events, with its humiliation in the OAS and the FSLN's determination to stick to a *junta* of its own choosing. Somoza supporters on Capitol Hill staged a ritual display of 'Communist-type rocket launchers and automatic weapons seized from Cuban-backed Sandinista terrorists', but by now it was a futile gesture. By 15 July, Somoza's departure was a certainty. Aides could be seen packing suitcases at the Bunker. The Somoza-owned airline LANICA refused to accept any currency but dollars, and the *cordoba* changed hands at 30 to the dollar, three times the official exchange rate. There was financial chaos, and Somocistas invaded the American Embassy in the rush for exit visas. Sandinista intelligence uncovered a plot for thirty National Guard officers to kidnap and assassinate Somoza. Any US involvement in this projected coup was a matter for speculation, but the Americans still believed that they might salvage the National Guard and retain some ability to manoeuvre, although they now accepted the new five-person FSLN-designated Junta as a reality.

The collapse of the last bastions of *Somocismo,* and the installation of Sandinista power, was accompanied by two days of bizarre events.

19 July: Patria Libre

Granada, the most conservative city in Nicaragua, fell in the early hours of 17 July. Chinandega was already under Sandinista control, and the Esteli barracks had been overrun. In the east, the 'Roberto Huembes' front took the provincial capital of Juigalpa and advanced westwards. Managua was encircled.

Somoza's last military option had been a secret visit to Guatemala to seek assistance from the Central American Defence Council (CONDECA). But Honduras, Guatemala and El Salvador had refused their support to Somoza in the OAS, and were in no mood to rescue the crippled regime. Somoza then retired the entire General Staff of the National Guard and at dawn on the 17th, as the Sandinistas drove into Granada, took his closest political allies and senior military officers with him on an aircraft for Florida. In command of the Guard he left Colonel Federico Mejia, second-in-command of the Managua police. But Mejia, with no control over his forces, slipped out of the country, too, without leaving any instructions for his successor, an obscure lieutenant-colonel named Fulgencio Largaespada.

By definition, the *Guardia* could no longer fight effectively once its raison d'etre had gone. The only thing which kept them fighting now was a blind instinct for survival. As a coherent military force, the *Guardia* had collapsed weeks earlier. Already expanded from 7,500 to 15,000 men in the wake of the September insurrection, its structures dissolved with the desperate drafting of thousands of new recruits in the final weeks of the war. As defeated provincial units fled in civilian clothing, their place was taken by press-ganged civil servants, relatives of soldiers, peasants from Somoza's *fincas* and workers from his factories, and hundreds of twelve- and thirteen-year-old children seized in military swoops on refugee camps and poor *barrios,* who were thrown into uniform and pushed out untrained to the battle front. 'An army truck grabbed me and took me to the EEBI,' was one story from a thirteen-year-old. 'When we arrived they stuck me in a pair of army trousers and a shirt four sizes too big, then gave me an ancient Enfield rifle without telling me how to use it.'[31]

Somoza's interim successor was a Liberal Party time server. 'The idea was that at eight in the morning somebody or other called Urcuyo was to take over — I had real trouble remembering the name at first, and more than likely I'll have forgotten it again in a couple of weeks,'[32] said Fidel Castro. To most Nicaraguans, too, the name meant little. Francisco Urcuyo Malianos was Somoza's president of the Chamber of Deputies, appointed to the post after the fall of Cornelio Hueck. His only function was to hand over power to the new Junta, but under orders from Somoza in Miami he went on television to announce his intention to serve out Somoza's term until May 1981. In the forty-three hours of his presidency, he was unable to assemble a cabinet (only four Liberal deputies were left in the country), the National Guard collapsed, and by 3.30 a.m. on the 19th Urcuyo was on a plane to Guatemala.

In the language of the State Department, there are 'controlled' and 'uncontrolled solutions'. Urcuyo's role in the transfer of power was implicit in the Junta's July 13 statement, and offered a point of convergence between Junta plans and the last scraps of a US strategy. Washington's hope for a swift, orderly and 'controlled' handover would have prevented the FSLN taking Managua by force and might have preserved some remnants of the Somoza state. But Urcuyo, as a loyal functionary of that state, carried through Somocista logic to the end and wrecked the Americans' final gambit. Urcuyo's order that the 'irregular forces' should lay down their arms, and *Somocismo*'s obstinate last-ditch attempt to preserve its institutions only guaranteed their absolute destruction. When the news of Somoza's resignation came, the Frente had made a rapid evaluation of the state of their forces and ordered a mass advance on Managua, calculating that they would need three days to take the capital and wipe out the last of the Guard.[33] Urcuyo's flourish gave the FSLN the margin it required. Negotiations on the ceasefire and transfer of power collapsed. In one of the heaviest nights of fighting in the whole war, especially on the Frente Sur where the Guard still controlled much of Rivas, the FSLN destroyed the remnants of *Somocismo*.

Radio Sandino woke the nation on the morning of the 19th with martial music, folksongs, the Sandinista anthem and the slogans of victory. It broadcast the first instructions of the Junta ordering discipline, vigilance, and generosity to the defeated enemy. The CDCs/CDSs were told to take on the tasks of local administration. Columns from Leon were the first to enter the capital. The forces of the Frente Norte converged with those of the Frente Oriental commanded by Luis Carrion in Boaco and Chontales. At 3.30 in the afternoon more columns arrived from Esteli. From all parts of the country, thousands of armed Sandinistas drove into the streets of Managua on commandeered armoured cars and decrepit cattle trucks. Red and black flags appeared everywhere. But even before the guerrilla forces arrived, the people of Managua had taken the city. Their first targets were the EEBI and First Armoured Battalion installations, then the smaller barracks, until it seemed that the whole population of the city was armed and firing volleys into the air from their liberated weapons. For the whole of the next day the streets were filled with family reunions after years of clandestinity and combat. 'It was pandemonium. Parents didn't know how to find their kids among the guerrilla columns because everyone used *noms de guerre.* It was no good asking for Rafael or Maria, but if you asked for 'Eagle' of the Frente Norte or 'Heron' of the Frente Sur, then the combatants would know who you meant.'[34] Briefly, there was administrative chaos, the nights still shattered by gunfire from triumphant but indisciplined *milicianos* or from roving bands of National Guard terrorists. It was the chaos which only an absolute power vacuum can bring, the removal of an entire state structure. One member of the National Directorate summed it up: 'The dictator's departure confirmed our theory that *Somocismo* was a coherent structure. We took out the heart and the body fell. Now we must fill the empty space.'[35]

Notes

1. Interview with resident of Barrio Bello Horizonte, Managua, July 1979.
2. Humberto Ortega, 'El Desarrollo de la Ofensiva Final' in *Barricada,* 30 December 1979.
3. Bayardo Arce, Press conference: 'Victorias de 1979 y Perspectivas', reprinted in *Barricada,* 31 December 1979.
4. *Observer,* 1 July 1979.
5. Luis Carrion, interview with Jorge Timossi of *Prensa Latina,* August 1979.
6. Bayardo Arce, *loc. cit.*
7. *Ibid.*
8. Carlos Nunez, *Un Pueblo en Armas,* p. 21.
9. Quoted in *Barricada,* 25 July 1979.
10. Nunez, *op. cit.,* p. 39.
11. Interview in Managua, August 1979.
12. *Latin America Political Report,* Vol. XIII, No. 27., 13 July 1979.
13. Quoted in Roger Mendieta Alfaro, *El Ultimo Marine,* p. 153.
14. Humberto Ortega, 'The Strategy of Victory', interview with Marta Harnecker.
15. Carlos Mejia Godoy y el Taller de Sonido Popular, 'Credo' from the *Misa Campesina,* CBS Records, Costa Rica, 1977.
16. Carlos Mejia Godoy y Los de Palacaguina; 'El Garand', from the collection of songs *Guitarra Armada,* cassette published and distributed by COSOCAN, Barcelona, 1979.
17. Tomas Borge, mimeographed interview, April 1979.
18. *Bases Programaticas del FSLN para la Democracia y la Reconstruccion de Nicaragua,* (mimeo), 1979.
19. James Petras, 'Whither the Nicaraguan Revolution?' *Monthly Review,* October 1979, pp. 14-15.

20. *Ibid.*, p. 14.
21. *Programa de la Junta de Gobierno de Reconstruccion Nacional* (Managua, Ministerio de Educacion, July 1979).
22. Alejandro Bendana; 'Crisis in Nicaragua', in *NACLA Report on the Americas,* Vol. XII, No. 6, November-December 1978, pp. 32-33.
23. *Nicaragua: El Pueblo Frente a La Dinastia* (Madrid, IEPALA, 1978), pp. 96-104.
24. These were Judge Stolz's conclusions from a visit to Nicaragua in August 1977, seeking to disprove the testimony on human rights violations by the National Guard given by Fernando Cardenal and other priests. Quoted by the US journalist Jeffrey St. John in *Human Rights and Revolution: A Case Study in Moral Confusion* (Washington D.C., Council on American Affairs, 1978), p. 73.
25. *Latin America Political Report,* Vol. XIII, No. 14, 14 April 1978.
26. *Newsweek,* 18 June 1979.
27. Interview with Sergio Ramirez in Costa Rica, May 1979.
28. *Latin America Political Report,* Vol. XIII, No. 25, 29 June 1979.
29. *Bohemia,* Havana, July 1979.
30. *Latin America Political Report,* Vol. XIII, No. 25, 29 June 1979.
31. Interview in Managua, July 1979.
32. Fidel Castro, speech at Holguin, Cuba on the 26th anniversary of the assault on the Moncada barracks, reprinted in *Granma,* Havana, 28 July 1979.
33. Nunez, *op. cit.*, p. 122.
34. Interview in Managua, February 1980.
35. Comandante Henry Ruiz (Modesto), in *The Guardian,* 21 July 1979.

PART 3
The People in Power

Introduction

The Challenge

'If the bourgeoisie want to call this process Communist, that's their problem,' declared FSLN Party Organisation Secretary, Carlos Carrion, towards the end of the first year. 'Let the Revolution be judged by its real social achievements and the New Man it creates,' added Junta member, Sergio Ramirez, 'and not by the ideological labels which some people try to pin on it.' The FSLN's Revolution is passionately anti-dogmatic, a dramatic break with the orthodox Marxism of Latin American communist parties since World War Two.

The euphoria of the July 19th victory died down quickly, to be replaced by an energetic enthusiasm to build the new Nicaragua. But the Sandinistas' aim was to make the spirit of the revolutionary war permanent. When Tomas Borge speaks of 'building paradise on earth', this in no sense suggests utopianism. It means that the new society cannot be a simple reorganisation of economic relations. That reorganisation must, through permanent education, through raising the cultural and ideological level of the workers and peasants, be matched by a radical transformation of the mental patterns of individuals. In contrast to the inhumanity of capitalism, the new society would mean the rational control by people of things.

To those who sought to pigeonhole the Revolution by sterile attempts to prove that it was a 'second Cuba' or a 'repeat of Chile', the Sandinistas responded with pragmatism and flexibility. The Nicaraguan Revolution, they insisted, was something completely new. It imitated no previous model. Instead it offered the rest of Latin America an example, by proving that military dictatorships – so long the norm of domination in the countries of Central America and the Southern Cone – were vulnerable to the armed insurrection of a united people. It had given proof of the need for revolutionary violence against the institutionalised violence of the state. And it had shown that in the guerrilla struggle itself – in the example of individual fighters, the mass heroism of the people, the principle of clemency towards prisoners – came the first signs of the new revolutionary humanism, the 'New Man' described by Che Guevara.

Observers began to take stock of the unique features of the Nicaraguan Revolution: the necessary and all-important tactical alliance with the private sector, the carefully constructed friendships with non-socialist countries, the ability to exploit the weaknesses and divisions of a hesitant US presidency. They noted, too, the massive participation of women in the armed struggle and in the tasks of reconstruction. This was unprecedented in Latin American history, as was the contribution of the Church. For the FSLN showed Latin America that the revolutionary humanism of a political and military vanguard was quite compatible, in practice, with the Christian humanism of the mass of the Church. And even the most cynical observers came to admire the generosity of a revolution which refused to exact vengeance on its defeated enemies, preferring to punish them with the example of a new and superior morality.

But as the Frente is fond of pointing out, winning the war was the easy part. After a honeymoon period with the bourgeoisie which lasted roughly five months until the end of 1979, the contradictions in economic and political interests could not help but surface. How was the Revolution to reactivate the economy, attack dependency and satisfy the basic demands of the masses for social change? – all this without placing at risk the hard-won unity with a middle-class which continued to own the majority of the means of production, and which saw the overthrow of Somoza as a source of new opportunities after decades of economic suffocation? The FSLN's vanguard role within the alliance could not be seriously questioned, but the concept of political pluralism which this alliance represented depended on the bourgeois parties formally endorsing Sandinista hegemony. This was bound to be put to the test.

Nor could the ideological definition of the Revolution remain imprecise for very long. The ideological umbrella of nationalism and anti-*Somocismo*, while powerful during the insurrection, could hardly be expected to stretch to cover the divergent demands of a frustrated middle class and a victorious mass movement. As the tensions emerged, the Sandinistas only reiterated that their primary commitment was to the poor, to a political and economic system which would end illiteracy, disease, malnutrition and slum housing, and to a system which would bring political power to the workers and peasants.

The Frente devoted those first five honeymoon months to an intensive structuring of the mass organisations and organs of the new state. It was a task which offered great promise and equally great problems. The old apparatus of domination had been completely swept away, but the new state power had to be consolidated swiftly drawing on a revolutionary movement with few members out of their twenties and almost no-one with governmental or administrative experience. Nicaragua would for the first time have a central ministry of economic planning, a ministry of agrarian reform, a ministry of social welfare. The errors of inexperience were inevitable, as were the shrill claims of the bourgeoisie that it was the only class capable of running the new state.

Management of the economy presented perhaps the most severe challenge. Left in ruins by Somoza's bombing, corruption and mismanagement, the country could only hope to breathe again by reactivating the existing economic base — an export-oriented agricultural economy which was the living embodiment of dependency and underdevelopment. This in turn meant that popular demands could only be met by increased output, efficiency, labour discipline and wage restraint. It was a potential minefield, which could only be safely negotiated through effective mass mobilisation and a rapid raising of political consciousness. The insistence of the FSLN minimum programme on restricting state ownership in the first place to former Somocista properties also brought its tensions, above all in the field of agrarian reform. Would the 2 million acres of confiscated farms prove sufficient to meet the overwhelming demand for land? And would the young regime, faced with its own administrative limitations and the low level of mass political education, avoid the pitfalls of state capitalism?

To stave off economic disaster, the Sandinistas also required a large injection of foreign aid with no strings attached, and a renegotiation of the US$1.64 billion foreign debt on favourable terms. This in turn imposed restraints. Any premature moves against the preserves of the bourgeoisie, especially the free activities of opposition political parties and the right-wing media, would be guaranteed to invoke the wrath of the USA, endangering the Sandinistas' indispensable friendships abroad and their requests for aid from foreign governments. Yet the latitude granted to political mobilisation by the Right would be sure to enrage a mass movement which would identify opposition manoeuvres as a frontal attack on the very basis of the revolution. By the end of 1979, the elements of the new state were in place, and the battle began in earnest to implant a clear understanding in the mass organisations of the patient tactics which the Revolution demanded.

Inevitably, sectors of the bourgeoisie were by now beginning to display outright hostility towards the Sandinista Government, and the pluralism of the Revolution granted them a political platform and a free press from which to launch their attacks. For the latter part of the first year of the Revolution, ideological warfare moved into the forefront. It was a critical test of the Frente's pragmatism. The private sector had to continue producing; the mass movement had to be consolidated; national unity had to be preserved; the party of the Sandinista Revolution had to be patiently formed; groups on the far left who saw national unity and class alliances as a sell-out to the bourgeoisie had to be won over or outflanked. And what impact might the freely expressed propaganda of the Right have in remote peasant areas which the Revolution was slow to reach? Among the ethnic minorities of the Atlantic Coast, untouched by the insurrection? And in driving a wedge between the Catholic hierarchy and the rest of the Church, whose alliance with the FSLN was so vital?

In such a conflict, the dynamic relationship between the Frente and the people, which had underpinned the success of the insurrection, would inevitably be the object of the closest scrutiny. The response of the popular organisations to the threats from the Right in early 1980 — the flight of capital, rundown of production, speculation, false propaganda — was swift and impressive. But popular demands and state policies, vanguard orientation and mass action: these had to converge. The Sandinistas had to avoid the ever-present dangers of both spontaneism from a politicised and indignant mass movement, and of bureaucratisation of a revolutionary leadership under attack from a private sector which refused to accept the rules of the game as spelled out by the FSLN. The umbilical relationship between the FSLN and the mass movement had to be strengthened, and the seeds of genuine democracy sown in the factories and farms, in the schools and in the *barrios*.

At least three vital factors worked in favour of the Revolution during its first year: the overwhelming and durable popularity and moral authority enjoyed by the FSLN; the continuing inability of the right-wing bourgeoisie to act in a unified or decisive manner; and the ambivalence and weakness of the Carter Administration. All of these gave the Revolution a breathing space in which to consolidate, to prepare for aggressions by a future US Republican government, to meet internal right-wing opposition which would look to Washington for support, and to defend itself against the hostilities of the governments of Honduras, El Salvador and Guatemala and the depredations of regrouped Somocista National Guards on the borders. This meant not only securing the economic base of the country, but preparing for the active defence of the Revolution. It meant consolidating the combat strength and political awareness of the new armed forces, creating a nationwide structure of people's militias, developing an efficient security apparatus to head off inevitable foreign and domestic attempts to destabilise the Revolution. And all of this without resorting to the repression of opposition groups.

The Sandinistas came to power, too, knowing the inevitable impact of their Revolution on the growing popular struggles in nearby El Salvador and Guatemala, and fully aware of the interrelated importance of the revolutionary movements of Central America. The consolidation of Sandinista power in Nicaragua would strengthen the Salvadorean and Guatemalan Left. Likewise a popular victory in either of those countries would allow Nicaragua, starved of local friends and deeply committed to internationalism, extra space in which to consolidate.

These, then, are some of the tensions which would face the Sandinista Revolution in its first year, and they are the subject of the pages which follow. Under growing pressure from the Right, the Sandinistas insisted that national sovereignty and social justice would always, inevitably, take priority over tactical unity with those who sought to restore the class privileges of the private sector. The commitment to working-class interests would never waver — it was, after all, the entire reason for the FSLN's existence.

The tensions facing the FSLN at home, and the importance of the Nicaraguan Revolution to popular struggles elsewhere in Central America, were swiftly understood by Washington, and its policies towards the new Nicarague would be a vital test case of the US strategy of blocking the advance of the Left in the Region. Give the Sandinistas time, and support the private sector from within, argued the Washington liberals. Nicaragua is already lost to international communism, said the hawks. For both tendencies in Washington, one tactic was fundamental. This tactic was exposed in a document prepared by dissenting members of the National Security Council, State Department, Department of Defence and CIA in the final months of the doomed Carter Administration. They pointed to the major role the Western media were playing in an orchestrated attempt to sensitize public opinion to the policy goals of the United States in Central America. Nicaragua was the immediate target of this media offensive, and the tactic was twin-pronged: to isolate Nicaragua by drawing a curtain of media silence across the Revolution, and to discredit the new government by crude anti-Communist reporting of the 'second Cuba' variety.

This media offensive is, above all, the rationale for Part III of this book. My primary aim is to break the silence, to give a factual report of what is happening in the new Nicaragua. If it does so at the expense of a more detailed theoretical exposition, this is the result of a conscious decision on my part, and one which seems to me, on reflection, to be substantially correct. This is not the moment to write a volume entitled 'Socialism in Nicaragua'. The FSLN — if we are to accept the conventional 'second Cuba' thesis — has not yet produced its equivalent of the Second Declaration of Havana. But for now, let the facts speak for themselves.

11. Building the New Order

The Plaza de la Revolucion, where the new Junta had been received a year before, was not large enough to hold the anticipated turnout for the Revolution's first anniversary celebrations in July 1980. Instead, a quarter of Nicaragua's population — 600,000 people — crammed into the newly built Plaza 19 de Julio to show their overwhelming support for the Sandinista Revolution and the achievements of its first year. They lined up behind the portraits of Sandino and Fonseca, the red and black flags of the FSLN and the banners of their mass organisations, which by now had grown to represent more than half a million members. Urban workers gathered under the placards of the Central Sandinista de Trabajadores (Sandinista Workers' Federation: CST); they were joined by the peasants and rural workers of the Asociacion de Trabajadores del Campo (Rural Workers' Association: ATC), the women of the powerful Asociacion de Mujeres Nicaraguenses 'Luisa Amanda Espinoza' (Association of Nicaraguan Women: AMNLAE, named after the first woman militant of the FSLN to die in combat); and the youth and children of the Juventud Sandinista 19 de Julio (Sandinista Youth 19th of July) and the Asociacion de Ninos Sandinistas (Association of Sandinista Children: ANS). The heaviest concentration of all, though, marched to the square under the hand-lettered banners of the Comites de Defensa Sandinista (Sandinista Defence Committees: CDS), which had blossomed from the embryonic *barrio* groups of the 1978 insurrection into a fully fledged national structure present in every community.

Around the edge of the vast square, monumental hoardings carried the central slogan of the first anniversary: 'Sandino Ayer, Sandino Hoy, Sandino Siempre' ('Sandino Yesterday, Sandino Today, Sandino Always'). The crowds watched martial parades by the troops of the Sandinista People's Army, transformed from a guerrilla force into a politicised national army, and the militias — from young adolescents to elderly market women — of the recently created MPS. Away in the middle distance, the backdrop to the rally was provided by the volcanic hill of Asososca, with the massive white letters 'FSLN' set into its side. 'We didn't sleep in the *barrio:* we had mass demonstrations all night and then came here on foot first thing in the morning,'[1] said a CDS member from the south-western Managua *barrio* of San Judas. A young peasant from the cotton-growing north-west echoed the same enthusiasm: 'We left Chinandega at one in the morning. There was hardly anyone left in the town. Everybody wanted to come, even the literacy teachers. But they had to stay behind to celebrate the victory with their pupils.'[2]

As the Chinandega peasant suggested, the crowd might have been still larger but for the absence of the 70,000 *brigadistas* of the Literacy Crusade, completing the fourth month of their involvement in the Revolution's most critical first-year political programme. The *brigadistas* returned to a similar mass welcome a month later, but they missed the speeches by Fidel Castro and former Venezuelan President Carlos Andres Perez, and the presence on the platform of Nicaragua's new international allies, with strong delegations from the Socialist countries, the Non-Aligned Movement and the Socialist International. 'It would be inappropriate for me not to draw attention to the presence on this platform of delegates and personalities from the most varied, the most wide-ranging systems, ideologies and political colouring,' was Castro's way of noting their significance. 'Nevertheless, something binds us all together, all of us including even the North Americans.' The US Government — although President Jimmy Carter had declined the invitation — was represented by its Ambassador to the United Nations, who quietly led his delegation from the platform before the singing of the Sandinista anthem, 'We fight against the Yanqui/Enemy of Humanity'.

FSLN Comandante Daniel Ortega, representing both the government Junta and the Sandinista National Directorate, took the opportunity of the 19 July rally to announce a new decree enabling the state to take over control of idle farmlands in a major extension of the agrarian reform programme. Ortega's declaration was important as much for its timing as for its content, a powerful assertion of the FSLN's confidence in moving against one of the private sector's most intransigent acts of resistance to Sandinista policy. Obviously not all those present were entirely happy at the Revolution's show of strength and popularity. While small anti-FSLN left-wing groups — insignificant during the insurrection but now suddenly vocal — vied for prominent positions at the front of the crowd, representatives of bourgeois parties and the private enterprise organisation COSEP buttonholed the large contingent of visiting foreign journalists to voice their anxieties and complaints at the course of the Revolution. 'Excessive militarism' protested the bourgeois daily *La Prensa,* a cry eagerly taken up by much of the visiting Western press. With a receptive audience, dissident right-wing voices deplored the FSLN's vigorous moral support for the Salvadorean struggle, lamented the presence of Castro, of Grenadan Premier Maurice Bishop and a delegation from the USSR, attacked the predominance of the Sandinista *rojinegro* over the blue and white flag of Nicaragua, and accused the FSLN of marginalising the private sector from the decisions of government and committing a breach of faith by refusing to announce a timetable for elections. But when questioned more closely, they admitted the massive and durable popular support for the Frente and their own lack of a solid political base. And they remained silent when Comandante Tomas Borge, the only surviving founder member of the FSLN, asked the crowd to take a prolonged oath of allegiance. 'We renew our commitment to be intransigently loyal to the basic aims and the immediate tasks of the Revolution,' said Borge. 'That is, the realisation of full democracy and the social, political and economic liberation of the Nicaraguan people.'

Towards the Sandinista State

A battle is underway in Nicaragua for the future configuration of the state. The FSLN's 1979 victory, by ensuring the military overthrow of the Somoza state apparatus, has created the preliminary conditions for a popular revolution. The implementation of the Minimum Programme of the Sandinista Government will not be hampered by the survival of old structures of power. In crucial contrast to Guatemala in 1954 or Chile in 1973, neither the local bourgeoisie nor its US backers will be able to use the existing machinery of the state to undermine revolutionary advances from within. Nonetheless, the insurrection was made possible by the programmatic unity of divergent class forces, and the first question asked of the FSLN in victory was whether it would have the internal strength to control and direct a multi-class alliance, without allowing capitalist participation to subvert the Revolution's long-term strategic aims. To a large extent that question has already been answered. Sandinista control of the armed forces, and the weak alternative strategy and programme of the bourgeoisie, are the basic guarantees of success in the transitional phase to a new state. The bourgeoisie has no confident and united political leadership, and its only unifying force is not one of the right-wing political parties but an economic class grouping (COSEP); this has made the FSLN's task easier. As the Revolution consolidates itself, the evident pluralism which it offers — freedom of political representation for all bourgeois parties and organisations except those allied to Somoza — and the economic guarantees provided to 'patriotic businessmen' have drawn broad sectors of the Nicaraguan middle class behind the Revolution and away from the blandishments of the Right. The insurrectional strategy depended from the first on the FSLN's ability to recruit wide support from the 'floating' majority of the middle and petty bourgeoisie and to make that support permanent. In victory the pattern has continued and deepened, with a new bloc of centre and left parties giving formal coherence to the plan. National unity defended by armed strength continues to be the cornerstone of the Revolution. 'People, Army, Unity: Guarantee of Victory — that is the slogan at the very core of this Revolution,' Comandante Henry Ruiz reminded delegates to the first assembly of the Association of Rural Workers (ATC).[3] And Comandante Carlos Nunez, at the same assembly, commented that 'only national unity could give us victory, and only this same national unity — under new conditions — can enable us to sustain the victory.'[4]

The concept of unity is conceived of at three levels: within the FSLN itself, within the mass working-class movement, and in the nation as a whole. Logically enough, the difficulty of achieving and maintaining unity increases at each level. In the FSLN it is absolute. The three tendencies are dead and buried, assigned their proper place as the necessary product of particular historical circumstances. Within the mass movement, conflicts persist, but only seriously in the urban trade unions, for reasons which will be fully discussed in Chapter 13. Nationally, the threats to continuing class unity are graver, despite the ideal – again expressed by Nunez – that in the new regime 'we ought to find the organisations of the popular masses, private enterprise, the Church, middle-class political groupings, the Left, all those who wish to be there.'[5] But a profound contradiction exists between the Revolution's determination to place the working class at the centre of the stage, and the need to guarantee private sector cooperation to pull the country out of economic disaster.

In transposing national unity from its first, anti-Somocista phase to its second phase as part of a defined revolutionary programme, the Frente has inevitably encountered resistance, whether from clearly defined counter-revolutionary groups who employ internal or external aggression, or from the lack of political clarity of other sectors (both bourgeois and working class) who can and must still be won over to the side of the Revolution. This second phase of national unity has as its main thrust the defence of the long-term interests of Nicaragua's workers and peasants, and was expressed succinctly by Comandante Jaime Wheelock in an answer to journalists: 'We consider that national unity revolves around two great forces in this country, which are the workers of the city and the workers of the countryside.'[6] Like the three tendencies, the debate over the relative importance of the peasantry and the urban proletariat as a revolutionary class is a thing of the past. The worker-peasant alliance in Nicaragua is not a rhetorical demand, but a political reality and a strategic obligation for the FSLN. It is also the continuation of the Frente's long-standing project of working-class unity, first given concrete form in the 1970 Congreso Obrero-Campesino-Estudiante (Worker-Peasant-Student Congress), which brought together 100 peasant leaders, 80 trade unionists and 75 student activists at the National University to lay the foundations for unified revolutionary action. It is around the focus of this central peasant-trade union-student alliance that the Sandinistas' other alliances with divergent class forces should be understood. There is no contradiction in practice between their past definition of these latter alliances as 'temporary and tactical' and their present-day potential for lasting and strategic bonds. Because of the insistence in every minimum programme on the removal of the National Guard and all vestiges of *Somocismo,* the alliances involved no defence of existing bourgeois institutions, and they took full account of the national peculiarities of the Nicaraguan bourgeoisie as a class. The theoretical validity of including the bourgeoisie in a revolutionary platform has been borne out in the practice of radicalising as much of that sector as possible. Even after a year of revolution, the FSLN was unwilling to accept that the bourgeois parties currently aligned with *Sandinismo* were the only ones which could be won over. The doors were left open, and active recruitment continued.

The major lesson of the 1960s was that the FSLN could not enter into any kind of popular front headed by historically weak and vacillating bourgeois parties. Alliances were proposed only in the latter part of the next decade, when the FSLN had (or could rapidly achieve) unchallenged hegemony over the opposition movement, and when the political situation had matured into crisis. From 1977 onwards, there was no likelihood of the alliances falling under bourgeois leadership because of the character of the Nicaraguan state. Apart from the Conservative Party, none of the political groupings of the middle class had any institutional relationship with the state. They were not a legal parliamentary opposition and had no vested interest in *Somocismo*. Carlos Nunez again provides the analysis of their potential: 'When the revolutionary movement is strong, the petty bourgeoisie invariably tends to embrace revolutionary interests, and if we make strenuous efforts to educate them, to instil in them discipline, the example of the behaviour, the self-sacrifice of the proletariat, we can have them on our side permanently.'[7]

In the power vacuum brought about by the overthrow of Somoza, these groups have not even a toehold from which they can plausibly rebuild a bourgeois state during a post-revolutionary period in which the FSLN enjoys unquestioned dominance and moral authority. There are, quite simply, two roads which they can travel: to fulfil their nationalist and democratic aspirations — both fundamental to *Sandinismo* — by aligning themselves with the Revolution, thereby coming to terms with the gradual erosion of their class privileges; or they can turn overtly to the right-wing counter-revolution. In this way, the middle and petty bourgeoisie are a vital ideological battleground, a group which the Right cannot afford to lose in its fight for the future structures of the state. To choose the second option of counter-revolution implicitly means the acceptance of armed force, since there is no other way in which the Sandinista Government can be brought down. Yet the only indigenous armed force which could conceivably be pitted against the Sandinista Army is a reassembled National Guard, but this military machine's whole identity is Somocista. Memories of the 1979 war, aside from questions of class interest, make this improbable in the short term.

None of this should imply that the bourgeoisie is without economic and political influence in the state today. Like the FSLN, Nicaraguan businessmen have learned many lessons from Cuba, and many who might have left the country have chosen to stay in an attempt to prevent Nicaragua's 'Cubanisation'. And each class is manoeuvring from its real or perceived position within the government to advance its own class porject. While the large direct representation of workers' and peasants' organisations in the government gives the popular classes the strength to press their demands, there is a real dichotomy in the bourgeoisie's attempts to use its apparently large share in government and state positions. On the face of it, the bourgeoisie started with two of the five members of the Junta, numerous cabinet ministers and 11 of the 47 members of the Council of State, a body which shares legislative powers with the Junta. This would appear to give bourgeois parties and politicians a representation far greater than their real popular support would warrant. But it is important to recognise how these bourgeois representatives perceive their own position. They fall into two distinct categories: those who fight from an openly anti-Sandinista position from within the state, such as the representatives of the Democratic Conservative Party, the Social Christian Party or COSEP with their seats on the Council of State; and those who accept willingly a role assigned to them by the FSLN as part of its project for a multi-class government during the present phase of the Revolution.

Two cases illustrate this paradox well. The most celebrated was the resignation of two Junta members in April 1980. The departure of Alfonso Robelo followed a period in which he had actively sought to undermine the course of the Revolution from his position in the Junta, behaviour which among other things divided his party, the Movimiento Democratico Nicaraguense. He and Violeta Chamorro were replaced by two other bourgeois figures, one of whom was Rafael Cordova Rivas, a leader of the Democratic Conservatives. But Cordova Rivas had actively distanced himself from the hostile stance of his party over the previous months, and in accepting the call of the FSLN National Directorate to join the Junta showed that he was prepared to accept the Frente's strategy and a government platform which frontally attacks the prerogatives of the bourgeoisie. None of this, of course, prevents the right-wing parties from attempting to use Cordova Rivas and others like him in government for their own purposes.

The second case was that of Jose Francisco Cardenal. Cardenal's battleground was the Council of State, a more explicit expression of the FSLN's vision of future power structures. When Cardenal was named as Vice-President of the Council, he denounced the appointment as 'a hellish conspiracy of the Communist machine', a clear enough indication that he was not prepared to use his position as a COSEP leader to endorse an FSLN strategy. Cardenal resigned and left for the USA, despite the insistence of the American Embassy in Managua that COSEP should take up its six seats on the Council of State.

The two cases demonstrate the contradiction which the bourgeoisie faces in playing a minority role in the state. Its representatives are faced with a clear choice: accept FSLN guidelines for responsible subsidiary participation, or write themselves out of any long-term influence in shaping state policies. In taking on positions of authority, bourgeois politicians thereby explicitly endorse the FSLN's government strategy, and this has been spelt out clearly: 'The structure of the government, for all the names that some people have tried to pin on it, is another instrument for promoting the historic project of the working classes.'[8] A Cordova Rivas is prepared to accept that premise; a Cardenal is not. Openings for subversion from within are limited. Most of the key ministries of the revolutionary government – Agricultural Development, Planning, Education, Social Welfare – are either new creations or radically transformed. The Centre and Right cannot use the ministries as an instrument for retaining a bourgeois state or seriously blunting the

political direction of the FSLN. From within the government, the worst
they can do is to impede its work by the inefficiency, bureaucracy, corruption and abuse of power which many lower and middle level civil servants and
technicians have carried over from the Somoza era.[9]

Nationalism and Class Struggle

In each of the Central American countries, as in pre-revolutionary Cuba, there
is an unusual degree of interpenetration between the class struggle and the
fight for national liberation. The Central American convergence between local
capitalist exploitation and the strategic demands of the USA reached its
zenith with the Somoza dictatorship in Nicaragua, providing a further context
for the FSLN's insistence on incorporating the anti-Somocista bourgeoisie
into the national liberation struggle. The recovery of national sovereignty
was essential to the bourgeois democratic aims of the Nicaraguan middle
class. At the same time, the nationalist appeal of *Sandinismo* was crucial in
the mobilisation of the masses, and the resolution of the national question
has opened the way for the working-class to project its demands as a class-
based anti-capitalist struggle, in which the identification of Somoza with
United States imperialism (rapidly assimilated during the course of the
insurrection) can be enriched by a grasp of the common character of
Somocismo and capitalism as a whole.

There has been considerable debate on the primacy of the national liberation struggle in Nicaragua, and criticisms that the FSLN is only capable of
leading the Revolution in its nationalist, 'bourgeois-democratic' phase.[10]
But American intervention and the monopoly of power exercised by the
Somozas have both blurred the class contradictions of Nicaraguan society
and impeded the development of class consciousness. The war in Nicaragua
was quite literally a military fight for national survival, and as in Cuba
the victory brought what Debray has called 'the euphoria of unanimity'[11]
from each group ranged against the dictator. If the FSLN have assigned
primacy to the fight for national liberation over the class struggle, it is
because one is the precondition for the other. And any apparent underplaying
of the class struggle during the first months of the Revolution is for
eminently sound tactical reasons. When Castro visited Nicaragua, it was not
only to admire but to learn, and to offer some advice. That advice might be
summarised as: 'Avoid the early mistakes we made in Cuba, the political
rejection by the West, premature frontal attacks on the bourgeoisie, economic
isolation.' In an important interview with *Prensa Latina*, Comandante
Humberto Ortega elaborated on the FSLN view of the Revolution's early
months:

> In order that our struggle should not become acute, it is necessary to
> fulfil the programme which both the Frente and the anti-Somocista
> bourgeoisie supported. We have to fight, therefore, against various

forms of deviation. The situation of Nicaragua must necessarily be seen in the context of the domination which imperialism continues to exercise over this continent, and so you can see why it is not in our interests to sharpen the contradictions.[12]

The relationship of the FSLN to the bourgeoisie and the constant danger of American intervention help to explain the apparent contradiction between the radical form of the Frente's armed struggle and the moderation of their immediate political objectives. Again remembering Cuba, foreign — and particularly Western — aid must not be allowed to dry up, existing international friendships must be bolstered as a shield against intervention, middle-class support must not be forfeited. Anti-imperialism remains a powerful cement to bind together bourgeois groups whose loyalty might otherwise waver.

The Sandinista priority is to create internal and external conditions which will buy the Revolution time and breathing-space, in which the class character of the process can consolidate itself and the class struggle be played out on favourable terms. Comandante Henry Ruiz, speaking to a crowd demonstrating against the action of the ultra-left Frente Obrero, could not have been more explicit about the purpose of the transitional phase: 'The aim . . . is to free ourselves from exploitation and create truly human conditions of equality and justice. But that, companeros, needs a solid material base to work from. And that is why at certain times the Revolution may confuse those who wish to be confused.'

The comment was aimed at a small left-wing group which had attempted to take advantage of many workers' low level of political awareness and drive a wedge between the immediate demands of the working class and the strategic design of its vanguard. Having built a national insurrection in a country whose tradition of organisation and class consciousness is notoriously poor, the FSLN faced the danger of a natural hiatus in working-class energies after the overthrow of Somoza, a spell in which no automatic assumptions could be made about transferring insurrectional mobilisation into the organisational demands of national reconstruction. There were genuine risks that the masses might become defensive or apathetic. In the immediate post-insurrectional period, continuity of action had to be assured among the most militant sectors of the mass movement, while the least advanced groups had to learn a new relationship with the state and appreciate that the destruction of the Somocista system, far from ending the class struggle, merely created the conditions in which a resolution of class conflicts became possible. And both groups had to learn, through intensive propaganda and education, that their own creative energy was the basis for fulfilling the Revolution's strategic goals. A Sandinista propaganda document of early 1980 made the point forcefully: 'Correct revolutionary work is centred on the *strategic;* it is there that the true strength of a political project lies.'[13]

The class struggle, of course, possesses a dynamic which the FSLN can neither fully dictate nor control, and in the first months an urgent priority was to close the gap between the strategic vision of the Frente and comprehensible demands for immediate social transformation. That task is based on a reaffirmation and redefinition of the FSLN's vanguard role. The Frente assumed revolutionary leadership in a period of crisis, with the coexistence of an illegitimate ruling class and an uncoordinated mass movement. It was a crisis in which the nature of the bourgeoisie and the military failed to produce a means of damping down the class struggle, either through a civilian reformist alternative or a Nasser or Peruvian-style nationalist military solution. In 1979 and 1980 the vanguard has reasserted its leadership. At a September meeting to restructure the Sandinista People's Army, each of the FSLN's nine-member National Directorate received the title of 'Comandante de la Revolucion', no mere honorific but a formal ratification of the National Directorate as the ultimate political authority in Nicaragua, a significance not lost on the opposition bourgeoisie. At the same time, the Frente has moved to translate its popular support into solid class-based organisations which are increasingly capable of independent action within the strategic framework set forth by the FSLN. Within days of the July victory, another slogan began to appear throughout the country: 'Organisation, Organisation and More Organisation.'

The wisdom of the Insurrectionals' analysis of class dynamics in Nicaragua is increasingly clear. At the heart of most scepticism about the Frente's class alliance expressed by foreign Marxist analysts was a fear of political reassertion by the bourgeoisie after the fall of Somoza. But the assessment of class forces was also predictive, arguing that the weakness of the bourgeoisie would allow the revolutionary forces to take a firm initiative after the victory, driving an irreversible wedge into bourgeois power by immediately consolidating the mass organisations and the armed forces, demonstrating the poverty of the bourgeois alternative and refusing, from this position of strength, to comply with opposition demands for the institutionalisation of bourgeois power structures such as traditional elections or a quasi-parliamentary Council of State representing the political forces in existence *before* the victory. The original proposals for the Council of State were outlined in the Junta's government programme of June 1979, and many of the bourgeoisie's attacks on the government have been on alleged 'infringements' of this document which — because of when it was issued — obviously could not take into account the radical shifts in power over the succeeding months. Within five weeks of taking power, on 21 August, the Junta issued a second major document, the Statute on the Rights of Nicaraguans. This reiterated the commitment of the Sandinista Government to political pluralism and the effective defence of human rights, and contained one paragraph which more than any other alarmed the bourgeoisie and pointed to the overall direction of the government in cutting away capitalist prerogatives:

Property, whether individual or collective, fulfils a social function. Therefore it may be subject to restrictions with respect to ownership, benefit, use and disposition, for reasons of security, public interest or utility, social interest, the national economy, national emergency or disaster, or for purposes of agrarian reform.[14]

To the private sector, the practical implications of such statements have led inevitably to complaints that the political atmosphere is prejudicial to capitalist activity. Their hostility has led in turn to attempts to undermine the country's economic recovery, and each specific confrontation or new piece of legislation has drawn a clearer demarcation between the unity of pro-Sandinista forces and the overtly counter-revolutionary position of those who refuse to cooperate. A law forbidding the running down of capital industry, passed early in 1980, caused particular conflict, the more so because its effective application depends on the vigilance and mobilisation of factory workers through their mass organisations which the private sector's right wing continue to denounce as having 'no legal existence'.[15] Comandante Luis Carrion, commenting on the anti-decapitalisation decree, noted: 'The purpose of unity is to reconstruct in the interests of the people, and if anyone does not agree with these objectives, then we do not want them in the alliance.'[16]

The COSEP November communique reserved its greatest venom for the mass organisations, which represent the most direct threat to a future bourgeois state. In attacking them, COSEP played its familiar card of attempting to divide the revolutionary leadership: 'To sum up, all these points are manifestations of a Party-State confusion and of inconsistencies with pluralism, which give many people grounds for wondering whether some leaders intend to lead Nicaragua gradually towards a totalitarian dictatorship.'[17]

The structures of power which COSEP and its allies fear are being shaped pragmatically by the FSLN. Neither the Council of State nor the CDS represent a final vision of popular power; each is open to modification according to the future course of the Revolution. Similarly, the Sandinista Party — although a key concern — has not yet been formed. During the insurrectional period, the FSLN formed purely conjunctural instruments of dual power, and in the constantly shifting dynamic of the Revolution's first year, there is no reason to suppose that the organisation and functions of the CDS as presently constituted will remain any more unchanged than did the MPU in 1978-79. The MPU, as such, disappeared because it no longer responded to the needs of the moment, although the local organs which it created may be durable. In a similar way, the group of Los Doce served a specific historical function and then ceased to exist. This argument of permanently evolving and self-refining organs of popular democracy, which the Frente aims to have perfected by the 1985 elections, applies with particular force to the creation of the party. The Nicaraguan Revolution took place in the absence of a mass party because the Sandinistas believed that organisations specifically geared to the needs of the armed struggle were more appropriate, and that the party itself could only be built as the core of an unfolding revolution. There was no temptation to create a party prematurely, and even less now in the face of right-wing pressure for the Frente to 'reveal its true ideological character'.[18] Even at the height of the FSLN's internal divisions, the Tendencia Proletaria spoke above all of creating the 'embryo' of the future mass party. 'Embryo' in fact is the FSLN's favourite description of the mass organisations, and above all of the CDS.

> We in the FSLN do not see ourselves as the final repository of revolutionary ideas. That would be dogmatic, and we do everything possible to avoid dogmatism or the rigid application of any political theory in our vision of future popular power. That principle has guided the FSLN throughout its history as an organisation. We look to the masses constantly to enrich our vision, and when we talk of the CDSs as the 'embryos' of popular power, it is because we have no preconceived idea of what that power will look like. The CDSs are the best current example we have, because they involve the whole people and function in a highly democratic way which guarantees a continuous dynamic interplay between the vanguard and the masses and avoids the risk of bureaucratisation. The actual structures of popular power in the long term will be forged through necessities and experience.[19]

The Economic Inheritance

The backcloth to this struggle for the future state, and the root of most of the immediate restraints facing the FSLN, is the unprecedented collapse of the Nicaraguan economy. 'We must get used to living in a war economy,' insisted Wheelock.[20] There are five complementary reasons for this crisis:

(1) The destruction of the country's productive capacity as a result of the war: Each sector suffered in different ways. Textile production, for example, was badly hit by the systematic bombing of major factories, while the reactivation of the fishing industry was damaged by the theft of the fleet by fleeing National Guardsmen and delays by the Honduran Government in returning these stolen boats. Nevertheless, material damage to the economy as a whole – and the capital required for rebuilding plant – was less than the US$2.5 billion originally estimated. 'Information from the private sector was largely at fault,' commented one economic adviser. 'The business community's aim was to restore the economy to the wasteful levels of the Somocista period'.[21] The conclusion of the report on Nicaragua by the United Nations Economic Commission for Latin America (ECLA) was that production levels for 1979 had fallen back to those of 1962, with annual *per capita* income plunging to US$585.

(2) A breakdown of the country's distribution network and creeping paralysis of the state apparatus in the second half of the 1970s: This applies both to the internal distribution of goods and to foreign markets. Regional markets within Central America (representing 22% of Nicaragua's exports markets in 1977)[22] suffered badly from the war and from the economic crisis in El Salvador during 1980, and have to be recaptured in a climate of inevitable short-term export restrictions. After the war, production shortfalls and increased internal demand led to many traditional regional exports being reserved for

domestic consumption. There were, for example, no exports of cooking oil, flour or cotton derivatives during 1980.

(3) The disruption of the 1979 agricultural cycle, with domestic and export crops left unplanted: The worst affected crop was cotton, Nicaragua's second biggest export earner, with a 1980 loss of $100 million and only 20% of normal acreage planted. As well as the loss of foreign currency, Nicaragua was forced into short-term imports of basic foodstuffs, particularly severe in the case of beans and rice (with maize, the staples of the Nicaraguan diet). For several years before the Revolution, Nicaragua had achieved self-sufficiency in both crops. The country also needed an immediate injection of capital for infrastructural repairs to the agricultural sector, including large tracts of coffee-growing land abandoned or diseased under Somoza, and for the import of seeds, fertilisers and insecticides.

(4) An immediate cash crisis caused by the flight of capital before the insurrection and the depletion of state reserves: After Somoza's final ransacking of the Treasury, the Government of National Reconstruction found only US$3.5 million in reserves, not enough to pay for two days' worth of imports. The cash-flow problem was exacerbated by the necessary rise in public expenditure on social programmes in 1980.

(5) Nicaragua's US$1.64 billion external debt, the highest *per capita* debt of any Latin American state: Some $600 million of this was scheduled for repayment in 1979 alone, a sum greater than the country's total income from exports.

Economic recovery was further threatened by three additional factors: the uncertain degree of cooperation from a bourgeoisie which retained majority ownership of the means of production; the extent to which the working class would accept a prolonged period of austerity without interrupting production; and the shortage of experienced administrative and technical personnel. Low state salaries (even a minister earns a maximum of US$1,000 a month) mean that the private sector can aggravate this problem by seducing personnel with offers of salaries which the state cannot match.[23]

On 22 October 1979, the Junta and the National Directorate of the FSLN set up seven working groups to programme the transitional phase of economic recovery. Two months later their results were revealed in the 1980 Programme of Economic Reactivation, known more commonly as Plan 80.

Plan 80: The Initial Economic Strategy

'We are setting out on the road to build not only a New Economy, but also a New Man.' (Plan 80)[24]

Sandinista strategy for the first year aimed to reactivate the existing economic base of the country at the same time as initiating the future transformation of the economy. Although the state has control over the financial

201

system, foreign trade and natural resources, ownership of the means of production remains largely in private hands, and the twin aims of Plan 80 represent a delicate balance between economic reactivation, pure and simple, which would favour the preponderance of private ownership, and simple tranformation towards state control, which would interrupt the recovery of production and threaten the economic basis of the necessary tactical unity with the private sector.

Balance of Public and Private Ownership

	1978		1980	
	Public	*Private*	*Public*	*Private*
Agriculture	—	100.0%	19.1%	80.9%
Manufacturing Industry	—	100.0%	25.0%	75.0%
Construction	39.9%	60.1%	70.0%	30.0%
Mining	—	100.0%	99.0%	1.0%
Services	30.8%	69.2%	54.7%	45.3%
GDP Total	*15.3%*	*84.7%*	*40.8%*	*59.2%*

Source: Comite de Coordinacion Economica, Ministerio de Planificacion in *Datos Basicos sobre Nicaragua* (Managua, SENAPEP), p. 14.

The Plan itself set seven political targets: the defence, consolidation and advance of the revolutionary process; the reactivation of the economy in the interests of the masses; the maintenance of national unity; the construction of the Sandinista state; strengthening the Area of Public Property (APP); establishing and maintaining internal and external balances; and initiating the process of transition to a new economy.[25] The current phase of reactivation will last for at least two years, a period in which the overriding concern is to re-establish former production levels. The Ministry of Planning saw Plan 80 as the forerunner of a medium-term economic plan for the 1981-83 period, although in the light of the first year's results it seemed unlikely that a three-year plan would be feasible even by the end of 1980. By the most optimistic forecasts, 1982 is the earliest that the state can expect to start diversifying and restructuring the economy.

For the moment, immediate production targets have been to return to the 1978 level of economic activity for both export and domestic markets. Within the existing economic base, the priorities for reactivation carry a heavy dose of economic nationalism, the first steps towards breaking Nicaragua's economic dependency. This makes sound economic sense and appeals to the nationalism of both the workforce and the anti-Somoza capitalists. 'The first priority is to increase the productive capacity of the country in internal food supply for domestic consumption and to reduce its financial dependency on imports.'[26] In addition to food production, the priorities for state financing are the textile, pharmaceutical and building material industries, with state credits through the Banco Nacional de Desarrollo (National Development Bank) following three broad criteria: the use of Nicaraguan raw materials, aggregate value and generation of local employment. Although the metropolitan distortions of *Somocismo* will take years to eradicate, Plan 80 also made modest attempts to stimulate industry outside the Managua area. In figures, the target for 1980 was to capture US$966 million in income, divided between export earnings and essential foreign aid. Of this sum, 87% was destined to finance the imports needed for economic recovery, 10% for unavoidable capital payments and just 3% to build up currency reserves.

These are the bare bones of a transitional mixed economy whose actual performance has been conditioned by a series of imponderables. How would the private sector behave in view of the Plan 80 statement that this was the first stage towards an economy where·it is planned that 'the programming action of the state over the private sector will deepen'?[27] How efficient would the new Area of Public Property (APP) be? What degree of organisation and discipline would the trade unions achieve in meeting production targets and accepting austerity? And what external factors — fluctuating world prices for Nicaraguan exports, economic or military aggression against the Revolution — might impede economic recovery?

The tensions between the active role of the mass organisations (particularly the APP which effectively functions as a school for workers'· control) and the aspirations of the private sector have been the key dynamic in economic performance during the first year since the Revolution. Plan 80 was quite explicit about the need for the workers' organisations to participate fully in drawing up, evaluating and controlling economic strategy. The broad outlines of the Plan were presented to the mass organisations for comment and criticism at an early stage, although their representatives were not as vocal as the government had hoped. However, their reticence in planning meetings was a natural feature of a mass movement in its infancy, and in October 1979 still affected by a feeling of vertigo about the active role assigned to it in shaping state policies. The mass organisations have now more than found their feet, and their contribution to the 1981 plan was expected to be much more decisive. In the latter months of 1979, many businessmen still felt angered by the apparent distinction made by the government between their role and that of the mass organisations: 'This programme is the fruit of the shared efforts of some 200 state technicians and advisers and the representatives of the popular organisations, and the *consultations* carried out with private enterprise.'[28] The key argument, therefore, is not whether Nicaragua has broken sharply with the capitalist system — that has not and could not have happened despite the state's 40.8% share in gross domestic product — but over which political groups determine the speed and direction of Nicaragua's *future* move away from a capitalist economy.

The rules of the real relationship between the state and the private sector within the initial mixed economy have been clearly spelt out. They offer a firm commitment to state financing for private enterprise: 'The point is to unite salaried workers with small producers and artisans, with professionals and technicians, in a single powerful bloc of national unity. It is also a question of integrating patriotic businessmen, offering them the state support necessary to reactivate the private sector within the production targets in this programme.'[29] As well as reflecting the FSLN's commitment to pluralism, the decision to finance private sector recovery is something which the government has little option about. It is a risk, but a necessary one, which Jaime Wheelock touched on:

> We are resolutely pressing ahead with the democratic project for a pluralist mixed economy, in which all the forces of the country, including minority groups, can participate and be represented. We are doing so by virtue of a thorough understanding of our national situation, and at the same time a sense of realism which takes into account the fact that we have emerged from a punishing war, that we have to rebuild our country and that all forces who wish to take part responsibly will have full guarantees, the full support of the Revolution.

To the private sector, short-term guarantees are one thing, but fears that they have no place in the Sandinista economy in the long run have always held back full COSEP cooperation with Plan 80. In the course of often tense planning meetings to work out the details of the Plan, the private sector reached the point of threatening to withhold investment. The government's answer, as given by Orlando Nunez of INRA, was quite simple: 'We replied that they'd never invested before and we didn't expect them to do so now. In the past working capital came from state loans. We'll find it for them now as well. All we want them to do is to guarantee production.'[30]

The initial reaction of the private sector was supportive: they too, gauging the mood of the country, act with their own form of realism. A typical statement came from Ismael Reyes of the Chamber of Industries (CADIN), a member of COSEP: 'All of us industrialists are in favour of a fairer order for the working class'.[31] The apparently rapid change of line from COSEP's attempts to blame the government for the slow resumption of production, and their accusations in the 14 November communique that private business had seen 'a rapid erosion through doubt, insecurity and even mistrust . . . of the atmosphere of optimism which followed the victory', had much to do with the strong tone taken by the FSLN as Plan 80 was unveiled. On 30 December, Comandante Henry Ruiz, newly appointed as Planning Minister in a cabinet reshuffle which coincided with the launching of the Plan, put the government position firmly:

> [The danger is] that private enterprise will back out of its responsibilities, fail to put its weight behind the Plan and wait to see what we do. That attitude of wait-and-see is criminal, because it leaves all the work to the state in the full knowledge that the state alone cannot

solve all our people's problems without the assistance of the private sector. We try to be objective about our own needs and at the same time objective about the aspirations of private enterprise. So that when we talk of financing the private sector, we do so realistically, in the same way that we have behaved throughout the struggle. These are areas of real concern. However, if private enterprise does not start moving, if it plays a waiting game, then the Revolution will take whatever measures necessary – the unproductive *latifundio* will disappear for one thing. If private enterprise fails to understand that the secret of harmony is for all of us to work together for the good of the people, they will have made a catastrophic mistake.[32]

Accumulation For Whom?

There was little then in the initial provisions of Plan 80 to frighten off the private sector. With no expectation of investment, the worst economic crimes which the bourgeoisie could commit would be a refusal to produce – which would be not only economically but politically damaging in that it would prevent the government fulfilling its commitment to reduce unemployment through job creation in the private sector – and any attempt to run down or decapitalise the factories. In such a climate of programmed economic reactivation, the risks for Nicaraguan capitalists were almost nil, with no expectations of fresh private capital accumulation through new investment, but merely the use of existing fixed capital to be supplemented by working capital from the state bank and the promise of assured (if limited) profit margins. Not surprisingly, many businessmen have grasped the advantages of this access to state finance, and have preferred to resume production while allowing the state to take all the risks. It is a chance which the FSLN is prepared to take, accepting that it is impossible to restart production by decree and that sweeping nationalisations at present would only produce a further drop in output.[33] The private sector, too, accepts many of the realities of the situation. Speaking about the private sector's constant dialogue with the Junta and the FSLN National Directorate, COSEP leader Enrique Dreyfus commented: 'The FSLN is intelligent, capable and pragmatic, and private enterprise is responsive to reality. The terms of reference are therefore pragmatic'.[34]

At the same time, many capitalists realise that they are caught in a cleft stick over investment. 88% of all current investment already falls on the public sector,[35] and as private investment continues to stagnate, businessmen feel less and less in control of the country's future economic direction. As this private sector crisis deepens, businessmen see around them the tangible evidence that workers – albeit unevenly – are taking an ever greater role in both production and distribution, and are in the words of Plan 80 'progressively increasing their capacity to influence economic policy decisions'. And while the Frente is prepared to define the ground rules to accommodate as

many 'patriotic businessmen' as possible, it has shown itself inflexible with
capitalists whose response to their loss of muscle takes the form of direct
attacks on the working class, in whose interests the economic reactivation
programme must be seen to work. Under Plan 80, the transitional economy
aimed at a steady increase in working-class purchasing power and consumption levels and a growing capacity on the part of the state to accumulate
capital without either adding to the country's external debt or generating
inflation which would hit the working class. The strategy depends, among
other features, on a revision of the tax system so that taxes fall progressively
on the most highly paid, and on an efficient system of price controls and
distribution of essential goods. As these policies took root, the frontal
attacks launched by bourgeois groups increased. They took various forms:
not only the running down of capital and production boycotts which we have
mentioned, but also attempts to subvert the distribution networks controlled
by the state and mass organisations, as well as refusal to comply with labour
regulations or to implement the terms of factory *convenios colectivos*
(worker-management agreements). In the midst of a popular revolution,
working conditions in many plants remain unchanged. In the Laboratorios
Recipe Factory, for example, workers waited for almost four months without
a reply from management on a series of demands for environmental health
improvements and the introduction of Saturday working to allow day release
to work on the Literacy Crusade. In such cases, successful negotiation
depends primarily on the organised strength of the plant union, backed up
by the knowledge that when the state intervenes, it will do so on behalf of
the work force.

One paragraph of Plan 80, above all, summarises the state's ability to
direct private sector action and confront the bourgeoisie where necessary:

> We count on the advantage of a state apparatus which will allow not
> only the articulation of the extensive public sector, but also the
> channelling of private sector activity by means of the state control of
> commerce and banking. In addition, we can count on the exceptional
> degree of support from the people's organisations, which allows the
> government ample margins of flexibility in the management of the
> economy.[36]

The state is to be the future pivot of capital accumulation. But the critical
moment has not yet been reached, and will not be until full economic reactivation is achieved in 1982 or 1983. At that point, the question will have
to be answered: how is state capital accumulation to be used? It is here that
the Plan 80 concern for the rapid consolidation of the Sandinista state
becomes so vital. Before this take-off point for economic restructuring, the
state must be strong enough to resist any bourgeois challenge on future
economic direction. That strength must embrace both the formal apparatus
of the state and the coherence of the mass organisations as the architects of
state policy, as well as the productive capacity of the APP, whose industrial

sector – known as the Corporacion Industrial del Pueblo (COIP) – was running at 83% of its full capacity by the end of 1979. Increasingly, too, it means winning the battle over distribution as well as production. To soften the inevitable collisions with the private sector in the short to medium term, the FSLN has made a double-edged appeal, based on the bourgeoisie's remaining potential for radicalisation and on its simple self-interest as a class. The second part of that appeal is, in a nutshell: 'Produce, accepting lower profits and higher taxes, or commit class suicide'. In many industries, though by no means all, there is evidence that the message has been received and understood.

The State Sector

Direct state control of the economy, as we have seen, accounts for 41% of Nicaragua's 1980 GDP, and the Area of Public Property employs a fifth of the economically active population. The APP is made up of a number of elements: all industries and farmlands owned by Somoza and his allies; subsequent areas of nationalisation, including all natural resources, the finance system and foreign trade; government; and a majority of services. On the face of it, these represent major inroads into capitalist ownership in Nicaragua, but the reality is often more complex and ambivalent.

On the positive side, control of finance and trade gives the state a tighter grip on the direction of the economy than its percentage stake in the means of production – still well under half, and less than 20% in the key agricultural sector – might lead one to suppose. The 25 July decree nationalising the banking system met with little opposition from the Right. Although the private sector surely realised that the takeovers of BANIC, BANAMERICA and a series of smaller banks were a major step towards state control of the economy, loosening the leverage which the bourgeoisie derived from its stockholding, businessmen largely accepted the step as an inevitable one and were relieved to see the state inherit the economic headaches of the finance system. In addition, the tense relationship between the big, pro-Somoza bourgeoisie and the rest of the private sector helped to soften the blow. The presidents of both BANIC and BANAMERICA, with their close personal ties to the dictator, had fled the country in the months preceding the victory, and both had in fact been expelled from the ranks of COSEP.[37] The new government soon followed up the bank nationalisation decree with a recall of all high currency notes of 500 and 1,000 *cordobas*, closing the borders temporarily to prevent Somocistas re-entering the country with stolen currency. The move recovered a useful 180 million *cordobas*, but also provoked the first anti-government demonstrations from small savers irritated by being offered government deposit certificates (redeemable in six months at 8% interest) in exchange for the withdrawn notes.

Armed with this control over banking and foreign trade, the government set about reactivating the crippled industrial and agricultural sectors. The

People's Industrial Corporation (COIP) took over 168 factories from Somoza
and his associates, which are now managed in eight major groups – plastics,
textiles, timber, foodstuffs, pharmaceuticals, building materials, paper,
metal and machinery. The total value of these confiscated industries was
US$197.3 million, and they represented a quarter of all industrial plant in
Nicaragua, employing 13,000 workers of the 65,578 strong industrial labour
force. The speed of COIP reactivation outstripped that of the private sector.
By the beginning of 1980, 81 factories were back in full production and only
17 were still standing completely idle, most of them in the textile industry.
Four months later, the Junta was able to announce that the figure had risen
from 81 to 99, and that the large textile plant El Porvenir would soon be
ready to resume production.[38] In terms of their immediate economic benefit
to the state, however, they were a mixed bag. While the condition of some
came as a pleasant surprise – Somoza had owned many of the most dynamic
industries producing exports for the Central American Common Market –
others were insolvent.[39] Plan 80 drew attention to these initial problems
of state ownership: 'The majority of Somocista enterprises were one of the
most important vehicles for the flight of capital, for which reason their
financial situation is still very precarious.'[40] The anomalies of the state's
inheritance from Somoza faithfully reflected the climate in which industry
and agriculture operated under the dictatorship. Because of Somoza's control
of the state, his factories and farms were protected from free market competition, cushioned by protective legislation, and often ran at a loss, financed
by unsecured loans and Somoza's constant transfer of assets from his private
property to the state and back again to provide phantom collateral for
foreign lenders.[41] Conversely, although many smaller private businesses went
to the wall during the economic collapse of 1979, the privately owned sector
which remains is potentially more dynamic, having survived for so long in
adverse conditions. COSEP is well aware of this: it is one of the private
sector's major advantages.

For all the difficulties experienced in reactivating industrial production,
the Revolution faced its most critical challenge in the vital agricultural sector,
both export crops and basic foodstuffs (beans, rice and maize) for domestic
consumption. Here the recovery of production levels went hand in hand with
the need to initiate a convincing transformation of social relations in the
countryside through an agrarian reform programme which limited itself
initially to the confiscation of all Somoza-owned lands. Agricultural exports
must keep the economy afloat in terms of foreign exchange, domestic
crops must satisfy the anticipated rise in local demand and purchasing
power, and the Revolution must give the peasantry and rural labourers both
political power and improved living standards. The economy still depends
overwhelmingly on the performance of agriculture, which accounts for three-
quarters of foreign currency earnings (chemical products, the major industrial
export, earned a little over 25% of the value of coffee exports in 1978).
Only 52% of the population lives outside the towns, but in fact nearer 70%
is directly or indirectly dependent on agriculture for their livelihood.[42] Job

creation programmes are indeed designed to maintain this balance, with Plan 80's fight against unemployment aiming to create 50,000 new jobs in agriculture — 53% of all new employment.

Agricultural Export Figures For Five Major Crops, 1978

	Total Earnings (US $)	*As % of All Exports*
Coffee	199,600,000	30.9%
Cotton	140,912,000	21.8%
Meat	67,733,000	10.5%
Sugar	19,614,000	3.0%
Bananas	4,799,000	0.7%

Source: Ministerio de Comercio Exterior (MICE).

The confiscation of Somoza's properties gave the Sandinista Government control over 2,012,000 acres of land, 75% of it fully productive. The state also inherited 600 tractors, 28 crop-spraying aircraft and 198,000 head of cattle.[43] Literally overnight, the Sandinistas were faced with the problem of administering their huge inheritance, equivalent to 19.1% of the country's agricultural production. The new agrarian reform institute, INRA, found itself at full stretch. Nor was the dilemma purely an administrative one: to extend expropriations to other parts of the private sector during the first year would certainly jeopardise the economic cooperation of landowners, while state control of less than a fifth of agriculture was unlikely to satisfy the peasants' urgent demand for land. In the case of the two major export crops, the public ownership figure was even lower. The state owns a mere 13.3% of cotton lands, and only a little more — 15% — of coffee plantations.[44] While the control of export marketing breaks into the private sector's crucial direct links with overseas markets, these patterns of ownership presented the state with two sharply differentiated problems. Privately owned cotton is predominantly in the hands of large and medium-sized planters, many of them loyal to Alfonso Robelo's MDN and other right-wing parties. Their willingness to restore full production in early 1980 after the previous year's disastrous 80% decline in cotton exports was a key test of the private sector's willingness to cooperate with the new government, and its potential capacity for economic blackmail. Coffee ownership was an entirely different proposition. It is 70% owned by a vast network of small peasant producers without any clearly defined political loyalties. Here, the battle was to be for their organisation and cooperativisation, and for their allegiance either to the state or to the private enterprise lobby in the growing conflict over distribution and internal trade.

The clamour for land from the dispossessed peasants and small proprietors who produce 24% of the country's agricultural output (including 80% of basic grains and almost 100% of vegetables) cannot be easily or rapidly satisfied. The inequalities of land ownership generated by Somocista capitalism will take years to remove. The Revolution found that tiny farms of less than 10 *manzanas* (17.2 acres) account for 41.6% of all properties, but only 2.2% of land area. The large *latifundios* of more than 500 *manzanas* (860 acres) are by contrast only 1.8% of all properties, but take up a full 47.5% of all agricultural land.[45] And that land is the most fertile in the country, the result of decades of theft and expulsions by the cotton and other land barons. These big private estates employ 300,000 agricultural labourers — almost nine-tenths of the economically active rural population — for the four months of the annual harvest. For the rest of the year, these labourers scratch out a subsistence living growing basic grains. The state must now supply them with cheaply rented lands and credit, for *Somocismo* — which directed 90% of agricultural credits towards large scale export crop cultivation — traditionally left the peasantry in the clutches of money-lenders. The social consequences of these rural inequalities are alarming: 68% rural illiteracy, 94% of homes in the countryside without drinking water, infant mortality running at 120 per 1000.[46] To combat these evils requires massive financing, and from an economy in crisis; to fail to combat them is to place at risk the sympathy of the peasant population for the Revolution.

If we have examined the challenges to industry and agriculture separately, it is precisely because the economics of *Somocismo* brought about a complete dislocation of the two sectors. Nicaragua presents the common phenomenon of a predominantly agricultural economy whose needs are not serviced in any sense by local industry. The particular form of distorted industrialisation stimulated in the 1960s by the Central American Common Market left agriculture totally dependent on imported inputs — seeds, fertilisers, insecticides, machinery, plant and technology, vehicles and spares. Nor were local agricultural raw materials processed in the country for domestic consumption: exported cotton fibre, for example, had to be reimported as finished cloth. Realistically the eradication of these economic distortions can only be a middle-to long-term objective.[47']

In the move towards state regulation of the economy, Nicaragua will at least avoid the head-on conflicts with US and foreign capital which for Cuba marked a decisive point in the early development of its Revolution. Direct foreign investment in Nicaragua is far less significant than in Cuba and the Sandinistas' only move against foreign capital has been the decrees nationalising natural resources, giving the state control over mining, fisheries and forestry. Some areas, like fishing companies and the geothermal energy project at the volcano of Momotombo near Managua, had already passed into public ownership with the decree confiscating Somoza's own properties. But here again, the economic weight of these confiscations is offset by the political dilemmas presented by industries located (with the exception of the goldmine of El Limon in the *departamento* of Leon) in the Atlantic Coast province of Zelaya, whose population, even after a year, remained largely marginal to the Revolution. Nicaragua's gold and silver mining centres at Bonanza, Siuna and La Rosita in Northern Zelaya were nationalised by decree on 2 November 1979. They had been owned previously by the American and Canadian Neptune, Rosario and Septentrion mining companies, and while production levels are currently low — 1979 gold earnings were a mere US $7.9 million[48] — prevailing high gold prices and the previous owners' short-sighted attitude to investment and seam exploration offered major possibilities for expanding the industry into a significant foreign currency earner. But the mines of Northern Zelaya are a microcosm of the Revolution's most delicate industrial and trade union problems. COIP industries everywhere are a vital breeding-ground for future relations of production, but for the moment they are administered by state managers, not yet by the workers themselves. In the mines this has often proved disastrous, for they are one facet of the FSLN's uphill struggle to integrate the Atlantic Coast region into the mainstream of the Revolution.

'Nicaragua is really two countries — the Pacific and the Atlantic', Nicaraguans are apt to remark, and there is much truth in the comment. Although the jungles and savannahs of the Costa Atlantica to the east constitute half the country's land area, only 193,835 people live there — under 9% of the national population.[49] Ethnically, they are quite separate from the mainly *mestizo* population of the west, a complex mixture of black descendants of slaves imported by the English and three indigenous Indian tribes. In the northern part of this region, Miskito Indians predominate — the largest of the indigenous groups. On the coast, English-speaking blacks are the majority, while small remnants of Sumo and Rama Indians cling to their precarious identity near the Honduran border and in the south. Frequently the Sumo and Miskito will have nothing to do with each other, the relic of ancient conflicts over land. Isolated black communities have at least five distinct ethnic and linguistic groupings. Many Miskito Indians hark back nostalgically to the region's days as a British protectorate ruled by London-designated 'kings', and see the Revolution as granting them the freedom to further their separatist dreams.

The Atlantic population works in the goldmines and fishing ports, or the lumber camps and sawmills of the interior. Others are plantation labourers or subsistence farmers, and in the remoter areas pre-capitalist forms of agriculture survived. Internal transport is almost non-existent, the area accessible from the Pacific only by a daily DC-3 and riverboat services, or an earth road from Matagalpa to the mining settlement of Siuna, open for two months of the year. Even so, many Costa Atlantica inhabitants were profoundly ambivalent about the integration offered by the Sandinista Revolution. 'Somoza neglected us, but at least he left us alone' was one comment which reflects a widespread mistrust.[50] The *costenos* did not participate actively in the insurrection; many indeed only learned of it weeks later. All this makes it fertile ground for the counter-revolutionary Right, and as the Revolution faces growing threats from that direction its biggest challenge is to come to terms with these real cultural and racial obstacles which can, all too easily but mistakenly, be reduced to security problems.

In the nationalised goldmines, ramshackle collections of timber and zinc buildings deep in the hilly rain forests of the north, the Miskito work force has begun to come to terms with the Revolution, but major obstacles remain. As the miners disappear underground on the morning shift, the racism inherited from the American mineowners becomes apparent. Those who disappear in the cage are wholly Miskito; the surface workers and office personnel are *mestizo* or white. 'It's no good trying to teach these Indians a skill' was the comment of one surface worker who remained behind after the Revolution. 'After a couple of months here, they just get bored and drift back to their villages.'[51] It was unavoidable that such attitudes should survive the Revolution, for they were deeply ingrained in the personnel who remained. All mining company transactions were conducted in English, and the FSLN had no ready supply of trained technicians to decipher them. To make matters worse, the Miskito workers have no tradition of trade union organisation, and although now affiliated to the Sandinista Workers Federation (CST), each of the three main mines came out on strike within months of the July victory and little early headway was made in educating the workforce politically about the reasons for the Revolution's inability to improve their wages and working conditions overnight. Faceworkers, exposed to the near certainty of early death or disability from silicosis, still earned a basic wage of US $0.47 an hour in mid-1980. The first appointed union officials proved both corrupt and inefficient. And, to make matters worse, plant managers and technicians brought in by the state mining agency, CONDEMINAH, were often accused of insensitivity to local problems in an area where the Sandinista Revolution is still largely seen as 'a change of government in the west.' CONDEMINAH Director-General Enrique Lacayo explained: 'There was tremendous distance between the state and the miners in Bonanza, a great lack of trust on the part of the workers. In Rosita we had a complete disaster. The officials we appointed kept aloof from the work force. They worked according to totally petty-bourgeois criteria.'[52] With a critical shortage of trained personnel and political cadres, the Revolution continues — inevitably — to come up against similar problems, though to a lesser degree, in other publicly owned COIP industries. On occasion, the result can be a breakdown of confidence between workers and government, a perception of the state as merely 'the new boss'.

Finally, the conflict over distribution is emerging as a crucial facet in the Nicaraguan class struggle, as it did in the Chile of Allende's Popular Unity. It would be the wildest ultra-left fantasy to consider nationalising the vast network of tiny *comerciantes* who control local trade in Nicaragua. Furthermore, unemployment has swelled their numbers still more. In Managua's Mercado Oriental alone, the number of street traders leapt from 6,000 to 10,000 in the first three months of the Revolution. However, there is legal provision for partial state control over distribution through the Ministry of Internal Trade (MICOIN). 'In particular cases, and where the national interest so demands, the state shall have powers to purchase part of a product in order to ensure direct distribution to the consumer.'[53] The enemies here of course are speculators and hoarders, and the key to successful food distribution lies in the harmony between state agencies (ENABAS and MICOIN) and the evolving role of the mass organisations, in the CDSs' efficiency at controlling distribution and identifying and understanding how speculation works. Already there have been major problems over adequate sugar and salt supplies, and speculators have been aided and abetted by accusations from the right-wing daily *La Prensa* that government production figures are inaccurate. This is a point to which we shall return later.

Over the first year, *campesino* producers received guaranteed high prices for their food produce, not only as a result of the generosity of state financing but because prices were conditioned by a market with built-in shortages after the war, and where purchasing power rose with the strengthening of the social wage. This has generated a 20% increase in food demand,[54] and with greater consumption levels the battle for mass organisation control of pricing and distribution assumes even greater importance. For the moment, the main channels of food distribution at ENABAS-regulated prices are the Expendios Populares, controlled by the Sandinista Defence Committees; factory-based Consumers' Cooperatives set up on the initiative of the CST; rural foodstores run by the ATC; municipal markets overseen by local revolutionary *juntas;* and finally the network of small shopkeepers and independent tradespeople. In the first four, without having actual ownership, the state and mass organisations exercise considerable powers of control. It is the last group, which is still the largest, around whom the battle is still being fought.

Socialism and a Mixed Economy

One thing was clear in all this, both in Plan 80 and in every major pronouncement of the FSLN on the economy and the concept of national unity: the private sector was to have a major role in economic reconstruction, but that role had to be understood as secondary, secondary on the political plane to the hegemonic role of the FSLN, and secondary on the economic level to the overriding interests of the workers and peasants.

By the end of the Revolution's first year the challenge from the Right was mounting, and foreign support for one or other sector of the bourgeoisie ranged from Carter Administration doves to the paramilitary death squads of Guatemala City and San Salvador. It would be dangerously naive to suppose that each strand of reactionary opinion pitted against the Sandinistas wished to drown the Revolution in blood and reimpose a right-wing dictatorship, or that private sector opposition to the government was a monolithic plot in which the CIA pulled the strings. The lack of bourgeois reforms in Somoza's Nicaragua left a fragmented class which overwhelmingly accepted the need for armed insurrection, and reluctantly accepted the need for this to take place under left-wing leadership. After the victory, large segments of the middle class also accepted the new guidelines for capitalist activity. Others adopted a wait-and-see approach, some opted for economic sabotage, others still for active collaboration with the armed Right. These are crude categories, with an infinite variety of finer shadings, but in general they held true until the early summer of 1980, when the resignation of Alfonso Robelo from the ruling Junta made for a clearer alignment of forces.

But the private sector's attempt to wring concessions from the Government of National Reconstruction proved after a year that they were not strong enough economically to project a restoration of a capitalist economy which could satisfy the class interests of the dominant sectors of the Right. The space for ambiguity had shrunk, and the battle lines between the Revolution (in which we include a substantial part of the petty bourgeoisie) and those who oppose it had been clearly drawn. The tactics which the Right would adopt thereafter depended on the course of events in Central America, the degree of unity which the Right could muster, and its willingness to accept the premise that the current balance of forces ruled out any idea of supplanting the Sandinista Government short of using armed force.

By April 1980, COSEP and its class allies had shown that whatever their rhetoric about displaying 'a patriotic spirit in the interests of the majority of the Nicaraguan people', they were unwilling to accept the 'rules of the game' as laid down in Plan 80:

> Private enterprise is considered an active subject of reactivation, especially in critical areas such as agriculture, industry, exports and internal trade. The participation of private enterprise in economic reactivation, through its technical contribution and the productive investment of its profits, will allow the 'rules of the game' to be defined progressively in the course of the process, in which private enterprise will discover – not theoretically but historically – the original role which it can play in building the new Nicaraguan economy.[55]

An 'original role' was not enough. COSEP demanded influence over government as its birthright. The Sandinista Government had shown its good faith promptly. On 7 August 1979 the Junta restored to INDE and the Chambers of Commerce the legal titles stripped from them by Somoza. In return, the bourgeoisie offered only complaints that 'the private sector feels itself absent from the decisions of government', 'provisional allies in an uncomfortable coexistence'.[56] The Democratic Conservatives for their part spoke of a 'climate of social anarchy', complained that 'the businessman must have economic incentives' and demanded that the aim of the agrarian reform should be to 'transform the proletarian into a property owner'.[57] Much private industry continued to stagnate. On 8 February 1980, *Barricada* praised small businessmen's willingness to pay taxes, contrasting this with widespread tax defaulting by the bigger industrialists. The tone of private sector complaints became more strident, to the extent that Enrique Dreyfus, president of INDE, actually claimed at the Institute's conference on 29 February that civic action had been more important in bringing down Somoza than the armed struggle! On 28 March, Vice-Minister of Planning Federico Cerda spelt out in cold figures what FSLN good faith and business intransigence had meant. In 1980, state credits committed to the private sector would total 3,247 million *cordobas*, of which 953 million would go to industry, 1,797 million to agriculture and 497 million to commerce. Against this, private sector hostility meant that only 296 of Nicaragua's 663 industrial enterprises were operating at full capacity, with a major crisis of reactivation in textiles, which it had been intended would earn more than 100 million *cordobas* in exports during 1980. To justify its economic vandalism, the private sector resorted to a favourite tactic: accusing the FSLN of breaking alleged written agreements offering solid guarantees to bourgeois economic interests. COSEP invoked the by now legendary Pact of Puntarenas, supposedly witnessed by US and Latin American politicians, and drew an angry response from Sergio Ramirez:

> No such Puntarenas Pact or anything like it exists. I think some people in this country, carried away by the old mentality that prevailed in Nicaragua in the time of Somoza, still think in terms of pacts. It would be ridiculous to suggest that the FSLN or the Junta ever signed any sort of pact. Signing pacts also used to mean signing them in the presence of foreign representatives. Perhaps what we are being reminded of is that we made a commitment in front of foreigners. We never committed ourselves to any kind of concessions.

Meanwhile, the mass organisation denunciations of economic sabotage flooded in. The Plastinic Factory was accused of falsification of invoices and tax evasion; the US multinational Sears of concealing capital and sacking workers while continuing to obtain loans from the National Development Bank; the SOVIPE engineering company of threatening to close down its plant because of an alleged lack of raw materials. Several companies were charged with undermining their Nicaraguan operations in favour of outlets in other Central American countries: Standard Steel was accused of stockpiling raw materials in Guatemala and running down its Managua plant; the INCA metalworking plant of doing the same in Honduras; Sears (again) of shipping out capital and goods to Costa Rica and El Salvador. The CST reported that 29,000 workers in Managua alone were not receiving the minimum wage levels laid down under the Somocista code, even before the Junta's June wage decree which was in turn boycotted by hundreds of local employers.

In the countryside, it was a similar story. Landowners were accused by the ATC of systematically neglecting harvests, herds and machinery. The Standard Fruit Company was alleged to be draining capital from the seventeen banana plantations which it leased to local concessionnaires in the *departamento* of Chinandega, while continuing to pay its 3,800 workers starvation wages averaging only US $30 a month. Hundreds of farm labourers were laid off by coffee plantation owners who claimed that their crops had been affected by the *roya* coffee blight, a claim refuted by ATC officials and inspectors from the Ministry of Labour. There was growing pressure on idle lands as a result of *latifundistas'* refusal to rent them out as before to small peasant farmers. The landowners retorted angrily that the government was turning a blind eye to 'illegal' land invasions.

But the government's major fear was how this economic assault from groups unwilling to accept the rules of the game would affect prospects for the crucial cotton crop. INRA had set a planting target of 179,000 *manzanas* (307,880 acres) of which the private sector controlled 87%. A handful of large landowners were responsible for bringing in 40% of the 1980 crop. 'Our target for cotton production,' said Planning Minister Henry Ruiz, 'is in plain and simple terms a matter of life and death to pull us out of economic stagnation.'[58] There were very real reasons for the government's anxiety at this critical test of private enterprise intentions. The cotton planters of Leon and Chinandega were among the most influential members of the Nicaraguan bourgeoisie, not only through their vigorous role in COSEP and the agricultural producers' union UPANIC, but as a substantial part of the power base of Robelo's MDN. Preparations for cotton planting began in late April, and on the 22nd of that month Robelo resigned from the Junta, accusing the government of a drift towards 'totalitarianism'. INRA waited anxiously for cotton planting figures to come in. When they did, they proved an encouraging token of the FSLN's persuasiveness and the remaining good sense of the private sector. True, they were down on expectations, but only by 21%, with a final count of 141,139 *manzanas* (242,759 acres) sown.

Consolidating the Economy

At the end of the first year Arturo Cruz — formerly president of the Banco Central and by now a member of the Junta — noted that 'all available indicators point to a vigorous process of reactivation, significantly stronger in the COIP and in small businesses.'[59] As far as agriculture was concerned, on the one hand Nicaragua's abundance of natural resources and fertile agricultural land, its relative diversification of export crops and intensive use of farmlands traditionally left idle, made for optimistic mid-term forecasts. But at the same time, Cruz's statement is another way of saying that private sector recovery gives grounds for anxiety, and even in the key agricultural sector results have been variable. In an interview with *Barricada*, Agriculture Minister Jaime Wheelock ascribed this to a number of factors: the post-Revolutionary expectations of rural workers, their lack of political education (with its inevitable corollary, the large amount of potentially productive time necessarily spent on political organisation and trade union study), the difficulties in establishing the labour discipline necessary for the transitional period, and some initial peasant resistance to the notion of cooperativisation. But he reserved his harsh comments for the private landowners' group UPANIC, protesting that 'the private sector is going to have to make quite major concessions if it is to live with us in the new society.'[60]

Notwithstanding private sector hesitations, first-year economic figures when published showed Cruz to be substantially right. Results were encouraging. Of major agricultural products, only beef exports failed to measure up to Plan 80 targets. The crippled textile industry accounted almost single-handedly for the shortfall in industrial output. In the period from July 1979 to December 1980, inflation fell from 84.3% to 17.5%.[61] Unemployment too was slashed, surpassing the aims of Plan 80, although businessmen carped that this reflected above all the expansion of the state bureaucracy. The Frente conceded the point, and now speak of streamlining the government during 1981. It is a minor quibble, and a glance at basic statistics will confirm that the FSLN can be satisfied with the economic results of their first year in power.

Job Creation in 1980

Sector	Plan 80 Target	Actual New Jobs
Agriculture	50,000	44,700
Industry	10,000	7,700
Construction	15,000	5,400
Other Production	–	1,800
Services	20,000	31,700
Commerce	–	21,000
Total	*95,000*	*112,300*

Source: *Plan 81*, p. 22.

Agricultural Production in 1980

Crop	% of Production Target Achieved
Cotton	102.2
Coffee	104.2
Sugar	112.1
Beef	91.5
Rice	130.5
Maize	120.3
Beans	102.1
Sorghum	175.0

Source: *Plan 81*, pp. 31-3.

Agriculture had exceeded almost all targets. Equally encouraging was productivity in the processing of export crops, helped along by regular Workers' Production Councils and thrice-annual Production Assemblies. In sugar for example, where the state owns five of the six refineries, productivity in one refinery leapt after the Revolution by 95%. Industry meanwhile restored 91% of 1978 production levels, showing real growth of 7.3%

over 1979. Largely offsetting losses in the textile industry was a windfall, which even the best planned revolutions need. It came from the problematic goldmines of the Atlantic Coast, the result of a steep rise in world prices. Here, Plan 80 had aimed for 60,000 ounces of gold with an export value of US $23.4 million. In the event, production rose to 67,000 ounces and export earnings leapt to US $39.9 million.[62]

Thus both internal factors, which the FSLN and the Government of National Reconstruction can to a large extent influence, and external factors such as the foreign debt, condition the rate of economic recovery. By mid-1980 – despite the successes of the first reactivation plan – there were definite signs that the demand for austerity would be even greater in 1981, with genuine threats of shortages, further wage restraint and middle-class discontent at income redistribution, falling levels of luxury consumption and the distribution of essential goods to favour the working class. After 1979's 'Year of Liberation' and 1980's 'Year of Literacy', 1981 was officially titled by the FSLN 'Year of Defence and Production' with the secondary title 'Year of Austerity and Efficiency', 'During this year,' said Cruz bluntly, 'we have consumed too many non-essential imported products. We cannot be content with current levels of output. We are carrying an external debt out of all proportion to our productive capacity. The cost of the petroleum we consume and the servicing of the debt takes up 60% of the currency earned by our exports, which seriously threatens our scope for reinvesting the surplus generated by our people.' And this despite the preferential terms granted on oil supplies from Mexico and Venezuela. Imports were bound to rise far above the abnormally low $360 million of 1979. Plan 80 called for imports of $773 million, but in fact these rose to $870 million, largely as a result of increased internal demand which could not be satisfied by local industry, and uncontrollable fuel bills.[63]

In facing its external debt, the new Nicaraguan Government had to face one of its starkest political decisions: whether to follow the initial inclination to declare the debt 'the responsibility of the international community', and so risk financial blacklisting by the West; or to renegotiate the debt on favourable terms. It went for the second option, refusing only outstanding sums for arms shipments from Israel and Argentina. The US $1.64 billion total debt is made up 70% of government debts and the remaining 30% (roughly US $500 million) of loans contracted by BANIC and BANAMERICA, inherited by the state when the banking system was nationalised. The main sticking point in the renegotiation was with private banks – mainly North American – which had financed Somoza on harsh terms towards the end of his rule. 'The money was often lent to private Nicaraguan companies. But the loans were guaranteed by state entities such as INFONAC (the industrial development agency) and BAVINIC (the housing development bank). The private companies were generally owned by the Somoza family or its associates, and were often already mortgaged to the hilt. But the international banks made their loans on the basis of the state guarantees, rather than the strength of the borrowers.'[64]

During the protracted renegotiation of the debt, which started in Mexico City in December 1979 and ended almost nine months later, the private banks (led by Citibank) put up stiff resistance to terms which, when finally agreed, were considerably more lenient than those traditionally supplied to wayward Latin American governments. Both sides gained from the agreement: the bankers by avoiding the precedent of default and winning recognition of commercial interest rates; Nicaragua by winning a five-year grace period — the crucial time-scale for effective economic restructuring — and keeping the necessary measure of goodwill from Western financial institutions. Nonetheless, the closeness of a Ronald Reagan presidency and bankers such as Citibank is a further element in the threats which Nicaragua will face from a Republican White House in 1981 and after.

Washington and other enemies of the Sandinista Revolution are well aware of the objective problems of the Nicaraguan economy, not only the external debt but the difficulties of getting agricultural and industrial production going again, the existence of a parallel dollar market and the possible threat of a devalued *cordoba,* inflation, unemployment and the continuing need for foreign aid. They will use these as a framework for economic destabilisation. It is easy to predict the methods they will resort to in heightening the crisis: withholding much-needed aid and undermining the leadership of the Revolution by encouraging strikes and popular discontent, speculators and the production saboteurs of the Right.[65]

In the short term there is no chance of Nicaragua applying to private lenders for aid. Low currency reserves mean that the country could offer no security of repayment. For the first three years at least, aid will have to come from 'soft' lenders, whether sympathetic foreign governments or multilateral agencies. By the end of 1979, the government's International Reconstruction Fund (FIR) had received loan offers of US $490 million. Of this total, $370 million was delivered in 1980, although this included $177 million in loans already promised to Somoza by the World Bank, the IDB and USAID, and now diverted into new projects. Repayment terms, with average interest of 3.9% and a thirty-two-year repayment period, are the customary soft terms offered by the multilateral agencies. Elsewhere, cash has come from the international friendships built by the FSLN in the late 1970s. Nicaragua has received US $130 million in straight donations, primarily from Mexico, Venezuela, Cuba, West Germany, Holland and Sweden, and $128 million in government loans — including $30 million from the GDR — with as much again awaiting ratification.

In contrast, the Revolution's most celebrated battle over foreign aid has been the $75 million package requested by President Jimmy Carter immediately after the war, and destined 60% for the Nicaraguan private sector. On 11 September 1979, Assistant Secretary of State for Inter-American Affairs, Viron Vaky, promised that the $75 million would be despatched 'in a week'. A year later, as the pre-election crisis of Jimmy Carter deepened and the conservative line in the administration's divided Central American policy asserted itself, the loan had still not been sent. It is beyond

the scope of this study to analyse fully the Congressional debates and secret
hearings which blocked the aid package, but the issue mirrored the split
between the Republican Right, which believes that Nicaragua is already lost
to 'international Communism', and the Democratic Liberals whose hope was,
to bolster the private sector and salvage bourgeois democracy in Nicaragua.
In February, COSEP showed its own enthusiasm for the State Department
line by sending a high-level delegation to Washington led by Enrique Dreyfus
to lobby senators for the upcoming debate. Five months later, Nicaragua's
Foreign Minister Miguel D'Escoto praised what seemed to be final Congressional approval of the $75 million: 'This is a triumph for the progressive forces
of Congress, led by our great friend Senator Sorinsky and Ambassador
Laurence Pezzullo who has played a very important role . . . ' He also
approved 'the desire of President Carter not only to maintain but to deepen
friendly relations with Nicaragua and to respect our right to self-
determination.' With a Reagan victory in November 1980, any hopes of the
US Government continuing that respect are dead. Nicaragua has entered a
phase of outright Washington hostility, and its carefully constructed friendships with the Socialist countries, the Non-Aligned Movement, social
democracy and other Latin American democracies become a more pressing
strategic priority than ever.

Notes

1. *Barricada,* 20 July 1980.
2. *Ibid.*
3. *ATC Asamblea Nacional Constitutiva: Memorias* (Managua, SENAPEP, 1980), p. 74.
4. *Ibid.,* p. 11.
5. *Poder Sandinista,* No. 12, 10 January 1980.
6. Press conference after the resignation of businessman and MDN leader Alfonso Robelo from the government Junta, 23 April 1980.
7. Carlos Nunez, 'La Revolucion y las Organizaciones de los Trabajadores' in *La Revolucion a traves de Nuestra Direccion Nacional* (Managua, SENAPEP, 1980), p. 69.
8. Bayardo Arce, *El Papel de las Fuerzas Motrices antes y despues del Triunfo,* speech to assembly of teaching staff of the Universidad Centroamericana (UCA), Managua, July 1980.
9. Particularly in the first months of the Revolution, corruption and abuses continued to be widespread as the new machinery of government took shape. These practices were both acknowledged and severely criticised by the FSLN. See for example Tomas Borge, *Los Derechos Humanos y la Revolucion Nicaraguense,* speech to Interamerican Human Rights Commission, 10 October 1980 (Managua, Ediciones Patria Libre, 1981), pp. 40-2. In later months, FSLN complaints were increasingly directed at administrative incompetence and the frequent failure of bureaucrats to implement government programmes swiftly enough.

10. Within the country, these criticisms came initially from two left-wing groups hostile to the FSLN: the Partido Comunista de Nicaragua (nominally loyal to Moscow but rejected by the USSR which regards the Partido Socialista Nicaraguense as its fraternal party) and the small Movimiento de Accion Popular-Frente Obrero, a pro-Albanian group. Both subsequently moderated their criticisms and declined in influence after mid-1980. For a fuller discussion of their role, see Chapter 15.
11. Regis Debray; *A Critique of Arms*, p. 63.
12. Interview with Jorge Timossi, August 1979.
13. *Linea de Propaganda de la Revolucion Sandinista: Documento de Estudio* (Managua, SENAPEP, 1980).
14. *Statute on the Rights of Nicaraguans*, 21 August 1979, Section 2, Paragraph 27.
15. COSEP communique to the Junta and FSLN National Directorate, 14 November 1979.
16. *Barricada*, 3 March 1980.
17. COSEP, *loc. cit.*
18. Interview with Democratic Conservative Party (PCD) politician, Diriamba, July 1980.
19. Interview with FSLN militant, Managua, March 1980.
20. Jaime Wheelock, speech to *Asamblea de Compromiso*, Ministry of Agricultural Development, 14 July 1980.
21. Dr. Valpy Fitzgerald, economic adviser to the Ministry of Planning, interviewed in *Latin America Weekly Report*, WR-80-09, 29 February 1980.
22. Banco Central de Nicaragua, *Informe Anual 1977*, p. 53.
23. Interview with FSLN comandante Omar Cabezas, Managua, August 1980.
24. *Programa de Reactivacion Economica en Beneficio del Pueblo*, (Managua, SENAPEP, 1980), p. 13.
25. *Plan 80*, p. 21.
26. *Ibid.*, p. 73.
27. *Ibid.*, p. 128.
28. *Ibid.*, p. 6.
29. *Ibid.*, p. 13.
30. Reprinted in *Latin America Weekly Report*, WR-79-08, 21 December 1979.
31. *Barricada*, 6 January 1980.
32. *Barricada*, 30 December 1979.
33. See *Intercontinental Press*, 27 December 1979.
34. Interviewed in the news magazine *Ya Veremos*, Managua, June 1980.
35. *Plan 80*, p. 70.
36. *Ibid.*, p. 114.
37. *Latin America Economic Report*, Vol. VII, No. 31, 10 August 1979.
38. *Mensaje de la Junta de Gobierno de Reconstruccion Nacional al Pueblo Nicaraguense* (Managua, SENAPEP, 1980), p. 18.
39. Dr.Valpy Fitzgerald in *Latin America Regional Report*, RM-80-03, 21 March 1980.
40. *Plan 80*, p. 20.
41. *Latin America Economic Report*, Vol. VII, No. 42, 26 October 1979.

42. *Datos Basicos sobre Nicaragua*, p. 7.
43. *Mensaje de la Junta de Gobierno de Reconstruccion Nacional al Pueblo Nicaraguense*, p. 11.
44. *Datos Basicos sobre Nicaragua*, p. 23.
45. *Objetivos y Alcances de la Reforma Agraria Nicaraguense* (pamphlet), (Managua, INRA, 1979).
46. *Ibid.*
47. *La Revolucion y el Campo*, (Managua, INRA, 1980) p. 5.
48. *Plan 80*, p. 57.
49. *Datos Basicos sobre Nicaragua*, p. 7.
50. Comment by a Miskito Indian from the Atlantic Coast port of Puerto Cabezas, interview in Managua, February 1980.
51. Interview with a machine-shop foreman at Bonanza, Zelaya Norte, August 1980.
52. *The Open Veins of Nicaragua* (report by the Nicaragua Solidarity Campaign to the National Union of Mineworkers) (London, NSC, 1980).
53. *Plan 80*, p. 54.
54. *Latin America Weekly Report*, WR-80-33, 22 August 1980.
55. *Plan 80*, p. 14.
56. COSEP communique, 14 November 1979.
57. El Partido Conservador Democrata; Una Esperanza para Nicaragua in *La Prensa*, 8 December 1979.
58. *Barricada*, 30 December 1979.
59. In *Un Ano Despues* (Managua, Oficina de Divulgacion y Prensa de la Junta de Gobierno de Reconstruccion Nacional, 1980).
60. *Barricada*, 29 June 1980.
61. *Programa Economico de Austeridad y Eficiencia* (*'Plan 81'*) (Managua, Ministerio de Planificacion, January 1981), p. 82.
62. *Ibid.*, p. 53.
63. *Ibid.*, p. 66.
64. *Latin America Economic Report*, Vol. VII, No. 42., 26 October 1979.
65. See analysis of CIA and other subversion by former CIA agent Philip Agee, translated into Spanish as *La CIA y sus Objetivos: Como Trabaja la Contrarrevolucion* and published in the CST newspaper *El Trabajador*, Managua, March 1980.

12. Revolutionary Democracy and Revolutionary Power

A People in Arms

'A new National Army will be organised . . . composed of combatants of the FSLN, soldiers and officers who have behaved with integrity and patriotism in the face of the dictatorship's corruption and repression, and those who have taken part in the struggle to overthrow the Somoza regime.'[1]

The definition of the new army, written at the height of the war, had to assume the survival of some remnants of the National Guard, although the institution as such would disappear. But the stupidity of 'someone or other called Urcuyo' assured the destruction of the Guard, the possibility of creating a wholly new state, and military control of that state by the revolutionary vanguard. Furthermore, FSLN control of the armed forces had been a basic element of the understanding reached by the Frente and the bourgeois opposition during the war. 'Even more important, it is a direct reflection of reality. That is to say, it corresponds to the fundamental role played by the FSLN in the military overthrow of the dictatorship.'[2] Finding 'honest elements' of the National Guard proved virtually impossible: a couple of pilots for the new Sandinista Air Force, a police Major, and finally the short-lived Minister of Defence Bernardino Larios, who made no public appearances, was replaced by Humberto Ortega in the December cabinet reshuffle and subsequently had to be sentenced to eight years in prison for leading a conspiracy to assassinate the FSLN National Directorate.

The existence of a people's army is the cornerstone of the Nicaraguan Revolution. The FSLN has put an end to two decades of bitter experiences for the Latin American Left, in which governments came and went while armies remained. The Frente's own history as a revolutionary organisation has exactly spanned — and drawn the lessons from — those two decades. In the 1960s it refused to be drawn into the *foquista* excesses which led to disastrous defeats in Venezuela and elsewhere; by striving to create unbreakable links with the masses. In the 1970s, the other lesson — of a people united but without arms, as in Chile — is too obvious to be stated here. Liberal militarism may have been in the heads of some younger Tercerista *recruits*, but it was anathema to the FSLN's vision of the armed

223

struggle as the highest expression of the mass struggle. The phrase 'People's Army' is no mere turn of rhetoric. To any visitor, the sight of teenage soldiers giving each other piggybacks outside the Casa de Gobierno, *comandantes* dancing in the street in religious festivals, the atmosphere of relaxed trust between the people and the military, make it an immediate reality. To idealise this face of the Sandinista People's Army (EPS) would be wrong: another side of the coin is the dismissal of hundreds of troops for indiscipline. Both show the roots of the new army. Luis Carrion, speaking to troops at the Selim Shible military school, named after an early FSLN martyr, traced the uniqueness of the Sandinista army: 'We have this difference from almost every revolutionary experience in the world: elsewhere, regular armies were clearly formed, and in the course of a relatively prolonged struggle were consolidated and structured. The participation of the masses in the war was less direct. Our own case is quite different, and for that reason the kind of army we have in victory is quite different.'[3]

By the end of the war, the FSLN had more than 15,000 combatants under arms. Eighteen months earlier the National Guard had outnumbered them by ten to one. Of these 15,000, 2,000 formed a regular army on the Frente Sur and Frente Nor-Occidental. Another 3,000 were guerrilla forces in the north and east. But more than 10,000 were irregular militias and spontaneous combatants in the urban areas. Carrion went on to compare the combat effectiveness of these different groups, and the lessons which the FSLN had learned from the mass struggle: 'I remember when we used to theorise about military organisation in clandestinity, we would draw the distinction between what we called 'select' units, and the militia units with less combat capacity, less experience, less training. But the fact of the matter is that when the offensive came, all those ideas melted away: in most cases the most combative units turned out to be the irregular militias.'[4]

The heterogeneous make-up of the FSLN's forces in the insurrection presented real political and military obstacles to the subsequent formation of a disciplined, politicised army. The last days of July were chaos, with few units intact, troops straggling back to the capital from the various battlefronts and *milicianos* careering through the streets in commandeered vehicles daubed with FSLN slogans. Within days, Managua's fields and empty lots were crammed with wrecked cars and military trucks. On the 29th, the National Directorate took the first steps towards structuring the army, naming Humberto Ortega, Carrion and Borge to the Comandancia General, and appointing Joaquin Cuadra, a leading *comandante* from the Frente Interno, as head of the General Staff of the EPS. On 22 August the first new units were formally created. In an interview with *Prensa Latina*, Carrion described the Sandinista military's most urgent priorities:

'One of our major concerns currently is to blend the different forces — the regular army units of the Frente Sur, the guerrilla units, the urban combat brigades, spontaneous mass combatants and militias — into a single entity. It is very important to explain to each of them their complementary role in the war to overcome the natural tendency towards fragmentation.

Our idea is to build a relatively small army, with great mobility and combat readiness. There are basic economic reasons for that, which prevent us from having a different or larger scale army. According to our experience, this army should be intimately related with a force capable of taking up arms at short notice: the militias, who played an essential role in the war. We will have two kinds of militias: one permanently mobilised, and another with relative mobility.

But the character of our popular army will not come from its operational structure, but from its politicisation and its objectives . . . In it, there is a large percentage of workers, both rural and urban. There are also many students. As far as age goes, it is basically a very young army. The average member is 20 or 22 years old. There is also a notable number of women, for whom special units will be created.[5]

The EPS then has made no pretence of being an apolitical force. Its explicit aim is to defend the conquests of the Revolution. It has a seat on the Council of State, its soldiers were given priority in the *alfabetizacion*. Military training intermingles with constant political education. At first, these classes concentrated on building a consciousness of the EPS as the direct inheritors of Nicaragua's tradition of mass struggle — the war against the military adventures of William Walker in 1856, Indian uprisings of the 1880s, the resistance of Zeledon, and above all Sandino. From there, they moved on to building awareness of the class character of the army. In the police, now created as an autonomous force for the first time, the emphasis was on their role as servants of the people. The army has been constantly alert to the dangers of infiltration by both right-wing Somocistas and cadres from the ultra-left Frente Obrero and Partido Comunista. The low level of political consciousness affects all ranks, and is more acute among men than women. While women have often put their political understanding into civilian tasks, the hundreds of disaffected working-class youths who joined the armed struggle in the final months must be kept in the EPS at all costs, for it is here above all that the Revolution, through constant political education and practical experience, can best hope to build them into fully-fledged Sandinista cadres.

For the first six months, the question of the militias became a fraught political debate. The Nicaraguan ultra-left angrily accused the FSLN of 'disarming the people' a cry taken up by some Marxists abroad. But the restructuring and temporary demobilisation of the militias responded to an objective political necessity. Although there was brief discussion of a permanent disbanding of the militias, in view of the possible later introduction of compulsory military service, two factors convinced the FSLN that they were essential: Nicaragua's vulnerability to attack, and the people's own will to take part in the armed defence of the Revolution. The country's geography lays it open to Somocista attacks in rural areas; its northern border is easily penetrated by exiled National Guardsmen in Honduras. These areas cannot be secured by the small EPS alone. A wave of terrorist murders as early as October 1979 and the paralysis of factories by hostile capitalists have made the defence of offices and workplaces even more urgent. As the Frente took stock of the situation, it was made clear that temporary demobilisation was a necessary stage in making the militias more effective in the long run.

During the war, despite their heroism, the danger of unstructured militias had become apparent. In provincial areas especially, the relationship between militias and Sandinista regulars was often ambiguous, and the lack of clear discipline led more than once to unnecessary loss of life. In Managua, as the insurrection dragged on, the local people's commando units began to take their own risks, and in desperation at their independent attacks on National Guard and economic targets — which threatened to disrupt the carefully laid insurrectional plan — the FSLN tried to assign one regular militant to each group of twenty *milicianos* to bring them directly under Frente orders. In the last days of the war, the number of *lumpen* youth who took up arms complicated the situation still further. 'Not all the *muchachos* behaved as we would have wished. The conduct of some left a lot to be desired. Some went in for robberies and abuses of their new authority, which forced zonal commanders to call them to order in the strongest possible terms.'[6] In the first days after the victory, the militias took charge of internal security and checkpoints in the absence of centralised military control. Each *barrio* had its own passwords, vehicles could be stopped for document checks a dozen times in the course of a single kilometre, safe-conduct passes were issued arbitrarily. Anyone wearing a red-and-black kerchief could take advantage of the situation, and many did. Throughout July and August an informal dusk-to-dawn curfew was imposed. From 6 p.m. onwards the sound of gunfire was unremitting, and no Managuan knew whether from militias, un-captured National Guards or common criminals. The chaotic distribution of arms from looted National Guard posts on the 19th made matters worse, and the Frente was profoundly disturbed: 'The FSLN has the highest regard for the people's militias. They symbolise all that is beautiful about this Revolution. We believe that the militias have a vital role to play. For that reason, we are making major efforts to improve their organisation, their technical skill and their discipline, so that they can really turn themselves into an effective fighting force.'[7] At the same time, the Frente appealed for all irregular forces to turn over their weapons to the Sandinista authorities, and warned that force would be used if necessary to disarm those who resisted. 'We make this appeal to our militia comrades: there are many people, criminals and opportunists, who are taking advantage of the present situation of chaos and disorder, exploiting the sudden and complete collapse of Somocista power by seizing arms. We know that there are all sorts of elements out there, disguised as militias for their own criminal purposes.'[8]

Operation Puno Sandinista (Sandinista Fist) was put into effect swiftly to recover unauthorised weapons. The operation yielded a total of 5,000 guns. Insubordinate militias were dismissed, armed criminals were imprisoned. As the wartime militias broke up, their members went in different directions.

Those over eighteen with the greatest political experience were incorporated into the EPS, although the lack of a guaranteed wage at first prevented many from joining up: 'I fought in the war, now all I want to do is to join the Sandinista Army. But how can I? I have a wife and three children to feed.'[9] The Sandinista Police drew much of its initial strength from former combatants who were factory workers with no jobs to return to. Their factories had been bombed out and they were now sleeping rough, unfed. The younger *muchachos* went back to school. Some adolescents turned to crime, and others held on to their weapons and became part of the Milicias Populares Anti-Somocistas (MILPAS), armed wing of the ultra-left MAP-FO.

Now, a year later, the Frente is well on its way to its target of 300,000 armed workers' and peasants' militias. In the December cabinet changes, Comandante Eden Pastora moved from the Ministry of the Interior to become Vice-Minister of Defence with special responsibility for building the new Sandinista People's Militias (MPS). The choice of Pastora, commander of the attack on the National Palace and with Borge the Sandinista leader with the most charismatic personal following, was a shrewd one. Immediately after his appointment to his new post, Pastora announced that the MPS would be formed within a matter of weeks, directly answerable to the Ministry of Defence, and open to anyone aged between sixteen and sixty who identified with the aims of the Revolution. The official inauguration came on 24 February as part of the Sandino anniversary celebrations, with a march-past of 1,200 uniformed *milicianos* in the Masaya sports stadium. By the time of the 19 July rally, almost 100,000 were armed and trained.

At the Masaya rally, Pastora described the functions of the MPS: to defend the country against internal acts of aggression; to ensure the security of factories and farms, towns and villages; to take part in joint military operations with the EPS and the Sandinista Police against armed counter-revolutionary groups, especially in rural areas; and to be mobilised into medical and reconstruction brigades in the event of natural disasters.[10] Borge added an important extra function in a December speech to the Sandinista Police: the security of the media – the offices of *Barricada*, the Sistema Sandinista de Television and Radio Sandino. In each case, the militias would be formed by the media workers themselves.

The strength and dedication of the militias was one of the most visible advances in Nicaragua over the middle months of 1980. In every factory, farm, office and government department, groups of *milicianos* undergo military training at dawn and after working hours each day. Although there are few women militias in rural areas, their presence in the cities is striking, especially among the market women of Managua's Mercado Oriental. Their ability to respond rapidly to military crises is impressive. In mid-1980, a band of ex-National Guardsmen moved in from Honduras to attack the FSLN command-post in the small northern village of Quilali. The Frente called for 400 rural militias to support the EPS search operation, and within hours Quilali was filled with 600 militias from the Esteli and Ocotal regions. Instead of sending them home the army kept the 200 extra volunteers on the spot as reinforcements until the operation was completed.

By February 1980, the first factory militia units were in action, working in close cooperation with the CST to guard against bosses' production boycotts and to prevent the physical sabotage of plant, as in the famous dispute at the El Caracol food-processing plant. One hundred of the 300 workers at the METASA plant in Tipitapa promptly enlisted in the militias, accompanied by similar proportions in the 'vanguard' factories of TELASA in Granada, FULESA, MAYCO and La Cementera. In the Area of Public Ownership, factory militias operate with the full cooperation of the state; in privately owned enterprises they are predictably a major point of conflict between nervous factory owners and the work force; in worker-occupied plants they are an essential facet of workers' control of production. In the countryside too, despite a slower start, the participation of peasants and rural labourers in the MPS is now well established. Two members of the Credit and Service Cooperative at El Jobo near Esteli gave the following account of their involvement:

> We've been integrated in the militias for a month now, a very short time in other words, but, for all that, we've made quite a bit of headway, since all the *companeros* are interested and turn up punctually for training. In fact, every single member of this co-operative takes part. Our aim is to build a really strong militia platoon here at El Jobo. We began to organise when *companero* Rito came up from Esteli, and he made us realise the importance of forming the militias. We've been working on it ever since then. We reckon that we have to be ready to defend ourselves against attacks from outside the country, and from inside too, and we also have to be well organised in case there's any attempt to sabotage the cooperative. Among us, there are militias who are members of the ATC, others too from AMNLAE and from the CDS: we're all joined together in a single platoon. There are about 40 of us divided into three squadrons. Each squadron has a person in charge, and the three together have an overall *responsable* and a political secretary. So far we've only had weapons training with the Garand and the M-16. As a rule, we have one afternoon's training a week, and then every Saturday afternoon too, usually for about an hour and a half at a stretch.

The El Jobo militia's political secretary added:

> Right now, we have to get all the mass organisations together behind this scheme, because building the militias is going to be the basis for defending this Revolution of ours. Another important thing is that, since we haven't been started for very long, we still work a bit slowly, but we're learning. My job as political secretary is to give a political meaning to the militias, more or less pass on to them the things I've learned. The trouble is we can't do much political study because we've

got very few books. What I'd like would be for some *companeros* who have got a bit more political training than me to pass on their experience to us, people who have got books at home . . . There are some women involved in the militias . . . they take part because as members of the community it's a duty and a need. And we're seeing that in training they do everything the same as a man, just as well. The main thing is that we all have to be ready to stand guard over what we produce, make sure that no-one tries to boycott production. That's why we're in the militias.[11]

A year into the Revolution, the military threat has grown from exiled National Guardsmen and their Central American and Washington backers. The necessary defensive steps which the FSLN must take to meet this of course pose questions about the compatibility of vertical military command and the ambitiously non-hierarchical democratic structure of the mass organisations. The questions apply with particular force to the militias, now nearing a combat strength of 300,000 — an eighth of the population — and under the direct command of the regular armed forces. Its members are factory workers, market women, peasants, students and white-collar employees, each accustomed to playing an active role in the appropriate mass organisation. The most politically advanced will come to terms with the contradiction; others left vulnerable by the mass passivity imposed by the Somoza era may well opt for the ease of accepting vertical orders in all spheres of activity.

Within the EPS, a similar tension is apparent. Military ranks were established only in the spring of 1980, a firm and unquestioning chain of command as in any other national army. But simultaneously, the education of political cadres in the army was advancing rapidly. 'As a member of the party cell in my army unit,' reflected one soldier, 'it's normal for me to question and debate the opinions of a *companero* who outranks me in military terms. But when it comes to military orders, I must of course obey that person unhesitatingly. A *comandante*'s actions may be above reproach in the military sense, since he or she has reached that rank because of outstanding qualities which we all recognise. But within the party, such a person is treated as an equal. And that can be very confusing.'[12] Permanently alert to the dangers of border attacks or even a full-scale invasion from the north, the troops of the EPS must also spend long periods shut up in barracks. The risk here is of separation from the community, both physical and political. It is a problem which the FSLN, hearteningly, is very much aware of, and making real attempts to solve by continuing to encourage the greatest possible interplay between the army and the civilian population, especially by involving soldiers directly in the productive process. 'To fail in this would be a betrayal of the people, a return to the elitism of the National Guard. The EPS must be seen at all times as no more than an expression of the people in arms. If we fail here, we are betraying the most basic principles of Sandinista democracy.'[13] It is time now to look at how these principles of

Sandinista democracy operate.

The FSLN and Direct Democracy

With the March 1979 unification of the FSLN, the three leaders of each
tendency had taken the name of Joint National Directorate. On 26
September, at the organisation's first assembly of cadres and militants, the
word 'joint' was dropped from the title, formally burying the three
tendencies. In those early months of the Revolution, the internal
commissions set up by the FSLN scrupulously followed the principle of equal
representation by each of the former tendencies, with Borge (GPP), Carrion
(TP) and Humberto Ortega (Tercerista) taking charge of restructuring the
armed forces; Ruiz (GPP), Nunez (TP) and Tirado (Tercerista) responsible
for building the mass organisations; and Arce (GPP), Wheelock (TP) and
Daniel Ortega (Tercerista) handling relationships with the Junta – a
commission which later looked to the structuring of the state in general. The
balance has persisted in subsequent stages of the internal reorganisation of the
Frente and reaffirms the complementary role of the tendencies in the insurrection.

At the level of junior and intermediate cadres, identification with one
or other tendency did not always break down so rapidly. The division of
labour before 1979 meant that there was still some imbalance in certain areas
of work and geographical regions, for example a predominance of TP cadres
in urban organisation, a reluctance to abandon long-held GPP loyalties in the
more remote towns of the north, Tercerista strength in the armed forces. In
itself this was quite logical, and was only damaging to the extent that
individuals (rarely in key positions) continued to adopt sectarian attitudes.
At first it was not uncommon to find Proletarian activists meeting as a group
and bemoaning the ideological weakness and bourgeois mentality of recent
recruits, or to hear Tercerista combatants from the Frente Sur complaining
of the prominence given to 'Marxist hardliners', both groups in their way
falling victim to the image of a divided Frente portrayed outside Nicaragua
and by reactionary groups inside the country.[14] But this kind of problem is
now seen in perspective as a challenge to the FSLN as a whole, and after the
first year the tendency mentality is effectively dead at all levels.

The three pillars in the reorganisation of the FSLN in peacetime are the
groundwork being laid for a Sandinista Party, the structuring of the armed
forces and the strengthening of the mass organisations, three tasks which are
coordinated at the provincial level by the Frente's Comites de Direccion
Departamental (CDDs). In a year, the strength of the mass organisations has
grown dramatically. The CST now groups together 170,000 workers, the
ATC 106,000 rural labourers, AMNLAE 25,000 women, the Sandinista
Youth 15,000 – with a further mass influx at the end of the Literacy
Crusade, and the CDS 220,000 people at *barrio*, block and village level. In
an interview with the weekly *Poder Sandinista*, Jaime Wheelock outlined the

importance of the mass organisations: 'The organisation of the working class in trade unions will be the basic support of the Revolution, and likewise the rest of the mass organisations. The organised people must prepare themselves to run the state, through all the channels which the Revolution is creating.'[15]

The phrase 'prepare *themselves*' is instructive. There is no intention that the mass organisations should become mere appendages of the FSLN, designed to execute leadership decisions. Their role is an independent one. This class independence, and the primary role assigned to the mass organisations by the FSLN, was taken further by Carlos Nunez in a speech to the CST: 'The CDS . . . what are they but the result of all the efforts of the FSLN and other revolutionary organisations to give the popular classes a form of organisation through which they can express their concerns, their worries, their criticisms, and say how far they want to take this revolutionary process? . . . This happens in the context of creating organisations with a true class character which embrace the productive sectors of the nation.'[16]

It is only natural that the mass organisations should express a class character independent of the bourgeoisie. Less obvious, but equally important is their independence from the state. The numerical strength of the mass organisations is impressive, but it is only part of the story. The rush to organise is only to be expected in the immediate aftermath of a mass insurrection. A more relevant concern is *how* and *why* they organise. There is no shortage of problems here: on the one hand the acute shortage of political cadres, on the other hand the different origins of each of the mass organisations and their distinct tasks before the Revolution. The CST, for example, grew out of clandestine factory committees whose tasks included frontal attacks on the state and the sabotage of factories and machinery. They were sometimes formed spontaneously, and sometimes at the instance of FSLN cadres. The ATC was more directly a creation of the Frente in giving the rural workers and peasants an instrument to express their demands for land. The CDS were intimately linked from the beginning to the United People's Movement, working around the immediate tasks of the insurrection and with hugely varying levels of political awareness in different areas of the country. AMNLAE began life as a small pressure group of predominantly middle-class women, and rapidly acquired a mass character.

Each of the mass organisations was then asked to adapt to radically new tasks after the insurrection, and to interlock with the others around common political objectives. This was perhaps easiest for the CDS, which were by their very nature the least tied to specific sectoral loyalties, and were already active at a national level before July 1979. The main task of the mass organisations today is to organise the defence of the Revolution in every sphere: the political, the economic and the military. These three facets of their work fuse together, above all, in the central need of the mass organisations to stimulate production. This, of course, raises the whole question of their relationship to the state, when much of their initial rationale was the destruction of the state. That relationship has often been tense. Like the mass organisations, the revolutionary state is new and has evolved rapidly. Often this has meant the state lagging behind the demands and flexibility of the mass organisations, and the role of the CDS especially is one of vigilance over the new state. In the early months, this sometimes meant the adoption of parastatal functions by the CDS — the very feature which the right-wing opposition criticised so fearfully. It was a response to the inadequacy of the nascent state, as Carlos Nunez made clear: 'They behaved as parastatal organs because they failed to find in the state the receptiveness, dynamism and flexibility required to solve real problems.'[17] Perhaps the most important point here is that the FSLN has invariably sided with the mass organisations where such conflicts with the state have arisen, and stressed the active role of the mass organisations in transforming the state apparatus.[18] During the first year of the Revolution, the May 1980 installation of the Council of State with a built-in majority for the mass organisations was the most notable example of the dynamic convergence of the people and the machinery of government.

The independent status of the mass organisations is also highlighted by their relationship with the future Sandinista party. There is no intention that they should be swallowed up in the party, but rather that they should serve a dual function as a breeding ground for party militants and a rearguard for the party when it is formed. Their critical role in evaluating and improving government decisions is fundamental. In mass demonstrations, whether to mark anniversaries, repudiate the activities of the CIA in Nicaragua, condemn the manoeuvres of ultra-left trade union groups, or support a new government decree, their presence and numbers are vital in gauging approval and understanding of measures taken. If a demonstration is small, it is direct evidence that policy should be rethought.

The same procedure applies at the local level. In Jalapa, a small town near the Honduran border, the local Junta of Reconstruction was dismissed at the instigation of the town's mass organisations and replaced with a 'Popular Council of Government'. In Leon too, the country's second city, whose *junta* was the first to take office in June 1979, a new *junta* was appointed in February, its members named directly by the mass organisations. The Council of State's main source of suggestions for new legislation are what is termed 'Cabildos Abiertos' — open assemblies — in which Council representatives visit provincial towns and sound out local opinion in mass gatherings. In one town, the demands included a revision of the Somocista Labour Code, a reduction of the working day to eight hours for domestic servants, enforcement of paternity law, stricter measures against those guilty of counter-revolutionary propaganda, and an overhaul of the medical profession.

In a more structured way, the CDS have direct influence on every ministry whose policies affect local issues. This influence has two stages: through the CDS, the people identify their demands and bring them to the attention of the ministry concerned; when the demand is acted upon, the CDS ensure that policy is properly executed and make criticisms if it is not. This dialogue applies in every area: in the opening of Child Development Centres with the Ministry of Social Welfare; in food pricing and distribution with ENABAS (the Nicaraguan Institute of Basic Foodstuffs) and the Ministry of Internal Trade; in education with demands for improvements in school facilities and the mobilisation and security of literacy *brigadistas;* carrying out local vaccination programmes with the Ministry of Health; requests for electric lighting and new housing programmes through the National Energy Institute (INE) and the Ministry of Housing (MINVAH). Even within the ministries, the CDS have a formal representation which monitors government policy and performance through the Programmatic Coordinating Commissions (CPC) and the National Secretariat for the Defence of the Economy.

To the FSLN, all these are examples of the permanent dynamic which must exist between the FSLN, the government and the people. Writing in the national CDS newspaper, Sergio Ramirez of the Junta expanded on its importance:

'Grassroot opinions must be brought to the CDS representatives. This is a genuine political dynamic, the only dynamic which can make a revolutionary process possible, because if the leadership of the Revolution were locked away giving orders, giving guidance blindly without communicating with the masses and their organisations, without these organisations understanding the measures which are taken, and without the critical and creative support which these organisations must give, then the Revolution would simply not work.'[19]

The Vanguard and the Masses in Victory

From the moment of launching the attack on the San Carlos barracks in October 1977, the FSLN's role alternated between that of initiator and co-ordinator of mass action. The twenty-one months leading to the July 1979 victory taught the Frente the level of organisational capacity and political consciousness in the people's struggle, the moments in which the masses required inspiration through example, and the times when their revolutionary potential surpassed the leadership's expectations. These lessons have been used to enrich the relationship between the vanguard and the people in the first year of the Revolution.

The organic links which the FSLN created with the popular organisations, not only in the final crisis of *Somocismo* but over ten years of patient work through intermediate bodies, have made for a continuous interplay between leadership organisation and spontaneous mass action. The spontaneous energy which abounds in Nicaragua today is the FSLN's most powerful asset, but there has been a strict avoidance of spontaneism determining the overall policy and direction of the Revolution. In the insurrection of September 1978, there were critical moments in which leadership and spontaneity were out of phase, but the still fresh memories of the results of spontaneous action at that time have helped to discipline acts whose tactical importance has changed radically with the taking of power.

Land takeovers, for example, a major weapon of the rural poor against *latifundistas* in the struggle against Somoza, are not now in the interests of the government agrarian reform programme. The initial confusion of peasant groups at an apparent contradiction in FSLN advice ('I don't understand it at all,' commented one Chinandega peasant days after the victory. 'One minute seizing the land is revolutionary, then they tell you it's counter-revolutionary.'[20]) has been overcome to a large degree by ATC political education work, and land invasions have been few in the first year. The ATC and the CST have both faced the major task of explaining that land seizures and factory strikes, while having a defensive importance in relieving immediate exploitation and bettering living standards, were above all instruments in a strategy against the state. This political education underlines Ramirez' insistence on 'understanding the measures that are taken'. Explanation must be constant, patient and detailed, and in the many gaps which still exist, Humberto Ortega's determination to 'fight against various forms of deviation' takes on real importance.

Again, land seizures and factory strikes illustrate the point. Both weapons were used by ultra-leftist, anti-FSLN groups immediately after the Revolution as an attack on the nascent Sandinista state, which they accused of being 'bourgeois-democratic'. Where such conflicts arise, the FSLN call for open political debate about ultra-left errors, and it is important that the Frente never replace debate with repression, unless unavoidable. There have been two major examples of repressive action against the ultra-left, and both momentarily unsettled the principle of constant dialogue. In the first, the closure of *El Pueblo*, daily newspaper of the pro-Albanian Frente Obrero (FO) and the gaoling of a group of journalists, damage was minimal. It came at the end of a long process of publicised debate between FSLN and FO leaders, and was widely understood in terms of the threat posed to security by the FO's armed wing, the MILPAS (although the MILPAS were in fact peripheral to the state's judgment against *El Pueblo*). The second case of imprisonment of ultra-left politicians was of members of the Partido Comunista in May 1980, and was perhaps more damaging to the FSLN, although the PC was discredited among most workers. The lack of public understanding of the case enabled the PC to mount a small but effective campaign against the government's action in resorting to prison sentences rather than public debate.

These are isolated instances. Otherwise, the Frente has rarely acted without consultation and explanation, and is well aware of the dangers of moving faster than the advances in working-class political consciousness. Although this has meant caution about taking steps which the FSLN would have the power to take, any unilateral action could only be applied at the inevitable cost of bureaucratisation and an interruption of the critical dynamic between the vanguard and the people. That risk will of course increase as the Revolution comes under greater threat. Increasingly, the mass organisations are themselves capable of formulating demands which directly determine state policy; where they frame demands which are not immediately feasible for reasons related to economic restraints or the balance of class forces in a particular sector, the grounds for applying a brake are explained (wherever possible at factory, farm, plant or community level) and as a rule accepted because of the moral authority of the FSLN leadership. Conflicts, despite the lack of experienced cadres and the still yawning gaps in political consciousness, have been rare, and again this says much for the FSLN's historical relationship with the people and the determination never to let the vanguard become an elite.

Undeniably, the nature of that relationship and the conditions of the struggle in Nicaragua led to a low priority being given to the theoretical presentation of the insurrectional phase, beyond a basic grasp of its anti-imperialist character and the importance of organisation on class lines. The particular merit of the FSLN's leadership of the insurrection lay in its ability to grasp subjective conditions, its skill in agitational work and its capacity to respond to the objective crisis of *Somocismo* with action in readily under-standable forms rooted in the immediate realities and language of the people. In accelerating the subjective conditions for insurrection, the Frente brought out the people's *voluntad de lucha,* the combative will which has acted as a basis for developing more thoroughgoing class consciousness. They also saw the size of the organisation mushroom over two years, from a few hundred selected and trained militants to a military force of thousands with mass popular support from Nicaraguans of every class and the most widely varied levels of political development. Any initial purist complaints about the effect of this explosive growth on the clear definition of the organisation have been allayed by the convergence of leadership policies and mass demands in the first year. The political programme worked out through the insurrection, based on an appraisal of the uneven state of the mass movement, has proved a satisfactory expression of the working class's initial demands and provides a real platform for launching the Revolution's next stage.

The FSLN is intent on constantly renewing its popular support and moral authority. In Borge's words: 'We cannot simply capitalise on the prestige which we won in the war and think that this is enough. We have to win the support and respect of the masses every day, each minute, by knowing how to interpret the interests of the working people.'[21] There are innumerable anecdotes of Borge's own ability to win that support. Opening the Pedro Rivas Recalde Agricultural Complex near Managua, he was asked by a peasant woman, 'Comandante Tomas Borge, I want to beg you to see whether they can open an ENABAS food store here.' Borge replied, 'ENABAS? Yes, that's possible. But there's just one thing . . . You shouldn't beg for it, or even use the word "beg", because begging is a thing of the past. If you need some-thing, what you should do is *demand* it.' With his status as the oldest member of the National Directorate and only surviving founder of the FSLN, Borge unquestionably enjoys the widest popular support of any Sandinista leader, and there was a danger that a personality cult might grow around him, which ultimately could only serve those who wished to portray him as a Nicaraguan Fidel.

The collegiate leadership of the Frente carries forward a determined trend against any form of personality cult which began on the battlefield. Debray quotes a handbill posted in Matagalpa: 'The Northern Regional General Staff of the Frente Sandinista wishes to make it known that no combatant shall be allowed to take the title of "Comandante", "Don" or even "Senor", nor should these titles be applied to any other person. Sandinista comradeship forbids us from paying homage to anyone with titles. What we owe to each other are words of brotherhood. There is no greater homage for a Sandinista, whether a regular fighter or a militia, than to be called "hermanito" [little brother] or "companero".'[22] Within the National Directorate, each member has defined responsibilities, but the point is made repeatedly in speeches that any one Comandante speaking on matters of policy does so on behalf of all nine. Joint leadership, combined with the strengthening of the mass organisations, is also seen as a defence against any attempt to use position on the Directorate to further personal ambitions, a possibility which the Frente is realistic enough to recognise. A member of the FSLN close to the leadership explained:

> There has been a conscious attempt from the beginning to undermine any chance of elitism, to create the structures of popular power as quickly as possible so that no comandante can ever avoid scrutiny by the people, and criticism where it is necessary. If the point were ever reached where one comandante or another abused his position, that person could not remain in the leadership. This must be a vanguard which is permanently answerable, permanently subject to recall.[23]

The large number of personal visits to remote areas by members of the National Directorate, especially where local crises demand swift resolution, is of course born partially of necessity in the present absence of middle level cadres, but it also reflects the leadership's concern to remain permanently in touch with grassroots feelings and criticisms. Similarly, Radio Sandino's phone-in programme, *Linea Directa,* allows direct access to Sandinista leaders and criticisms both of policy and personal behaviour. For example, while the need for security and efficiency is widely appreciated, there has been strongly worded criticism of the leadership's use of confiscated Somocista houses and Mercedes Benz's, for so long the exclusive property of Somoza and the National Guard.

Human Rights, Security and Revolutionary Morality
The concern to demystify political leaders is one part of a sustained drive to create a revolutionary morality. Echoing Che Guevara, a repeated theme of speeches and propaganda is: 'In creating the new society, we must also create the new man and the new woman.' And in the days following the war, the most frequently broadcast speech on the two Sandinista television channels was Borge's insistence that the Revolution must continue to prove its legitimacy by demonstrating its moral superiority over *Somocismo*. His theme was

taken from Carlos Fonseca's famous phrase 'Implacable in combat, generous in victory'. Those hostile to the Nicaraguan Revolution waited in vain for mass executions and reprisals.

Instead, there were promises of a fair trial for captured Guardsmen and an abolition of the death penalty. The treatment of prisoners has been one of the Revolution's most controversial areas, and one in which the FSLN had directly opposed strenuous popular demands for retribution, especially in the cities which had suffered most at the hands of the National Guard during the war. One teenage Sandinista responsible for guarding prisoners in Leon described his own dilemma:

> Look, if's hard to feel any generosity at first for these people, when you know what they've done. I mean, I lost members of my family in the bombing of Leon, and when the Frente put me on guard duty in the prison, all I wanted to do was to take revenge. But with discipline and time your feelings change, gradually. You realise a lot of things: how most of the *Guardia* are only humble peasants, just like you. And the things you have to do, like giving the prisoners the same meal rations as the *compas* of the army when there isn't enough food to go round, when you see the effect that has. When the *Guardia* realise that they were fighting and killing people who are now sharing their food with them instead of torturing and killing them. Because that's what they believed, I mean that's what Somoza told them would happen if they lost, and they swallowed it . . . that we would rape their wives and murder their children. And now they see what really happens, and it's terrible for them. They realise that they were fighting for a lie. So when you see what this generosity means in practice, you know it's right.[24]

Nevertheless, dealing with more than 7,000 National Guard prisoners remained a major dilemma. Although their treatment has been humane, to the extent of including prisoners in the country's Literacy Crusade and seeking foreign aid to develop a prison system on the Scandinavian pattern, the captured Guardsmen are held in sordid, Somoza-built gaols designed for only 2,000 inmates. Each of the Frente's potential options carries potential ammunition for those who wish to attack the Revolution. Executions and summary justice have been rejected. The wholesale release of suspected war criminals would immediately double the strength of the regrouped National Guard in exile. As many as 2,000 of them are already camped inside Honduras, where they enjoy the protection of the right-wing Honduran military for their border incursions. As many again have joined the security forces and death squads of El Salvador and Guatemala, with still others allegedly receiving military training in secret camps in Florida. The actions of these terrorist bands is already a serious headache for the newly created State Security service, which with Cuban assistance is coming to terms with the threats to internal security. The FSLN's third option was to give a fair trial to all prisoners, with all the attendant difficulties in assembling evidence and the absence of adequate judicial machinery, resulting in slow trials and accusations of detention without trial and alleged human rights abuses. The FSLN opted for the third course and has duly been criticised by the Nicaraguan Permanent Commission for Human Rights (CPDH). The CPDH, however, all but disappeared after the Revolution, with Conservative, Socialist and Liberal members leaving the Commission, so that it was under the effective control of a handful of right-wing Christian Democrat politicians. Their accusations of human rights abuses by the FSLN have not been echoed by any relevant international body.

Setting up nine special tribunals and using the existing criminal code with maximum penalties of thirty years' imprisonment, the trials began in December 1979. The early proceedings were indeed slow, and seven months later the courts had processed only a tenth of all cases, with an almost 100% conviction rate. 'Changing the judicial structure of a country is something which takes time,' noted Borge. 'There are no grounds for thinking that we were not worried by the initial sluggishness of the courts.'[25] Towards the end of 1980, the bottlenecks cleared. Mass acquittals of those whose guilt could not be proven, and the speeding-up of judicial procedures meant that the last National Guard case was tried in February 1981. Securing eye-witness evidence and positive identification had often proved impossible, and most Guardsmen — who enjoyed full rights of legal representation — based their defence on non-involvement in combat duties, claiming to have been cooks, gardeners, chauffeurs or medical personnel. In one of its daily reports on the well-publicised trials, *El Nuevo Diario* voiced the common complaint that 'those who came before the tribunals yesterday were yet again blind, deaf, dumb and amnesiac.'[26]

Reports of isolated cases of torture, maltreatment and even execution in the first weeks after the insurrection were confirmed, but this was before the effective constitution of a new central government. What was heartening was the Frente's full recognition of such cases and the severe discipline handed out to offenders. In November, the leadership officially admitted the abuse of power by army members, particularly in remote areas where a vicious circle undermines local confidence in the FSLN: on the Atlantic Coast and in marginal communities like the Pacific beach resort and seaport of San Juan del Sur, lack of participation in the insurrection means that support for the Revolution is fragile, and this in turn is threatened by the undisciplined and arbitrary behaviour of local troops with the poorest level of training and political consciousness. Borge, detailing the problems of local indiscipline in the military, commented specifically on the murder of the former National Guard commander of the Atlantic port of Puerto Cabezas after his arrest, and promised a full investigation and punishment of those implicated. At the same time, 100 members of the armed forces were arrested — most in the northern area of Jinotega — and also in November the Junta announced that it was suspending the decree allowing for the 'confiscation of property belonging to the Somoza family or known Somocistas'. The decision followed widespread allegations that the term 'known Somocistas' was being interpreted arbitrarily by individual officials. The clean-up of the security forces was immediate and drastic, and by March the Ministry of the Interior was able to announce that since the Revolution 1,500 members of the Sandinista Police had been dismissed for abuses of authority.[27] To mark the forty-sixth anniversary of Sandino's death, Borge took the opportunity to remind his audience of the moral qualities required of a Sandinista militant:

> A Sandinista is someone who cares more for the people than for him or herself; a Sandinista is someone who fights corruption intransigently; a Sandinista is someone who makes every possible effort to eradicate from his or her mind all selfishness, all arrogance — features which at times are so widespread, not only at the level of the militant but among members of the armed forces. Because the fact that you wear a Sandinista uniform or carry a Sandinista identity card entitles you to no privileges whatsoever . . . To be children of Sandino, we must have superior moral values.[28]

The critical point to which Borge returned was the damage which abuses — and the failure to acknowledge abuses — could have on the relationship between the Frente and the Nicaraguan people: 'We have to work patiently every day to face up to these weaknesses, which have no place in a revolutionary. We are not the sort who try to hide our weaknesses, because our duty as Sandinistas is to lay our weaknesses bare in front of the masses.'

The Sandinista Defence Committees

Unlike the other mass organisations, the CDSs are tied to no particular sector. They embrace men and women, workers and peasants, cities and countryside alike. In their ranks are CST, ATC, AMNLAE and youth movement activists. Their functions touch every facet of political decision-making: production and distribution, social programmes, militia organisation. Based on the smallest unit of population — the urban block or *manzana* — a CDS is permanently accessible to every Nicaraguan.

For all these reasons, the FSLN has seen the CDSs as the most advanced form of the new democracy. The influence of the CDSs is felt in their weight on the Council of State. On the forty-seven-seat Council, they have nine members, the heaviest representation of any organisation, with two delegates from Managua and one each from regional groups of two or three *departamentos*. And recognition of their power is manifest in the way that the bourgeois opposition has singled out the CDSs as its main target. The Right's war against the CDSs has been an integral part of its fight for bourgeois constitutionalism: the attack has hinged on the fact that the committees have no 'legal' existence,[29] and recognising their *de facto* existence the Right has made futile attempts to demobilise the CDSs by demanding that the state circumscribe their functions, removing their political role and turning them into anaemic 'community development organisations'. The Right realises that it has lost this battle. The CDSs for one thing are too firmly rooted: one of their greatest strengths is that, unlike the Cuban Committees for the Defence of the Revolution which were formed to defend Cuba against attack in late 1960, the Nicaraguan ones grew organically out of the armed struggle and were in place when the Sandinista Government took power, effectively running the country for the first few weeks until the new state took shape. This is not to say that the CDSs have developed uniformly. There was a brief hiatus in their evolution towards the end of 1979, precisely because they were tied to no particular productive sector and their activities had to be harmonised with those of the emergent government.

In militant cities like Esteli or Masaya, the CDSs have evolved smoothly from their insurrectional work as CDCs. In Monimbo, for example, the needs of the insurrection brought a dramatic upsurge in community organisation:

> It's a funny thing: people tend to think that the Monimbosenos were always revolutionary. Well, it was just the opposite. We weren't born Sandinistas, we became Sandinistas. Political ignorance was tremendous. I'd say 95% of the people here supported Somoza, or thought they did. Whenever Somoza wheeled people out for some demonstration, the Monimbosenos would be there in force. AMROCS, Somoza's para-militaries, were strong here. So were the Somocista Women's Organisation and the Liberal Youth. Right up to the end there were *orejas* here. We were always used to assuming that Somoza, the Liberal Party, the National Guard gave the orders. People never participated in any decisions affecting their own lives. It's hard to overcome that, to learn that we're capable of thinking for ourselves. But in the war we had two advantages: we had a sense of community, and we were good with our hands. So we turned our skills to making arms, improvising weapons like the contact bombs.
>
> All that has stood us in good stead. As we began to organise the CDCs, the process taught us our own power, what we could achieve by being united. We used my own house as a medical centre in the war, and my *companera* still works on medical care with the CDS. She's giving courses of vitamin injections now. I ended up as *coordinador de manzana* [block coordinator]. The committees are even more vital to us now. Attendance hasn't fallen off. There's a problem here, of course, because at the same time this feeling for the community makes you want to throw yourself into your work, make the local economy healthy. That leads to some people saying they haven't got time for the CDS any more. We know that big economic changes won't come overnight, that we have to work for them, and so there's the temptation to say that the two hours I spend at a CDS meeting I could be here making a pair of shoes and earning a few pesos. But you have to get out

of that way of thinking, because that would mean letting other people do your thinking for you again, like before. The tradition of organising is very important to us now. Already on 15 June last year, in the middle of the fighting, we organised a meeting of 35 *manzanas,* with three central committees and health brigades in every part of the *barrio.*

Now some people complain that you can get better treatment if you are a CDS member. Well I see it like this: there are often queues in the clinics, because we still have shortages of medicine and doctors. Those who are not organised, through the CDS or in other ways, are probably the ones who wait longest and sometimes don't get attended to. Not because anyone discriminates against them: remember we're trying to build a whole health system from nothing: new clinics open, timetables are arranged, and the CDS are the natural means of passing all that information on and getting people organised. It's precisely for that reason that we want everyone to be involved in the CDS, so no-one will miss out on what they have a right to.[30]

Strength here came from the insurrection. In parts of Managua's *barrios orientales,* by contrast, many powerful CDSs still bear the stamp of their origins in the Christian base communities. And strength often has little to do with how long a committee has existed. The thirty-six CDSs of the Mercado Oriental were formed only in September 1979. The area was peripheral to the insurrection, but the solidly working-class composition of its inhabitants and their constant frontline fight in the economic war against speculators has made the market workers as militantly organised as any CDS in the country. Elsewhere, the CDSs initially undertook tasks which only reflected the absence of central government authority. On the Atlantic Coast, CDSs were abruptly set up as a reflex action to fill a vacuum, among people with no previous involvement in the Revolution, no sense of direction or historical perspective, and only the haziest idea of what 'Sandinista Defence' entailed. Atlantic Coast CDSs conducted marriage services and charged money for staging local fiestas — anomalies which could not and did not last. In February, feeling ran high in Puerto Cabezas when the government announced the temporary closure of a local radio station until it could be checked by Cuban technicians. When local Sandinista officials intervened in the protest demonstration, they discovered that the CDS had been instrumental in organising it, a situation which said as much about the autonomy of the CDS as it does about the specific political problems of the Caribbean area. It recalls Borge's insistence that anti-government action in the mass organisations should be construed as further proof of their independence. Again, Uriel Guzman of Monimbo touched on this: 'If one of the *compas* of the Frente, or someone in the government, does something wrong, commits some arbitrary abuse — and of course it happens — then that can be criticised in public, and the CDS meeting is the best place. We don't go to these meetings so that someone can hand down a line to us and tell us what to say — we won't let that happen any more. And if it means things that are unpopular, let's say them. No minority opinion is going to be suppressed in our CDS.'

In middle-class areas too, the CDSs have taken root, though in forms which are alternately genuine, amusing or opportunist. Red-and-black flags hanging from bourgeois houses may serve a populist purpose remote from the ideology of the FSLN, or they may be a token of true radicalisation. As on the Atlantic Coast, many middle-class CDSs have lacked a sense of direction. A resident of the elegant suburb of Los Robles in Managua, where the standard concerns of most CDSs — literacy, health education, water supply — are scarcely relevant, admitted when pressed that the only topic under discussion in the local CDS was how to promote tourism.[31] In areas like this, Sandinista militants and government officials living in houses confiscated from fleeing Somocistas have often acted as an important catalyst in giving a political dimension to local CDS work and integrating more middle-class support for the Revolution.

The original functions of the DCSs crystallised partly under FSLN guidance, and in part spontaneously. Many of them became sources of conflict. While organising volunteer brigades to rebuild roads was universally acceptable, CDS control of security and individual movement was controversial. At first the CDSs had wide security powers, detecting escaped National Guardsmen and infiltrated Somocistas, and this naturally involved processing of exit visas from the immediate local area. This gave great latitude to frequently immature committees, and some CDS officials began to denounce neighbours as Somocistas as a cover for settling personal and domestic disputes. Towards the end of the year, the CDSs made a thorough analysis of their teething troubles and future tasks. The problematic visas and letters of reference disappeared, not because of bourgeois attacks on CDS powers, but because the state was sufficiently consolidated to make these functions obsolete. Even so, the CDSs admitted that: 'A whole series of abuses were evident which were harmful to the people, for example the refusal to give letters of reference because of petty personal enmities. At the same time, many CDS officials and activists fell into arrogant ways, believing that their responsibilities turned them into the lord and master of the *barrio* and not the servants of their community'.[32]

From April 1980 onwards, there was a complete national reorganisation of the CDSs, and 'although humble people are still badly treated on occasion, such cases are now minimal.'[33] The national CDS office defined a series of new functions for the committees: they included maintaining the security of literacy *brigadistas;* organising street cleaning; garbage disposal; tree-planting and building playgrounds; 'defence of the popular economy' through price watchdog committees and action against hoarders; cooperativisation of small traders; political analysis of the media and propaganda; setting up cadre training schools with the aim of democratising the CDSs; people's clinics and pharmacies; vigilance against state bureaucracy; and campaigns against counter-revolutionary rumours. By this time between 10,000 and 15,000 CDSs were operating nationally, with an average weekly attendance of twenty members.

The work of the CDSs has been successful particularly in matters of health, food supplies and education. Their slogan became 'Organisation, Organisation and More Organisation'. By mid-February the CDSs reported that they had organised anti-polio vaccination campaigns for 80% of the country's children under five. The CDSs of fourteen *barrios* around Managua's Carretera Norte got together to build a maternity hospital on their own initiative in the Barrio La Primavera, and organised 148 people in voluntary CDS building and cleaning brigades. The CDS at national level put forward a plan to the Programmatic Coordinating Commission of the Ministry of Planning for the creation of 200 basic food supply centres in Managua and a further 450 in the rest of the country to improve food distribution. Each would be controlled by local CDS *Comites de Vigilancia*. Education has been taken out of the classroom and into the CDSs. 'This is the hour of non-formal education in Nicaragua', said Education Vice-Minister Miguel de Castilla.[34] 'The educational system is like a tidal wave, which shows itself in the mass media, in CDS meetings, in every facet of the class struggle. The school as an institution has lost forever all the mythical prestige it enjoyed in the past.' And Glenda Monterrey, a member of the Frente's *Comision Nacional de Organizacion*, added: 'The committees will be the basic vehicle for the people's political education.'

Although in practice many committees have fewer, the model composition of a CDS is nine members: a coordinator, plus secretaries responsible for organisation, education, propaganda, health, defence of the economy, community work, sport and culture. Cultural secretaries organise poetry workshops, peasant and worker theatre collectives and mobile cultural brigades to retrieve lost folk traditions. Mobile cinemas tour the *barrios* constantly, giving 3,000 film shows in 1980 which attracted audiences of 441,000 people.[35] The People's Cultural Centres set up by the Ministry of Culture are not forums for established artists but ways of promoting a collective concept of popular art through the CDS and other mass organisations, with the aim of reunifying a national culture broken apart by class and regionalism.

Nor are the nine functions of a CDS an exhaustive list of what they can do. Many committees have added roles appropriate to local needs. In the western Managua *barrio* of San Judas, the local committee set up a Productivity Commission to fight unemployment. Their original aim was to reopen a a local cinema and in the process create ten jobs. Applying to the government, they came up against frustrating bureaucratic delays, so they simply took over the cinema and ran it themselves. 50% of the profits were put towards creating further *barrio* employment, and the other 50% towards developing CDS cultural, health and education projects. With this as a basis, the San Judas committee then took over a machine-shop abandoned by Somocistas, restarted production and gave jobs to five local unemployed people with profits from the cinema. The third step was to open a clothing factory employing twenty-five people. This time the CDS tracked down rusting machinery left behind by a National Guard officer, renovated it and put the factory to work under CDS control. Money was a problem: 'We went to lots of places to find funding,' said one CDS member. 'At first there was no result, but we didn't lose heart. Experience told us that, if our aim was in the people's interest, if we persisted, we would get what we wanted. Finally we were given a grant from abroad through the Christian Solidarity Committee.' The clothing factory is now running successfully and the work force has grown. Like the Production Collectives set up by the Ministry of Social Welfare, the goods are sold direct through the factory or in the Mercado Oriental, avoiding the 60-70% mark-up of middlemen, and the surplus generated is going to create further jobs in San Judas.

The election of nine CDS representatives to the Council of State was the culmination of a long process of democratic structuring of the committees at national level. The first stage in the smaller *barrios* − those containing less than fifteen CDSs − was to elect one representative from each to form a Comite de Barrio Sandinista (CBS). In larger *barrios,* the unit was the CDS Council, composed of one elected coordinator for each of the CDSs' areas of activity.[36] In the case of a *barrio* vaccination programme, for example, the CDS Council health coordinator would plan the campaign in conjunction with the health secretary of each member committee. The next level was the Zonal Council, to which each *barrio* elected two representatives. For the Council of State elections, zonal delegates (Managua had 200 from eleven zones) chose their representatives to regional assemblies, which in turn received nominations for the nine seats on the Council. The nine eventually elected to serve were two accountants, two students, two peasant farmers, one office worker, one tailor and one factory worker. The second-line delegates (*suplentes*) were two peasants, a shoemaker, a tailor, a trade union leader, a small trader, a workers' representative on a local government *Junta,* an agronomist and a manual worker. *Barricada* called it 'democracy coming in off the streets.'[37]

Democracy Comes In Off The Streets

The postponement and enlargement of the Council of State was one of the FSLN's key battles against right-wing opposition in the first year. The original composition of the Council, which was to share legislative powers with the Junta, was outlined in the June 1979 programme of government.[38] It was to contain thirty-three members drawn from the following organisations: (1) the FSLN; (2) the seven member organisations of the National Patriotic Front (FPN) − the United People's Movement (MPU), Independent Liberal Party (PLI), Group of *Los Doce,* Popular Social Christians (PPSC), Social Christian trade unions (CTN), Frente Obrero, and Union of Radio Journalists; (3) the seven member organisations of the Broad Opposition Front (FAO) − the Democratic Conservatives (PCD), Social Christians (PSC), Nicaraguan Democratic Movement (MDN), Movimiento Liberal Constitucionalista (MLC), Moscow-line Socialist Party (PSN) and their trade unions (CGT-I), and

the right-wing unions of the CUS; (4) the six member organisations of the
private enterprise group COSEP – the Nicaraguan Development Institute
(INDE), Chamber of Industries (CADIN), Confederation of Chambers of
Commerce (CCC), Union of Agricultural Producers (UPANIC), Chamber of
Construction, Confederation of Professional Associations (CONAPRO);
(5) the National Autonomous University (UNAN); and (6) the National
Association of Clergy (ANCLEN).

These came to a total of twenty-three organisations, with no indication of
how the thirty-three seats would be allotted. None of the newly formed mass
organisations – not even the ATC (now more than a year old) nor the
women's movement AMPRONAC – was included. If the thirty-three-member
Council, with its power to amend Junta legislation by two-thirds majority,
had gone ahead, it would have placed state power heavily under the influence
of the bourgeoisie, which accounted for half of the Council's member
organisations: in other words, the Council would have been a travesty of the
real balance of forces by the end of the war. In mid-June, the FSLN certainly
still feared the survival of some elements of the Somoza state (exactly what
the FAO was hoping for), and must have felt it had little option but to
endorse such an arrangement. A month later the balance had altered radically
in favour of the popular forces. There was no longer real restraint on the
FSLN dictating the timing and composition of the Council. Its installation
could now be held back until such time as the emergent mass organisations,
duly consolidated at a national level, could take up their rightful position as
the dominant bloc on the Council. At the same time, the Frente's decision
was strengthened by the disappearance of some of the Council's original
members – Los Doce, the MLC – and the overtly counter-revolutionary
stance adopted by the Frente Obrero. In this setting, the vociferous right-
wing campaign for the immediate installation of the Council of State in its
original form was severely undermined. It was a campaign which the
bourgeoisie, almost by definition, had no chance of winning: the new
organisations proposed for membership were living proof of the hegemony
which the FSLN had won.

The formal decision to postpone and restructure the Council of State
came on 22 October. COSEP immediately launched a furious attack on the
government, which the Right accused of violating the alleged Pact of
Puntarenas which they suggested the government Junta had signed in Costa
Rica in the presence of Costa Rican and Venezuelan officials, giving guarantees of rapidly institutionalised structures of bourgeois democracy. The
government and Frente denied that any such pact existed, but the COSEP
tactic was clear and consistent – to accuse the FSLN and Junta of 'illegali-
ties' which might discredit it in the eyes of uncommitted middle sectors and
the deeply ambivalent US Government. The date which the FSLN chose for
the installation of the 'expression of the power of the organised people'[39] was
a masterstroke: it was 4 May, the 'Day of National Dignity' on which Sandino
had refused to sign the Pact of Espino Negro, a day which emotionally reinforced the national ideology of Sandinismo and exposed clearly to the people

the anti-nationalism of those who sought to restore bourgeois power structures.

The New Council of State: Allocation of Seats

Organisations envisaged in the original government programme are indicated with an asterisk.

Bloc 1: Sandinista Organisations		*Bloc 2: Members of the Frente*	
FSLN*	6	*Patriotico de la Revolucion (FPR),*	
CDS	9	*an alliance of pro-FSLN parties*	
ATC	3	Independent Liberal Party (PLI)*	1
CST	3	Socialist Party (PSN)*	1
AMNLAE	1	Popular Social Christians (PPSC)*	1
Sandinista Youth	1		
Armed Forces (EPS)	1	Total	3
Total	24		

Bloc 3: Private Sector Organisations and anti-FSLN Parties and Trade Unions

a) Members of COSEP		b) Right-wing Parties	
INDE*	1	Democratic Conservative Party	
CADIN*	1	(PCD)*	1
CCC*	1	Social Christian Party (PSC)*	7
Chamber of Construction*	1	Nicaraguan Democratic Movement	
UPANIC*	1	(MDN) *	1
CONAPRO*	1	c) Bourgeois-dominated Trade	
		Unions	
		CTN*	1
		CUS*	1
Total			11

Bloc 4: Independent Organisations
These do not constitute a formal bloc as such.
They are organisations broadly supportive of the FSLN, in some cases directly — the teachers union ANDEN is affiliated to the CST.

CGT-1 (Socialist Unions)*	2	Teachers' Union (ANDEN)	1
CAUS (Communist Unions)	1	MISURASATA	1
Journalists Union (UPN)	1	Association of Clergy (ANCLEN)	1
Health Workers Union		Higher Education Council (CNES)	1
(FETSALUD)	1		
Total			9

The consolidation of working-class power in the new Council of State was endorsed strongly by the mass organisations, which ever since the victory had pressed for full representation. The CDS had called for the Council to have a 'truly class character' and the reaction of the CST executive committee in Chinandega of 4 November was typical: 'The bourgeoisie wants to hide the undeniable fact that political and social conditions have changed profoundly since the triumph of the Revolution. Today it is impossible to conceive of the Council of State without the direct and representative participation of the organised working masses.' The Moscow-line PSN also, significantly, endorsed the fresh arrangement of forces. In an interview with *Barricada*, Socialist leader Luis Sanchez declared:

> Since 19 July there has been a significant regrouping of social, political and economic forces in the country. New mass organisations have sprung up like the CST, ATC and Sandinista Youth — in short, new organisations which enjoy great popular strength and mass support. This important role must be institutionalised. On the other hand, other organisations which were taken into account when the original plans for the Council of State were drawn up have disappeared, weakened or lost all influence, all political and social prestige.[41]

Parallel with the struggle between the Frente and the Right, there were smaller-scale disputes over the inclusion or omission of particular groups. The Social Christian leadership of the CTN was outraged that the Socialist unions of the CGT-I, with a smaller membership, should be allocated two seats. The Communist Party meanwhile was excluded altogether from the Council, because — according to Junta member Moises Hassan — 'it has placed itself outside the law', while on the other hand its union federation, CAUS, was included as a 'legitimate workers' organisation' despite having led a series of damaging strikes in February 1980. And there was unease in the Church hierarchy about the unanimous decision of the Catholic clergy to participate, aggravated by statements like this from Father Felix Jimenez: 'Our participation is a reflection of the class struggle which is taking place in our country, and logically within the Church itself as a part of our society. The struggle is a fierce one: some members of the Church are opting for a particular project, which they may refer to as social democracy or some other term. Others, in contrast, are opting for a programme which is thoroughly identified with the interests of the people.'[42]

The inclusion of the ethnic organisation, MISURASATA, in the Council was also problematic. 'At the beginning our relationship with the other mass organisations was difficult. They mistrusted us, perhaps because under Somoza there was an ethnic organisation called ALPROMISU[Alianza para el Progreso de los Miskitos y Sumos, founded in 1973], which had very dubious origins. But we're managing to integrate our struggles with theirs. Naturally we've developed at a slower pace, but if the Revolution continues on its present path then MISURASATA is ready to play its part in support.'[43] The FSLN's own strategy is certainly to build up MISURASATA as the basis of its support in the Atlantic Coast region, while simultaneously trying to head off the risk of separatist currents using MISURASATA as their vehicle. *Barricada* publishes a weekly edition in Miskito, the main indigenous language in that area, and foreign aid too has helped to integrate the Coast popula- tion into the Revolution (MISURASATA has received offers of technicall training in cooperativism and trade unionism from Cuba, Panama and Mexico). By its democratic procedures for electing its delegate to the Council of State, MISURASATA indicated the most important thing – it was begin- ing to function with the same internal democracy as the other popular organisations.

The founding session of the Council of State took place as scheduled on 4 May, presided over by the Supreme Court of Justice and in the presence of Archbishop Obando y Bravo. It elected Comandante de la Revolucion Bayardo Arce as its first president. 'This gives institutional form,' said Arce in his inaugural address, 'to the policy of national unity implemented by the FSLN, and also opens a forum for dialogue and a school for popular power.' One vice-president came from each of the Sandinista, independent and private sectors: Comandante Dora Maria Tellez for the FSLN, Plutarco Anduray for the Independent Liberal PLI, and Jose Francisco Cardenal of COSEP. Cardenal's prompt resignation and complaints at the abuse of 'my unsullied name as a democrat' was one of the more bizarre turns of the power struggle that was building up. It also hinted at a confusion which had been raging for weeks within the disunited bourgeois opposition. When the moment came to react decisively to a confrontation with the FSLN, the bourgeoisie vacillated as it had so often done before. Should the bourgeoisie boycott the Council of State? The PCD was hopelessly split on the issue, dividing into three opposing camps and mirroring the three Conservative factions which had originally united in the new party. COSEP made its decision to take part only after protracted discussions with the United States Embassy. Although eventually accepting the State Department's view that withdrawal at this stage would be suicidal, COSEP made its entry with an aggressive statement proclaiming private enterprise to be the 'motor force of the economy' – precisely the epithet often applied by the FSLN to the workers and peasants. By 4 May, only Robelo's MDN and the PCD had failed to nominate their delegates, and even within the MDN there was a vocal minority group opposing the Robelista position. The Social Christian PSC announced its representative, but like the other two right-wing parties failed to put in an appearance at the inaugural session. On 8 May, at the Council's first full debating session, a formal appeal was made to all three parties to take up their positions immediately. When they still refused, the CDS put up a motion giving the PSC, PCD and MDN an ultimatum, opposed by the PSN who felt it tactically wrong at this stage to force a confrontation. But the confrontation was there, whether the Socialists liked it or not, and its resolu- tion was not restricted to internal debate in the Council of State. It hinged on the FSLN's response to Robelo's resignation from the Junta; the appointment of two new Junta members from the bourgeoisie asserted the Frente's hegemony at this critical moment. It cut the ground from under Robelo's campaign to assume leadership of the private sector opposition, while maintaining the constant mobilisation of the mass organisations in defence of their majority position on the Council of State and against the *burguesia vendepatria*. In the face of this, it was natural that the MDN should prove the most intransigent of the bourgeois forces, but eventually it too followed the PSC and PCD into the Council. With COSEP already there, it would have been absurd for the MDN to remain isolated from the rest of the anti-Sandinista Right.

Fully constituted now, the Council of State set to work with its worker-peasant majority. Its functions were to approve Junta legislation, prepare an electoral law and constitution and present its own proposals to the Junta for new legislation. Within the Council, all voting is by simple majority, and any proposed legislation must be supported by at least ten of the forty-seven members. Since the bourgeoisie has eleven representatives, this means that right-wing proposals can gain the backing needed for full debate — but only if the bourgeoisie is agreed on the proposals. The Council of State may, in other words, bring a surprising indirect advantage to the Right by prompting it to overcome its traditional weakness of disunity. To the working class, meanwhile, the Council of State is an open reflection of the class struggle: 'For the CST, the aim was to elect as delegates the most responsible comrades, those who had a critical vision and firmly rooted class consciousness. Because the Council of State would give us the chance to confront the exploiting classes face to face: the bourgeoisie, the gentlemen of COSEP.'[44] In the same interview, the armed forces' representative, Comandante Hugo Torres, went further into the question of the responsibility which Council of State delegates had to the masses, both through the open assemblies (*cabildos abiertos*) which explain the functions of the Council at a local level, and in the heart of the mass organisations themselves: 'If we make a mistake and pass a law which is against the interests of the people, then the people must protest. And [if we fail them] . . . they must go as far as exercising their right to dismiss us as their representatives.'[45]

Popular Demands and State Policy

The events of April and May 1980 — the resignation of Robelo from the Junta and the installation of the Council of State — marked a watershed in the advance of the Revolution, and the culmination of its second phase. The first had lasted from 19 July to the end of December, characterised by a firm democratic restructuring of the popular organisations (of which the First National Assembly of the ATC was a high point) and a strengthening of Sandinista power in the Government of National Reconstruction which reflected the changing balance of class forces in the months following the war. The resignation of the entire Cabinet in December to make way for the publication of Plan 80 was critical. On 16 November Borge had told a conference at the Central American University (UCA) that: 'We have the arms, the mass organisations, and a government of honest people who are closer to the FSLN's line with each new day.' But the fight against bureaucracy in government, and consolidation of key ministries in line with the FSLN's strategy, had to be taken further. Six weeks later Daniel Ortega told *Barricada:* 'We are making structural changes which are in harmony with the interests of the Revolution: that is, the interests of the people.'[46] This involved not only the appointment of *comandantes* to key ministries (Humberto Ortega to Defence, Wheelock to MIDA, Ruiz to Planning) but the redrawing of ministry responsibilities and the establishment of new state agencies – the amalgamation of Agriculture and Agrarian Reform into a single ministry, the creation of COIP to administer the state industrial sector, and the inauguration of commodity agencies like INPESCA (fisheries) and ENCAFE and ENAL (coffee and cotton) for better centralised economic planning.

It was only natural that, in this first phase, there should be instances of unilateral action by government, due either to bureaucracy, the imperfect early development of the state, or the initial disorientation of a popular movement unaccustomed to shaping state power. The FSLN's task was to overcome this by strengthening the mass organisations and reforming the government where necessary. The aim was an improved articulation of the relationship between the masses and the state, to reach a point where popular demands and state policies would converge. The occasional case of unilateralism was not too detrimental – what mattered much more was the capacity of the mass organisations to identify such cases and condemn them. The Frente was greatly encouraged by the people's response to two early decrees which had not been the product of sustained dialogue with the masses, the more so since the actual measures taken were manifestly in the popular interest. The first was the 19 December decree to slash rents – a move welcomed for its content but criticised as a unilateral government decision; and the second was the early set of price controls on basic foodstuffs. Here, the CDS of the Mercado Oriental complained that the controls had been instituted without adequate consultation, a complaint based on the findings of communal assemblies of consumers and market traders organised by the CDSs themselves. As a result, the fixing of prices is now resolved by constant dialogue between ENABAS, the Ministry of Internal Trade (MICOIN) and the mass organisations. Plan 80 was the first major state policy document to reflect this dialogue, and it institutionalised mass scrutiny of future ministerial decisions by setting up a series of Programmatic Co-ordinating Commissions (CPCs) to cover a dozen areas of policy: finance, agricultural production, the Area of Public Ownership (APP), industrial production, supply, prices and consumer affairs, infrastructure and projects, labour and salaries, social services, education and culture, foreign affairs, and planning and information.

Plan 80 and the Cabinet reshuffle brought an end to the first period and opened four months of intense ideological struggle in which the Frente made it clearer that national unity meant unity around the interests of the working class. For the mass organisations, it brought the necessary *national* structuring of the CDSs and the militias and the institutionalisation of worker and peasant power in the Council of State. It was a key period in enriching the relationship between the popular organisations and the state, and it brought important new legislation in both the industrial and agricultural sectors which was directly stimulated by mass mobilisation. On 17 February more than 50,000 peasants and rural labourers marched to the Plaza de la Revolucion in Managua. They had come from every part of the country, even plane-loads from Waspan on the north-eastern border with Honduras carrying banners in Miskito. Through the ATC, they put pressing demands on behalf of both farm labourers and small peasant producers. To shouts of 'Don't hand back a single inch of land', the marchers demanded INRA confiscation of untilled 'intervened' farmland (whose owners were under investigation for their possible links with Somoza) and state action against private landowners who refused to resume production, meet minimum wage levels or implement recently decreed improvements in working conditions and social benefits. Edgardo Garcia, Secretary-General of the ATC, put the organisation's position on production boycotts, coinciding with the growing mobilisation of the CST around the same issue: 'Any coffee planter or other producer who does not wish to carry out harvests or who boycotts production will be denounced by us as an enemy of the Revolution. Through our own efforts we will get the production moving that they want to sabotage.' It was not just a statement of principle. The ATC had already moved in numerous cases to complete the coffee harvest where private plantation owners had left crops unpicked or had dismissed workers.

For small peasant producers, the marchers demanded a reduction in the annual interest paid on state loans from 14% to 5%, and the annulment of debts contracted with INVIERNO or other Somocista banks now under state control. They complained of delays by Banco Nacional de Desarrollo officials in processing loan applications, and – most significantly – insisted that a signature from the ATC should be the only condition required by a small producer for an application for state credit.

Wheelock's reply to the march was swift and decisive: 'We know that your demands are just, and this march gives us the confidence to advance and make further transformations.'[47] While he repeated the need for the agrarian reform to proceed in an orderly manner, avoiding 'anarchic and spontaneous actions', he insisted that 'there are elements among the landowners who must be hit hard if their lands are left idle . . . There is not the slightest intention on INRA's part to hand back a single inch of land.' He promised that the state would take prompt action to endorse the ATC's demands, while for the Junta Sergio Ramirez announced that a new decree was imminent. It came on 3 March, an immediate confiscation of all the *tierras intervenidas,* excluding only those owned by small producers, areas of less than 25 *manzanas* (43 acres) on the Pacific Coast or 50 *manzanas* (86 acres) elsewhere.

In the weeks leading up to the ATC march, Wheelock and other senior officials of INRA had been active in validating similar demands by other groups of farmworkers. On 12 February, the owner of the medium-sized

251

Hacienda El Callao near Managua had dismissed a number of labourers in-cluding ATC activists, and had refused to allow the work force to carry out the *pepena* – the final phase of the coffee harvest. Workers on the farm had responded by taking over the *pepena* themselves, selling the coffee beans directly to INRA and calling Wheelock in personally, demanding a state takeover of El Callao and alleging a long history of exploitation and economic sabotage by the owner. But one worker on the *finca* made it clear that the ATC understood very well the distinction between landowners who had blatantly infringed 'the rules of the game' and the rest of the private sector. 'Ernesto Solorzano is not representative of the private sector. He is betray-ing the alliance between our government and the private sector in order to feather his own nest.'[48] The direct action of workers at El Callao was supported by more than 100 farm labourers on neighbouring *fincas,* and the government's response was decisive. Wheelock visited the farm, dis-cussed the workers' grievances fully, and within forty-eight hours announced state intervention at El Callao.

Working-class mobilisation against some factory owners' attempts to sabotage industrial production produced very similar results to the ATC march, and at exactly the same time. Responding to a wave of factory occupations in February 1980, a decree by the Junta on 2 March against decapitalisation of factories again endorsed the principle of direct indepen-dent action by the working class, and implicit in both decrees was an encou-ragement of further class action along the same lines. While other Sandinista leaders attacked capitalist falsification of tax returns, alteration of export and import invoices, concealment of capital held abroad and failure to record the receipt of foreign currency, Carlos Nunez of the National Directorate made explicit the significance of the new decree: 'This decree,' he said, 'is the result of the direct action of the workers and their mass organisations.' He tellingly praised not only the efforts of CST-affiliated unions, but also those of other trade union federations: the building workers union SCAAS (loyal to the Socialist CGT-I) at the Sovipe plant, and Communist CAUS members at the Nicarao farm equipment factory.

Nicaraguan workers gained immense confidence from these victories, two examples of the new convergence between their own actions and the state's response. They realised, furthermore, that no decree could be effective unless followed up by further action to guarantee enforcement and uncover further abuses. *Poder Sandinista* had already stressed the point: 'Workers' control, expressed through their class organisations, must play a fundamen-tal role of vigilance . . . This is as important, if not more so, than the legal measures taken against illegal practices.'[49]

Of course, none of this means that every strongly felt working-class claim can automatically count on the same response from the govern-ment. As between the industrial and agricultural sectors, for example, the rhythm with which state control can push forward is necessarily different. On 11 March, within eight days of the new agrarian reform decree, many thought that the same principle could be applied to industry, and thousands of factory workers marched from the CST headquarters in Managua to the *Casa de Gobierno* to demand the confiscation of all factories under investigation according to the provisions of the new anti-decapitalisation law. Moises Hassan and CST Propaganda and Political Education Secretary Ramon Medrano explained to the demonstrators why this was impossible: 'We must be calm and patient,' said Hassan. 'There are certain limits which we cannot overstep now, since that would place the Revolution in danger. We have plenty of time ahead of us, and the measures which need to be taken will be taken at the necessary and opportune moment.'[50] Far from using this response to demobilise the demonstrators, Hassan and Medrano fully endorsed their action in organising the march, and turned in the second half of their reply to the need for industrial workers to remain organised and vigilant and to denounce further evidence of economic sabotage in their factories.

At every level of the mass organisations, Nicaraguans prize this access to dialogue with government. Talking during the same week as the new agrarian reform and anti-decapitalisation decrees, a member of the CDS in the Barrio Beatriz Castillo near the Managua lakeside, where only 5% of adult men have regular employment, pointed to the contrast between the present situation and the Somoza era:

> We've identified two main needs for this *barrio* through the CDS: the need for drinking-water and an electricity supply. We went to see INAA [the state water agency] and they've agreed to lay on piped water. Now next week we have a meeting with INE [the state energy agency] to see if it's feasible to get power lines installed. That may not be possible, because eventually the whole *barrio* is moving to a new site. But if it's not, we know that the decision will be reached through dialogue that we take part in as equal partners, and we'll understand the reasons and be involved in whatever future plans are made. Under Somoza, my God ... there was no chance for working people like us to approach the government. Or even if there was, you had to ask for an appointment six months in advance by telegram ... Somoza and his cronies were always too busy at the Country Club, drinking cocktails and highballs. Much more important things on their minds than talking about the problems of the people.[51]

A New Kind of Elections

Having lost its battle for the Council of State, the bourgeoisie launched an intensive campaign for rapid elections. From the start, the FSLN had resisted domestic and foreign pressure to call old-style *elecciones de guaro y nacatamales* on a time-scale dictated by the bourgeoisie, who insisted on 1981 or 1982 as an ideal date. The Right was realistic enough to recognise that such elections could only result in a massive popular endorsement of the

FSLN, but the aim of the campaign was not to win the elections but to insti-
tutionalise the structures of bourgeois democracy. To this, the Frente has
consistently counterposed a promise of elections for which the full reconstruction of the country and the development of embryonic working-class
power structures were a necessary precondition. As for the transitional
period, placards throughout Nicaragua proclaimed: 'The people have already
made their choice with blood.' Elections would be the formal seal on the
popular power being built through the mass organisations.

Marked by a context in which a worker-peasant majority had been
guaranteed in the Council of State, the bourgeois campaign concentrated on
unifying the existing parties of the Right, drawing floating sectors of the
middle and petty bourgeoisie away from the Revolution, and building
support among peasant groups in the most backward areas where armed
groups of former National Guard terrorists were operating. Crucial to the
campaign was an attempt to discredit the FSLN by making false claims that
the National Directorate had made a formal agreement in May to announce
an election timetable at the 1980 anniversary celebrations on 19 July. With
the world's press at its disposal on that day, the Right accused the
Frente of 'breaking promises' and undermining the basis of national unity.
When the celebrations passed off with no mention of elections, COSEP
angrily threatened to walk out of the Council of State. The ideological
battle for elections was spearheaded by *La Prensa,* which used the May-to-
July period to give front page coverage to every small meeting of Democratic
Conservatives, Social Christians and the MDN. When the PCD held a July
electioneering meeting among peasants in the remote southern area of
Nueva Guinea, *La Prensa* took the chance to attack a counter-rally organised
by the Juventud Sandinista, denouncing the crowd's chants of so-called
Communist slogans such as 'Popular Power'. The column-space devoted to
such petty incidents indicated not only the seriousness of the right-wing
press campaign but also the bourgeoisie's frustration at its own inability to
mobilise support around a real alternative to *Sandinismo.* It was the old-
problem of the Nicaraguan bourgeois opposition: their forms of organisation
were still largely those of the pressure groups set up to meet specific short-
term challenges during the Somoza era, with no strong political base, no
organised membership and no solid party structure to rely on. Unlike the
FSLN, the Right had so far failed to evolve new political structures adequate
to the needs of the post-Revolutionary situation.

Right-wing leaders also used the slow economic recovery of the country
as a further justification for prompt elections. Under the headline 'While
there is pluralism, there will be no Communism', Democratic Conservative
Emilio Alvarez Montalvan was given a full-page spread in *La Prensa*. He could
hardly have been more explicit about the Right's intention of using its
control of production as a political weapon:

> We must make it clear that a climate must be produced in the country
> which will increase production and the capacity to accumulate savings.

And elections are the only thing which will give us that peaceful outlook. Every society has its conflicts . . . Here, the man caught in the middle does not want to risk his money, nor does he want to invest. There is no hope in the future . . . The politician is to some degree a sportsman, and what he wants are the rules of the game.[52]

The Frente's reply made clear that such demands could not be isolated from an international context in which a Reagan election victory was an imminent possibility, and counter-revolutionary attacks within the country were being stepped up. Comandante Omar Cabezas, speaking at the inauguration of the Silvia Ferrufino Health Centre in Managua, drew out the connection:

This external aggression [from Honduras] is accompanied by an internal counter-revolutionary movement in Nicaragua. A section of the rich, a section of businessmen, is running around out there talking about elections, asking why we don't hold elections. An election now would cost us 40 million *cordobas*. We prefer to use those 40 million *cordobas* to build schools and hospitals. With the war, our people won the right to vote if they want to vote, and not to vote if they don't want to vote. The people are in the Council of State, and that pains the rich. The people are in government, in the army, and that pains them. So they think that maybe elections will bring the rich to power. They believe − or rather dream − that elections will enable them to snatch away from the people the conquests which they won by armed struggle.

The Frente refused to be drawn on an election schedule until it was ready. The moment came a month after the first anniversary with the return home of the literacy *brigadistas,* another superlative piece of timing. Humberto Ortega, speaking to the crowd of 350,000, preceded the announcement with a bitter attack on the right-wing campaign:

They try to discredit our armed forces, the government, the National Directorate. They indulge in rumour mongering, they ridicule our leaders, they seek to separate Christianity from Sandinismo . . . These reactionary sectors have also recently arrived at a sort of unity of 'mummies' and fossils, which through their electoral formulas are trying to turn back history and reinstate a regime of exploiters and oppressors: a false democracy, a false freedom.[53]

It is worth quoting at length from the National Directorate's announce-ment that elections are to be held in 1985:

For the Frente Sandinista democracy is not measured solely in the political sphere, and cannot be reduced only to the participation of the people in elections. Democracy is not simply elections. It is something more, much more. For a revolutionary, for a Sandinista, it means *participation* by the people in political, economic, social and cultural affairs. The more the people participate in such matters, the more democratic they will be. And it must be said once and for all: democracy neither begins nor ends with elections. It is a myth to want to reduce democracy to that status. Democracy begins in the economic order, when social inequalities begin to diminish, when the workers and peasants improve their standard of living. That is when true democracy begins, not before.

Once these aims are achieved, democracy is immediately extended to other fields: the field of government is broadened; when the people influence their government, when the people determine their government, whether this pleases some people or not. In a more advanced phase, democracy means the participation of the workers in the running of factories, farms, cooperatives and cultural centres. To sum up, democracy is the intervention of the masses in all aspects of social life. We point out all this to establish on a principled basis what the FSLN understands by democracy.

The National Directorate statement concluded:

After a year of the Revolution, we can responsibly state that the backwardness and the economic, social and moral destruction of the country is so far-reaching that we cannot expect the country to be reconstructed before 1985. For that reason, the National Directorate of the Frente Sandinista has decided that the organised Junta of Government must remain at the head of governmental affairs until 1985.

Therefore, our working people, our workers and peasants, our youth and women, the professionals and patriotic businessmen who are dedicated to National Reconstruction, should make ready in 1985 to decide on the programme of government and the country's best individuals, who will take charge of the government and continue to push forward with the tasks of our Revolution.

For its part, the Junta of Government of National Reconstruction . . . will commence an electoral process in January 1984.

Ortega added further comments which spelt out the FSLN's election message:

As everyone will have understood, the elections we speak of are very different from the elections desired by the oligarchs and traitors, conservatives and liberals, reactionaries and imperialists . . . Never forget that *our elections will be to perfect revolutionary power, not to hold a raffle among those who seek to hold power, because the people hold power through their vanguard — the FSLN and its National Directorate.* (emphasis in original)

Towards the Party of the Sandinista Revolution

To coincide with its election propaganda, the Right launched a vociferous campaign in the Council of State to define and regulate the activities of political parties. Its specific objective was to undermine the FSLN's authority to govern and to force it into a formal – and premature – announcement of the Sandinista Party. The Council of State move was headed by the Democratic Conservatives and supported by the eleven right-wing members of the Council as well as by the Communist union leadership of the CAUS. Alvarez Montalvan of the PCD led a typical attack on the FSLN in *La Prensa,* accusing the vanguard of having no legal constitution, of being a 'political party very much *sui generis,* a party with guns.'[54] The right-wing attack focussed on the confusion between party and state, and the supposed predominance of radical elements within what COSEP and its allies habitually refer to as the FSLN Party. 'The FSLN,' stated COSEP in a major attack on the government in late 1980,

> although *de facto* a political party, avoids defining itself as such, giving rise to a confusion between Government-Party-FSLN, with all that this implies – such as the unilateral use of confiscated television, radio and newspapers, the use of state economic resources for FSLN party ends . . . The creation of parastatal Sandinista bodies which are granted state buildings and economic resources to realise political activities . . . The army is the army of a party, not a national army.'[55]

COSEP's conclusion, like that of Alvarez Montalvan, was that the Frente had two options: to refuse to declare itself a party, in which case it would forfeit the right to govern the country and could not compete on equal terms with 'established' parties in any future elections; or to form the Sandinista Party immediately, in which case it could no longer lay claim to 'its own' army and police force. There is both cynicism and desperation in COSEP's attempts to brand the FSLN as a military force only capable of leading the armed stage of the struggle, after which it should quietly disappear and allow traditional elections to be wrangled over by the tiny parties of the Right. Nevertheless, the formation of the Sandinista Party is indispensable to the future development of the Revolution. But as with the Council of State and the elections, the party will be formed at a rhythm dictated by nobody but the FSLN itself. Carlos Fonseca's own graphic comment shortly before his death that 'to talk of a party today is to have your feet in Petrograd, or in Yenan, or in the Karl Marx Theatre in Havana in 1965 – it is not to have your feet in Subtiava or Waslala,'[56] was as true in early 1980 as it had been in 1976. It was only in September 1980 that Tomas Borge expressed the case for the party with real urgency. 'We have achieved the basic structuring of the revolutionary state,' he said. 'Now the time has come to devote our full attention to developing the Party of the Revolution.'[57] Before the July 1979 victory, the rhythm of the war and the pressures of clandestinity made party building impossible; thereafter, until the summer of 1980, the problems of consolidating the state were paramount, as was the Frente's emphasis on intensive political education work. One of the most tragic legacies of four decades of *Somocismo* has been the disastrous level of ideological awareness in Nicaragua, and the Frente's own absence of experienced cadres to form the basis of a party. The intermediate links between the FSLN and the people during the insurrectional phase, mass participation in the popular organisations – these are one thing, but the ideological clarity required for the party is quite another matter. To rush the creation of the party, in the absence of mass political consciousness, would inevitably produce a small elite organisation, separation from the people, bureaucratisation – all anathema to the basic tenets of *Sandinismo*. But the contradiction here for the Frente is to achieve ideological preparation at the mass level rapidly enough to counter an ideological onslaught from the Right, which will grow as the Revolution takes firmer root, and which still enjoys free access to its own influential means of communication and organisation.

So far, the Frente's public discussion of the future party has focussed more on the qualities required of cadres and the basic principles of democratic centralism which will govern the party, rather than on precise details of structures and timetables. Borge and other Sandinista leaders have spoken frequently of a party in which 'the leaders will be directly under the control of the organisation.' In a February speech, Borge emphasised that it would be

> a revolutionary party of a new kind, which bears no resemblance to the old and corrupt parties of the past, a party tainted neither by fear, nor sectarianism, nor elitism, nor anyone's personal ambitions. A party which will have flexible tactics, and at the same time will be capable of intransigence in the face of injustice and exploitation, intolerant of opportunism and other deviations into which revolutionary organisations can often fall . . . We understand, of course, that in order to create this kind of organisation we must pass through a period of political and organic maturing. It is not enough to wish for the existence of a high quality party; we must work every day towards its formation.[58]

That work has been slow and patient, its main emphasis on the formation of cadres and the gradual shaping of the FSLN's own internal structures of secretariats and departments. The final form is no more preconceived than that of the mass organisations. Like them, the stress is always on the word 'embryonic'.

Even so, the FSLN's Assemblies of Cadres and Militants – the third of these was held in September 1980 – have marked staging-posts in the advance towards future party organisation. Parallel to these assemblies, the Frente has set up Sandinista Base Committees (CBSs), whose task has been to grade future party members into three categories: *militantes* (those with a long history of active political work in the FSLN); *pre-militantes* (activists recruited during the most recent phase of the struggle); and *simpatizantes* (a category open to all those who share the political aims of the Frente and have a reasonable degree of political training).[59] The effort to train local cadres and structure these Base Committees into Sandinista Party cells fell to the regional FSLN Comites de Direccion Departamental (Departmental Leadership Committees: CDDs). The CDDs were born in February 1980, and the role of women as leadership cadres was very marked at this level: five of the fifteen CDDs were headed by women, including those for the major cities of Managua, Leon and Esteli.

Cadre training is taking place intensively within each of the mass organisations, and at shop-floor and farm levels. While each of the mass organisations must train its own activists, skilled in the specifics of trade union, rural or women's issues, an upward filtering of the best of these activists to become party cadres emphasises again the critical role of the mass organisations as party breeding-grounds and rearguards, while scrupulously maintaining their own autonomy. Propaganda committees of four or five people in each productive centre, constant political seminars and study circles, CDS propaganda units, leadership visits to the workplace: each of these is a forum for building the consciousness which the party requires. It is a long and difficult task.

'We face problems which other revolutions have not had to deal with,' noted Borge. It is these unique conditioning features of the Nicaraguan Revolution which define the issues that the new cadre must master − a lasting tactical alliance with the private sector in which the majority of the bourgeoisie remains in place; an inherited economic disaster; a mounting revolutionary struggle in at least two neighbouring countries. It means understanding the complex meaning of a transitional mixed economy and the permanent subordinate place which the private sector can win for itself by accepting FSLN leadership and diminishing profits; the demarcation line between 'patriotic' businessmen and the counter-revolutionary Right; the need to regenerate the economy through increased productivity, accepting austerity and labour discipline while resisting the economistic temptations offered by the ultra-left; a redefined vision of the state, for all its temporary shortcomings, as the ally of the working class; uncompromising internationalism (the cry of 'Long live proletarian internationalism', once the preserve of a handful of vanguard cadres, has now taken its place as a permanent feature of every mass meeting). Each new cadre must handle these concepts flexibly, not transmitting them blindly from the leadership to the rank-and-file but enriching them by learning from grassroots experience.

Above all, the party will seek this clarity. In December 1979, from his position within the Junta, Alfonso Robelo made attempts to pressure the Frente into something quite different: a broad multi-class party, the Partido Sandinista Unico, which would embrace all forces which had been active in the anti-Somoza bloc. To agree to such a plan would have seriously diluted the ideological force of the Revolution, as Robelo in fact intended, and the

Frente decisively rejected his proposals, a serious reverse for the MDN leader which contributed directly to his later slide into an overtly anti-FSLN stance.[60] Where Robelo proposed a single party, the FSLN proposed to create the broadest possible *front* of revolutionary and progressive organisations under Sandinista leadership, within which each party would retain full autonomy. To move towards a one-party state in Nicaragua today would be extremely dangerous, and the FSLN has not fallen into that trap, despite the stated willingness of other parties like the Socialists to fuse themselves into a single party. The Nicaraguan working class has organisations independent of the FSLN to which sectors of it are traditionally — and legitimately — loyal, and the Frente has had the wisdom to respect both this autonomy and the independent status of the parties of the bourgeoisie. Its aim was to revive a bloc similar in character to the National Patriotic Front of 1979, but responsive to the new needs of national reconstruction.

On 1 January 1980, the Independent Liberal PLI reaffirmed its unconditional support for FSLN leadership. It was the beginning of the new bloc. A little over a month later, Comandante Carlos Nunez was able to announce the first unity talks between delegates from the FSLN, Socialists, Independent Liberals, Popular Social Christians, even Robelo's MDN and the right-wing Social Christians. The previously hostile Communist Party of Nicaragua also decided to join in. By 19 February, in a conjuncture marked by the inauguration of the Comision Nacional Intersindical — the first major step towards trade union unity — a coordinating committee was formed by six of these parties. Only the Social Christians decided to reject this model of national unity. The committee called itself the Bloque Popular Patriotico, and agreed on the need to close ranks in the face of reaction and ultra-leftism, simultaneously endorsing the decision to postpone and restructure the Council of State in the interests of the working class. Events over the next three months made it inevitable that the MDN and Communists would withdraw, and in May the FSLN and the three remaining parties (PLI, PPSC and PSN) founded the Frente Patriotico de la Revolucion (FPR), making it clear that the door was still open for other parties to reconsider their position. The FPR was much more than a symbolic grouping of left-wing parties. Coming in the wake of Robelo's resignation from the Junta, it was yet another firm practical response to a critical turning-point in the Revolution, and a reaffirmation of the FSLN's vanguard role. Nor was the FPR purely a tactical device. It foreshadowed the role of political parties in the immediate future of the Sandinista state, one of guaranteed active co-existence. The FSLN has learned many lessons from previous revolutionary experiences. Not least among them is that the dictatorship of the proletariat is far from being the same thing as the prompt establishment of a one-party state.

Such a concept of pluralism will be put rigorously to the test. Four parties of the Right continue to exist and organise without hindrance, but they are preparing for all-out war against the FSLN, and have made it clear that they reject the Sandinistas' right to retain power. The Frente's ideological battle against these groups has not resorted to repression. In the coming years — perhaps months — however, mass demands for action against the right-wing parties' deliberate attempt to subvert the new democratic order will grow, and the FSLN will have to decide whether to endorse these demands. At the same time, four parties of the Left operate independently, with three of them accepting the FSLN's right to guide the Revolution. As individuals, there is no reason to suppose that their support of the FSLN will waver. But their raison d'etre, as for any political party, is the exercise of political power. In the coming period, though perhaps not for several years, they will have to decide whether their continued existence as parties is relevant.

Notes

1. *Programa de Gobierno de Reconstruccion Nacional,* Section 1, Paragraph 12.
2. Interview with Enrique Schmidt, Managua, August 1979.
3. Luis Carrion, speech to the Selim Shible military school, 8 September 1979, reprinted in *La Revolucion a Traves de Nuestra Direccion Nacional* (Managua, SENAPEP, 1980), p. 57.
4. *Ibid.*
5. Luis Carrion, interview with Jorge Timossi, reprinted in *Nicaragua, Patria Libre* (Havana, Casa de las Americas, 1979), pp. 191-3.
6. Interview with Frente Interno combatant, Managua, July 1979. The Frente Interno, because of its wide experience in organising irregular forces during the war, was initially responsible for restructuring the militias.
7. Luis Carrion, speaking at a National Directorate press conference, 29 July 1979.
8. *Ibid.*
9. Interview with former *miliciano,* Ciudad Dario, August 1979.
10. *Barricada,* 25 February 1980.
11. In *El Machete,* newspaper of the Asociacion de Trabajadores del Campo, No. 7, July 1980.
12. Interview with middle-ranking member of the Ejercito Popular Sandinista, Managua, January 1981.
13. *Ibid.*
14. Based on interviews with combatants from each tendency, July-August 1979.
15. *Poder Sandinista,* No. 6, 22 November 1979.
16. Carlos Nunez, speech to the Central Sandinista de Trabajadores, 7 October 1979.
17. Carlos Nunez, *El Papel de las Organizaciones de Masas en el Proceso Revolucionario,* speech at the Gruta de Xavier, 20 April 1980 reprinted Managua, SENAPEP, serie Orientacion Sandinista, No. 3 1980, p. 16.
18. The same April 1980 speech by Nunez contains one of the most complete statements on record of the FSLN's view of tensions between the mass organisations and the state. See *ibid.,* pp. 18-21.

19. Sergio Ramirez, interview in *Desde La Cuadra,* No. 2, July 1980.
20. Interview in Chinandega, August 1979.
21. Tomas Borge, *El Partido Sandinista y las Cualidades del Militante,* speech to Ministry of Interior staff, 20 February 1980, reprinted Managua, SENAPEP, Serie Orientacion Sandinista, No. 7, 1980, p. 15.
22. Regis Debray, 'Nicaragua – Una Moderacion Radical', originally published in French in *Le Monde Diplomatique,* the Spanish version was published in *Nicaragua en Lucha,* No. 3, Barcelona, COSOCAN, February 1980, pp. 8-23.
23. Interview in Managua, March 1980.
24. Interview in Leon, August 1979.
25. Tomas Borge, *Los Derechos Humanos y la Revolucion Nicaraguense,* pp. 36-7.
26. *El Nuevo Diario,* 9 July 1980.
27. See *Barricada,* 7 and 8 March 1980.
28. Tomas Borge, *El Partido Sandinista y las Cualidades del Militante,* p. 16.
29. COSEP communique, 14 November 1979.
30. Interview with Uriel Guzman, Monimbo shoemaker and CDS activist, Masaya, August 1980.
31. Interview with CDS member, Los Robles, Managua, July 1980.
32. Ronald Paredes of the National Office of the CDS, in *El Nuevo Diario,* 9 July 1980.
33. *Ibid.*
34. Interview with Miguel De Castilla, Deputy Minister of Education, Managua, March 1980, quoted in George Black and John Bevan, *The Loss of Fear – Education in Nicaragua Before and After the Revolution* (London, Nicaragua Solidarity Campaign/World University Service, 1980), p. 36.
35. *Plan 81,* p. 105.
36. See *Los Comites de Defensa Sandinista en el Proceso Revolucionario de la Nueva Nicaragua* (pamphlet), (Managua, Secretaria Nacional de Organizacion de los CDS, May 1980).
37. *Barricada,* 4 May 1980.
38. *Programa de Gobierno de Reconstruccion Nacional,* Section 1, Paragraph 2(b): Poder Ejecutivo.
39. *Barricada,* 13 November 1979.
40. *Barricada,* 5 November 1979.
41. *Barricada,* 22 April 1980.
42. Interviewed in *Barricada,* 8 May 1980.
43. Interview with MISURASATA regional organiser, Bonanza, Zelaya Norte, August 1980.
44. Interview in *Perspectiva Mundial,* 28 July 1980.
45. *Ibid.*
46. *Barricada,* 27 December 1979.
47. *Barricada,* 18 February 1980.
48. *Barricada,* 16 February 1980.
49. *Poder Sandinista,* No. 17, 14 February 1980.
50. *Barricada,* 12 March 1980.
51. Interview with members of the Comite de Defensa Sandinista, Barrio Beatriz Castillo, Managua, March 1980.

52. *La Prensa*, 2 August 1980.
53. 'Aplastar la Contrarrevolucion' speech reprinted in *Barricada*, 24 August 1980.
54. *La Prensa*, 2 August 1980.
55. COSEP, 'Analisis sobre la Ejecucion del Programa de Gobierno de Reconstruccion Nacional', in *La Prensa*, 22 November 1980.
56. Quoted by Victor Tirado Lopez, *El Pensamiento Politico de Carlos Fonseca Amador,* (Managua, SENAPEP, 1980), p.8.
57. Tomas Borge, 'Hacia el Partido de la Revolucion Sandinista', opening speech to the Third Assembly of FSLN Cadres and Militants 'Heroes de Nandaime', 13 September 1980.
58. Tomas Borge, *El Partido Sandinista.*
59. Interview with member of Comite de Base Sandinista, Boaco, August 1980.
60. Tim Draimin, *Nicaragua's Revolution*, NACLA Report on the Americas, Vol. XIV, No. 3, May-June 1980, p. 12.

13. A Strategy for Workers and Peasants

Transforming the Countryside

On 15 July 1979, four days before the end of the war, 1,061 peasant families in the *departamento* of Leon occupied 22,600 acres of Somocista-owned farmland and put them into full production. Even before the Sandinista Government had taken power, its agrarian reform programme was already underway. Decrees 3 and 38 of the new Junta gave to the state control of more than 2 million acres of prime land, and considerable scope for future agricultural development. For Nicaragua is a grossly under-used country. Only 7.4% of its surface area is under permanent cultivation, another 13.8% is pasturage, 31.5% is unexploited, and 47.3% is forested. But the problem of under-use is one which can be dealt with at relative leisure. The immediate challenge is the tension between reactivation of agricultural production on the one hand and transformation of social relations in the rural sector on the other. This is, of course, a dilemma that pervades the economy as a whole. 'We didn't invent this model of an economy dependent on agricultural exports,' commented one official of the agrarian reform institute INRA. 'But that's what we've inherited. The Revolution has to satisfy the demands of the rural masses vis-a-vis an agricultural structure which was designed to exploit them. To keep the country on an even keel, we have to generate as much production as we can of export crops, knowing that in the long run this may only reinforce the imbalance between the two halves of agriculture — exports and production for the domestic market. It's a frightening paradox.'[1] In 1979-80, agricultural production fell by 36.9%. The prices of leading export crops had also fallen on world markets. Emergency restoration of production was essential, but how could INRA simultaneously shift the emphasis away from export dependency without damaging the prospects of that recovery?

The concentration of so much farmland in the hands of Somoza and his allies fully stretched the new administrative capacity of INRA, starved like other government agencies of both finance and trained personnel. Politically, too, the restriction of the agrarian reform to Somocista lands was fundamental to the Frente's tactical alliance with the private sector, and avoided too many immediate conflicts with other private landowners. Nevertheless, friction over land was unavoidable. As well as the confiscation of

Somoza properties, the government 'intervened' farmlands whose owners were suspected of links with the dictatorship, freezing production while legal investigations were carried out. As these suspicions were often based on allegations by local peasants and ATC committees, the *intervenciones* became a major bone of contention between the state and right-wing landowners protesting their illegality, and a focus for future demands by the ATC, whose members were often frustrated at the delays in resuming production. Decrees 3 and 38 gave the government wide powers to extend the agrarian reform, by expropriating lands owned by tax defaulters, properties abandoned by their owners and farms left idle in defiance of legislation. Thus, although the initial state sector was deliberately and necessarily restricted, the legal framework existed to allow INRA to resolve land conflicts in favour of the peasants and rural labourers. In the privately owned sector, INRA's early strategy rested on guaranteeing cheap terms for peasants renting from big landowners; providing generous state finance for small peasant proprietors; and eliminating the obvious abuses by private landowners through the vigilance of the ATC. Private landowners angrily retorted that INRA was also sanctioning 'illegal' land takeovers by dispossessed peasants.[2]

INRA believed that agrarian reform, like every aspect of the Revolution, should obey specific national conditions. This meant keeping large agro-exporting concerns intact, stimulating basic grain production for local consumption, and resolving the ambiguities of a rural class structure formed by Somocista capitalism, where a high proportion of the rural population are wage labourers (but for only part of the year). With the need for a seasonal reserve labour force, most subsistence farmers had direct experience of plantation labour. This, coupled with the original powerbase of the FSLN among the northern peasantry, convinced INRA that there was no deeply rooted property instinct among Nicaraguan peasants, and that agrarian reform might therefore move directly from *latifundismo* to collectivisation, without passing first through a phase of redistribution of land into privately owned *parcelas*.[3] As events during the first year were to prove, this strategy required some modification.

Somoza, too, in his own way had tried to deal with agrarian tensions. Major land invasions had exploded with the expansion of cotton cultivation in the 1950s, and in 1963 Somoza's Congress passed an agrarian reform law, creating the Instituto Agrario Nicaraguense (IAN). It was the height of Alliance for Progress politics in Latin America, and IAN – like similar institutions in other Latin American countries – was the direct result of the US-sponsored Punta del Este Conference in 1961.[4] IAN's main thrust was the creation of resettlement colonies to relieve pressure on the land, in which peasant families were given plots of between 1 and 30 acres. But these plots did not give the peasant sufficient income for year-round subsistence, and the need to sell his/her labour during harvest time to supplement the family income was as pressing as ever. Somoza's 'agrarian reform' was, in other words, nothing more than a rationalisation of the reserve labour-force required by big landowners.[5]

265

At first, IAN resettled peasants near the cotton plantations of Leon and Chinandega, but the pressure on land showed no signs of easing. Somoza's next answer was to force peasants out to the agricultural frontier lands of the Atlantic Coast, creating the Proyecto Rigoberto Cabezas (PRIC) colony in the underpopulated region of Nueva Guinea. Here, in the inhospitable south-east, they were conveniently far from the pressure points of the north-west, and could also be relied upon as a reserve labour-force for the planned capital-ist expansion into the Atlantico. Such was Somoza's solution for the pressures on cotton-growing lands. It now remained for him to deal with the coffee-growing zones, where pressure on land was also acute, and which by the 1970s were buzzing with support for the FSLN guerrillas. INVIERNO, the Peasant Welfare Institute, was the third phase of Somoza's reform. Founded in 1975, again at the USA's behest, it simultaneously aimed to undermine support for the Frente, provide cheap labour for the coffee plan-tations, and guarantee the supply of basic grains for the domestic market. The latter two targets were achieved at immense social cost which guaranteed the failure of the first target. INVIERNO financed basic grain production by giving high-interest state loans to peasants who had previously been un-able to offer sufficient security to qualify for the old bank loan system. But the state's purchase prices for their crops were kept deliberately low. The result was poverty and debt, and the only way to survive was by selling one's labour for the coffee harvest. All this has a disturbing consequence for the Sandinista Government: not only is there acute imbalance between the two sectors of agriculture, but plantation labour has been profoundly stigmatised by the years of *Somocismo*. And that very plantation labour is the key to emergency economic reactivation.

For the first five months of Revolution, FSLN Comandante Jaime Wheelock was head of INRA, while the Conservative landowner Manuel Torres ran the separate Ministry of Agricultural Development. The subsequent restructuring of the government machinery brought the two together in an expanded Ministry (MIDA), with Wheelock taking overall charge in the December 1979 Cabinet reshuffle. It was a necessary step to consolidate Sandinista guidance of such a key area and to centralise state agricultural production, avoiding duplication of effort and giving clearer form to the improvisation of the first five months. Wheelock outlined the new ministry's priorities and problems:

> Decree No. 3 has confiscated large *haciendas* in full production. Sugar refineries, large rice and coffee plantations, dairy farms, all with quite a high level of technification. We definitely can't break up these productive units, they are simply not susceptible to division. What we are trying to do, instead, is to improve their technology, improve their administration, improve their infrastructure.[6]

This approach was logical: these enterprises are the heart of Nicaragua's export-earning capacity. But investment possibilities are limited. The meagre foreign aid allotted to agricultural development will only supplement the basic source of investment in infrastructure, which must be the generation of surplus within the agro-exporting enterprises themselves. Wheelock showed that INRA was acutely sensitive to peasant anxieties that investment would be directed at the big state farms instead of cooperatives and went on: 'We haven't made much progress as far as cooperatives are concerned, but as from this year we — together with the ATC and Procampo [the division of INRA responsible for stimulating small peasant producers] — are promoting a whole new movement of cooperativisation.'[7] By the time of Wheelock's comments, the Cooperativas Agricolas Sandinistas (CAS), in place before the insurrection as forms of clandestine rural support for the FSLN, were the most advanced form of collective land use, though still relatively few in number.

The basic unit of confiscated rural property is the Unidad de Produccion Estatal (State Production Unit: UPE). The units cover farms of every size and type, oriented both towards exports and the domestic market. While AgroINRA, the division in charge of major export facilities (sugar refineries, cotton and coffee processing plants etc.) holds only 90,000 acres, the UPEs account for almost two million. There are 2,200 of these production units, grouped together for administrative purposes into 170 state complexes.[8] Each is initially managed by an INRA-appointed administrator, though farmworkers are directly involved in the running of the UPEs and planning of production targets through their representation on the Administrative Council. The old psychology of domination dies hard — it is still common to hear farmworkers refer to the INRA manager as the *mandador,* the all-powerful foreman of the Somoza era — but in time these patterns of administration will give way to full worker control of production as the ATC advances its work in technical training and political education. This new relationship between workers and the state was a point which Wheelock, who more than any other Sandinista leader has touched on the risks of state capitalism, dealt with in his address to the December 1979 ATC Assembly:

> There are those who have said that what is happening is a replacement of the old *patron* by a new one — the state. Those who make this claim have failed absolutely to understand the significance of this Revolution: that the state now is not the same state, it is a state of the workers, a state of producers, who organise production and place it at the disposal of the people, and above all of the working class. Are these people wage labourers? No — they are producers of social wealth, and the consciousness of the producer is quite different from that of the wage labourer . . . He knows that each stroke of the *machete* is no longer to create wealth for a boss, but perhaps to create a new pair of shoes for a barefoot child who may be his own.[9]

But such a transformation, as we have seen, depends not only on the attitude of the state but on the inherited consciousness of the rural work force, for whom plantation labour is often still akin to slavery.

Decreases in Crop Production, 1979-80

	1978-79	1979-80	Changes in Output
	(tonnes)		*(%)*
Export Crops			
Cotton	113,436	23,000	− 80%
Coffee	65,090	55,200	− 15%
Domestic Food Crops			
Maize	254,150	172,500	− 33%
Beans	55,476	39,652	− 29%
Rice	59,800	37,536	− 37%

Source: Ministry of Planning.

Each major export crop has presented specific problems of reactivation. Coffee, in particular, was inherited in a lamentable state. Lands had been allowed to fall into neglect, with the *roya* coffee blight widespread under Somoza. By mid-1980, the Government of National Reconstruction was able to announce sweeping improvements, the introduction of new high-yield strains of coffee, and the rehabilitation by the state agency CONARCA of 12,000 *manzanas* (20,640 acres) of neglected coffee plantations. Sugar faced different difficulties, with exports suspended in June 1980 in the face of domestic shortages, but in the middle term the government is optimistic about expansion of the crop by a simple extension of area planted. The state owns five of the country's six refineries, excluding only the giant Ingenio San Antonio, and MIDA aims for a 20% increase in harvests during 1981, with the eventual intention of doubling sugar production by the end of the decade and diverting a proportion of the crop into cane alcohol as a petroleum substitute. In the case of cotton, the FSLN pins its hopes for economic recovery and social transformation on two complementary measures. First, in a decree announced by Comandante Daniel Ortega on the first anniversary of the Revolution, all idle lands were expropriated.[11] Second, cotton owners were obliged in 1980 to hire out their lands to peasants at greatly reduced rents. Large estates are the norm in Nicaraguan cotton cultivation, often owned by absentee landlords who made rich pickings under Somoza by renting them out for as much as US $200 per *manzana* (1.72 acres). Small farmers now have access to these lands at fixed maximum rents of $30 for cotton growing and $10 for cultivating basic grains.

The Peasantry

The sweeping nationalisation of idle lands announced by Daniel Ortega and the rigid enforcement of controlled rents are only two examples of the measures which INRA is ready to take on behalf of the peasantry in their fight against recalcitrant private landlords. On 21 December 1979, at the ATC's Assembly, Ortega had addressed the problem of lands stolen from peasants in the 1960s by landowners not technically linked with Somoza and who therefore had escaped the first phase of the agrarian reform. He made it clear that while investigations would be carried out according to scrupulous legal procedures, they would be unambiguously designed to restore such lands to their original peasant owners: 'We have to look for legal arguments, bring forward whatever evidence we have and make a bit of history . . . demanding that these lands be handed over to the *campesinos*.'[12] Wheelock had given similar assurances to a meeting of small coffee producers in the northern town of Jalapa, when they complained of economic sabotage by landowners smuggling coffee across the nearby Honduran border. 'If we find big landowners doing this', he declared, 'we will confiscate their *haciendas* to prevent them damaging the national economy.'

A later comment on how the agrarian reform might be extended in the problematic northern *departamentos* of Madriz, Matagalpa and Esteli was among the most radical statements of INRA's future intentions. In these areas, geography and patterns of land ownership mean that many peasants do not live within reach of wage labour opportunities and can only live from subsistence farming of basic grains on land rented out by local *latifundistas*.

> In those areas we can say: 'All right, gentlemen. By what right have you taken over the entire *departamento* of Madriz or Esteli? Don't you realise that for fifty years you have forced everyone else to live without land? We cannot accept the existence of landlords who have monopolised an entire *departamento* and kept the mass of people living in misery and exploitation.' As you can see, in areas like that we have to expropriate, we have to take those lands even if it means paying for them, so that we can redistribute them to the communities who work them. Now, instead of breaking these lands up, we can establish production cooperatives. Why should we fragment them? But if I am a small producer and I don't want to cooperate, this doesn't mean for a moment that I will be forced to. Every agrarian reform has to be voluntary.[13]

There are two options for the FSLN in the cooperativisation of the peasantry, and INRA has shown itself consistently sensitive to the need for flexibility between collective land use and *parcelizacion*. The first step forward in the organisation of small peasant producers was the Credit and Service Cooperative (CCS), which was relatively simply achieved. But the more advanced CAS, in which peasants join together their individual *parcelas* and cultivate them collectively, using the income generated to finance local infrastructure and communal social services, have been slower to get off the ground. In the first year, INRA's work with small peasant producers was

dictated by the need to defend the peasantry's class interests and the drive
for increased production. It centred on rationalising the production of basic
crops for domestic consumption (beans, maize, rice etc.); organising the
peasants economically and politically; heading off private sector attempts
to promote peasant organisations parallel to the state cooperatives; and
ensuring higher productivity and increased economic and political status
by offering easy access to state finance. In all these areas, the ideal was a
fusion of the planning role of the state and the organisational work of the
ATC. The ATC offered organisation to the 100,000 peasant producers
(divided between those farming basic grains and those involved in small-
scale export crop production, notably coffee where they handle 70% of
output), Procampo gave technical assistance, the National Development
Bank granted favourable state credits, and ENABAS, the Ministry of Internal
Trade and the rural CDSs controlled prices and commercial distribution.
This approach was not without pitfalls, and INRA was honest about the
defects in its first year strategy. Credit policies, in particular, needed to be
reassessed. In many cases, credit had only been provided for immediate
productive needs and not for long-term infrastructural investment. This
had alleviated short-term consumption problems but done little to stimulate
future economic growth. In the CCS, where private peasant ownership
persisted, credit had at times only worsened the inequalities within a cooperative, as only the better-off peasants could take full advantage of it. These
are teething troubles which INRA will have to overcome in future.

The state and the ATC can claim major successes in the political organisation of previously uncommitted peasant producers. Here the battle for their
loyalty is not with opposition trade unions, but with the powerful interest
groups of the private sector. Through the Chamber of Commerce, the Union
of Agricultural Producers (UPANIC) and the sectoral associations of cattle
ranchers, coffee plantation owners, cotton growers, rice planters and others,
the private sector has done everything in its power to steer small farmers
away from unionisation and state cooperatives, and to weld them instead into
an effective interest group at the service of the bourgeois lobby. The scale on
which these farmers operate is tiny, and so their economic position is
marginal. On the Pacific Coast, 23,000 of them farm 140,000 acres, a mere
4.5% of the region's cultivable land and the same size as a single INRA cattle
estate confiscated from Somocistas on the savannahs of Rio San Juan in the
south-east. In other words, the small farmers have little in the way of shared
vested interests with the *latifundistas*. Nevertheless the big landowners are
capable of many tactics to try and win them over. One anecdote, told by an
INRA veterinarian, may suffice:

> I was up in Somotillo, near the Honduran border, for a meeting
> between INRA, the cattle ranchers of FEGANIC [the ranchers'
> federation] and small peasant farmers. Half a dozen peasants turned
> up – the very poorest kind, those who have a couple of *manzanas*
> of land and a few scraggy cows – to tell INRA that their cattle had

been stolen by rustlers, maybe National Guards from over the border. What could the state do, they asked? In reality there was very little INRA could offer: not a question of bureaucracy, or lack of sympathy . . . there just isn't the money. But you could see the kind gentlemen of FEGANIC going into a huddle. Here was a chance to buy some peasant support. So they came up to the families, all smiles and sympathy. 'What a tragedy, my poor friend' (pulling out rolls of high currency bills from their wallets) 'how much were the cows worth? 20,000 *cordobas*? Here you are.' Half a dozen peasant families won over, just like that. And make no mistake, these people still have a lot of money. This kind of thing happens all the time.[14]

In the face of this kind of competition, the state has given the small farmers technical know-how and has fixed purchase prices for their produce. The ATC has helped by enforcing ENABAS food prices locally and has set up Comites Populares de Produccion (People's Production Committees) to persuade the small farmer to sell direct to the state. Although local supply problems remain, with a black market in basic grains, local distribution committees of the mass organisations are beginning to control the problem. The women's organisation AMNLAE is crucial here, and its work in the field of food distribution may be instrumental in shifting the consciousness of peasant women away from a domestic to a collective role.

As another basic step towards the incorporation of small producers into the mass organisations, the Revolution fought and won two major battles in key agricultural zones in the early months of 1980. First, small coffee growers from Matagalpa split from the Central Cooperativa controlled by big local landowners. And next the small cotton planters of Leon and Chinandega — two *departamentos* which between them account for 85% of Nicaragua's cotton production — set up their own independent cooperative. Wheelock was quick to point out the significance of the new cooperative movements. After the December ATC Assembly and the February mass demonstration to demand 'no return of intervened lands', they were, he declared, 'the third great event in the agrarian sector'.

This then, in summary, is INRA's great dilemma: how to maintain the delicate balance necessary between production for export and production of basic foodstuffs, how to service the needs of the rural proletariat and of the peasantry when most of the rural population is a mixture of the two. Year-round work is being created for seasonal agricultural labourers in production collectives through investment of part of the surplus generated by the UPEs. But the present dynamic of export-oriented growth will, if sustained, create a demand for a still larger rural proletariat and do nothing to improve domestic food supply. At the same time, enforced cooperativisation among landless peasants will reduce the work force available at harvest times in the export sector. Already the first cotton and coffee harvests have been faced with a labour shortage. In part, this is explained by the fact that the 40,000 or so regular migrant pickers from Honduras and El Salvador have stopped coming to Nicaragua, but, more critically, peasant producers – guaranteed an adequate flow of state finance and fair prices for the first time – are unwilling to revert to traditional seasonal work on the cotton and coffee harvests. The complexities of administering agricultural credit have also played their part here: credit facilities were sometimes granted too late to peasant cooperatives, resulting in maize and bean harvests coinciding with the ripening of export crops. But it is a question of ideology as much as economics. Peasants, having previously seen participation in harvesting the export crop as only a necessary evil in order to keep their family going during the remaining nine months of the year, are now happier staying on their own plot of land. Why should they go on migrating to the backbreaking labour of the cotton fields? The Frente's emphasis on voluntary work to bring in the 1980 harvests may help to change preconceptions about the social function of wage labour, but that change will only come gradually.

The Association of Rural Workers

Three-quarters of the rural population is now organised in the ATC or peasant cooperatives. The democratic basis of the agrarian reform and the special role of the ATC in allowing INRA to gauge grassroots feeling and measure the pace of reform was Wheelock's central theme in his address to the ATC Assembly in December 1979:

> It is vital to realise that agrarian reforms can never be made from above, that agrarian reform is a combination of great effort from the grassroots and the organisational efforts of their representatives at the superstructural level. I stress the importance of organisation. The ATC has a permanent place in INRA. You are a real power there, and what you say in INRA is as good as law.[15]

By mid-1980 the ATC could claim considerable success, having managed to organise almost one-third of Nicaragua's economically active rural population – 110,383 workers out of a total of 350,000. The breakdown of membership showed both the initial success of cooperativism and the problems still facing the ATC in correcting the imbalance in its strength on state and private farms. 48,712 of its members were organised in 397 credit and service cooperatives, 30,844 in 472 state farms and 21,552 in 621 private farms. In privately owned *fincas* today, capitalist exploitation often continues as before, and the ATC lacks sufficient committees on the spot to fight for basic improvements such as the implementation of minimum wage levels. At the moment of the 1979 victory, the ATC had affiliated regional committees in only four departments: Carazo, Masaya, Chinandega and Managua. Today its membership extends through all sixteen, having finally penetrated even the backward areas of Rio San Juan and Zelaya in the east where pre-capitalist modes of production still exist.

The organisation is proud of its long tradition of building a rural workers' movement in secrecy. They trace their struggle back to the resistance of striking sugar-cane cutters in Chichigalpa in 1945, an armed action which was put down by the National Guard with many dead. Throughout the 1960s spontaneous land struggles continued, often as undirected fights against starvation wages and inhuman living conditions. It was a movement which, as we have seen, first took on organised form as a result of the joint efforts of FSLN militants and religious groups. This process of organisation culminated with the formal foundation of the ATC in Diriamba in March 1978, bringing together Rural Workers' Committees from different regions of the agro-exporting Pacific seaboard. Their propaganda organ, *El Machete,* emerged as the first publication of a Sandinista mass organisation. The land invasions of Tonala and Sirama in the department of Chinandega were an early product of the new organisation, and in the ensuing insurrections of September 1978 and May-July 1979 'the ATC was able to convert itself into a powerful force of the FSLN, not only in building the armed struggle but in organising political action by workers and peasants in the rural areas.'[16] The Frente began to organise military training schools for ATC committees in response to National Guard repression of land takeovers and peasant demonstrations, and by September 1978 these defensive armed groups had moved on to an active combat role. Despite rudimentary arms, they provided cover for the Frente's withdrawal from the cities of Chinandega and Carazo where the ATC enjoyed greatest support, and throughout 1979 kept up a steady stream of harassment operations against Somoza's troops.

The history of the ATC, as the earliest of the mass organisations, exemplifies the dynamic relationship between the FSLN and the masses. Spontaneous peasant struggles were given form and direction under FSLN leadership, until a coherent class-based organisation emerged, formally independent but umbilically linked to the FSLN. The ATC's unconditional recognition of the vanguard role of the Frente was reiterated in the Declaration of Principles adopted at its December 1979 Assembly. It was a document which might also serve as a model for the democratic functioning of the other mass organisations. Article 4 stated:

> The ATC adopts as its own the principles of our vanguard, the FSLN, with regard to working methods and decision-making mechanisms which will guarantee internal democracy and the effective participation of the bases in the life of the Association. For that reason, we highlight the importance of criticism and self-criticism in the relationship between the grassroots and the leadership, and of the principle of democratic centralism, which means that rank and file opinion will be consulted and taken into account in all the Association's major decisions at every level.[17]

The Assembly itself was the culmination of a long process of local

273

elections which the FSLN hailed as an example of Sandinista democracy in action. In his speech to the Assembly, ATC executive member Francisco Lopez reported that:

> All rural workers affiliated to the ATC took part in assemblies where the objectives of this event were explained and 664 candidates were nominated to attend. Of these, 250 were elected as delegates to this Assembly. . . . There are 100 delegates representing the municipal, departmental and national offices of the ATC, which means that 60% of delegates are direct representatives of grassroots bodies.[18]

With two or three political meetings a week the norm in most UPEs, the ATC rank and file is increasingly capable of formulating its demands and understanding their political context. The ATC's main achievement, and its main challenge in the next phase of the Revolution, is perhaps not organisation for its own sake, but organisation around a new vision of the state. Labour discipline is improving. Land invasions were not widespread in 1979-80. Production targets have been satisfied. In helping to set up the Matagalpa small coffee growers cooperative, the ATC also won a more subtle victory, in rooting out bureaucrats from ENABAS, the National Development Bank and the state coffee agency ENCAFE who had connived with the private sector. It has pressed too, with growing success, for genuinely democratic local forums for liaison with INRA and other government departments. In the larger agro-exporting complexes, these worker demands have brought rapid social advances. At the German Pomares sugar refinery, for example, ATC efforts have resulted in a clinic staffed by fourteen social workers, *comisariato* selling seventy-five basic products at ENABAS-controlled prices, and a production collective turning out clothing which is free to the sugar workers and cost price to their families. On the uncultivated land at the complex, workers grow green vegetables to supplement their diet, in consultation with nutrition advisers from INRA.[19] This is an early sign of what the ATC aims to achieve throughout the network of state farms, and in time on private farms too.

On national issues, the ATC has been unwilling to move faster than its membership, reluctant to make demands which are not the result of direct rank and file pressure. On wages, even when the Frente Obrero was attempting to make political capital out of the economic crisis by organising sugar workers around demands for 100% wage increases, the ATC was unwilling to be pushed into a premature counter-claim. Instead, despite the fact that *campesino* wages after the Revolution averaged a mere 636 *cordobas* a month (US $63.60), and were in many areas as low as 360 *cordobas,* the ATC insisted on waiting for demands in line with the Frente's austerity programme to be communicated upwards from the grassroots. Only when this happened in May — a full three months after the Frente Obrero conflict — did the ATC leadership petition the Junta for modest wage increases.

The success of the ATC in countering ultra-left opportunism speaks volumes for the mutual trust between the organisation's leadership and its rank and file. Yet in itself this is not remarkable: in the major agro-exporting plants, the ATC has a firmly rooted historical relationship with the labour force. Furthermore, there is little activity by other unions in the rural sector. With the exception of the Social Christian CTN in certain sugar refineries, and the Frente Obrero (now a spent force), the ATC has not had to contend with hostile, established trade unions in the same way as the CST has had to do amongst urban workers. The ATC's progress in labour organising on the big Pacific Coast plantations is impressive, but hardly surprising. The bigger challenge is in organising the peasant producers, especially those who live all year round from their farming. Towards the end of 1980, there were signs that the ATC alone might not be the best way of achieving this. The ATC's own membership is only too familiar from first-hand experience with the contradictory class psychology of the peasants, small proprietors and rural proletariat. The first year brought a number of conflicts of interest at the grassroots level between these three sectors, precisely reflecting INRA's own dilemma. Many began to argue that, if the ATC as presently structured was not flexible enough to represent the interests of the small producer as well as the plantation labourer, then perhaps an entirely separate new mass organisation was necessary. The answer came at the end of the year with the emergence of the Asociacion de Pequenos y Medianos Productores (Association of Small and Medium Producers). Many ATC activists have crossed over to the new body, and although it may not yet qualify as a mass organisation in the same sense as the ATC or CST, its appearance on the scene is a further indication of the Revolution's readiness to experiment constantly with new and more appropriate forms of popular power and organisation.

Urban Unions and Class Unity

The Central Sandinista de Trabajadores (Sandinista Workers' Union: CST) has set itself four strategic objectives: the struggle for working-class demands which transcend the economistic basis of traditional Nicaraguan trade unionism; support for the revolutionary transformation of the state; increased levels of worker participation and control of production, especially in the Area of Public Ownership; and, above all, the fight for the class independence and unity of the urban proletariat.[20]

While there is considerable convergence between these aims and those of the rural ATC, the CST in addition has to overcome the Somocista legacy of a divided urban workers' movement. The ATC is an active protagonist of class unity, but it is the CST which has borne the brunt of the struggle for the loyalty of the urban working class. Although the Nicaraguan labour movement is traditionally the weakest in Central America, with only one in twelve workers unionised under Somoza and minimal penetration by the major international trade union currents, and although the CST now represents 70% of unionised labour, the FSLN's objective of a single unified *central* remains distant.

There are five other urban labour federations in Nicaragua today, with political stances ranging from the Right to the Ultra-Left. The popular support of these five federations varies widely. All are small, and frequently linked for historical reasons to specific trades or industries. Some have seen their power base seriously eroded since the Revolution. Others have grown around their original nuclei in particular industries as a natural consequence of the new freedom for trade unions. The Social Christian-oriented Central de Trabajadores de Nicaragua (CTN) claims that its membership has tripled since July 1979 to 65,000. It is affiliated to the World Confederation of Labour (WCL) and its Latin American regional organisation, CLAT. In contrast, the small Consejo de Unificacion Sindical (CUS), encouraged by Somoza for its virulent anti-Communism, has lost ground rapidly in its traditional enclaves of support among banana plantation workers and dockers. The decline in CUS support has further weakened the influence in Nicaraguan labour affairs of its North American backers, the AFL-CIO and American Institute for Free Labor Development. The CUS is affiliated to the International Confederation of Free Trade Unions (ICFTU) and its Latin American regional body, ORIT. On the Left, the two main non-Sandinista federations reflect the 1960s split in the Nicaraguan Socialist Party. The Socialist PSN's Confederacion General de Trabajadores-Independiente (CGT-I) is linked internationally to the World Federation of Trade Unions (WFTU) and its Latin American organisation CPUSTAL, has particular strength among construction workers; it has been the CST's strongest ally since the Revolution. In contrast, the Central de Accion y Unidad Sindical (CAUS), which is loyal to the Communist Party of Nicaragua and is without international affiliations, is a small federation with some strength in the textile industry, and has had major conflicts with the CST. It promoted a series of strikes in early 1980, although it did subsequently abandon its confrontationist positions. Finally, the small Frente Obrero (FO), trade union wing of the Movimiento de Accion Popular (MAP), was the product of an ultra-left split from the FSLN ten years ago. It has operated an armed wing, MILPAS, but what little influence it possessed fell away sharply after March 1980.

In taking the first steps towards urban working-class unity, the CST has come into inevitable conflict with four of these labour federations. But two important lessons have emerged. Non-Sandinista unions will only be won over by patient effort, a unified *central* cannot be created by decree or compulsion. And equally, whatever the position adopted by the *centrales'* leaderships, each is an established and legitimate working-class current.[21] As such they enjoy the traditional loyalty of much of their core membership, and are respected by the FSLN, which has learned not to divorce itself from any sector of the working class.

Immediately after the victory, the insurrectional Workers' Fighting Committees (CLTs) formed the nucleus of the new Sandinista labour *central*, adapting their role to the demands of the new state while remaining independent of it. In retaining this autonomy, the function of parallel structures of power changed, with the Junta and the government no longer perceived as bourgeois institutions counterposed to the power of the masses, but as part and parcel of the strategy designed to create that power. On 27 July 1979, spontaneously formed new committees and the old CLTs in factories throughout the country took the name of Comites de Defensa de Trabajadores Sandinistas (Sandinista Workers' Defence Committees). At the national level, these committees became the CST. Having spent the first year of its existence educating workers to understand their long-term class strategy, the CST unveiled in July 1980 its *Plan de Lucha,* the immediate fighting platform to be set against the old economism. The plan involved the enforcement in every factory of minimum wage levels and recently decreed wage increases; compliance with the terms of the *convenios colectivos* signed by management, workers and government; full respect by management for newly won trade union rights; a revision of the existing Labour Code; the organisation of voluntary trade union work brigades; and the establishment of outlets to distribute food at controlled prices in the factories. On the face of it, many of the demands seemed defensive, but their timing was crucial, involving a clash with reactionary factory owners who were concertedly opposing the legal framework of the new state.

Although, for the time being, the old Somocista Labour Code of the 1940s remains in operation, the state has suspended one of its major clauses: the prohibition of national craft or industry-wide unions. The organisation of plant-based unions (the only ones allowed) was one of the major obstacles to working-class strength under Somoza, but it is a tradition which has not died easily. The vast majority of new unions are plant-based, with only teachers, health workers, journalists, public employees and construction workers organised nationally, and four of these five are for white-collar workers. Only gradually are the advantages of industry-wide unity becoming apparent to workers. In the mines of the Northern Atlantic Coast, the situation is characteristic. In the last months of 1979, separate unions sprang up spontaneously in the major mining settlements of Bonanza, Siuna and Rosita. When CST officials and local miners' committees made an exhaustive study of working conditions and wage rates in the three mines, the effects of these divisions became clear. Not only did salary levels vary from one mine to another, but there were also discrepancies within the same mine, unequal pay for equal work, often on a racial basis. Wage parity in the mining sector is now a reality for the first time, and the first result of coordinated action came when the unions at the three mines joined forces to negotiate large cuts in ENABAS prices for beans, rice and sugar.[22]

As well as the fight for unity within individual industries, unions have also begun to unite on a regional basis. On 7 March 1980, immediately after major conflicts with the Communist-led CAUS, Social Christian CTN and ultra-left Frente Obrero, a dozen factories in Managua's industrial belt on the Carretera Norte announced their decision to form a 'regional trade union bloc' which arose 'as a necessity in the face of the destabilising campaign being waged by the CIA and certain pseudo-leaders of the workers' movement.'[23] The reference was, above all, to the leadership of the CAUS. These twelve factory unions were all CST affiliates and included the important food-processing plant of El Caracol and the Standard Steel factory.

There have also been examples of local and inter-plant cooperation on the drafting of *convenios colectivos,* which were signed at the rate of more than one a day during January and February 1980. Again, Managua factories were in the forefront, with more than 90% of the *convenios* being signed there. There was a remarkable consistency in the workers' demands. In the urban areas, the principal demand was invariably for increased worker participation in factory management and control of production; in the rural areas, the tendency was to demand improved social services. In both areas, the unions emphasised the need for job security and better health and safety provisions. These claims cut right across the populism of the Somocista Labour Code, and it may seem surprising that the abrogation of the Code has not figured prominently among working-class demands so far. But in practice the restrictive clauses of the Code can be ignored, and its populist provisions — never implemented by the dictatorship — can now be turned to workers' advantage through strict enforcement. It is pointless to draft a new Labour Code precipitately while the workers' movement is in a state of flux. The elaboration of a new code is one of the prime tasks of the Council of State, but it will depend on the course of inter-union discussions on unity and the full consolidation of the Revolution.

These discussions, which began in January, were underpinned by the repeated insistence of the FSLN leadership on the necessity of creating a *central unica.* The comments of Carlos Carrion, responsible for the Frente's National Secretariat of Party Organisation, were typical: 'The working class is one single class, and must be organised as one. That does not mean establishing it by force but through work designed to increase workers' consciousness of the importance of unity.'[24] And Tomas Borge, reflecting on the class unity of the right-wing bourgeoisie within COSEP in contrast to the divided state of the workers' movement, added: 'It is not correct that the working class should have different organisations; in practice, we would only be dividing it.'

As Carrion suggested, the discussion required extreme caution and sensitivity. Rather than challenging the legitimacy of the non-Sandinista *centrales,* the CST faced the task of painstakingly portraying Sandinista trade unionism as the correct option for the working class, restricting its attacks to the leadership of the other federations, not the rank and file whom it must constantly strive to attract. A *central unica* can only be formed through a long process of open and democratic discussion. Pressure, in the rare cases where it has been applied, has been counter-productive, and is easily used as an ideological weapon by the bourgeoisie. Fortunately, although both the CTN and the right-wing CUS have alleged harassment, their complaints have been trivial. The CUS accusation of FSLN intimidation boiled down to the impounding by the Sandinista Police of a motorbike belonging to a CUS official. The concept of pluralism invoked by the pro-bourgeois leadership of the CUS and the CTN has the clear purpose of dividing and weakening the working-class movement. A statement by their allies in COSEP, dressed up as a defence of working class interests but in fact another attack on alleged breaches of legality by the government, could hardly have made this more explicit: 'The repeated intention to create a single workers' *central . . .* is difficult to harmonise with the spirit of the Basic Statute which authorises freedom of association in Article 8 . . . *We insist on the importance of competition between workers organisations.'* (Author's italics)[25]

However, Somoza's brutal repression of the trade union movement ultimately works to the Frente's advantage. The low level of previous unionisation means that more than 90% of workers have no experience of trade unionism within a bourgeois state, and although formidable weaknesses in class consciousness may partially benefit organisations like the CTN in the short term, there is no question of Sandinista hegemony over the workers' movement or the concept of worker control of production being seriously challenged from a position of strength. There are certainly bureaucratic currents within the trade union movement, but there is no entrenched bureaucratic leadership. Against the class collaborationism of the CUS and the CTN, the CST can manifestly draw on its extremely democratic origins in factory councils and insurrectional committees. In the final insurrection, the June general strike was critical in showing the power of unified working class mobilisation behind a leadership which cut across the traditional sectarian divisions of the Nicaraguan labour movement.[26]

The first move towards a unified *central* came on 28 January 1980, with talks between the CST, Socialist CGT-I and Communist CAUS setting up a National Inter-Union Commission, the CNI. The CNI was to serve as an umbrella organisation, within which each *central* would maintain full autonomy. The CUS and the CTN refused to have anything to do with the talks. In May, the ATC joined the new Commission. Coming in the middle of a polemic between the CST, the Frente Obrero and the CTN over wage rises, the formation of the CNI was as much an immediate tactical need as a long-term strategic one. Unfortunately, the positions of the CGT-I and the CAUS contrasted sharply from the first. While the CGT-I solidly endorsed the Sandinista strategy, the unity moves came too late to head off mounting CAUS opportunism over the wages issue. The initial CAUS statement on the unity talks was guarded: 'The workers' demands must take into account the effects of the economic crisis, inflation and immediate needs.'[27]

Within a matter of three weeks, the meaning of the comment was clear. The CAUS, trying to make political capital out of continuing working-class poverty, paralysed eighteen Managua factories with demands for 100% wage hikes. The CAUS move presented the Frente with a delicate contradiction: on the one hand, it was politically damaging for the CAUS to leave the CNI a mere three weeks after its inception; on the other hand, the CAUS demands were wildly unrealistic and the opportunism was flagrant. The response from the CST Secretary-General, Ivan Garcia, was cautious: 'A full study will be carried out with the Ministry of Planning. We should not give any answers without first analysing the situation carefully.' In the event, the strikes were halted by the rank and file initiative of local CST unions. Two months later, the CAUS rejoined the fold on May Day, publicly recognising its errors – or to be more precise, realising that strike action had failed to win it the anticipated political advantage. CAUS leader, Manuel Perez Estrada, told *Barricada:* 'At the outset we had a lot of problems, especially those of us in the CAUS. Nevertheless, we don't feel any resentment, since we are dedicated to the unity of all sectors of the working class.'[28]

During the early months of the CNI, two of the five major national unions took historic steps which strengthened the principle of unity and reinforced the moral authority of FSLN leadership. The first case concerned the construction workers' union SCAAS (Union of Carpenters, Bricklayers, Assembly Workers and Allied Trades), traditionally linked to the Socialist CGT-I since the union's foundation in 1951. Immediately after the July victory, some SCAAS leaders tried to affiliate the union to the CST, a move resisted by the majority of the leadership who remained faithful to the Socialist Party. The conflict produced two parallel and divided construction unions, with most of the rank and file staying with the CGT-I. On 9 January, SCAAS members loyal to the Socialist Party marched on the Ministry of Labour to demand recognition of the CGT-I leadership. The possible effect, with the Socialist Party's major industrial base pitted against the FSLN, was calamitous. Five days later, the situation worsened. The relatively well-paid building workers laying out the new Parque Luis Alfonso Velasquez, a children's recreation complex in the ruined centre of Managua, downed tools in protest at a government proposal to reduce their working hours and wages in an effort to generate extra employment in the construction industry. From its miscalculation of the mood of SCAAS workers, the FSLN drew vital lessons. To make matters worse the three-day strike was exploited by the Frente Obrero, who tried to recruit disaffected workers and accused the FSLN of anti-working-class policies. Any insensitivity to trade union disputes could only work to the advantage of counter-revolutionary groups. On the third day, the government yielded, but the FSLN took the issue further and in doing so gained great prestige. It called mass assemblies of the SCAAS workers involved to discuss the initial rationale behind the reduction in working hours. Far from being intended as an attack on working-class living standards, they explained, the job creation scheme was part of a broader strategy designed to benefit the working class as a whole. In calling these SCAAS assemblies, the FSLN indicated publicly its willingness to exercise self-criticism, and accompanied the necessary government concessions with proof that it could mobilise and educate non-CST unions.

The call was made for the SCAAS to hold fresh elections to its executive committee. The union timed them to coincide with the launching of the CNI, and on 28 January representatives of twenty-two construction plants formally endorsed the creation of the new commission. A joint list of CGT-I and CST candidates was put forward and approved by 90% of the 3,000 building workers present at the SCAAS Congress. The successful outcome of the dispute, and the significance of the Socialist SCAAS being the first major union to commit itself to trade union unity, thereby cementing the close links which exist today between the FSLN and the PSN, was praised by both parties as a major triumph.

Five weeks later, in the second episode which strengthened working-class unity, the health workers' union FETSALUD, with a membership of some 15,000, broke its previous affiliation to the Social Christian federation and took up an independent position, appointing an interim executive committee. Ivan Garcia of the CST described the significance of the FETSALUD Assembly:

> The National Assembly of FETSALUD was held recently, on 2 March, and the union decided to disaffiliate from the CTN, to which it had been linked in spite of a history of considerable militancy. On disaffiliating, FETSALUD formed a national executive council, the great majority of whose members were Sandinista comrades. But we believe that the wisest course for the moment is to leave the union as an independent body, because we do not wish to impose decisions on their membership. We believe instead that it should be the mass of rank and file workers belonging to FETSALUD who should clarify their own position and then decide for themselves when and whether they wish to affiliate to the CST.[29]

Borge, summing up the lessons of the SCAAS and FETSALUD episodes, made a key statement of the FSLN's vision of working-class independence:

> 'Trade union unity is not something which the revolutionary government can impose. The Sandinista Government does not want an official or governmental union movement. What we need is a trade union organisation responsive to the interests of the workers. The working class in Nicaragua must have the right to say 'no' where appropriate, and must even have the right to confront the government when it is necessary.

Opportunism and Strikes: Unions versus the CST

The CTN has not, however, given up its hold over FETSALUD without a fight, and its efforts to divide health workers at the union assembly have contributed to the difficulties which the Sandinista Government has faced in the health sector. In addition to the destruction of five of Nicaragua's twenty-five hospitals during the war, and the death or flight of 500 of the country's 1,300 doctors, the government has encountered considerable resistance in its attempts to forge a new radical consciousness among members of a profession accustomed under Somoza — and CTN leadership

— to treat medicine as a commercial activity granting privileged social status.

No less serious have been the CTN's disruptive actions in the sugar industry, where it also enjoys some support. It is thus the only trade union *central* (apart from the Frente Obrero, which will be dealt with separately) to have come into direct conflict with the Sandinista ATC. The CTN organised strikes at both the Amalia and Benjamin Zeledon sugar complexes. At the Zeledon refinery, 1,600 workers struck in support of a 57% wage claim by cane cutters and a 100% claim on the part of other workers. At the Ingenio Amalia, 564 workers came out. At Amalia, where the CTN had the support of a majority and the ATC a minority, the Sandinista union adopted a technique which has become the norm: it focussed its attack on the CTN leadership in order to try and split it from the rank and file, simultaneously explained to CTN members that their leaders' actions could only benefit the bourgeois opposition, and that the wage rises demanded were incompatible with the country's economic recovery and the overall interests of the working class. In the case of the CTN, although workers at both sugar complexes returned to work without winning their demands, these tactics have not been notably successful. The organisation's membership has grown, and as it feels its relative strength and as conflict heightens between the Frente and right-wing groups like the Partido Social Cristiano, the positions of the CTN have hardened. Its tactics have also become more sophisticated and divisive. After boycotting the 1980 May Day celebrations, the CTN seized the opportunity of the 17 July Garcia Meza coup in Bolivia to confront the CST again. While the CST and the Sandinista Comite de Solidaridad con los Pueblos mounted mass demonstrations to denounce the coup, the CTN called its members out for a one-day work stoppage, supposedly in solidarity with the Bolivian working class. The action was criticised by the FSLN as an unwarranted interference with production, but received heavy coverage in *La Prensa* and appeared to many workers who failed to grasp its opportunism as a more radical internationalist initiative than that of the FSLN itself. Most critically, as the battle lines between revolution and counter-revolution become more sharply drawn, the CTN is aware that it can stagemanage a degree of international support, as Nicaragua's second largest labour federation, with the weight of CLAT behind it and support from Christian Democratic governments like Venezuela.

The CUS, by contrast, seems a spent force. Discredited by fifteen years of acquiescence with Somoza, it has seen its old membership transfer rapidly to the CST. Its sole hope of regaining ground is in US-owned enterprises, where its support was always centred. The prolonged labour dispute at Nicaragua's TEXACO plant was a fair example of the faith which American capitalists continue to place in the CUS. Here, the company management refused for six months to recognise a trade union, eventually provoking a workers' takeover of the plant. The management response was to grant a unilateral 20% wage rise, while still refusing to grant union recognition unless workers agreed to affiliate to the CUS. As part of their support for a CUS affiliate, management agreed to one of the workers' main demands, the installation of a union notice-board, but on condition that it should be used 'only for trade information, and nothing to do with politics'!

The threat posed to trade union unity by the CAUS was an altogether more serious matter, and the wave of CAUS-led strikes in early 1980 cannot be separated from the political position of the Nicaraguan Communist Party (PCdeN). Communist leader Eli Altamirano, around whom a personality cult is encouraged, has defined the FSLN as having a 'bourgeois nationalist ideology'. According to the Communists, the Frente is therefore only capable of leading the first stage of the Nicaraguan Revolution, which they continue to characterise as bourgeois-democratic. When that phase is over, according to this thinking, the PCdeN itself will move in as the authentic vanguard of the Revolution's 'proletarian' phase.[30]

Most disturbingly, one edition of the party bulletin *El Partido* called for the 'cautious infiltration' of the Sandinista Army to prepare armed cadres for the 'proletarian revolution'.[31] Their tactics in the trade union sphere, encouraging land seizures and strikes without regard to their economic or political consequences, have — like those of the Frente Obrero — a single end: to make headway as a party and build their membership. Their May Day assertion that the CAUS had seen the error of its ways should not be taken too seriously. During the anniversary celebrations on 19 July, a group of Communist Party and CAUS members attempted to gain a prominent position at the front of the crowd with thirty large banners. When asked by those standing behind them to lower the banners, which were blocking the view of the platform, PC militants seized red and black FSLN flags and trampled them underfoot.

The CAUS-led strikes began at the FABRITEX textile factory in Managua in February.[32] Within hours, Plasticos Modernos and sixteen other smaller factories had walked out in sympathy. In the Nicarao S.A. textile plant, workers of the CAUS-affiliated SITRATEX union had halted production in protest at management's decapitalisation of the plant and falsification of tax returns, calling on the state to take over the factory. But in the FABRITEX strike the declared aim was quite different: a 100% wage demand. The strike at FABRITEX was particularly worrying for the FSLN because of the relatively large size of the factory and the crucial importance of textile production — already badly hit by the war — to the success of Plan 80. FABRITEX is a high technology plant employing 819 workers. The state has a 48% share in the factory, whose production is destined 30% for export markets. Production figures by February were already falling well short of projected targets: the firm had been operating at only 18% of its capacity the previous September, and the aim was to achieve full reactivation by the following February. Instead, production levels had reached only 77% of those anticipated — figures which the CAUS union was well aware of through its participation in weekly worker-management production meetings. When the CAUS lodged a 100% wage claim on top of this, it was rejected by the National Inter-Union Commission, and the CAUS then opted for direct negotiation with management. The reply was a 6% offer, and the work force walked out. The FSLN response was threefold: a vehement attack on Alta-mirano and the CAUS leadership, a series of discussions between the CNI and representatives of the eighteen CAUS-affiliated unions, and the mobi-lisation of local CST unions and Sandinista Defence Committees to argue with the striking workers. At no point was there an attack against the CAUS work force itself at FABRITEX or the other factories. It was explained that their demands were economically impossible and their methods incorrect. But the dialogue was kept open. Asked by *Barricada* to comment on the wage claims, Carlos Nunez replied that: 'It is not a matter of condemning the attitude of the workers, but of appealing to their revolutionary consciousness, asking them to understand the situation and reconsider their wages policy, and explaining to them frankly – for that is their right – how their basic needs can be satisfied as a result of their own participation.'[33]

At one factory after another the workers went back, not least because of the efforts of the local CDS in explaining the errors of interfering with production. But the strikes did not end before a wave of popular anger at the actions of the CAUS leadership. The strikes had coincided with a further delay in the US Government's $75 million aid package and revelations of a secret CIA report on Nicaragua. To the mass of workers, there was more than a casual connection between the two events.[34] An anti-CIA mobilisa-tion of 50,000 workers also became an anti-CAUS march. Sandinista workers seized CAUS offices in Leon on 4 March and in Managua the following day. In Leon, the building was turned over to the Literacy Crusade along with the offices of the tiny ultra-left Movimiento Obrero Revolucionario (MORE). In Managua, the red PCdeN flag was seized and, in a piece of pure theatre, handed over to the CST leadership 'for safe keeping until there is a genuine Communist Party in Nicaragua', at an official ceremony 'to rescue Communism' staged in the presence of ambassadors from the Socialist countries.

The FABRITEX strike posed vital questions about the government's relationship with the working class. Under existing legislation, any boycott of production is illegal. This prohibition is a weapon designed for use against factory owners but is also, theoretically, applicable to striking workers. On the third day of the dispute, statements by Labour Minister Virgilio Godoy suggested that strike action might be formally outlawed, a move which would have had serious repercussions on trade union unity. As events later proved, it would also have created tensions with the CST's own rank and file.

Fighting Economic Sabotage: The State and the Unions
The state has intervened actively in both industrial and rural disputes. In cases of alleged decapitalisation or production boycotts by management, the state has not yet made a single judgment against the workers. In wages and conditions disputes, it has promoted *convenios colectivos* favourable to the work force, avoiding strikes by negotiating trade union recognition agreements, sickness benefits, overtime pay, industrial safety and hygiene improvements, trade union office facilities and study leave, and explicit

grievance and conflict procedures. But in June 1980 proof came that the economic crisis did not leave state factories with CST-affiliated unions immune from strike action. At the Plywood S.A. factory in Tipitapa, under 61% public ownership, the 600-strong work force struck over a 43% wage demand which would have given them parity with the 40 *cordoba* ($4.00) daily rate of other local factories. The important CANAL cement works and other smaller factories also suffered stoppages for wage claims.[35] In all cases, the initiative to strike was taken by the plant unions against the advice of the CST leadership. The CAUS attempted to exploit the division within the CST, but by this time the Sandinista leadership was rapidly alert to the danger. It was impossible, as well as politically undesirable, for the CST executive to resist pressure from its own rank and file, and the legitimacy of wage claims from the lowest paid workers was recognised. In some instances, the demands were met. In others, the government replied with strong measures to reinforce the social wage. Whichever the solution, each of the strikes was resolved rapidly through open dialogue between the leadership and plant workers, and in a few factories where the demands were considered unreasonable the Frente used these forums for further political education of newly formed local union officers.

From the earliest months of the Revolution, CST industrial action has been directed much more against uncooperative and openly right-wing factory bosses. In November 1979 the work force occupied the FANISA pharmaceutical plant. Here the owners had claimed that their economic situation made lay-offs inevitable, and had selectively dismissed Sandinista activists with compensation payments equivalent to four and a half months' salary. At the same time, they had justified a run-down of production by claiming a lack of raw materials, to which the workers' response was a takeover which restored maximum production levels. On the Atlantic Coast, 283 workers did the same thing in the Bluefields Manufacturing Corporation clothing factory, forcing management to grant a series of improvements in working conditions. And in March 135 workers took over Polymer SA, a local subsidiary of United Brands, to demand full implementation of promised wage increases and the removal of restrictions on union activity. Each action counted on full approval from the state, and the Frente pointed particularly to the 29% increase in output achieved by the Polymer workers. Every factory occupation has been used by the FSLN as a blueprint for workers' control of production as the most effective way of combating counter-revolutionary action in the private sector. Their importance grew with the 2 March decree against decapitalisation and economic sabotage, itself the direct result of the unions' increased capacity to detect these actions, assume control of the factories affected and stand guard over the productive process, if necessary with factory militias.

The immediate stimulus behind the March decree was the most celebrated of all the factory occupations: the food-processing plant of El Caracol. In late November 1979 the Campos family, owners of the plant, had signed a *convenio colectivo* with the union. When six weeks had passed without the terms of the *convenio* being observed, the workers struck and halted production, but after intensive discussion and self-criticism went back to work within hours. By February they had compiled an extensive dossier alleging economic crimes and the management's Somocista connections. While the majority of the Campos family had fled to Miami, two members had remained behind in Managua with the express intention – according to the Roberto Munguia Lorente union at El Caracol – of running down the plant and shipping out its remaining capital. On 19 February, the workforce voted by a majority of 121 to 10 to occupy the plant. In their deposition to Comandante Carlos Nunez, invited to a meeting the following day, the workers listed their accusations:[36]

* Management refusal to stock sufficient raw materials, only ordering new stocks when existing ones were exhausted. The Campos family had blamed this on insufficient deliveries from ENABAS and ENCAFE.
* Refusal to maintain machinery.
* Reductions in distribution of El Caracol products. The owners had begun to demand immediate payment on delivery from the Supermercado del Pueblo (People's Supermarket) where eight days' grace had previously been granted. Additionally, the owners had failed to maintain and repair company vehicles, automatically cutting distribution.
* Removing 'unprofitable' vitamin additives from children's food products.
* A reduction to single-shift working.
* Dismissal of 28 workers.

The union independently initiated new industrial safety measures, management was locked out, and the first day of the work-in succeeded in raising production levels by 20%. A four-person Comision de Vigilancia was set up and remained in the plant round the clock to prevent physical sabotage. On the 21st the state intervened through the Procuradoria General de Justicia, and using emergency powers sealed off management offices for investigation. To the FSLN, the messages of El Caracol and the simultaneous occupations of other Managua factories were clear. First, the independent initiatives of the working-class organisations and the policies of the state were converging rapidly. Second, the dividing line between 'patriotic businessmen' and the counter-revolutionary Right was becoming clearer. The February factory occupations had as much to do with a rash of economic sabotage as with an upsurge in class consciousness.

Two weeks later, Junta member Sergio Ramirez announced the new anti-decapitalisation decree. If capitalists were found guilty of this kind of economic sabotage, they risked confiscation of their factories by the state. The principles behind the El Caracol occupation became law. *Barricada* devoted a long editorial to the importance of the new decree for the Frente's concept of national unity:

> This is not an aggressive measure by the Revolution against private enterprise, but a response to the attitude of certain elements . . .
> Patriotic businessmen, those who are honest and support the Economic

Reactivation Plan, should support this measure which will reinforce
national unity and purge it of elements who discredit the important
role played by private enterprise . . . The time has come to put a stop
to business deliquency.[37]

The following week *Barricada* gave a full page to detailed explanations of how
decapitalisation could be detected, to help other workers to follow the
example of El Caracol. The degree of worker participation which this pre-
supposed, including access to a company's confidential records, convinced
many members of the bourgeoisie that the law did in fact undermine traditional private sector prerogatives. For the moment, there is still a certain
logic in this typical assertion by Jaime Chamorro of *La Prensa:* 'All decisions
count on the help and cooperation of what they [the FSLN] call the
"progressive bourgeoisie". They are indispensable because a country can't
maintain production or run an economy without the cooperation of the
class which *knows* about production.'[38]

Learning to Control Production

But the private sector's nightmare is how long it will continue to monopolise
knowledge about production, when all around it is the evidence of direct
state support for worker control — a mixture of legislation, propaganda and
specific structures for popular participation — and the correspondingly rapid
increase in workers' consciousness. Production councils are the basic
instrument of worker participation in both private and COIP factories,
suggested by the CST within weeks of the victory. In the factories where
these operate, each section or department nominates representatives to a
shop-floor Production Committee, and each of these comes together to
form the factory's Production Council, backed up by regular trade union
education circles.

   The need for Production Councils is as great in state industry as in the
private sector, not least to challenge the mechanical interpretation of the
slogan 'Raise Production' sometimes applied by state bureaucrats. The
Councils, and the larger Assemblies of Economic Reactivation (ARE) which
bring together all workers in a single plant, have the major aim of educating
the labour force about the technical, administrative and economic aspects of
production. On a secondary level, they strengthen class solidarity by bringing
workers from all parts of an industry into a single political forum,
overcoming the resistance which white-collar workers have felt in more backward industries like the mines to joining the same union as manual labourers.
The thrice-annual plant production assemblies follow three distinct phases:
production planning, mid-year monitoring, and evaluation and criticism. To
the CST, the ARE represent 'the forum which guarantees that workers will
know how an enterprise is being run. And the workers have the power to
dismiss any administrator, whether on the grounds of inefficient management
of the company or maltreatment of workers.'[39] In each ARE, a production
committee is elected, composed of representatives of the management (state

or private), each section of the plant, the executive of the trade union, and the CST. The first ARE took place at the large privately owned San Antonio sugar refinery. It had been proposed by the workers in the political education school of the refinery's CST-affiliated union, and a disconcerted management team headed by San Antonio's owners – a powerful Conservative family – found itself answering questions and criticisms from 700 worker delegates on themes ranging from the routine maintenance of plant machinery to the effect on the industry of falling world sugar prices. The workers' mood was one of optimism and energy, a mounting self-confidence at their capacity to master the complexities of production. Since San Antonio, private sector AREs have seen that mood grow. In private enterprise then, the understanding of worker control may be either a direct response to capitalist aggression – as in El Caracol, where an already politically conscious union had begun to warn of the rundown of raw materials two months before taking action – or a gradual process of transforming production relations, accepted by the more flexible members of the private sector. In running COIP (i.e. state) industries, worker participation is more direct and immediate. The third, and most advanced, form of worker control is the case of factories abandoned by their owners and now run directly by the work force.

At the milk-processing plant of La Completa, worker control became a reality after the owners had fled the country:

> On 13 August the plant was taken by six *companeros:* a mechanic, someone from the production line, and four assistants. They opened the doors to the rest of the workers who were waiting and, in all, 82 came to work. We immediately took steps to organise security, we formed groups to clean the place up. We couldn't let the factory disappear, because that would have harmed the economy. We wanted to recover the factory and restart production and create employment – half the work force had been laid off six months before the insurrection. Frankly, at first, we took over the plant more because of the economic crisis than anything else, but as our awareness of the Revolution grew, we began to put the question of wages into the background. We worked for two months without pay. During that time the trade unions in the rest of the dairy industry – La Selecta, La Perfecta, Lacmiel and Eskimo – gave us economic help so that we could get by.[40]

At the important Amolonca food-processing plant in Chinandega, the same story applies. Again the owner fled the country, this time leaving debts of $1 million. With no working capital, a democratically elected factory committee began to run the plant, in cooperation with AgroINRA, which granted 25% of normal salaries until production at Amolonca could generate enough capital for regular wages. Amolonca now works smoothly under the direction of the committee, which maintains the machinery, organises security, and sets production targets and budgets.[41] For the FSLN, Amolonca is a likely model for the factories of the future. 'Here the workers have a consciousness of being producers, not wage labourers. It's our first experience of a factory council.'[42]

The Battle for Production

'Raise Production – Crush the Counter-Revolution. That's no jingle, companeros, it's no simple slogan. It really is the second part of the defence of this Revolution.' (Comandante Henry Ruiz)[43]

The front page of *Barricada*'s 27 January 1980 edition carried banner headlines praising the 215 workers of the Jose Daniel Amador CST-affiliated union at the privately owned Sandak shoe factory in Managua, for what it called 'exemplary proletarian consciousness' in increasing productivity. The story was part of the FSLN's continuous propaganda for higher production levels, in which notable examples of working-class discipline are held up for emulation by other groups. This time the choice of factory was significant. Sandak is a joint Nicaraguan and foreign venture which turns out 25,000 pairs of low-price shoes each week, largely using local raw materials, for the domestic market and regional exports to other Central American countries. In the Area of Public Property, the APP, emulation of workers' efforts is not a problem; in the private sector it can be critical, and if examples like Sandak can also illustrate the model conduct of factory owners, they can serve a double propaganda purpose.

One of the major battles for the new trade union movement has been to convince workers that high productivity and the acceptance of austerity in private industry does not serve the interests of the factory owner but of the working class as a whole. As well as providing a model for other workers to follow in the conduct of COIP (state) factories, the CST and the ATC have thrown themselves behind the campaign for weekend voluntary work, which has been devoted especially to bringing in the harvests. Here the voluntary *domingos rojinegros* (red and black Sundays) play a crucial role in overcoming workers' confusion over the abrupt shift in trade union demands from a reduction in working hours to the encouragement of voluntary overtime. The first voluntary work brigades, formed mainly by government employees, began to organise for the coffee-picking season in November and December 1979. Within weeks, the truckloads of volunteers leaving Managua became a regular Sunday routine, and the first concerted national day of volunteer labour was timed to coincide with the anniversary of Sandino's death. On that Sunday – 24 February – in the 'emulacion de Sandino', 10,374 workers contributed 58,207 hours of voluntary labour in vital agricultural areas. Yet the actual production which such days achieved was secondary to the class consciousness which they stimulate in workers – especially those employed outside the APP – about the new social function of production. On occasion, the *domingos rojinegros* have been counter-productive in strictly economic terms: when a desperate need arose for voluntary labour to complete the coffee harvest, inexperienced coffee-pickers damaged many of the bushes, affecting their yield during the following season. But even this has its own political value in teaching middle-class urban volunteers the complexities of what was previously seen as un-skilled rural labour.

Voluntary work on harvests is also combined with political education work among the rural labourers. In this interview Alberto Martinez, FSLN Political Secretary in San Rafael del Sur, some 50 kilometres south-west of the capital, described how this happened in the nearby Julio Buitrago sugar production complex at Montelimar.

We started when the sugar crop began to come in, on 13 December. Our work consists of a campaign of propaganda, agitation and con-sciousness-raising among the peasants who work in the sugar complex. To bring about real political consciousness among the cane-cutters we had to make direct contact with them and make them see the importance which production – in this case the sugar crop – has in the Revolution. And to achieve this the different mass organisations got together, the Juventud Sandinista, the CDS, the Sandinista Rural Police, and the Political Secretary of the FSLN, to plan this campaign. We suggested a number of things: to hold agitational meetings which would begin before the workers set off for the fields, that is at 5 a.m. We distributed mass organisation propaganda materials on the theme of raising production. . . we even made a banner which said *'La marcha hacia el corte de la cana no se detiene!'* ['the march towards the sugar harvest cannot be stopped!'] And in order to create a more effective link between the mass organisations and our *campesino* comrades, we are working ourselves on the harvest one hour a day during the week. On Sundays, and during the later stages of the harvest, we aim to increase this direct participation in their work. On this complex, 90% of the area sown with sugar cane is administered by AgroINRA* and the other 10% is owned by small peasant producers. The ATC has seen what we're trying to do here and it has made them keen to join in too. They are now planning to put together propaganda material about the importance of the sugar harvest. There are ten ATC commi-ttees here on the various *haciendas* which make up the complex, and they give political orientation as well as organising training seminars for the peasants in conjunction with INRA. We have created incentives for those *companeros* who work outstandingly in the cane cutting . . . we give them a red and black armband as a token of recognition from the FSLN. Their response has been really encouraging, there's

* AgroINRA is that section of the Agrarian Reform Institute responsible for the mana ment of large mechanised state farms and agro-exporting complexes with processing facilities.

tremendous interest in the political message which we're trying to put across. And we're hoping that those who distinguish themselves most in their work and their political development will go on to become members of the Frente. For us too, it has been a valuable political experience, because we feel that the whole exercise has helped to develop the peasants' political consciousness and bring more people into the Revolution directly, as well as strengthening the links between the vanguard and the people.

Revolutionary Austerity

Nicaragua's economic crisis is an objective fact. All the advances in workers' control, and the successful fight against trade union opportunism and economism, can only make sense if the working class is able to understand its response to the crisis and the rationale behind the FSLN demand for 'revolutionary austerity'. Although the Frente's moral authority is a major reason for the erosion of economism, no amount of popular support will automatically mobilise people around a policy of austerity. In areas where the CAUS and the Frente Obrero have support, the demand for austerity has been portrayed as a consequence of bourgeois influence in the government. Nothing, of course, would have suited the private sector better than a traditional policy of bourgeois austerity, revitalising private enterprise at the expense of the working class. Instead, the FSLN has had to convince the people that austerity is an objective necessity which affects all classes.[44] The workers and peasants must have solid proof that the initial redistributive policies of the state, as well as the long-term strategy, directly benefit the working class. In the Frente's own words: 'Austerity must be the answer to a concrete problem and not an externally imposed principle. We must distinguish clearly between the austerity produced by an unjust structural situation, and the austerity required to make the revolutionary project a reality. The sacrifice itself must be given a class content.'[45] To achieve this mentality, the FSLN faces a series of related challenges — to hold down real wages and combat inflation, which was running at 84% by the end of the war[46]; to generate employment, in part by asking workers to make direct sacrifices on behalf of the unemployed; to take immediate steps nevertheless to alleviate what Dora Maria Tellez referred to as *bolsones de miseria* (pockets of misery)[47] among the most marginal groups; to prevent the CAUS and other ultra-left groups from taking advantage of the economic crisis; and to apply the politics of austerity in different ways to the APP and the private sector.

The bourgeoisie, too, has had to accept a drop in living standards. Consumer fetishism has been a prime target for the propaganda of the media and the mass organisations, and the state has applied selective taxes and import controls to non-essential consumer goods which only the middle classes can afford. Reforms in direct taxation have brought the state an additional US $200 million in the first year, a sum used directly to increase the social wage of the working class through increased public expenditure on social services, which is a means of increasing popular demand without aggravating inflation. The alternative demanded by the CAUS would have been economically disastrous: to create increased demand through salary hikes, in excess of the projected supply of basic consumer items. Politically as well as economically, the first option was the only logical one: 'The people would not tolerate paying for reactivation with their hunger, after paying for the country's liberation with their blood.'[48]

Tomas Borge, as ever, had the unfailing knack of explaining in simple terms the inflationary threat of 100% wage demands. To accept the demands of the CAUS would have put an additional US $301.3 million into circulation and, speaking to the peasants of the Pedro Rivas Recalde agricultural complex, Borge outlined the implications:

> Let's suppose that each of you earns 1,000 *cordobas* a month, and we decide to double that to 2,000. What would happen? There would be more money on the street. Isn't that so? So the goods we have would be bought up very quickly, with more money around, and we would start to have shortages. And when shortages start, things begin to get more expensive. So that within a short time your 2,000 *cordobas* would buy the same that 1,000 *cordobas* bought you before. For that reason the problem is not to increase the amount of money in your wage packet, but to reduce the price of goods so that there is less money circulating in the market, and the money you do have can be used to buy more things.

Nevertheless, the Frente was well aware from the outset that the immediate problems of the lowest paid could not be solved by social wage increases alone, and that the increasing social wage would in the main bring its greatest benefits to the urban working class. Dora Maria Tellez pointed to the special situations of the rural miners, and especially of the poorest peasants, and asked for the active cooperation of the mass organisations in identifying other such 'pockets of misery.' 'These sectors do not receive the benefits of the social wage — transport price freezes, better hospital care, free medicine, more schools and public parks, subsidies on basic foodstuffs. These peasants don't benefit because they have no access to transport, they don't benefit because they are not affected by the law reducing rents, the improvements in hospital care. We must attend promptly to their problems.'[49] In reality, improvements in social infrastructure could not reach these groups quickly enough to avoid the need for wage increases large enough to ensure real growth in purchasing power but limited enough to have only a marginal inflationary effect. Tellez went on to analyse the relationship between austerity in the private sector and in the Area of Public Ownership, and the damaging effect on working-class interests of large wage increases in either sector:

> If we increase real wages in private enterprise, who foots the bill? The state bank which has had to lend the businessman the money to

reactivate his company. That bank is the people's. And where has it had to obtain the money for these loans? From taxes which are insufficient to meet the country's financial demand, and from foreign loans. But the businessmen make profits, the CAUS will say. That is true. But what happens to those profits? Part of them are recovered through a 6% tax on assets, which returns to the people in the form of more schools, hospitals, food subsidies . . . Then they will ask, does that not still leave some profits? Again, this is true. But the point is that these people will not invest in the country unless they are guaranteed profits . . . If real wages are increased to any large extent in the APP, then we suffer a reduction in the surplus which can be generated. And if that happens, what are we going to reactivate the economy with? How can we invest? How can we sow our crops?

Creating Jobs

The government's attempts to reduce unemployment — running at 34% in Managua alone — have also called for working-class sacrifices. Plan 80's target was to create 95,000 new jobs: 50,000 in agriculture, 20,000 in services, 15,000 in construction and 10,000 in manufacturing industry. In addition, unemployment and class tension increased as always with the end of the coffee harvesting season in late January. But the government has met its targets in most areas by investment in job creation programmes. NACLA illustrated this with a good example from the public sector, the medium-sized Metasa metal manufacturing plant: 'In the first nine months since the triumph, Metasa has created 139 new jobs, a 46% increase. At the same time, the salary of plant workers has risen an average of 24% while that of the higher paid administrative staff has dropped 15%, reducing administrative salaries to only twice that of the poorest paid workers.'[50]

The major exception has been the construction industry, where reactivation has been slow. Marcial Quintero, a 32-year old Managua construction worker, is typical of many unemployed in the industry:

> I have been out of work for five months, getting by as best I can by working as a porter in the Mercado Oriental, selling newspapers, one thing and another that my *companeros* have found for me, because we all help each other out in this time of crisis. I live in one of the most marginal *barrios* of Managua, with my wife and four children to support. There are about 15,000 building workers now, but only 5,600 of us have regular work . . . Still, we have great confidence in the Revolution. They've promised to find us work in the coming months. We know that the government is planning building programmes in various parts of the country, and we're ready to go anywhere for the same salary as we were earning before. A bricklayer like me earns 140 dollars a month, but we hope that will go up as the demand for labour increases. The government has also promised to build 200 new houses for members of the SCAAS, which I belong to, in the Barrio

Waspan in Northern Managua. Things like this are great achievements, although for the time being neither I nor thousands of other *companeros* have even got the bus fare to travel to the union offices.[51]

A major step towards improving conditions for workers like Quintero was the appeal in December 1979 for workers to give up their *treceavo mes*, or 'thirteenth month', salary paid at Christmas, instituted by Somoza as a populist concession after the January 1978 strikes. That, at least, was how it was depicted by Jaime Wheelock and Junta member Moises Hassan, who proposed that the *treceavo mes* should be donated by all those earning more than 1,500 *cordobas* (150 dollars) a month to a state fund designed to create jobs for 20,000 unemployed workers. But the issue became divisive, with many workers regarding the payment as rightfully theirs, the token of a small working-class victory over Somoza. The CST encouraged workers to contribute, with partial success, but the decision was an individual and voluntary one. Class solidarity had a long way to go, and the Frente appeared to have misjudged the workers' willingness to make such a dramatic financial sacrifice.

A further attack on unemployment has been headed by the Ministry of Social Welfare, with the creation of State Production Collectives (CEPs). Their aim was outlined by Antonio Jarquin, in charge of the programme in the Ministry:

> The programme aims to generate units capable of absorbing manpower and giving employment by means of artisan and manufacturing activity. Second, it aims to make available to the people a series of basic goods at the lowest possible price. This is because sales will leave out the middlemen, the speculators. Each CEP will have a distribution unit to guarantee this. These will be modes of production in which exploitation will disappear . . . The participation of women is vital. The problems of women will not be solved simply by incorporating them into productive activity. It's a question of establishing a new mode of production. The collectives depend on the community collectively assuming the domestic tasks of the women. That's why we are creating community laundries, dining-rooms, ironing centres, childcare collectives. Production and social services are a single bloc.[52]

The CEPs are certainly one of the Sandinista Government's most exciting projects, for the way in which they link production, the social wage, women's rights and mass involvement. An organic relationship to the local CDS is fundamental to their success. By the end of 1980, it was planned that a total of eighteen would be functioning. They began with clothing workshops in Esteli, Managua and Nagarote, and these were followed by carpentry shops and collectives producing building materials, toys and foodstuffs in different parts of the country.

Making the Social Wage Stick

Enforcing the various components of the social wage depends on the creative energy of the mass movement and the state and has inevitably brought each into open conflict with the Right. Sandinista leaders alleged that many entrepreneurs had used their workers' *treceavo mes* donations to finance their factories' capital needs; private medical care continues to flourish in opposition to the state health system; food hoarders and speculators are constantly at war with the CDS; despite gifts of buses from Spain and Mexico, public transportation is still inadequate and private 'cowboy' operators ignore the flat one-*cordoba* fare on urban bus rides. While the state — assisted by Cuban volunteer teachers — has taken the main responsibility for educational improvements, opening 50,000 new primary school places in rural areas, the independent efforts of the CDS and the trade unions have been crucial to the extension of health care. The advances in health provision in Ciudad Sandino, a large satellite town on the edge of Managua, are typical:

> When something new is built, the people are really involved in making the decision. Look at the clinic here for example: that was planned by the people. All the CDS got together, and collections were taken on every block, the work was shared out. The whole project was put up to the central offices of the CDS, and many people contributed, working for nothing to make it possible. A carpenter might come along one day and say 'I'll lend a hand today', or the next day it might be a bricklayer, or sometimes even *campesinos* would come in from the hills and say 'Here I am, what can I do to help?' It was all voluntary. That was how we built our clinic. And over there, where Somoza's famous Office of Health was, we've turned that into a People's Pharmacy. We sell medicines there at controlled prices. The clinic is always overflowing with people. We still lack the equipment for operations, but that's another project we have. Even so, many people who used to have to go to the Hospital Velez Paiz in Managua can now be treated right here in Cuidad Sandino.[53]

The enforcement of food price controls, too, depends on the vigilance of the mass organisations. In its 17 October edition, *Barricada* conservatively estimated that prices for basic consumer goods had risen by more than 100% since the Revolution.

The scarcity of basic items was caused primarily by the interruption of the agricultural cycle in 1979, made worse by the uncooperative attitude of landowners, financial problems and the action of speculators after the Revolution. Throughout the first year, the government also had to contend with periodic shortages of individual crops, the delayed effect of planting problems. Maize was scarce from April to June, beans in June, rice in January, April and June, and the state had to compensate for shortfalls by temporary imports. In the early months, foreign aid and $10 million worth of food purchased abroad satisfied local demand and stopped speculation, but as emergency aid dried up and ENABAS sought to extend its national food distribution network, speculators began to operate on a large scale. Sugar and salt were immediate targets. By the end of the first year, ENABAS had managed to set up 799 food distribution points, with another 194 in productive centres, and the state had the capacity to control 40% of local crop production, compared with an average of only 5% in other Central American countries. The Ministry of Internal Trade (MICOIN) aims to extend this to 75% by 1982, but until then speculators retain considerable room for manoeuvre. When there is a shortage of any item, the mass organisations respond in two ways: on the one hand, a propaganda and information drive to give the public accurate facts on prices, real output and availability; on the other, direct political action against speculators. The success of propaganda is impressive: during the alleged sugar crisis of mid-1980, popular opinion placed the blame squarely on hoarders, despite a private sector campaign to blame the government. In every municipal market, stalls display current ENABAS pricelists and the streets are hung with CDS banners bearing slogans like 'Against those who speculate with the people's hunger — POPULAR POWER '. In Managua, the thirty-six CDSs of the Mercado Oriental, the country's largest distribution centre, organised a mass campaign against profiteers in close cooperation with the state. When *campesino* producers arrived in the capital to sell their beans to middlemen, the CDSs intervened to have the goods sold to ENABAS at the same price, with the state guaranteeing resale prices which undercut the private merchants.

Price Fluctuations

	Early 1979 (Cordobas)	October 1979 (Cordobas)	February 1980 MICOIN-ENABAS fixed prices (Cordobas)
Cooking oil (gallon)	28.00	40.00	38.80
Maize (*quintal:* 220 lbs)	45.00	95.00	1.00 (lb)
Eggs (dozen)	6.00	12.00	9.00
Milk (litre)	1.00	2.00	2.85
Salt (pound)	0.25	0.60	0.60
Soap (1 bar)	2.00	4.50	3.75

Source: *Patria Libre*, No. 2.

CDS action has also been crucial to the success of government measures to improve working-class housing. The ECLA report on Nicaragua after the war estimated that 80% of all Nicaraguans lived in homes unfit for human habitation, a total of 300,000 housing units in addition to the 4,200 homes destroyed by Somoza's troops. As a first step, the government took over the so-called *repartos clandestinos* in October 1979, 200 *barrios* whose private landlords were denying adequate water supplies, drainage and electricity to their residents. The *repartos* are now publicly owned, and the state is responsible for services and rents. On 19 December, the government decreed massive cuts in all rents, to take effect from 1 January. For houses costing less than $50 a month – the vast majority of working-class homes – rents were cut by 50%. From $50 to $100, the cut was 40%, and for houses costing more than $100 the maximum annual rent cannot exceed 5% of the property's market value. In the case of inadequate slum dwellings, the decree gave the state power to take possession and impose rent reductions of more than 50%. As the third stage of the low-cost housing programme, slums will be torn down and replaced by brick and concrete houses with all services. It is a programme which will help during 1981 to combat the still alarming level of unemployment in construction. *Barrios* which lack access to power lines, like those by Managua's lakeside, are being physically transplanted. In others, the Housing Ministry MINVAH has set up housing banks coordinated by the CDS, which decide on the location of new houses and organise *brigadas de autoconstruccion* in which the residents themselves build their homes with technical advice from MINVAH, paying off the initial capital cost of around $3,000 per unit to the state over a period of 20 years.

Plan 80 aimed to increase working-class living standards by 20% in real terms during that year as a result of the social wage, even before the structural transformation of the economy. In fact, the true rise over the first year was probably closer to 10%. For the middle class, restrictions on imported luxuries and the progressive reform of taxation brought a drop in living standards, but only around 6-7%. This was an important move towards undermining capitalist prerogatives in line with Sergio Ramirez's comment that 'the welfare of the people, rather than profits, must come first', but probably as much as the Frente wished to risk in the first year to avoid a large-scale desertion of bourgeois support. Despite all the social measures described here, working-class purchasing power failed to keep pace with inflation, and it was inevitable that across-the-board wage rises for the lowest paid would have to be made. Plan 80 had calculated that a family of six needed an income of at least 950 *cordobas* ($95) a month for basic subsistence, even with price controls. By mid-year many workers were still earning less than that, often with families larger than six.

The Comision Nacional Intersindical, meeting on 31 May, blamed the failure to reach Plan 80's targets on the increases in food prices, which they attributed directly to speculation. The social wage alone, they claimed, could never compensate. The union leadership could hardly escape the pressure building up from the grassroots, the kind which shortly afterwards led to the Plywood and CANAL strikes. The CNI requested an across-the-board rise. for the lowest paid, and the state complied. In late June an increase of 125 *cordobas* a month was decreed for 300,000 workers – almost half the economically active population – earning less than 1,200 *cordobas*. The rise was backdated to the 1st of the month, despite vigorous private sector opposition, and the CST insisted that its rank and file give priority to attacking employers who refused to comply. Although the wage rise carried an inflationary risk, it was the result of popular pressure, communicated democratically through the mass organisations and endorsed by them. On other occasions, the FSLN has held back working-class demands by explaining why they were tactically wrong. But on the wages issue, after a year of restraint, this was out of the question.

Notes

1. Interview with regional official of INRA, Boaco, July 1980.
2. COSEP, *Analisis sobre la Ejecucion del Programa de Gobierno de Reconstruccion Nacional,* p. 10.
3. Jaime Wheelock, ' No Hay Dos Reformas Agrarias Iguales', interview with Xavier Arguello, in *Nicarauac,* Managua, Ministerio de Culture, No. 1., May-June 1980, p. 61.
4. See Alan Gilbert, *Latin American Development – A Geographical Perspective* (Harmondsworth, Penguin, 1974), p. 161. The Punta del Este Charter called for 'the effective transformation of unjust structures and systems of land tenure and use with a view to replacing *latifundia* and dwarf holdings by an equitable system of land tenure.' Outside Central America, the Latin American nations who complied most readily with the Charter were Venezuela (1960), Colombia (1961), Chile (1962), Brazil (1963) and Peru (1964). In none of these countries could the resulting land reform programmes be said to have made real progress.
5. *La Revolucion y el Campo* (Managua, INRA, 1979), p. 10.
6. Jaime Wheelock, *loc. cit.,* p. 60.
7. *Ibid.*
8. *Latin America Weekly Report,* WR-80-33, 22 August 1980.
9. Jaime Wheelock, speech to the National Assembly of the Asociacion de Trabajadores del Campo, in *ATC Asamblea Nacional Constitutiva: Memorias,* pp. 34-5.
10. *Mensaje de la Junta de Gobierno de Reconstruccion Nacional al Pueblo de Nicaragua,* p. 12.
11. *Barricada,* 20 July 1980.
12. Daniel Ortega, speech to ATC Assembly, *Memorias,* p. 26.
13. Jaime Wheelock, interview in *Nicarauac,* No. 1, p. 66.
14. Interview with INRA official, Managua, January 1981.
15. Jaime Wheelock, speech to ATC Assembly, *Memorias,* pp. 37-8.
16. ATC General Secretary Edgardo Garcia, speech to ATC Assembly, *Memorias,* p. 17.
17. ATC, 'Declaracion de Principios', *Memorias,* p. 54.
18. Francisco Lopez, Report to ATC Assembly, *Memorias,* p. 4.
19. MIDA-INRA, *Boletin Informativo,* 1980.
20. Interview with CST General Secretary Ivan Garcia, Managua, March 1980.
21. Ibid.

22. *The Open Veins of Nicaragua* (London, Nicaragua Solidarity Campaign, 1980).
23. *Barricada*, 8 March 1980.
24. *Barricada*, 13 December 1979.
25. COSEP communique, 14 November 1979.
26. *El Papel de los Sindicatos en la Revolucion* (pamphlet) (Managua, CST/ CGT-I joint publication, 1980), pp. 6-7.
27. CAUS communique (mimeo), February 1980.
28. *Barricada*, 29 April 1980.
29. Interview with Ivan Garcia.
30. In the newspaper of the Partido Comunista de Nicaragua, *El Partido*.
31. *El Partido*, August 1979.
32. This account of the FABRITEX and other CAUS-led strikes is drawn from a number of sources: *Barricada*, 18-28 February 1980; a large number of mimeographed broadsheets from the CST, CDS and other mass organisations; and several interviews with factory workers and union officials, Managua, February-March 1980.
33. *Barricada*, 20 February 1980.
34. See interview with *Comandante Guerrillera* Dora Maria Tellez, in *Barricada*, 6 March 1980.
35. *Intercontinental Press*, 21 July 1980.
36. *Barricada*, 21 February 1980.
37. *Barricada*, 3 March 1980.
38. Interview with Jaime Chamorro, Managua, February 1980 (quoted by kind permission of Reggie Norton, former OXFAM field director in Central America).
39. Julio Rojas, CST delegate to the Council of State, interviewed in *Perspectiva Mundial*, 28 July 1980.
40. La Completa factory worker interviewed in the CST newspaper *El Trabajador*, No. 3, 16 February 1980.
41. *Poder Sandinista*, No. 7, 6 December 1979.
42. Mimeographed FSLN leaflet, undated.
43. Henry Ruiz, speech to ATC Assembly, *Memorias*, p. 74.
44. Adolfo Gilly, *La Nueva Nicaragua — Antimperialismo y Lucha de Clases* (Mexico City, Editorial Nueva Imagen, 1980), p. 33.
45. *Linea de Propaganda de la Revolucion Sandinista — Documento de Estudio* (Managua, SENAPEP, 1980), p. 6.
46. *Plan 81*, p. 82.
47. Dora Maria Tellez, interview in *Barricada*, 6 March 1980.
48. *Plan 80*, p. 116.
49. Tellez, *loc. cit.*
50. Tim Draimin, *Nicaragua's Revolution* (NACLA), p. 24.
51. In *Ya Veremos*, Managua, June 1980.
52. *Barricada*, 20 December 1979.
53. Interview with Juana Cruz, shopkeeper in Ciudad Sandino, July 1980.

14. Consolidating the Revolution: Five Essays

Building Friendships against Intervention

In winning the struggle against Somoza, the FSLN was different from most other liberation movements in the breadth of its international diplomatic support. At the heart of Nicaragua's own feelings of solidarity lies a deep identification with Cuba, Vietnam and the popular struggle in El Salvador, and most analysis of Nicaraguan foreign policy has dwelt obsessively on these friendships and the opening of diplomatic relations with Socialist and Arab countries. However, this is to miss the point about Nicaragua's concept of non-alignment. For the FSLN, an unsolicited visit to President Jimmy Carter by three members of the Junta was an equally important affirmation of national independence. The importance of alliances in the Western capitalist world was nowhere better illustrated than in the effort to mobilise aid for the 1980 five-month Literacy Crusade. The Crusade was the central political project of the first year, a unique blend of ideological consolidation and the social ideals for which the war had been fought. There would be no shortage of attacks from the West on the Crusade's overtly politicising purpose, yet its profound humanitarian content was the perfect instrument for putting Western sympathy for the Revolution on the line. 'We know who our natural allies are,' a senior figure in the Crusade remarked candidly. 'But we also know who the friends are that we need. The biggest single threat we face is military intervention from the north. If that looks like happening, all the left-wing support in the world won't prevent it. But with friends like Mexico, the EEC, even in the USA itself . . . well, that would be a different story.'[1]

In the event, fully 99% of the $20 million in aid for the Crusade came from the West, with USAID providing the single largest donation of more than $2 million.[2] While *La Prensa* was jubilant at the generosity of the capitalist world, the FSLN also had reason for deep satisfaction. The friendships built up so painstakingly in the fight against Somoza had survived remarkably the first year of popular revolution, and the wisdom of Nicaragua's foreign policy has been to accept foreign support from whatever source, while remaining lucid about the widely differing motives which underlie each country's solidarity and turning them to Nicaragua's advantage.

Nicaragua's spectacular entry into the Non-Aligned Movement at its sixth summit in Havana in August 1979 provided many of the keys to the new foreign policy. Speaking on behalf of the Junta, Daniel Ortega had this to say:

> We are entering the Non-Aligned Movement because in this movement we see the broadest organisation of the Third World states that are playing an important role and exercise a growing influence in the international sphere, in the struggle of people against imperialism, colonialism, apartheid, racism – including Zionism – and every form of oppression. Because they are for active peaceful coexistence, against the existence of military blocs and alliances, for restructuring international relations on an honourable basis, and are for the establishment of a new international economic order.[3]

In the course of his speech, Ortega went on to express Nicaraguan solidarity with the liberation of Grenada, Iran, Kampuchea and Uganda in 1979. He demanded US abandonment of the Guantanamo base in Cuba, Puerto Rican independence, Panamanian sovereignty over the Canal Zone, independence for Belize and stated Nicaragua's commitment to the reunification of Korea and the withdrawal of American troops, and the ratification of the SALT II treaties. Among countries fighting for their liberation, he singled out Nicaraguan support for POLISARIO, SWAPO, the Patriotic Front of Zimbabwe and the frontline states, and the self-determination of East Timor. As well as paying tribute to the support of Castro, President Rodrigo Carazo of Costa Rica and President Jose Lopez Portillo of Mexico, ex-President Carlos Andres Perez of Venezuela and General Omar Torrijos of Panama, he reserved special words of solidarity for the PLO and the people of Vietnam, reiterating Nicaragua's recognition of the Government of People's Kampuchea.

With the exception of Castro's visit on 19 July 1980, no foreign leader has been given the same reception as Vietnam's Pham Van Dong the previous September. With monumental portraits of Ho Chi Minh and Che Guevara flanking those of Sandino on the front of the National Palace, the welcome for the Vietnamese premier reflected the close identification of the FSLN with the Vietnamese struggle. There were indeed many parallels: the decades of suffering under foreign aggression, the maturity of a guerrilla strategy in which the Sandinistas frequently cited General Giap as an inspiration. Like the Vietnamese Revolution, the Sandinista victory was above all that of a people standing alone, with powerful international solidarity but little direct foreign assistance. In both countries, the heroism of the people became a byword. And in both revolutions the leadership acted with great pragmatism, suspending the language of Marxism in favour of a nationalist struggle which would incorporate the broadest sectors of a 'patriotic bourgeoisie', following a flexible blend of national liberation and socialisation according to the circumstances prevailing at critical moments of the struggle. In rejecting decades of US domination, the Nicaraguans also rejected any international policies which would tie them directly to another power bloc, and must have felt a strong attachment to Ho Chi Minh's Vietnamese Way. Like Ho, the Frente soon found itself under criticism for taking a firmer hand against the ultra-left than against bourgeois dissidents. And like Ho, they saw the early tactics of the Far Left as a serious miscalculation of national conditions – specifically the all-important tactical alliance with the private sector – and a mechanical reading of revolutionary theory which took no account of the need to 'make haste slowly'.

Nicaragua's close ties with Cuba have made crucial votes in the United Nations the object of intense scrutiny from the Right. While voting with the Socialist bloc in recognition of the Heng Samrin Government in Phnom Penh, Nicaragua abstained in successive votes from condemning Soviet action in Afghanistan. During a high-level mission to Moscow on the other hand, Soviet leaders were reportedly irritated by a speech from Tomas Borge insisting on Nicaragua's independence on the Afghanistan issue, although the meeting yielded a fraternal joint statement from the FSLN and CPSU. In subsequent weeks the Sandinista media were at pains to analyse the Afghan situation to the Nicaraguan people, and a major article by Comandante Bayardo Arce in *Barricada* drew a firm distinction between Soviet intervention and imperialism, while roundly condemning US support for 'counter-revolutionary forces'.

Much internal and external hostility to the Sandinista Government has predictably centred on supposed Cuban and Soviet involvement in the country's reconstruction. In February 1980, a secret Congressional session to study a proposed American aid package of $75 million heard CIA evidence of 'Cuban-Soviet hegemony' in Nicaragua, and a major – if comical – condition placed on the aid by the right-wing Republican lobby was that not a cent should reach schools staffed by volunteer Cuban teachers. Among the wilder rumours which have circulated, backed to the hilt by Robelo since his resignation and avidly consumed by *La Prensa*, have been stories of Cuban missile bases in Esteli and 'Ontelemar' [sic],[4] Soviet spy ships disguised as trawlers to monitor American submarine movements off the Caribbean coast. *La Prensa* has gone as far as to allege that the Sandinista Police carry out political arrests on instructions from the Soviet Embassy in Managua. The residual prestige of *La Prensa* and the enduring anti-Communism bred by Somoza mean that some of these stories have gained credibility among the people, a fact not lost on the Nicaraguan Right.

Real or imagined Cuban assistance has also bruised one or two of Nicaragua's regional friendships. The Panamanian Government, which saw itself as a crucial source of military know-how to the FSLN, has been offended by the role assumed by Cuban advisers since the victory.[5] And domestic events in the Andean Pact countries, which were such a valuable source of diplomatic support during the insurrection, have weakened Nicaragua's backing from Latin American states. To add to the July 1980 coup in Bolivia and the steady rightwards lurch of the Christian Democrat government in Venezuela, relations with Colombia (never the most reliable of allies) have touched bottom. The reason has been Nicaragua's assertion of territorial rights over a 200-mile ocean shelf and its refusal to recognise the Barcenas-Meneses-Esguerra Treaty signed during the United States occupation in the 1920s, which ceded the Caribbean islands of San Andres, Providencia, Roncador, Serrana and Quitasueno to Colombia. Nicaraguan claims to the islands have been widely depicted in the Colombian press as part of a Cuban strategy to establish military bases in the Caribbean.

Perhaps the major lesson learnt by Nicaragua in handling its friendships with the West has been that the capitalist world is no monolith. At the level of world powers, there are fundamental strategic rifts between West Germany and the United States. At the level of aspirations for Latin American leadership, there is intense competition between Mexico and Venezuela. Exploiting these contradictions has helped the consolidation of the Nicaraguan Revolution as the four countries jockey for position in Central America. To the West German SPD Government, Washington policy towards Central America under the Carter Administration was fatally flawed. The SPD saw clearly that neither the State Department's advocacy of cautious reformism (but excluding the Left), nor the Pentagon/National Security Council line of arming traditionally friendly military regimes was capable of bringing long-term stability to the region. Bonn is also convinced that the events of the last two years have broken US economic domination of Central America. More than any other Western government, German foreign policy is shaped by a pragmatic need for foreign markets, and stability coupled with increased local purchasing power could make Central America an attractive target for West German exports. The Bonn-Washington division, which began with SPD political and financial support for the FSLN, reached crisis point over El Salvador, culminating in glacial meetings between SPD Vice-President, Hans Jurgen Wischnewski, and the State Department, after which Secretary of State Edmund Muskie ruled out any possibility of joint US-West German policy in the area.

West Germany would be strenuously opposed to any direct military intervention in Central America. For Nicaragua, the public divisions on strategy and the conflicts of economic interest within the capitalist world are a useful defence, especially as they are likely to heighten during a Reagan presidency. At the same time, the FSLN recognises that there is no monolithic Social Democratic intention towards Central America, an analysis which appears to have escaped Washington, which treats the West German Government, the SPD and the Socialist International as a single indivisible force encouraging Central American Marxism. The FSLN and El Salvador's Coordinadora Revolucionaria de Masas (CRM) came as observers to the Socialist International regional conference on Latin America in April 1980 and saw resolutions condemning the USA over El Salvador and Puerto Rico, as well as heated debates between the Latin American and West European Social Democrats on trading policies and the relationship between the Socialist International and Latin American communist parties. The principal split within the movement on Nicaragua is between the West Germans and Portugal's Mario Soares — which is ironic, in view of Germany's role after the

Portuguese Revolution, but consistent with West German pragmatism. Bourgeois democracy offered stability against a volatile revolution in Portugal; no Social Democratic solution is plausible in Nicaragua. Soares's unsuccessful attempt to steer Robelo's right-wing MDN into the Socialist International was the culmination of a long personal crusade to avoid the 'Cubanisation' of Nicaragua. To Soares, who had led an SI mission to Managua only two weeks after the Sandinista victory, the political purpose of massive Social Democratic aid was clear. Soares may also have grasped a contradiction in West German policy not lost on the right wing of the SPD, that a socialist revolution might not in fact create the favourable markets required by German capital. Within the SPD, as within the Socialist International as a whole, there are clear distinctions between the foreign policy position of the Government and the ideological sympathies of the party's left wing, and indeed the fear that this tendency might become dominant in German support for Nicaragua alarmed foreign policy advisers in Washington.

The SPD's Friedrich Ebert Foundation has been the most visible face of German Social Democratic involvement in Nicaragua, channelling aid and technical assistance and sponsoring a highly publicised Conference of Support and Solidarity in February 1980. The platform given to the Salvadorean Left and the radical tone of the conference resolutions must have worried Soares, who was among the participants.[6] For the FSLN, the significance of the conference was in maintaining the active friendship of democratic governments who had lent their weight to the anti-Somoza struggle. Sergio Ramirez of the Junta traced their support back to the previous year's seventeenth meeting of the OAS: 'It was in those days of struggle that a new kind of political behaviour emerged. That framework of democratic support for the Nicaraguan Revolution made us realise that we could form a bloc of democratic unity opposed to the interests of imperialism . . . We are a test case for Latin America. We are well aware of the role we are playing.'[7]

Turning to countries closer to home, the notion of an informal anti-imperialist bloc is nowhere more vital than in the Caribbean. Prominent visitors to the July 1980 anniversary celebrations were Prime Ministers Maurice Bishop of Grenada and George Price of Belize, reinforcing the unity of English and Spanish-speaking radical governments in the region against US efforts to subvert the Left in the wake of the Grenadian and Nicaraguan victories. The FSLN's close ties with the Caribbean are also a vital pillar of domestic policy, bringing the alienated minorities of the Atlantic Coast behind the Revolution by emphasising that Nicaragua's cultural identity is not only Central American and Latin, but Caribbean and Black.[8]

Nicaragua is also a test case for the regional leadership aspirations of Mexico and Venezuela, the region's two biggest oil-suppliers. Mexico, proud of its record as the only Latin American country not to break diplomatic relations with revolutionary Cuba, continues to mix radical foreign policy rhetoric with the ruling PRI's history of internal repression and corruption. Venezuela, in shifting smartly to the Right under COPEI President Luis Herrera Campins, has made overt attempts to interfere in Nicaraguan affairs (offering $20 million in aid as a direct bargaining counter for Christian Democrat inclusion in an expanded Junta) and has acted in concert with Washington over Central American policy, notably in giving outright support for the beleaguered military-Christian Democrat Junta in El Salvador. Both countries represent an essential source of Central American oil supplies, and Mexican oil wealth, in fact, lies close to the heart of Washington's dilemma. The United States cannot afford to antagonise Mexico for fear of losing access to the oil. But can it tolerate Mexico's public demonstrations of friendship with Castro, the FSLN and the Salvadorean Left, if this is likely to lead to Washington's ultimate nightmare of the Central American revolution reaching the oilfields on Mexico's southern border? For Nicaragua, the joint Mexican-Venezuelan scheme for subsidised oil exports to the region, by undermining economic dependency on either power, is a neat resolution of the contradiction between Venezuela's regional interventionism and Mexico's 'Hands off Central America' posture, and keeps both friendships alive.

The best evidence of the importance of these friendships to Nicaragua as a defence against intervention is the coverage given to them by the Sandinista media. Visits during 1980 by Herrera Campins and Mexican President Jose Lopez Portillo were front-page splashes surrounded by lavish protocol; they were given as prominent treatment as relations with Cuba, El Salvador and the Socialist bloc. If these friendships prove durable – and there is every reason to suppose they will – 'intervention from the north' will not prove easy.[9]

Overcoming the Ideology of Somocismo

Arce's article on the myth of Soviet imperialism and press coverage of Social Democracy are attempts to strengthen public perception of the new foreign policy. Widespread acceptance of *La Prensa* scare stories shows how far there is still to go in educating people to understand Nicaragua's new political direction. Signs on the Managua airport road still read 'Welcome to Nicaragua: Another Diners Club Country'. Taxi-drivers grumble that Tomas Borge wants to implant Cuban-style Communism in Nicaragua. When asked what Cuban Communism is, they confess they have no idea beyond that bred into them by Somoza. Other Nicaraguans will frequently say: 'There is no trace of Communism here, just *Sandinismo*. Everybody is Sandinista here. We've never known what democracy was, so how can we know what Socialism is?'

Somocista repression was not only maintained by force and coercion, but by ideological control and an occasional necessary dose of populism. While the votes of peasants were bought in what the Frente refer to as *'elecciones de guaro y nacatamales'*,[10] the capitalist values expressed for decades by the media and the acquiescence of the formal opposition parties have left a people notoriously hostile to Socialism. During the pre-Revolutionary period, as well as creating dual power structures, the FSLN developed a parallel

ideological and cultural hegemony which definitively broke the legitimacy
of the Somoza state. Once ideological consensus had been challenged, it
crumbled irreversibly until Somoza's only means of control was violence.
Traditional 'soft' propaganda was no longer effective. In its place came crude
and rabid anti-Communism, pitted against the Frente's own propaganda
which revealed the economic and political essence of *Somocismo*. The old
consciousness had been destroyed, but the task remained to build the new
mass consciousness, which could only develop partially and unevenly in the
climate of a revolutionary war. An FSLN militant gave this view of the
problem of political consciousness:

> Tell a Nicaraguan factory worker – as much in the CST as in the other
> labour unions – that we are building a system in which workers will
> control the means of production, in which income will be redistributed
> to benefit the proletariat and he will say 'yes – that's what we want.'
> Call it Socialism and he will tell you he doesn't want any part of it.
> Tell a peasant – in whom the problem of political education is even
> more acute – that the revolution is all about destroying the power of
> the big *latifundistas,* that the agrarian reform and the literacy campaign
> will incorporate the peasantry into political decisions, show how the
> Council of State and the mass organisations are giving that person a
> voice at every level of government, and he will be enthusiastic, he will
> recognise that this is right and just. Mention the word Communism and
> he will run a mile. Or ask most Nicaraguans what they think of Cuba,
> and they will tell you the truth – that the Cuban people are our
> greatest friends, that Cuba is defending our Revolution in countless
> ways, that they know someone whose kid is studying on the Isla de la
> Juventud [Island of Youth, where Nicaraguan children are studying in
> an international school alongside children from Ethiopia, Mozambique
> etc.] . Remind them that Cuba is a socialist state, and that still presents
> a contradiction. But the important thing is that it makes them reflect
> on their prejudices, it makes them challenge mentally the fixed image
> they have a Cuba with the reality of Cuban solidarity which they can
> see all around them.[11]

In this sense, Fidel's own comment to the crowd on 19 July that 'you remind
me so much of our own people . . . being here, we Cubans feel as if we were
in our own country' is no mere platitude. It is a suggestion which may have a
profound effect in breaking down ideological fears and ignorance. Nevertheless, the paradox of Cuban solidarity is that its most visible thrust – the
provision of volunteer teachers and health workers – has been directed at the
areas of greatest social deprivation, the most remote rural areas and the non-
Spanish-speaking Atlantic Coast, where the level of political consciousness is
at its lowest. The natural resistance of the Atlantic Coast population to a
'Spanish' revolution has at times been aggravated by the influx of Cubans.
The work of Cuban advisers in the fishing industry, or Cuban technicians

in a Miskito radio station, have been seen locally as 'jobs for foreign communists' in a region of acute unemployment. Fearful of aggressive atheism, some deeply religious older people have been unwilling to receive treatment from Cuban doctors. There are not many of these cases, but with each one a new rumour spreads and is eagerly fuelled by local Somocista and right-wing groups. In this atmosphere, local discontent with the initially slow pace of social change has occasionally reached flashpoint over the Cuban issue, among a local population which may feel alienated, politically and culturally, from the Revolution. One such flashpoint came with riots in Bluefields in October 1980. The immediate spark was trivial — most said it was over the appointment of a Cuban fishing boat captain in a town where regular employment in the fishing industry is rare. But whatever the cause, within hours the dispute had been exploited by Somocistas, ultra-leftists, Conservative businessmen, separatist groups and common criminals. It took the Frente three days to calm the town, avoiding military repression of an already explosive situation. The dilemma was an acute one: the FSLN decided that a large military presence was the only remedy, but transporting troops in from the capital risked further local resentment. EPS troops *were* flown in, but they were handpicked and only left Managua after protracted briefing on the political background to events in Bluefields.

The FSLN's attempts to bring about the economic and political integration of the Atlantic Coast have often been resented. 'They have a poster which says "The Atlantic Coast: the awakening giant",' said one local resident. 'But we don't need them to wake us up — we're awake already.'[12] After a year, the Revolution has made little headway in the region, a dilemma worsened by the difficulty in locating well-trained FSLN cadres with an awareness of local cultural patterns and the need to move at a different pace from the rest of the country. So long as the Revolution fails to consolidate its support on the Costa Atlantica, the area remains a fertile ground for counter-revolutionary activity. The Frente pins much of its hopes on two things: the ethnic organisation MISURASATA, which is represented on the Council of State, and the drive to bring the area into the Revolution via the east, by building friendships with Grenada, Jamaica and other Caribbean nations, and stressing Nicaragua's identity as a Caribbean country with cultural traditions distinct from those of the Pacific Coast majority. MISURASATA originally had difficulty gaining acceptance from the other mass organisations, but is now gaining ground through its interventions in the Council of State and its organisational capacity among groups such as the mineworkers.

Like the other mass organisations, MISURASATA's main difficulty is the political education of its own membership. A CDS activist from Managua described the way this affected the early growth of the CDSs: 'One of the major difficulties is the lack of *companeros* with a clear political vision. As the committees were formed spontaneously, some people who were not up to the job and others who were simply opportunists began to manipulate certain CDSs for their own purposes.'[13]

The major successes of the Frente's early propaganda work have been to teach the political independence of the working class from the state, and the class independence of the proletariat from the bourgeoisie. These basic gains by the mass organisations have driven bourgeois ideology into a corner, without using explicitly Marxist terminology, but they have not destroyed it. The damaging legacy of *Somocismo* is seen less in the overt acceptance of capitalist ideology than in the survival of patterns of apathy, a reluctance on the part of the workers and peasants to take independent and militant initiatives. The initial purpose of Sandinista propaganda was to consolidate the anti-imperialism of the mass movement, to deal with the basics of *Sandinismo,* not to instil obedience to leadership positions, but rather to stimulate creative analysis by the working class of its own history so as to provide a basis for independent class action. The early stages were difficult, and leadership cadres found themselves frequently frustrated by the people's reticence in articulating their demands. The CST, for example, was criticised for not demanding ENABAS food distribution points in the factories, and for remaining silent about the need for effective consumer-protection laws. But, as the FSLN admitted in subsequent self-criticism, this tentative early behaviour reflected the limitations — perhaps necessary ones — of initial political education and propaganda work.

Cupertino Perez, a peasant from the Comuna Julio Buitrago in Leon, described the content of early political education: 'Quite often in the after-. noons or evenings, the commune secretary has been giving us political talks, about how terrible it was to live under *Somocismo,* how long *Somocismo* lasted, or about the thought of Sandino, and the importance of the Revolution now.' It was often very basic, with the twin dangers that the propaganda of *consolidation* would cease to be in step with the demands of the Revolution and the future needs of the working class and the ever-present risk of triumphalist propaganda leading to mass passivity in the euphoric early months.[14] One of the negative results was a delay in restarting production, with the working class unsure of what was expected of it and what it was capable of. In some cases, little explanation was given of actions taken by government.

The mood changed abruptly with the publication of Plan 80 and an intensive propaganda effort around the tasks of economic recovery. *Barricada* stressed the need in an important editorial which was also an appeal to the mass organisations:

> When publishing front-page news about the inauguration of a new production complex, for example, our treatment of the story has too often been confined to political speechmaking at the expense of hard facts. There has been too little analysis of the participation of the workers, their aspirations, how they organise. The same thing happens with our support for the campaign against bureaucracy, which has been inadequate, because solid examples and proposals for alternative action are lacking. We believe that this self-criticism by *Barricada* should act

as a guide to Sandinista militants, mass organisations and propagandists. We appeal to them to intensify their efforts to strengthen the propaganda of production . . . New forms of organisation, propaganda and mobilisation and new revolutionary attitudes to our work are essential if we are to keep moving forward, and we should open the debate without delay. A political debate rooted in reality, in hard facts.[15]

The development of the weekly newspaper, *Poder Sandinista,* first published in mid-October by the FSLN's Secretaria Nacional de Propaganda y Educacion Politica (SENAPEP), became crucial to political orientation. Its first issue was launched in the middle of a two-month series of 'Political and Trade Union Formation' seminars run by the CST, and it shared the seminars' aim of encouraging a critical dialogue which would strengthen the links between the Frente and the mass organisations. *Poder Sandinista* centred its attention on propaganda around production and the role of the mass organisations in the state. Starting from basics, it provided a dictionary of production which gave workers definitions of basic political concepts such as social class, profit, means of production and surplus value. In March, in the midst of a national debate about economism and working-class strategy, it tackled the central issue of trade union demands in a revolutionary society:

The historical components of the relationship between capital and labour have always been framed in four stages: (a) the demand for a guaranteed minimum wage; (b) the demand for a real wage with purchasing power; (c) the demand for a social wage (which the state guarantees in the form of services, education, health care, housing etc.) and for improvements in working conditions; (d) the demand for extending workers' participation in the decision-making process, both inside and outside the workplace. Traditionally in capitalist societies, these demands have tended to be lodged in this order of priority, but today they should be the other way round.[16]

The Propaganda and Political Education Secretariat set itself three distinct functions: agitation and propaganda, publications, and political education. Agitprop covered the intensive use of the Sandinista media (*Barricada, Poder Sandinista,* Radio Sandino, the Sistema Sandinista de Television, etc.) The visual media have made a concerted attack on ingrained cultural values as well as laying the foundations of a new ideology. Legislation prohibits all sexist advertising and television advertisements for tobacco and alcohol. Although Sandinista TV is virtually obliged by a shortage of material to continue using some US-produced programmes, there is a ban on all those glorifying crime or involving propaganda for the US armed forces, as well as children's programmes based on 'super-hero' images.

Sandinista publications concentrated at first on the basic writings of Sandino, Fonseca and members of the FSLN National Directorate, and brief

309

biographies of 'Heroes and Martyrs of the Revolution', the latter as part of a sustained campaign to honour the memory of those who died in combat, whose lives provide examples for the working class to emulate. But now, with the need for intensive theoretical cadre training, SENAPEP has moved on to editions of the most important works of Marx, Lenin and Che Guevara. Finally, work on political education covers the organisation of cadre schools and cooperation with the ATC and CST in their independent educational work. The ATC runs five-day courses for peasant activists at the Escuela Piquin Guerrero, and the CST regular seminars and a trade union radio school *Habla la CST* ('The CST Speaks').

There is an evident tension here between the dynamic of national unity and the rhythm dictated by the need to raise the theoretical level of FSLN militants and build a Sandinista Party. Businessmen who see CST study groups analysing pamphlets by Lenin are more than ever convinced that their days are numbered. The first anniversary of the Revolution was a time of growing ideological struggle, with the Right claiming that the systematically anti-capitalist drift of mass education work was actively contradicting the commitment to national unity. After the propaganda of consolidation in the final months of 1979, and the propaganda of production in 1980, the use of Marxist-Leninist study tools in party building from mid-1980 on is, in the bourgeoisie's favourite phrase, evidence of the Frente 'revealing its true identity'.

But the lack of adequate cadres must be solved urgently. Many of the FSLN's most experienced militants — trade unionists, peasant leaders, *barrio* organisers — were killed in the insurrection. In government, too many young Sandinista militants lack administrative and technical skills, while at the same time too many technicians lack political consciousness. The battle against bureaucracy in government is as much a reflection of these deficiencies as of the survival of Somocista working habits. Although it is correct to draw a distinction between the formal executive arm of government and the other emerging forms of popular democracy, the fact remains that the FSLN must ceaselessly monitor the performance of the executive from within, if it is to fulfil efficiently the function ascribed to it by Bayardo Arce as an 'instrument for promoting the historic project of the working classes'. This means two things: having Sandinista militants present as capable administrators at every level of government, and transforming as many administrators as possible into Sandinista militants.

In the mass organisations, meanwhile, the battle for class consciousness and independent action is slowly being won. The growing convergence between mass organisation initiatives and state policy means that the over-reliance on leadership intervention is being reduced. The critical phase here was roughly from November 1979 to February of the following year. As the National Directorate shut itself away for discussions on Plan 80, the trade union movement momentarily faltered. Ultra-left groups like the MAP-FO and the Partido Comunista began to make headway. When the leadership came back into circulation at the end of the year, its members promptly undertook extensive tours of the country. In the rash of industrial conflicts in the first two months of 1980, Borge intervened to resolve a Managua construction workers' strike, Ruiz to head off Frente Obrero activity in the San Antonio sugar refinery, and Nunez to ratify the factory takeover at the El Caracol food-processing plant. The first steps were taken towards the unification of the trade union movement. These incidents are now less frequent and interventions by leaders less necessary as each plant builds its own cadres capable of identifying the class interests of the workers and defending them against the aggression of the bourgeoisie and the ultra-left.

Cultural Insurrection: The Literacy Crusade[17]

'It is only possible for literacy to have real meaning in a country which is going through a revolutionary process.' (Paulo Freire)

Cuba took two years to launch its campaign against illiteracy. The Nicaraguans began their National Literacy Crusade, described by Bayardo Arce as 'a strategic task to consolidate our Revolution', barely eight months after the Sandinista victory. Of all the early exercises in political education, the Crusade was without doubt the most important. For two weeks before the 23 August rally, 'war communiques' from sixteen *departamentos* had declared one village after another 'territories free from illiteracy', until the Crusade's planners were able to announce the final results: 406,056 newly literate Nicaraguans, slashing the country's illiteracy rate from 50% to a mere 13%.

Especially in the more remote rural areas of the north and east, the *brigadistas* had carried out their task in the face of formidable obstacles, not only insects, malaria, dysentery and the monotonous rice and beans diet of the peasant population, but sniper attacks from the remnants of the National Guard, who carried out the threat they had broadcast from their clandestine radio station Volveremos (We will return) in Honduras. Counter-revolutionary attacks left seven *brigadistas* dead. Another forty-nine died from road accidents, drowning and disease. Remarkably, only 4% of the 85,000 teachers dropped out during the five-month campaign, most of them in the first few weeks. The Frente was well aware that in addition to the physical hazards involved, the *brigadistas* had been working with the sector of the population most vulnerable to ideological attack, peasants who in many cases were reluctant to cooperate with the agrarian reform and the ATC because they feared Somoza would return to take reprisals against those who had supported the Revolution. In his speech of welcome to the returning People's Literacy Army (EPA), Humberto Ortega noted:

> It is the duty of you young Sandinista guerrillas to prevent our peasants who live out there where no news reaches them, from being

confused by the reactionary bourgeoisie and the counter-revolution . . . You are the main thread which binds us to those peasants. It is the responsibility of each one of you to ensure that every *campesino* remains a Sandinista . . . because it is out there that the counter-revolution moves, the mummies, the clapped-out Conservatives and oligarchs, with their talk of farcical elections.

The first to be taught, however were the soldiers of the EPS, 30% of whom – or some 2,500 – were illiterate. In the new armed forces, literacy had the specific political function spelled out by Carlos Carrion, the FSLN delegate to the Literacy Crusade: 'In the people's army we want every comrade to be able to read and write, so that he or she can understand all our country's problems, and understand that the army is not a separate distinct institution isolated from the struggles of the masses.'[18] Seven weeks later, on 24 March, the rest of the country began to learn. The language and style of the crusade was military – 'war communiques', 'literacy guerrillas' and 'battle fronts'. Beginning so soon after the insurrection, this was no accident. Many of the teenage members of the EPA had themselves fought, and their power of mobilisation and discipline drew heavily on still fresh memories of the armed struggle. The EPA was organised into six battle fronts identical to those of the FSLN during the war, with each sub-divided into brigades, columns and squadrons. The basic unit, the squadron, was composed of thirty teachers of the same age and sex, drawn wherever possible from the same school or college. The main force of the EPA was supported by 3,000 part-time Workers' Literacy Militias (MOA) and 30,000 more Urban Literacy Militias (GUA) who taught people in city homes and markets. Like the regular military forces of the EPS, they shared a single purpose: to create and defend popular power.

The logistics of moving 60,000 teenage teachers around a mountainous country with only a rudimentary communications system were complex, and the task – like that of protecting the *brigadistas* in the field, sustaining their morale and integrating middle-class urban students into a wholly unfamiliar peasant environment – fell largely to the mass organisations. With 60% of the *brigadistas* female, the women's movement AMNLAE took on a major role, giving the teachers support in the field through the Comites de Madres (Mothers' Committees). The Juventud Sandinista and the teachers' association, ANDEN, bore the brunt of mobilising *brigadistas* at the outset, and the CST took charge of organising the Workers' Literacy Militias. The ATC looked after food, accommodation and transport in isolated communities linked only by river or horse-trail, and in the northern *departamentos* of Madriz, Nueva Segovia and Jinotega they set up local ENABAS stores where there were problems of food distribution. The ubiquitous CDSs drew up a national plan of logistical support for the Crusade and provided the basic forum for dialogue with local communities. As for communications and security, military metaphor became a military reality, with responsibility shared between the EPS and local units of the newly created Sandinista

People's Militias. At the level of national planning, each of the popular organisations occupied a seat on the National Literacy Commission. Taken together, these practical proofs of the capacity of the mass movement were one of the central triumphs of the Crusade.

Another was the political education of the *brigadistas* themselves. Although their initial motivation was never in doubt, the Literacy Crusade has won an entire generation of Nicaraguan youth over to a clear under-standing of the Revolution, and – as the FSLN would have wished it – not through propaganda but through practical experience. This response from Ivan, a 17-year old *brigadista* from Masaya, was characteristic:

> It's not a question of making a decision . . . I didn't 'decide' to take part in the Crusade. It's more like an obligation. I mean, how can you believe in the Revolution and not join the literacy brigades? Last year in the insurrection I took up a gun; this year it's an exercise book, but I don't see any real difference. It's all part of the war to liberate the country. I want to go into the countryside too, and learn what it means to be a peasant in Nicaragua, to get rid of this stupid idea that here's the town and there's the country, and they're two different things. We're all in this Revolution together.[19]

When they evaluate their experience in retrospect, the *brigadistas* dwell most on their relationship with the *campesinos* and the initial problems of acceptance. These are constant themes of the field-diary which each teacher kept and a frequent topic of discussion in the regular Saturday evaluation meetings which the literacy squadrons held throughout the five months of the Crusade. The urban-rural mistrust fostered by *Somocismo* produced initial reserve in many peasant areas, at times bordering on open class antagonism. This was overcome by the astute way in which the FSLN threw the Literacy Crusade into the debate over production. Opportunistic right-wing propaganda against the Crusade, often from those who were actively sabotaging the production effort, took the line of 'Surely the government's priority should be to devote resources to production. What is the point of teaching peasants to read and write if we can't give them enough to eat?'[20] The Frente's response was to draw the human resources for the campaign from economically unproductive sectors (school and university students), while the EPA and MOA programmed their classes for evenings and weekends to avoid clashing with working hours. *Brigadistas* threw themselves for the rest of the day into the productive activities of the peasantry – planting and harvesting, care of livestock, milking, local handicrafts – and provided the country with a temporary labour force which did not interfere with job creation programmes for the unemployed. The *brigadistas'* efforts – often more enthusiastic than competent at using the long-bladed *machete* or baking corn *tortillas* – helped break down the resistance of peasant families, and by August close personal bonds had developed between teachers and learners. The potential of the Crusade itself to relieve unemployment was

313

also grasped. Of the equipment used in the programme, only hurricane lamps could not be produced locally.

> In Esteli for example we produce the rucksacks which the *brigadistas* use to carry their teaching materials. Small things which we can turn out cheaply and at low cost to avoid unnecessary imports. Through the work of AMNLAE and the Social Welfare Ministry, we have managed to set up a Production Collective which has given work to 90 unemployed local women. So far we've produced 15,000 rucksacks, as well as uniforms for the *brigadistas* and the ordinary clothes which we sell here at controlled prices through the People's Clothing Store.[21]

Right-wing attacks on the Crusade were clearly directed at the political content of the teaching materials, and motivated by a fear that five months of political education would bring the peasantry solidly behind the Revolution and render them impervious to bourgeois counter-propaganda. Alfonso Robelo himself, at that time still a Junta member, led the assault, which gained credibility because it came from within the government. In a speech to MDN members at Chinandega on 11 March, he attacked the Crusade: 'We should not be talking of literacy which can be manipulated to domesticate the minds of the marginal population: that would be criminal.'[22] After his resignation, the tone of the attacks became more hysterical. The Crusade was now accused of being an instrument of Communist indoctrination. Robelo, meanwhile, had sent his own teenage children to study in the USA.

These attacks found fertile ground among many bourgeois families, who were reluctant to grant parental permission for their children to participate. As a result, only one-third of the *brigadistas* came from middle-class homes. Parents who did comply, although initially nervous about the overtly politicising aims of the campaign, overcame their qualms through first-hand experience of the Crusade in action and their own first contact with the realities of peasant life. Again, the planners' astute reading of the situation vindicated the FSLN's belief that the Revolution had to move at a pace sensitive to the people's political limitations, and could still win over sizeable sectors of the middle class. Unrestricted parental access to the *brigadistas* was allowed. Some made regular weekend visits to the more accessible areas; others undertook ten-day treks into the mountains by jeep, mule and canoe, and returned home transformed by what they had witnessed.

The educational materials which so alarmed the bourgeoisie were the twenty-three chapters of the literacy primer *El Amanecer del Pueblo* (Dawn of the People). The teaching methodology embodied many of the theories of the Brazilian educator, Paulo Freire, who had spent a week in discussions with the Crusade's planners. It was based on a creative discovery of words and oral dialogue through the use of photographs illustrating the principal themes of Nicaraguan history and rooted in the experience of the learners. Freire's 'generative' words were contained in key sentences which carried the political message of the Revolution: '*Sandino, Guide of the Revolution*' (Chapter 1); '*The Popular Masses Made the Insurrection*' (Chapter 5); '*The Sandinista Defence Committees Defend the Revolution*' (Chapter 6); '*The Revolutionary Workers' Organisations Promote Production and Watch over the Revolutionary Process*' (Chapter 8); '*Agrarian Reform Will Restore to the People the Production of the Land for the People*' (Chapter 10); '*Our Democracy is the Power of the Organised People*' (Chapter 21) and so on. The photograph accompanying Chapter 10 is typical. It shows men, women and children harvesting maize. One man wears a cap with the name INRA; another a baseball cap with a picture of Sandino. In practice, this photograph stimulated thought and discussion on agricultural products, the role of INRA, the division of agricultural labour between the sexes, child labour, Sandino, the role of the peasantry. The training of the *brigadistas* concentrated on their ability to sustain and enrich this dialogue by understanding thoroughly the political concepts involved and enabling the peasant learners to discuss openly their own experience, ideas and opinions accumulated during the years of the dictatorship.

The deployment of the *brigadistas* to remote areas and the resources of the mass organisations also allowed the government to achieve results over and above those of the Crusade itself. The most important of these political byproducts were the *brigadistas'* involvement in the campaign to eradicate malaria, health education and preventive medicine programmes, the search for mineral deposits, archaeological remains; collection of samples of flora and fauna; compilation of Nicaraguan popular culture — songs, poems and folk legends; recovery of the oral history of the war of liberation by means of 2,000 taped interviews with eye-witnesses; and censuses designed to assemble. information on patterns of employment, agricultural resources, and local trade and distribution.

After five months of intensive teaching, difficulties of course remained. The illiterate ethnic groups on the Atlantic Coast were not integrated into the first phase of the Crusade. Their turn came on 31 September, and the teaching materials used with the Miskito, Sumo, Rama and black English-speaking communities took special regional factors into account. They were the only departure from the Crusade's intention to produce a single, identical primer for use with all social groups, a decision fundamental to the unifying political strategy of the campaign. The delay in bringing literacy to the Atlantic Coast reflected political sensitivity, not neglect. The Atlantic Coast teaching materials, produced with the help of Caribbean literacy experts, were for minorities whose cultural traditions, need for economic integration and often uneasy relationship to the FSLN dictated a more gradual approach.

A long term question, and absolutely fundamental, was: how could the government sustain the impetus created over five months of unprecedented progress, and avoid the dangers of dependency on *brigadistas* whose role could only be temporary? The answer came in the creation of autonomous peasant organisations. The original classes of five or six, or Sandinista Literacy Units, became Popular Education Collectives (CEPs) coordinated

by the *campesinos* themselves. Initially, the CEPs maintained the reading level
of the newly literate and helped slow learners to complete the primer, during
a 'sustaining' phase which preceded the October creation of a Vice-Ministry
for Adult Education. The permanent programme of adult education has
taken up where the Crusade left off. In the words of one of its planners:
'The method is popular participation, dialogue, education for awareness. It is
reference to history as it is lived . . . overcoming the contradictions between
the people's and the official language. It is equipping people for permanent
and universal self-education. It is to weld the education and the organisation
of the masses into one endeavour.'[23]

To the bourgeois Right, this was all profoundly threatening. As the
Crusade ended, the FSLN's National Directorate and the Crusade's coordinator, the Jesuit priest Fernando Cardenal, were inundated with letters
of gratitude and commitment from those who had participated as learners.
But one letter from a newly literate peasant went addressed to the
'Distinguished Gentlemen of the Democratic Conservative Party, the MDN,
the Social Christian Party and the Social Democrat Party' (the latter a small,
violently anti-Sandinista right-wing party formed after the Revolution and
subsequently disowned by the Socialist International). The letter's message,
in rhyme, was simple:

Ahora ya se leer,
Ahora no me vuelven a joder.

(Now I can read/Now you won't push me around any more.)

The Dialogue between Marxists and Christians

Cardenal's presence as director of the Literacy Crusade, and the massive
support given to it by both Catholics and Evangelicals, is only one facet of
militant Church involvement in the Sandinista Revolution. His brother,
Ernesto, is Minister of Culture and the Maryknoll priest, Miguel D'Escoto,
Foreign Minister. Throughout the mass organisations, especially in the CDS
and the ATC, Christian activists hold key positions. In the rural areas as
in many urban slums, the Church can be the most important force for
legitimising the Revolution. On the remote Atlantic Coast, the dominant
Moravian Church is fundamental in mediating between the Frente and a sus-
picious local population. When the FSLN took power, one of the first public
celebrations of victory was a mass officiated at by the Archbishop of
Managua, Monsenor Obando y Bravo. The relationship between the Church
and the FSLN takes its place along with the alliance with the private sector
and the extraordinary range of international friendships as a further unique
feature of the Nicaraguan Revolution, and is a priority in the consolidation of
national unity.

The convergence of Marxism and Christianity is explained by particular features of Nicaraguan history in the last decade, breaking radically with a tradition in which the Nicaraguan Catholic Church was as loyal an ally of the ruling class as any in Latin America. In the 1930s, the Bishop of Granada was infamous for publicly blessing the arms of United States Marines setting off to fight Sandino. The change began with the Second Vatican Council, and particularly with the Latin American Bishops' Conference at Medellin, Colombia, in 1968. After Medellin, parish priests, pastoral communities and even the Catholic hierarchy broke from their long-standing complicity with Somocismo. Nicaragua presented a textbook case of what the new Theology of Liberation was all about: 'a situation of injustice which may be described as one of institutionalised violence . . . revolutionary insurrection may be legitimate in the case of evident and prolonged tyranny which dangerously threatens the common good of a country.' The upsurge of post-Medellin thought in Nicaragua coincided with the appointment of a new Archbishop in 1971 and the Managua earthquake and political chaos of the following year.[24] As early as 1970, the first Catholic organisations emerged in which spiritual and class concerns overlapped. In that year, one of the leaders of the Juventud Obrera Catolica (Catholic Workers' Youth), Father Francisco Mejia, was imprisoned and tortured, and the bishops demanded the excommunication of those responsible.

The most famous affirmation of this new theology was Ernesto Cardenal's contemplative community on the archipelago of Solentiname, founded in the mid-1960s. At first 30 couples settled there, with the group eventually growing to between 800 and 1,000. 'Some left early on, believing that Ernesto was teaching Marxism because he was challenging traditional interpretations of the Scriptures and portraying Christ as a proletarian fighting against injustice.'[25] That community, as we have seen, produced the FSLN combatants for the 1977 assault on San Carlos, which Cardenal himself described:

> Why did they do it? For one reason only; their love for the Kingdom of God . . . When the moment came, they fought with great bravery. But they also fought in a Christian way. That dawn in San Carlos, they tried repeatedly to reason with the Guard by loudhailer, so that they could avoid shooting. But the Guard replied with machinegun fire, and very reluctantly they too had to shoot. Alejandro Guevara, one of my community, entered the barracks when there was nobody left but dead and wounded soldiers. He was going to set fire to the barracks, so that there would be no doubt of the success of the attack, but refrained from doing so out of consideration for the wounded Guardsmen.[26]

As Solentiname moved closer to the FSLN, the Catholic hierarchy became more openly anti-Somocista, while never committing itself to the Sandinista alternative. Opening the academic year at the National University, Monsenor Obando y Bravo said: 'A situation of violence is crushing the masses. I make a clear distinction between basic or institutional violence rooted in socio-economic structures, and the violence of the oppressed which it engenders.'[27] None of the bishops had attended the April inauguration of the ruling trium-virate, but instead had issued a pastoral letter condemning the government and declaring Church support for 'a completely new order'. In response, government repression against the Church was stepped up, and Obando y Bravo complained that Somoza was interfering with Archdiocese mail and telephones and condoning break-ins to his offices. After the earthquake, tension between Somoza and the bishops increased, reaching its height during the 1974-77 state of siege, when the National Guard took over chapels in the north as temporary barracks. The bishops also complained that in the eastern and northern area where National Guard counter-insurgency operations were concentrated, 'in some villages the military commanders are demanding a special permit for every Catholic religious meeting.'[28] The denunciation was a recognition by the hierarchy of the role in the rural zones, where the Church was traditionally weak, of the new radical grassroots church, the Christian Base Communities (CEB). As the political conflict grew, the Church offered the only sanctuary there was for those fleeing the regime's persecution. Those involved in the CEB were offering an interpretation of the Scriptures encouraging the right of the poor to create independent grassroots organisations to defend their interests, thereby placing the Church inevitably at the heart of the class struggle.

In the late 1960s Christian groups made their first contacts with the FSLN in organising the first Rural Workers' Committees, and Capuchins began to organise agricultural cooperatives, which the Frente increasingly saw as a continuation of the tradition of Sandino in the 1930s. In 1967 these Christian groups were instrumental in bringing together 300 delegates to the first Congress of Peasants in Matagalpa, and by the end of the decade 300 Ligas Campesinas (Peasant Leagues) and Sindicatos Campesinos (Peasant Unions) were functioning.

By 1975, a formal and militant break had been made between these radical Catholic groups and the bourgeois opposition. During the state of siege, the Organizaciones Cristianas de Nicaragua complained that *La Prensa* and the traditional opposition media were in the hands of 'bourgeois sectors opposed to the Somoza dictatorship, but not committed to the true liberation of the Nicaraguan people.'[29] For influential church groups to make such a distinction was remarkable. Their position also necessarily created tensions with the hierarchy, which never abandoned its links with the bourgeois parties.

After the head-on confrontation with Somoza over the 1972 appointment of the triumvirate, Archbishop Obando y Bravo and Bishop Salazar of Leon expressed their support for the Christian Democrat line, and in August 1974 a strongly worded pastoral letter criticising the forthcoming elections and declaring that 'nobody can be forced to vote in the interests of a particular group' came in the middle of arrests of bourgeois political leaders including Pedro Joaquin Chamorro who had urged an election boycott. The attachment to a bourgeois solution persisted right up until Obando y Bravo's flight to Caracas with FAO leaders in July 1979 to seek a renegotiated Junta. In late 1977, the Archbishop accepted his role as mediator of the national crisis at the instigation of the COSEP-INDE lobby, and in the bishops' response to the crisis the following January the hierarchy, despite its apparent legitimisation of armed struggle, made it clear whose project they favoured: 'Once more we say to our people that we are by your side ... we are in agreement with those who are trying to solve the country's problems using civilised means.'[30] By July, their position had hardened, and although the substance of the bishops' demands were still those of the FAO, there was certainly sufficient common ground with the FSLN's Minimum Programme for the Catholic hierarchy to be considered part of the Frente's platform of broad national unity. The main demands were these:

* A new socio-political order which would enable the majority of the people to live in human conditions as regards food, health, education, housing, employment, land, wages and human rights.
* Genuine rights to form political organisations (outside of the traditional parties), organise trade unions and elect government authorities.
* Genuine structural reforms in taxation, land ownership and business, which would redistribute the wealth of the nation more equitably, closing the immense gulf which separated the minority who were rich from the great mass of the poor.
* A far-reaching campaign to clean up public administration.
* A reorganisation of the armed forces on the basis of serving national – not party or personal – interests.
* The resignation of President Somoza.[31]

These demands from the hierarchy placed the necessary seal on the convergent relationship that had been growing up between the FSLN and the 'base Church' over the previous decade. The CEBs' activity both in rural and urban communities, and actions such as Church occupations in protest against human rights violations, had led the FSLN to look for ways of bringing Marxists and Christians together, and the hierarchy's mediation in the 1974 Chema Castillo raid and the 1978 National Palace attack had – despite the ambiguity of Archbishop Obando y Bravo's position – given the Church a considerable degree of credibility. The FSLN and the 'base Church' had arrived at a fusion of action, a discovery of common areas of political concern through practice and not through theory, because the sections of the Church most directly linked to the working class were challenging the elitism of traditional Catholic theology and presenting arguments about the Scriptures, like Cardenal, in a way directly relevant to the everyday political realities of the people, a democratic and non-doctrinal reading of the Christian faith.[32] In the zones which were to become the centres of the popular insurrection, the CEB were making active preparations for the war, and the dividing line between a CEB and a Comite de Defensa Civil often became hard to draw. Some of the most combative of Managua's *barrios orientales,* such as Nicarao and 14 de Septiembre, became virtual no-go areas for the *Guardia* as the result of the joint efforts of the Frente and the Church. In Esteli too, community organisation was a reality a full three years before the 1978 insurrection. The Colombian priest, Father Julio Lopez allowed his parish house in the Barrio El Calvario to be used as the Frente's command-post in September:

> The Frente first approached me for organisational and political help in 1975, and I gave it willingly. This *barrio* was the most militant and best organised in the whole of Esteli, and our *comites de base* formed the nucleus of what would become the CDCs and then CDSs. We divided Esteli up into 56 zonal committees in preparation for the insurrection, and work was in hand as early as March. Outside the town, we tried to instil revolutionary consciousness in the peasants by taking loudspeaker vans round the valleys playing Carlos Mejia Godoy's 'Misa Campesina'. The local women would bring the communiques of the Frente into Esteli hidden in pots of food, and we priests would then distribute them. Many of the kids here who joined the Frente did so out of their Christian convictions, and the Church continues to play a fundamental role in the CDS today.[33]

Christians constantly strove to find biblical parallels for the armed struggle: 'During the NationalGuard assault on the Barrio Riguero in Managua, there was an old man who used to read to the guerrillas each time there was a lull in the fighting from the Book of the Maccabees, to keep their spirits up with stories of the victorious guerrilla war of Judas Maccabee and his brothers against the Hellenic imperialist aggressors who persecuted the people of Israel.'[34] Many Christians themselves joined the armed struggle, the best known of them being the Spanish missionary of the Sacred Heart Gaspar Garcia Laviana, who became a *comandante* on the Frente Sur. After working with the Frente for three years, he announced his decision to take up arms in December 1977 in an open letter which quoted the papal encyclical 'Populorum Progressio'. He had worked for years in a peasant community. 'I tried to salvage the situation in a Christian way, in the pacifist sense, trying to lift the people through their own resources or those of the government. But I realised that all this was a lie, a big deception. I began to get discouraged to see that so much work brought no result . . . because people went on living the same.' The figure of 'Comandante Martin', his *nom de guerre*, has been a vital example for the FSLN in giving practical proof of the convergence of revolutionary *Sandinismo* and Christian values. 'Martin' was killed in combat a year after joining the armed struggle.

Since the Revolution, the FSLN has continued to insist on the compatibility of revolutionary and Christian thinking. The Right has attempted to turn the Church into a propaganda weapon, and the divergence between the popular Church and the hierarchy has become a critical debate. The tone of the bishops' first pastoral letter after the victory,[35] fearful of losing support, was timid and restrained despite expressing 'confidence in the high ideals which have inspired our movement of liberation'. The document also demanded the immediate restoration of press freedom (in other words the reappearance of *La Prensa*), a move in fact made by the new Junta within days after a brief spell in which the FSLN's *Barricada* was the only newspaper in circulation. The people were angered by the bishops' reticence, as they were by the complete silence of Pope John Paul II on a war which had cost 50,000 lives; in contrast, the right-wing press in Central America enthusiastically seized on the pastoral letter. A Salvadorean daily promptly headlined 'Church Opposes Nicaraguan Government.' The Frente's own view was put in a document to its first Assembly of Cadres: 'With the Catholic and Evangelical churches we must develop closer relations at the diplomatic level, following a generally cautious policy which seeks to neutralise wherever possible the influence of conservative pastors and to have closer ties with priests sympathetic to the Revolution, at the same time as stimulating the religious sectors of the Church.'

Although the bishops are not interested in wielding political power as such, the tone of their major pastoral letter in November was interesting. They could see their own position counterposed to the appeal of a popular church, and could not afford to lose their influence over the faithful. In its main paragraphs, the document made these comments:

> As far as the freedom of party political organisation is concerned, it seems essential to us that the Nicaraguan masses should have a conscious and active participation in the revolutionary process: this should be brought about through the existing organisms of direct popular democracy and those which will be created as a result of national dialogue. Different forces have contributed generously to the historic process and no-one should place obstacles in the way of their contribution. At the head of these forces, it is clear that the FSLN has won itself a place in history.[36]

An extensive paragraph on socialism followed; it concluded that, 'if socialism means the exercise of power from the perspective of the masses, and increasingly shared with the organised people so that there is a genuine transfer of power towards the popular classes, it will find nothing in the Christian faith but motivation and support.'[37] In fact, their wishes for the Nicaraguan Revolution were couched in language which, while perfectly compatible with the FSLN's own vision, began over subsequent months to sound closer to that used by Alfonso Robelo: 'We are confident that the revolutionary process will be something original, creative, profoundly national and in no way imitative. Because, with the majority of the Nicaraguan people, what we aspire to is a process which moves firmly towards a fully and authentically Nicaraguan society, neither capitalist, nor dependent, nor totalitarian'.[38]

The hierarchy's dilemma is that it cannot afford to lose its own support to the dominant influence of *Sandinismo,* yet it fears the loss of its autonomy, all the while knowing that any overt criticism of the Revolution, whose moral authority is undisputed, would lead to an erosion of its own position. The Church is alarmed by the continued presence of priests in government, and by the way in which the lay Delegates of the Word – who played a vital role in the conscientisation of peasant communities – have moved into the mass organisations. In the religious festival of Santo Domingo in August 1980, the government's vigorous support for the ceremony and the way in which the Frente's leadership took to the streets to join in the festivities, far from reassuring the bishops, led them to fear a secular takeover off religious activity.

As the Right attempts to exploit these divisions, with the Association of Christian Businessmen unilaterally proposing the evangelical organisation CEPAD for membership of the Council of State, an important current of progressive religious thought has crystallised into the so-called Theology of National Reconstruction. This centres on the Jesuit priest Alvaro Arguello, director of the Historical Institute at the Central American University; he also holds a seat on the Council of State as the representative of the Association of Nicaraguan Clergy (ANCLEN). This tendency promoted a seminar soon after the Revolution entitled Christian Faith and Sandinista Revolution, attended by members of the Junta and the National Directorate. It defines the relationship between the Church and the FSLN in the light of statements such as Fidel Castro's 'there are no contradictions between the tenets of religion and the tenets of socialism'[39] and the assertion of the Mexican Bishop of Cuernavaca, Monsenor Sergio Mendez Arceo, that: 'Marxism is a search for the welfare of all. Capitalism is anti-Christian.' Arguello's Instituto Historico has launched a series of educational pamphlets, the *Folletos Gaspar Garcia Laviana,* designed to reassure Christians about Marxism and resist the growing anti-Communism of bourgeois propaganda which has sought to drive a wedge between the Frente and the Church.

By May, the row within the Church over the political role of priests became public. Following a directive from Rome, the Nicaraguan bishops demanded that: 'Now that the exceptional circumstances have ended, Christian laymen can carry out with equal efficiency public tasks at present the responsibility of some priests.' Nine of the priests concerned replied promptly to the bishops' criticisms. They included the Cardenal brothers, Miguel D'Escoto and Edgard Parrales, deputy director of the Social Security Institute. In reasserting that 'our loyalty to the Church and our loyalty to the poor cannot be in contradiction', they warned that the unity of the country must be mirrored by the unity of the Church, and that the only people who could get any advantage from the bishops' statement were reactionary propagandists.[40]

Three months later, Bishop Salazar of Leon dismissed a popular Salvadorean priest from the northern parish of El Viejo and refused to enter into any discussion about his reinstatement. The reaction of the people was an immediate and overwhelming repudiation of the Bishop's action, an occupation of the church at El Viejo and then of Leon Cathedral.[41] These frictions are bound to continue, and the Nicaraguan Church now faces a historic test, one which the Catholic Church in Cuba failed. The Cuban example, of the Church turning against the Revolution and thereby forfeiting its influence, is clear to the Nicaraguan bishops. They recognise that they could be marginalised if they adopted the same position as the Cubans, but at the same time they do not wish to identify with the Revolution to such an extent that the Church loses its own independent identity. As the bishops agonise over this dilemma, the evidence is clear that the mass of the Church's rank and file has already made its decision.

Organising Women: AMNLAE

'As we organised the first CDCs for the insurrection in the barrios orientales *of Managua, so many husbands were terrified when they saw the degree of involvement of their wives. Terrified by women taking the initiative, fighting, organising. In so many households, the men were less committed to the Revolution than the women. And the woman, with her double oppression – oppressed by* Somocismo, *oppressed by* machismo – *had to make the choice between her husband and the Revolution. It was extraordinary how many of them, thousands, opted for the Revolution.'* (Fatima Caldera, AMNLAE Activist)[42]

If the participation of the Church was unprecedented in Latin America, the massive incorporation of women into the armed struggle and the inroads which the Revolution has made into traditional sexual attitudes are no less remarkable. In Nicaragua, *machismo* reached grotesque proportions even by Latin American standards. In the Somoza era, a television advertisement for a well-known brand of rum typified prevalent male values. It showed two birds clawing each other bloodily to death in a cock-fight, as a sonorous voice-over announced 'Cock-fights and rum . . . for men who are *really* men'. The women who joined the struggle against Somoza, and in doing so questioned their own status in Nicaraguan society, were not merely heroic individuals. They had set themselves the task of building a mass women's movement loyal to the FSLN, capable of voicing the demands of Nicaraguan women after the overthrow of Somoza.

In this they were heirs to a rich tradition of women's participation in *Sandinismo*, although their organisation was a recent phenomenon. From the early 1960s, the FSLN had pointed – as had Sandino himself – to the notable role played by women in Zeledon's resistance of 1912, and the presence of fighters like Blanca Arauz, Conchita Alday and Maria de Altamirano in the anti-imperialist war of the 1930s. By 1969, the Frente's revolutionary programme embodied a series of points on the liberation of women, and in the final insurrection a number of women – Dora Maria Tellez, Monica Baltodano, Leticia Herrera – became guerrilla *comandantes*.

'There were columns in which the entire command was composed of women, women who commanded hundreds of men without any problem.'[43] With the example of the three women combatants in the 1977 attack on San Carlos, and the major role played by Dora Maria Tellez in the National Palace seizure, thousands of women joined the FSLN in the final stages of the war. The photographs of dead combatants which filled the early editions of *Barricada* proved the point eloquently: a full 30% of the Frente's fighting strength at the end were women. In addition, during the insurrection, thousands of working-class women provided support for the combatants with food, shelter and medical services, making bombs and storing ammunition. In themselves, these rearguard tasks would have made little impact on many male combatants' stereotyped view of the female role. Their importance was in conjunction with the role which women played at every military and political level. Men learned through visible practice, not through theory, that women were capable of equality in every aspect of the struggle.

Nicaraguan women's history of political organisation at the national level is only three years old, and from the beginning it has counted on notable strength among working-class women. AMPRONAC, the Association of Women Confronting the National Problem, was born in September 1977. It began to function when the state of siege was lifted, part of the intense revival of political mobilisation. It functioned legally and openly, with a relatively innocuous title, and many prominent middle-class women were active in its leadership. Within months, as the Chamorro assassination polarised political opposition to the dictatorship and the bourgeois opposition lost direction, AMPRONAC faced a critical moment of definition. The movement retained a broad platform designed to attract women of different political persuasions. AMPRONAC defined its aims being: (1) to encourage the participation of women in the resolution of the country's problems; (2) to defend the rights of Nicaraguan women in all sectors and all aspects — economic, political and social; and (3) to defend human rights in general.

But 'the advances of the popular struggle against the dictatorship brought about significant changes in our organisation. We were transforming ourselves from a small organisation of 80 women into a popular organisation with an ever greater will to fight.' This new phase opened with the celebration of International Women's Day in March 1978, when the AMNLAE leadership confronted not only its relationship to the growing mass struggle but also the debate about specific feminist issues. As a statement by one of their leading militants revealed, the two considerations became inseparable at this point, the balance between them being dictated by the rhythm of the Revolution: 'The contents of Women's Week would not satisfy the big international feminist movements because it gave greater emphasis to the general struggle of our people for a free country. But it did relate to the real needs of Nicaraguan women.'[44]

AMPRONAC's activities at this time — hunger strikes, church occupations, protests at human rights abuses — may appear to have been essentially defensive. Yet the key point was not that these activities reflected the early dominance of bourgeois women, but that they came to represent the part which the women's movement, with its current strength and social composition, could most effectively undertake within the overall strategy of the FSLN. Actions like the occupation of the UN building in Managua had enormous international repercussions against the dictatorship. The growing stature of the movement became more apparent towards the middle of 1978, as AMPRONAC worked more directly with the FSLN and the newly formed ATC and more women joined the armed struggle. AMPRONAC did not suffer a major split between women sympathetic to the FAO and those loyal to the FSLN. Instead, its newly recruited militants were overwhelmingly Frente members or sympathisers. AMPRONAC worked closely with the MPU in *barrio* organisation, and its identity as an overtly Sandinista organisation was sealed with its July 1978 national conference at which 150 women from nine cities committed themselves firmly to the Frente. The democratic regional election procedures for the conference indicated that AMPRONAC was now effectively functioning as a mass organisation, paving the way for its role after victory.

AMPRONAC became AMNLAE. It now has a seat on the Council of State, contains 25,000 members, and has a local structure of neighbourhood committees each headed by a coordinator, a propaganda secretary and a political development secretary. Debate in these democratically functioning local committees touches on every theme from literacy and social welfare programmes, through the role of women in the military and the trade unions, to questions of sexual politics, childcare, contraception and abortion. Outside the formal structure of AMNLAE, women are active in the other mass organisations, especially the CDSs where they outnumber men in many urban committees.

AMNLAE has, despite all this, faced formidable obstacles in consolidating its drive against *machismo* and sustaining the victories which women won for themselves in combat. It has based its struggle on pointing to the objective conditions of Nicaraguan women: their economic oppression as the worst paid of industrial workers, their domestic enslavement, the contrasting situation of urban women (many of whom are single parents) and rural women (who are in a more stable male-dominated family environment where traditional roles are harder to break down).

The vehicle for educating women is the AMNLAE newspaper, *La Voz de la Mujer* (Women's Voice), which supplanted a *Barricada* women's page, edited by a collective of two journalists, five women from AMNLAE, and four from the other mass organisations. Like all the publications of the mass organisations, *La Voz de la Mujer* has aimed to stimulate debate and polemic, in this case around the central demand for women's incorporation into production and national reconstruction. AMNLAE's concrete achievements have been numerous: setting up women's production collectives and Child Development Centres (CDIs) whose purposes are to collectivise childcare, release women from domestic oppression and allow their full participation in

economic activity; a complete ban on sexist advertising and on the
commercial exploitation of women; and advances in paternity and divorce
legislation. Women, as teachers, learners and organisers, played a dominant
role in the Literacy Crusade, a direct response to the marginalisation and
higher illiteracy of peasant women. Women have directed major social welfare
programmes such as the rehabilitation of prostitutes and the *Quincho
Barrilete* programme for street waifs. And they have assisted in forming an
independent organisation of six-to fourteen-year-old children, the Asociacion
de Ninos Sandinistas (ANS), which has built on the militant participation of
young children in the insurrection. In a conversation in Managua in early
1980, three members of the ANS – all aged eleven – described the organisation, aims and political significance of the Association of Sandinista Children:

> *Elias:* 'To get kids affiliated to the ANS, we organise them by grade. A
> committee is formed in each school and those committees take charge
> of all the students. The slip which they fill in with their personal
> details is kept on file, and then we indicate the work they should do.
> We already have about 5,000 affiliates in schools.'

> *Moises:* 'We hope that children will have enough schools, playgrounds,
> a different kind of Christmas. We want children and their mothers to
> have hospitals, we want there to be no more kids forced to sell chewing-
> gum in the streets.'

> *Jose:* 'The ANS has to be a serious organisation, because this is where
> we're going to build the revolutionary cadres of the future.'

In the family – which AMNLAE still affirms as the basic unit of society –
this kind of militant maturity among children, coupled with the new consciousness of their mothers, has dramatically altered the internal dynamic
of family relationships.

Yet there is much talk within AMNLAE of the dangers of a *reflujo* – a
loss of impetus – in women's attitudes. The risk was present in all the mass
organisations, but more so in AMNLAE. *Machismo*, though on the defensive,
was still an ever-present enemy of women's integration into the revolutionary
process, and women have had to assert their new militancy in many
unfamiliar spheres, such as the industrial unions. A prominent woman
militant of the FSLN replied to the point when it was put to her by an
American feminist interviewer:

> You ask me if there has been a loss of impetus. Perhaps in certain
> sectors, yes. Among the petty bourgeoisie it's possible that there are
> some women who say 'OK, I've done my bit. Now let's rest for a while.'
> But not among the women of the people. Among proletarian women,
> among peasant women, those who suffered the repression most
> directly, you don't find that. The woman who went through the

insurrectional struggle can no longer be apathetic. She can no longer be a woman isolated from her social context. Perhaps she might fall back a little at first, but I am sure that sooner or later she will become involved again.[45]

By the end of the insurrection, *machismo* had genuinely been forced back to the defensive. The extent to which it has temporarily regained ground lies in a number of factors; the tendency of many men to see female militancy as a product of the military phase of the struggle only; the reassertion of a powerful myth of motherhood, which subverts recognition of women's equal capabilities in favour of a traditional approval of the female role as provider; the breathing space given to men by AMNLAE's own need to take stock of its future strategy; and the primacy it has given in the present stage of the struggle to achieving women's rights through the consolidation of the Revolution.[46] These are battles which AMNLAE has faced, above all, in the industrial working class, where male attitudes have been slowest to change, and in the armed forces. The organisation has been concerned, despite the assertion of equal pay for equal work, by the passivity of women and the lack of a specific women's struggle in the trade unions.[47] In the CST, male workers have been unwilling to address the issue as men, and have only responded in limited ways where AMNLAE pressure has forced them to do so.

But the most visible change in Nicaragua in the Revolution's first year is a conscious demilitarisation of women, the result of a military regulation minimising the exposure of women to potential combat situations. The hundreds of armed female combatants on the streets of Managua are a thing of the past, and the move to reassign women to secretarial, guard and political education duties was resented by many women who had given proof of their equal military ability on the battlefields.[48] Many women have left the EPS. When the first officer ranks were created in February 1980, the lists contained only fifteen women out of a total of 230. Three held the rank of *comandante*. Yet although there are frequent complaints from female soldiers of the residual *machismo* of rank and file troops, this is not the whole story. Paradoxically, the exodus of women from the military is an indication of their political capacity and commitment to the Revolution. While many male combatants came to the armed struggle with minimal political consciousness, the class composition and political experience of women was quite different. If they have now left the armed forces, it is because they are better placed than men to fill positions as intermediate and leadership cadres in the government and the mass organisations, using for the benefit of the Revolution the technical skills which traditional patterns of training have given them. Thus the Social Welfare and Education Ministries are strong in female ex-combatants, many of whom combine their state duties with an active role in AMNLAE.

In assessing its relationship to international feminist currents, AMNLAE has been presented with a wide range of Western and Latin American models, and has opted for a course which has more in common with the Bolivian Housewives' Committee than with the European and North American radical feminism. AMNLAE's most notable visitor, in November 1979, was the Bolivian miner's wife Domitila. In contrast, AMNLAE leaders have often been irritated by Western feminists' attempts to transplant the struggle of women in advanced capitalist countries to the Nicaraguan situation. In the view of Gloria Carrion, executive secretary of AMNLAE: 'When Western feminists come here to interview us, very often the first question is: "What are you doing about abortion, or sexual politics?" Of course, these are important questions for women; but we have to go one step at a time, and our priorities are determined by our social, political and historical circumstances.'[49] For the moment, AMNLAE's struggle for the full equality of women, the full integration of women into society, cannot be separated from the overall struggle of the mass organisations to consolidate the Revolution. This assertion in no sense conflicts with AMNLAE's recognition that there is a specific women's struggle. A January 1980 document of the organisation contains the important statement: 'We believe that the basis of the problem of women lies in the enslaving subjection of women to domestic labour. Domestic labour must be recognised as the material obstacle which limits the full integration of women into society.' Comments like this provide a context for women's participation in the effort to reconstruct Nicaragua, and suggests that ever deepening demands will emerge from the Nicaraguan women's movement according to the dynamic of AMNLAE's own development as a mass organisation and the speed with which Nicaragua's Revolution can be consolidated.

Notes

1. Interview with Literacy Crusade Official, Managua, July 1980.
2. Final Ministry of Education figures, September 1980.
3. Daniel Ortega's speech to the Sixth Conference of the Non-Aligned Movement is translated in full in Pedro Camejo and Fred Murphy (eds)., *The Nicaraguan Revolution* (New York, Pathfinder Press, 1979).
4. This particular allegation, contained in an AP cable, presumably refers to the airstrip at Montelimar on the Pacific coast.
5. *Latin America Weekly Report*, WR-79-08, 21 December 1979.
6. *Barricada*, 2 March 1980.
7. *Barricada*, 29 February 1980.
8. See 'Nicaragua in the Caribbean Context', in *Latin America Regional Report*, RC-80-07, 22 August 1980.
9. For further analysis of the background to this section, see editions of *Latin America Weekly Report*, especially 'European Socialists Look to Latin America', WR-80-15, 18 April 1980; 'Central America a Key Feature of the President's Latest Grand Tour' WR-80-28; 18 July 1980; and 'A Bridge Too Far from Bonn to Washington', WR-80-34,

29 August 1980.

10. *Guaro* is cheap alcohol; *nacatamales* are a Nicaraguan delicacy of ground maize and meat.

11. Interview with FSLN militant in Ministry of Planning, Managua, July 1980.

12. Interview in Managua, February 1980.

13. Interview in Managua, August 1980.

14. *Propaganda de la Produccion* (collection of articles from the weekly *Poder Sandinista*), (Managua, SENAPEP, 1980), pp. 27-8.

15. *Barricada*, 12 December 1980.

16. *Poder Sandinista*, No. 21 , 13 March 1980.

17. Parts of this chapter appeared originally in George Black and John Bevan, *The Loss of Fear − Education in Nicaragua Before and After the Revolution*, (London, Nicaragua Solidarity Campaign and World University Service, 1980).

18. *Ibid.*, p. 61.

19. Interview with literacy *brigadista*, village near Masaya, March 1980.

20. Interview with businessman, Managua, February 1980.

21. Interview with women in Esteli, March 1980 (AMNLAE).

22. *La Prensa*, 12 March 1980.

23. Quoted by Alicia Sanchez in 'Literacy Crusade − An End and a Beginning', *Nicaragua Today* (bulletin of the Nicaragua Solidarity Campaign), No. 2, October 1980.

24. 'The Churches in the Nicaraguan Revolution', Paper by Michael Dodson and Tommie Sue Montgomery, presented to the Latin American Studies Association National Meeting, Bloomington, Indiana 16-19 October 1979, pp. 2, 7.

25. Interview with Dona Olivia de Guevara, a long time resident of Solentiname, Managua, February 1980.

26. Ernesto Cardenal, 'Lo Que Fue Solentiname, in IEPALA, *El Pueblo Frente a la Dinastia*, p. 92.

27. *Nicaragua − Combate de un Pueblo, Presencia de los Cristianos* (Lima, Centro de Estudios y Publicaciones, 1978), p. 54.

28. *Ibid.*, p. 58.

29. *Manifiesto a las Fuerzas Cristianas Solidarizadas con la Lucha Revolucionaria del Pueblo Nicaraguense*, June 1975.

30. *Mensa je del Espicopado ante la Gran Crisis de la Nacion*, Managuan, 28 January 1978.

31. *Mensaje del Episcopado ante la Gran Crisis de la Nacion*, Managua,

32. Dodson and Montgomery, *loc. cit.*, especially pp. 8-9, 12-16.

33. Interview with Padre Julio Lopez, Esteli, March 1980.

34. Quoted by Jose Arguello in *Nicaragua en Lucha*, No. 3. Barcelona, COSOCAN, February 1980.

35. *Carta Pastoral del Episcopado Nicaraguense − Compromiso Cristiano para una Nueva Nicaragua*, Managua, 17 November 1979.

36. *Ibid.*, pp. 7-8.

37. *Ibid.*, p. 9.

38. *Ibid.*, p. 10.

39. Fidel Castro, Statement to Jamaican priests, 1977, quoted in *Folletos Populares Gaspar Garcia Laviana*, (Managua, Instituto Historico

Centroamericano, 1980), No. 1., p. 23.
40. *Latin America Weekly Report*, WR-80-21, 30 May 1980.
41. *El Nuevo Diario*, 31 July 1980.
42. Interview with Fatima Caldera, Oficina de la Mujer del Ministerio de Bienestar Social, Managua, February 1980.
43. Humberto Ortega, interview with Marta Harnecker.
44. Megan Martin and Susie Willett (Eds.),*Women in Nicaragua* (London , Nicaragua Solidarity Campaign, 1980), p. 36.
45. Nora Astorga, interviewed by Margaret Randall in *Nicarauac*, No. 2., July-August 1980, pp. 42-3.
46. Interview with Luzmylia Blandon, member of the teachers' union ANDEN, Managua, July 1980.
47. This issue has received extended coverage in the AMNLAE newspaper, *La Voz de la Mujer*. See for example interview with Rosa Maria, thirty-nine-year-old factory worker in *Voz de la Mujer*, No. 1, May 1980.
48. Interview with three female EPS soldiers, Rivas, February 1980.
49. Martin and Willett, *op. cit.*, pp. 35-36.

15. The Threat of Counter-Revolution

How the Counter-Revolution Works

Right-wing terrorism against the Sandinista Government began on 19 July, 1979, the very day of victory. Since then, far from letting up, attacks by groups of former National Guardsmen have escalated, their rhythm closely matching each fresh conflict between the FSLN and the right-wing private sector. With the collapse of the Guard, 7,000 of Somoza's troops were taken prisoner. But another 5,000 escaped to El Salvador, Honduras, Guatemala and the USA. On the weekend following the Sandinista victory, a car-load of heavily armed Guardsmen machine-gunned the Camino Real Hotel near Managua Airport, which was the temporary headquarters of members of the Government of National Reconstruction; they wounded several FSLN guards stationed at the entrance. At night, Somocistas who had taken refuge in Red Cross centres and the Salvadorean and Guatemalan embassies slipped out under cover of darkness to fire on FSLN patrols and road-blocks. These first attacks, for all the shouts of 'Somoza will return!', were desperate and leaderless acts of revenge. They formed part of no political strategy. But almost immediately, Anastasio Somoza Portocarrero began to shuttle between Miami and Guatemala City, reassembling the remnants of the Guard into an effective fighting force, and the 2,000 housed in temporary refugee camps across the Honduran border began to overcome their demoralisation and launch systematic strikes into Nicaraguan territory.

In this initial climate of Somocista violence, the dangerous temptation was for many Nicaraguans to see the term 'counter-revolution' only as a description of *armed* attempts to re-install the dictatorship, failing to take precautions against the more insidious attacks on the Revolution. Since then, understanding of the process has matured, in two distinct phases. As political education took root, the rush of enthusiasm to correct the original narrow definition swung popular feeling briefly to the opposite extreme: 'counter-revolutionary' became a blanket insult for Somocistas, criminals, incompetent workers, and even traffic offenders! The word threatened to lose all meaning. When a Venezuelan internationalist working for INRA died in a drowning accident, the local CDS accused his fellow-workers of 'counter-revolutionary negligence' in allowing him to become exhausted through overwork. Happily, the consolidation of the mass movement and the rising incidence of economic and ideological assaults on the Revolution led to a more solid grasp of what counter-revolution meant. People began to ask the most pertinent questions: was it any longer adequate to portray National Guard terrorists as isolated psychopaths, or did they form the military spearhead of a defined right-wing strategy? Did the terrorism of the extreme Right abroad relate directly, or coincidentally, to economic destabilisation by the domestic opposition? What points were there in common between ultra-left groups and the Right, and was there conscious collaboration between them? What role was the CIA playing in fomenting discontent? And how did the Right set about creating an artificial climate of crisis? What were the ideological weapons at its disposal?

Direct economic attack on the country by the USA was difficult in the case of Nicaragua, because of the traditionally low level of direct US investment and the limited space for manoeuvre by American financial agencies. The threat was also counterbalanced by the substantial levels of aid flowing in from Nicaragua's Social Democratic allies and the disarming effect of the government's willingness to renegotiate its external debt. For the US to withhold its direct aid (a not very significant $75 million, in any case) proved both an ineffective and internationally unpopular weapon, not least because of the open split in Washington between those in the Carter Administration who saw aid as a way of defending private sector interests in the country and those who argued for a total freeze on bilateral assistance. A much more promising line of attack for those in Washington who wanted to subvert the Sandinista Revolution was to support the efforts being made by the Nicaraguan Right to sabotage economic recovery by running down production levels, encouraging the flight of capital, smuggling, hoarding and speculating, and strikes in key economic sectors. For the latter, anti-FSLN groups on the Left could prove useful tactical vehicles.[1]

The Right faced complex problems in furthering this strategy. In their favour was the fact that the private sector still controlled a majority of industry and agriculture, but this was offset by a number of factors: the state's control of finance, foreign trade and a portion of internal distribution; the capacity of the popular organisations to respond effectively to sabotage; the serious divisions within the opposition bourgeoisie over its attitude to the economic reactivation programme; and — by the Right's own admission — its lack of a popular base. Its response, in crude terms, was as follows: to build its own power base in areas where the FSLN had yet to consolidate its support — the Atlantic Coast, the most marginal peasant groups and small traders (traditional Somoza strongholds), and any remaining middle-class 'floaters'; to try and weaken mass support for the Frente; to assess the chances of strategic unity between the 'civic' opposition and sectors of the armed extreme Right; and to overcome the historical disunity of the Nicaraguan bourgeoisie. The final point was perhaps the most serious dilemma for the opposition, since any attempt to unify the Right would almost certainly derive from the opportunism of one or other group within the bourgeois leadership, whose own sectional economic aspirations were not necessarily those of the private sector as a whole. At the time of writing, there is still no unified right-wing opposition to the FSLN, but the signs are that it may be imminent, and since his resignation from the Junta in April 1980, Alfonso Robelo has been clearly bidding for its leadership. Within the private enterprice organisation, COSEP, Robelo's MDN has certainly established its political ascendancy.

Logically then, the main thrust of the counter-revolutionary Right has been in the ideological sphere, choosing accusations which would simultaneously hit the most vulnerable areas of the Revolution and gain the likeliest consensus support in Washington. These campaigns[2] have concentrated first on undermining the moral authority of the Sandinistas and casting doubt on any anti-capitalist measures taken by the government. To attack the vanguard role of the FSLN, the criticisms levelled suggest that the Frente is an exclusively military organisation, incapable of running a country at peace. There are personalised attacks on Sandinista leaders, rumours of splits between 'radicalising' and 'restraining' influences in the National Directorate, accusations of economic incompetence (especially in the Area of Public Ownership), constant criticisms of the armed forces, rumour campaigns about food shortages, Cuban advisers, local abuses of power. Second, there are tactics destined to show the bourgeoisie's dedication to 'pluralism' as opposed to an FSLN hell-bent on 'totalitarianism'. Democracy is equated exclusively with 'free elections', socialism in other countries is denigrated, the Literacy Crusade is attacked as an instrument of indoctrination, the Frente's objective of labour unity is depicted as an assault on trade union freedoms, the CDSs (and, in particular, their security functions) are labelled the equivalent of the *orejas* of the Somoza era, and attempts are made to define the FSLN as 'anti-religious' and weaken the Revolution's base of support among the progressive clergy and a still deeply religious population.[3] (This campaign had an interesting counterpoint in ultra-left accusations that the FSLN had 'betrayed Marxism' by building such a close relationship with the Church.)

As a last resort, the Right has had recourse to acts of open provocation, hoping thereby to push the FSLN into repressive actions which can be depicted as attacks on the right to free association, press freedoms, political pluralism, human rights — matters which Washington now considers important in Nicaragua for the first time. The right-wing parties and press have been the loudest champions of the extreme left Frente Obrero and the Nicaraguan Communist Party in their confrontations with the FSLN. Since the Revolution, the Permanent Human Rights Commission has become a virtual instrument of the right-wing Social Christian Party, acting as an apologist for National Guard prisoners. Through the privately owned local media, with eager assistance from Western press agencies, the Right has launched an aggressive anti-Communist campaign attacking other revolutionary movements in the region — most notably in El Salvador — and playing its full part in the process of 'softening-up' public opinion to accept possible US military intervention in Central America.

One year on, the possible emergence of a unified right-wing opposition was the biggest internal threat to the FSLN. But, paradoxically, the Sandinistas' first ideological skirmishes were not with the Right but with the far Left. It is worth looking in some detail at who the *ultristas* are and what tactics they employed to attack the Revolution from the Left.

More Revolutionary than the Revolution? The Ultra-Left

'There are groups dedicated to confusing the masses. Since they believe that what we have is a bourgeois revolution, they tell workers that they must fight to install socialism here. As their basis for this, they will tell the peasant, for example, that his house needs repair, that he is starving, that he has no money, that he is unemployed. And there is no doubt that all this sounds very sympathetic and attractive to someone who is hungry, someone who needs to be properly clothed, someone whose family needs a breadwinner. But these elements do not dare address themselves to the most advanced sectors of our people. They aim their propaganda at the most backward sectors, because they know that there they have some chance of confusing people.' (Commandante Carlos Nunez, speaking about the ultra-Left).

Nunez's comments accurately describe the tactics of several groups who have tried to exploit the gap between the legitimate wishes of the Nicaraguan masses and the immediate capacity of the state to transform social relations. Their aim is to outflank the FSLN and strengthen their own power base. On the far Left of Nicaraguan politics, two groups are insignificant – the tiny Trotskyist Liga Marxista Revolucionaria and the Movimiento Obrero Revolucionario (MORE), the latter despite its proven links with the Communist Party. The FSLN's three major confrontations with the Left have been with the CAUS/Communist Party, discussed in Chapter 13, a prolonged running battle punctuated by uneasy truces; with the internationalist Brigada Simon Bolivar, and with the Movimiento de Accion Popular-Frente Obrero (MAP-FO).

Of the many Latin American international brigades which fought alongside the FSLN, the Brigada Simon Bolivar was always a maverick. Organised in Colombia by the Partido Socialista de los Trabajadores (PST), it embraced combatants from Chile, Uruguay, Venezuela, Mexico, the USA and other Latin American countries, subscribing to varied ideologies. The combatants entered Nicaragua during the last days of the war on the Frente Sur. Other sympathisers actually attached themselves to the Brigade after 19 July. More than anything, the freedom with which they operated indicated the FSLN's early problems of imposing centralised military authority on irregular fighting units and the Brigada Simon Bolivar took advantage of the post-war chaos to dress in FSLN uniforms and carry red and black flags in order to convince people that they spoke with FSLN authority. The PST leadership encouraged a simplistic move to socialism, exhorting workers to strike and peasants to seize private land. As the Frente became aware of the threat of a newly arrived foreign group posing as an alternative revolutionary leadership, it called leaders of the Brigade in for meetings where it stressed the need for internationalist units to be integrated swiftly into the single Sandinista military command. The response was aggressive. When the FSLN arranged a meeting with all Brigade members on 14 August, it found itself confronted with a demonstration of 1,000 workers who had been brought there – supposedly by an FSLN contingent – in the belief that they were to lobby the Sandinista leadership on wages and trade union questions. The demonstration was the last straw, and the Frente expelled sixty non-Nicaraguan members of the Brigade to Panama.[4]

Six weeks later there was more trouble from the Left. On 3 October, State Security arrested five members of the Nicaraguan Socialist Party, accusing them of having collaborated with Somocistas. Although there was no suggestions that the PSN itself was involved in activities against the government (indeed it has been the FSLN's most active supporter), the incident raised the possibility of direct collaboration between the extreme Right and the Left, with the common aim of undermining FSLN authority. Suggestions of this came to a head with the most serious ultra-Left attack on the FSLN – the activities of the Frente Obrero. December and January are the months of traditional unemployment in Nicaragua, and, as the FSLN had predicted, it was a period used by the Frente Obrero to accelerate a political and military campaign against the new government. Like the Brigada Simon Bolivar, but in sharp contrast to the Communists who at least recognised the initial vanguard role of the FSLN, the Frente Obrero denounced the FSLN from the outset as having sold out the Revolution to the bourgeoisie. But the FO was not a new organisation: it had a very particular history. It was formed by FSLN dissidents in 1970 and expelled by the Frente in 1972 after revelations of a plot to assassinate the entire FSLN leadership. It was never able to carry out its threats, largely because it did not succeed in recruiting enough cadres. Right from the early 1970s there were allegations that its members had close ties to Somoza's Office of National Security (OSN). Although its ideology was not consistent, the FO's basic orientation was towards Peking, and it held this line until the Chinese invasion of Vietnam, when it switched its allegiance to Enver Hoxha's Albania. Towards the end of the decade, it managed to build a limited base in the working class, and had its own student movement, the Comites de Lucha Estudiantil Universitaria (University Students Fighting Committees: CLEUS). During the FSLN split it attempted to masquerade as a fourth Sandinista tendency, the so-called FSLN Autentico.

With this dubious ancestry, the Frente Obrero found fertile ground among the dispossessed peasantry and some urban slum-dwellers. Its name alone (Workers' Front) tricked many uneducated workers into believing that the FO was acting legitimately in the interests of the working class. And if its name was likely to deceive naive workers and peasants, the acronym of the FO's armed wing, the MILPAS, was even more cleverly chosen. To any

Central American peasant, the *milpa* is a cornfield, the plot of land cultivated by subsistence farmers. In the peasant value system, the *milpa* has an almost religious significance. The Frente Obrero encouraged land invasions and the spontaneous takeover of privately owned urban land by the unemployed, criticising the government for the measured pace of the agrarian reform and accusing the FSLN of being the hostage of a bourgeois reformist government. Its strategy, in other words, was little different from that of the Brigada Simon Bolivar – an immediate uncontrolled passage of socialism which would, of course, have destroyed the Nicaraguan Revolution. In September, the MAP-FO made its narrow sectional ambitions clear. Instead of supporting the FSLN initiative to delay the Council of State and ensure its worker-peasant majority, the MAP-FO joined the Right's campaign for the immediate installation of the Council in its original form which included the Frente Obrero. Better a quasi-parliamentary organ reinforcing bourgeois strength with FO representation than a class-based Council from which the FO was absent.

Trade union activity by the FO and attacks by its newspaper, *El Pueblo*, were stepped up with the publication of Plan 80. *El Pueblo* demanded the 'active sabotage of the economic plan in order to bring power back into the hands of the people'. This was no idle threat. The FO encouraged the walk-out by SCAAS building workers in January, denouncing the Parque Luis Alfonso Velasquez job creation scheme as an attack on working-class interests, and of course trying to swell its own ranks by recruiting disaffected SCAAS members. But it concentrated its main energies on the sugar refineries. 'Generally they operate where we (the FSLN) are weak, where our cadres and militants have not been able to go to explain the country's economic situation.'[5] The FO had formed a 'Comite Agrosindical' on Somoza's old sugar estate of Montelimar, where Somoza's paternalism towards his own employees worked to the Frente Obrero's advantage. The FSLN faced tremendous problems there. Somoza had kept on 3,000 under-employed workers on the estate, an anomaly which the ATC and INRA tried to rectify by rationalising the labour force, giving the maximum amount of full-time employment and launching a local job creation programme to generate work for those left unemployed. The FO moved in rapidly, and with some success, to exploit discontent.

Its attacks at the Ingenio Monterrosa and the huge Ingenio San Antonio, both in the *departamento* of Chinandega, were even more damaging. There is an urban and rural proletariat of 25,000 in Chinandega, which is an important focus for the economic reactivation programme. The *departamento* contains not only the two sugar mills, but the country's main port (Corinto), banana plantations, cotton gins, important cooking-oil and food-processing plants and chemical factories for crop-spraying. The paralysis of economic activity in Chinandega was a serious affair. By 31 January, both San Antonio and Monterrosa were in the third day of an FO-led strike. The sugar crop is particularly vulnerable to work stoppages: stacked cane rots quickly and the molasses contained solidifies if not promptly processed. The ATC calculated that daily losses at San Antonio alone were upwards of half a million cordobas.

At Monterrosa, FO leader Alejandro Gutierrez told workers that it would be necessary to fight another civil war — this time against the FSLN — to attain genuine worker and peasant power. The FO deceived workers at Monterrosa into believing that a number of local cane-cutters had been arrested, and announced its plan to take several truckloads of workers to Managua to protest against their detention. Instead, they drove the Monterrosa workers to San Antonio to persuade labourers there to boycott a mass assembly being addressed by Comandante Henry Ruiz, the new Minister of Planning. FO activists stormed the platform to prevent Ruiz from speaking. Although they temporarily disrupted the meeting, the attack was ultimately a failure. When the FO left, the mass meeting carried on and 4,000 San Antonio workers elected a new union leadership as planned. From San Antonio, the FO and the Monterrosa workers went on to Managua. On arrival, the workers discovered that, far from protesting against the detention of fellow-labourers from Monterrosa (who were in fact at liberty in San Antonio), they were expected by the FO to demonstrate against the closure, five days earlier, of the FO newspaper *El Pueblo*. Having spent the night in Managua, the Monterrosa workers returned home the next day angry and exhausted, and met FSLN and CST leaders who explained the consequences of their strike. It was not an easy task, since the FO had genuine support at Monterrosa, but eventually a majority decided to call off the strike in exchange for promises of immediate social wage improvements. As well as assuring prompt attention to local health and housing problems, the Frente promised that an ENABAS basic grain store would be installed in the refinery. The FO did not give up, and at San Antonio they played their final card — the deployment of their armed MILPAS. When San Antonio workers called off their stoppage, cane cutters returning to the fields were met by FO supporters who slashed the tyres of their trucks and threatened workers with guns and *machetes*.[6]

The FSLN undoubtedly made mistakes in its handling of the sugar refinery disputes. In a key economic area, it had failed to anticipate the degree of support for FO demands, and the response which finally settled the strike was the result of an emergency decision rather than careful forward planning. In Monterrosa especially, the Frente Obrero succeeded in convincing the work force that the FSLN's anti-FO stance was also an *anti-worker* one. To add fuel to this argument, units of the EPS had briefly detained the Monterrosa workers in Chinandega as they made their way to Managua, 'pointing their guns at them threatingly' according to a *Barricada* article criticizing the incident, an almost unique case of confrontation between the Sandinista military and rank and file workers. For the rest, the Sandinista counter-offensive was directed at the FO leadership. The FSLN media took up the fight. They reported Tomas Borge's accusation that the FO was following 'mechanical ideological formulae' which failed to understand Nicaraguan history. One cartoon in *Barricada* portrayed an FO activist floating on a

cloud above a group of workers, with his head buried in a book, and the
caption 'Having seized political power, proceed to . . .' It summed the FO up
nicely.[7] And FSLN Party Organisation Secretary, Carlos Carrion, made it
clear that the FSLN had no quarrel with the working-class demands ostensibly being put by the FO, only with their timing and motivation: 'This minis-
cule organisation is quite ignorant of the situation of the country and the real
problems we face. They make a series of proposals which are totally pie in the
sky. These proposals are very nice, very interesting, but quite unrelisable.'[8]

Just as the sugar strikes had less to do with economic demands than with
FO retaliation for the 23 January closure of their newspaper *El Pueblo*,
the Frente's counter-attacks concentrated less on the strikes than on the
reasons for closing the paper which had provided their ideological basis.
The paper had circulated freely during the final weeks of the war in Managua,
but the January closure was not the first time the FSLN had halted its
production. In late July 1979, *El Pueblo* had been closed during the short
spell of post-war censorship which also silenced *La Prensa*, and its director
Melvin Wallace had been briefly detained. For the next six months, *El
Pueblo*'s attacks on the Revolution (or in its own phrase 'the Sandinista phase
of the Revolution') had intensified. It had declared support for a tiny new
organisation in Leon, the Movimiento Popular Revolucionario, whose
declared aim was to 'rescue the CDSs from Sandinismo'. It had denounced
the Literacy Crusade and employment creation programmes as reformist exercises in pacifying 'unstable social sectors', and criticised voluntary work weekends as exploitation means of enriching a bourgeois state. In its final edition,
it had lambasted Plan 80 for giving 'great opportunities to the bourgeoisie and
the businessmen and few benefits to the exploited masses'. It was intolerable provocation, and the EPS moved in to occupy the building and arrest
El Pueblo's editors. Although the move was welcomed by most of the
FSLN's supporters, the Frente went to considerable lengths to explain the
need for repressive action against a paper with a circulation of only 2,000
copies, and the vulnerability of the young state to what it called 'ideological
diversionism'. Although Comandante Walter Ferreti of State Security
displayed two large caches of MILPAS arms, which Frente Obrero leader
Isidro Tellez admitted were connected to his organisation, the charges
initially brought against the eight-ultra-leftists arrested did not relate to illegal
possession of arms. Instead, they invoked the law for the Maintenance of
Order and Public Safety, which prohibited 'the written publication of proclamations or manifestoes designed to harm popular interests'. During the trial
of the eight, Judge Victor Manuel Ordonez referred to an article in *El
Pueblo*'s 21 January edition calling for 'the replacement of the government
with another truly capable of defending our self-determination in the face
of attack [from international reactionary forces]'.

Press freedom was one of the major democratic liberties won by the
Sandinista Revolution, and the Frente did not take the decision to close
down *El Pueblo* lightly. Nevertheless, the move was met with a barrage of
criticism — from Pedro Joaquin Chamorro Barrios of *La Prensa*, from the

CTN, and from right-wing broadcasters on Radio Mil and Radio Mundial. Their reaction in the name of pluralism reinforced one of the Frente's basic arguments: if left-wing opposition to the government had no realistic hope of providing convincing alternatives, whose interests were being objectively served by the antics of the ultra-Left? Recalling the early allegations of collaboration between the Frente Obrero and Somoza's OSN, FSLN leaders began to wonder aloud who had paid for the MAP-FO's expensive printing equipment, and why *El Pueblo* had escaped Somoza's Black Code which had shut down even the bourgeois *La Prensa* for a year. They pointed, too, to the extensive coverage given by *El Pueblo* to the activities of the Social Christian Party and the amount of advertising space which the PSC had purchased in return for the favour. If the FO was harming economic recovery and dividing the working class, it was playing straight into the hands of the Right.

El Pueblo's printing works were handed over to the Literacy Crusade as anti-FO demonstrators had demanded, but the episode was not over. The Frente Obrero had repeatedly assured the FSLN that its armed wing, the MILPAS, had been dissolved after the Revolution and all weapons handed over to the Sandinista military. But in the month after the closure of the newspaper, one arms cache after another was discovered, often with the initials MILPAS burned into the gun-stocks. A wave of hold-ups and attacks on Sandinista patrols followed, producing a climate of real tension in Managua. Reorganisation of the EPS was still incomplete. The Casa de Gobierno was still guarded by teenage soldiers in jeans and T-shirts, and civilian trust in the Sandinista armed forces was momentarily shaken. Any youth carrying a machinegun in the street might, in fact, be a member of the MILPAS or a soldier of the EPS.

But from April 1980 onwards, MILPAS attacks declined. The Frente Obrero had lost its temporary initiative, and there was a high desertion rate among its members. In June, Wheelock and Borge held private talks with the leaders of the rump that remained. They came away encouraged: 'At bottom, these people now have positive attitudes. We have found them receptive to our arguments, to the point of examining the possibility of incorporating them into the tasks of the Revolution, respecting their right to criticise but not to act subversively.'

The Robelo Resignation

After their disorientation in the early months, sections of private enterprise began to spoil for a fight. At government level, the first fissure came some nine months after the Revolution when Junta member, Alfonso Robelo, announced his resignation on 22 April 1980. The FSLN National Directorate held a press conference the next day to offer their comments. Comandantes Arce, Wheelock and Humberto Ortega noted that its ostensible reason, the enlargement of the Council of State, had been merely a pretext.

'In recent months,' declared their prepared statement, 'Engineer Robelo had been questioning a series of FSLN initiatives.'[9]

Robelo's development in nine months of power spoke eloquently of his opportunism and his inexperience as a politician. Within a week of the victory, he had been in Cuba as a member of the FSLN/Government of National Reconstruction delegation to the Moncada anniversary celebrations, returning home with ecstatic praise for the 'clarity of Comandante Castro's thought'. Robelo even began to sell off some of his business interests. Nonetheless, he remained the private sector's hope for leverage within the government, and was sharply reminded by his own MDN members – alarmed at this apparently spectatular conversion to *Sandinismo* – of where his loyalties lay.

In January, he served notice of his intention to pursue personal and private sector interests from within the Junta, when the MDN published its *Ideario Politico*. It was an extraordinary document: a mix of half-baked reformism, private sector propaganda and resonant nationalism appropriated from the writings of Sandino. It stressed the vital role played by the private sector in the 1978 strikes, credited the FSLN with 'more courage than fighting resources', claimed prominent MDN involvement in armed combat, and now proposed transforming the MDN from a movement into a fully fledged party. In the name of 'political pluralism', Robelo's own preface to the manifesto depicted the MDN as leading a march towards 'a process of socialisation in freedom, a political, economic and social system which is authentically revolutionary, genuinely Nicaraguan'.[10] Education and the military would be apolitical: 'Programmes of study . . . shall not be aligned to a specific political ideology',[11] and 'the police and army shall both be at the service of the homeland, and not of a particular ideology or party.'[12] To round off, the MDN manifesto left its readers with resonant phrases from Sandino, Pedro Joaquin Chamorro and Nicaragua's great national poet Ruben Dario. Robelo signed the preface with Sandino's own seal of *'Patria y Libertad'*. In itself, the language may seem innocuous enough, an empty populism which would cut little ice with the Nicaraguan masses. But Robelo sought to turn the very basis of *Sandinismo* – a specific national solution which did not imitate foreign models – against the FSLN, appropriating the language of Sandino without the class substance. Just as seriously, the key paragraphs on education, private enterprise and the military aligned Robelo clearly with the main lines of current right-wing propaganda, and it used his position within the government to do so.

Robelo took pains to confuse his two roles as MDN leader and Junta member, and in public appearances it became hard to tell in which capacity he was speaking. The rift began to open with the events of February and March (the ATC march, the factory occupations and the decree against decapitalisation of industry). By early March, Robelo must have been convinced that his future no longer lay with the Junta. At this point, *La Prensa* took up his case with a banner headline 'Applause for Robelo and Attacks for the Government'.[13] Robelo had attended a meeting of private traders on 9 March to hear complaints about ENABAS and government attempts to monopolise domestic commerce. As the private traders reserved their most bitter attacks for the CDSs, and announced their intention of 'declaring war' on the government, Robelo declared his full sympathy for their grievances.

He had just returned from a private visit to the USA, where he had lobbied for the speedy release of the Carter Administration's $75 million aid package to bolster the private sector, and had held talks with Deputy Secretary of State, Warren Christopher. Major MDN meetings in the following weeks received headline treatment in *La Prensa*. On 11 March, Robelo appeared in the MDN stronghold of Chinandega. 'Singular speech by Robelo' commented the headlines.[14] It was singular indeed from a serving member of the Junta. He demanded prompt 'free elections' and firmer guarantees for private business, and implicitly accused the FSLN of breaking the terms of the 1979 government programme. On 16 March, with three fellow Junta members out of the country, he repeated the same themes to an audience of 5,000 in Managua, for the most part well-heeled *capitalinos* who booed the appearance of red and black Sandinista flags in the crowd. The Junta's press office came out with a terse statement: 'Companero Robelo has full freedom to express his personal opinion as leader of the MDN. This demonstrates the political and ideological pluralism which exists in the country.' *Barricada,* seeing the way in which Robelo was sliding, was more forthright. In its 18 March editorial, the paper condemned him for attempts to 'conceal the true roots and class character of the MDN'. The CST, more bluntly still, accused Robelo of being 'a rat who took refuge in *Sandinismo* when the ship of the oligarchy was sinking'.

Why then, if the split was so deep, did Robelo not resign in mid-March? The answer can be traced back to the special position of the MDN within the private sector. The Movement had been formed in 1978 by a small but dynamic business sector in response to the failures of the traditional bourgeois parties and coalitions. Its leadership had from the start been highly personalist. Robelo had been an appropriate private sector figure for inclusion in a Sandinista Junta because the MDN's power base had been more stifled by *Somocismo* than any other organised capitalist group. The MDN was not tainted by a history of collaboration with the dictatorship. From the moment the new party was formed, Robelo had been set on unifying the bourgeois opposition under MDN leadership, and the sustained determination of the FSLN after the Revolution to attack capitalist prerogatives provided him with a new opportunity. An abrupt resignation in March would have hampered his efforts to build a solid political base and US support from a position of credibility within the Junta. Instead, he opted to wait for a single major conflict which might allow him to mobilise the whole disarrayed private sector behind his resignation. In the event, this meant hanging fire for a full month after his 16 March Managua rally, until the Council of State expansion came up for a Junta vote.[15]

The Junta split 2—2 on the decision to amend the Fundamental Statute and enlarge the Council. In the absence of Daniel Ortega, who was touring

Africa, the casting vote was made by proxy by another member of the Frente's National Directorate. At the 21 April press conference to announce the new decree, Sergio Ramirez explained that: 'There should be nothing surprising about this. We have followed the same procedure on other occasions, since Comandante Ortega is a representative of the National Directorate of the FSLN and may perfectly well be replaced by another of its members.'

In itself, the Council of State vote provided Robelo with a *pretext* for resignation. Equally important was the timing, and a series of events over the previous weeks helped convince him that resignation now would place him at the head of a powerful backlash against the FSLN. His US trip – though the results are not publicly known – may have been one consideration. So may Venezuelan remarks that preferential oil supplies were linked to 'the extent that Nicaragua advances in the process of democratisation'. On 18 April, a meeting of all four bourgeois parties and COSEP at the Social Christian Party headquarters indicated that the Council of State issue was important enough to draw a united response from the Right. Finally, and most cynically, Robelo saw considerable tactical advantage in linking his resignation with that of Violeta de Chamorro on 20 April, a decision communicated to the Junta in advance on the grounds of ill-health and exhaustion. Chamorro subsequently reiterated that her resignation had no political overtones.

In a brief letter of resignation, Robelo accused the FSLN of 'deviation from the goals of our Revolution'. In reply, the National Directorate described his action as 'an abandonment of the Revolution at a moment when he thought it would bring him greater political advantage'. The resignation rebounded badly on Robelo. The Frente moved quickly to nip the crisis in the bud, and the Right failed to coalesce in the way Robelo had hoped.

First, the MDN itself was far from being a united force. Although its national council issued a statement in line with Robelo's resignation letter, accusing the Council of State of being a 'totalitarian-style apparatus', warning signs within the party should have alerted Robelo to its shortcomings as a credible political force. After the 16 March rally, two of the MDN's leading members, Industry Minister Fernando Guzman and Vice-Minister of Internal Trade Pedro Antonio Blandon had left the party in protest, undermining any hopes Robelo may have entertained of a mass walkout from the government of high-ranking MDN officials. Nor did the party's rank and file all welcome the resignation: three prominent MDN local officials from Leon and Chinandega condemned Robelo for his failure to consult the party's bases.[16] The other right-wing groups also failed to act decisively. COSEP closeted itself away for discussions with the US Embassy, and the Democratic Conservatives for heated internal debates on party tactics. In the end, as we have seen, none of them boycotted the Council of State, although some delayed taking up their seats.

The FSLN reacted in three ways: by reasserting the principles of national unity, its unswerving commitment to the pre-eminence of working-class interests, and its refusal to respond to the artificial 'crisis' with concessions; by mobilising the mass organisations immediately and linking their protests to the broader class issues involved; and by smoothly replacing Robelo (and Chamorro) on the Junta with two more representatives of the middle class. For COSEP, the identity of the new Junta members mattered less than the manner of their appointment. For almost a month, the Junta continued with three members, while holding regular meetings with the private sector. At the end of April it lifted the state of emergency in force since the victory and reinstated *habeas corpus*, thus defusing one of the bourgeoisie's main constitutional arguments against the way in which the revolutionary state was being run. And on 18 May, the FSLN National Directorate – by simple direct nomination, which removed any lingering doubts about a conflict of authority in the government – named former Central Bank President, Arturo Cruz, and Conservative lawyer and UDEL leader, Rafael Cordova Rivas, to the two vacant places on the Junta. In their brief acceptance remarks, Cruz and Cordova Rivas further undermined the threat posed by Robelo. 'Political pluralism has been maintained,' said Cordova Rivas. 'It has never ceased to exist. A clear example of it is the Council of State, in which political parties of differing ideologies are represented.'[17] He denied categorically that Washington threats to break diplomatic relations had influenced the new appointments. Cruz, meanwhile, stressed the importance of his own 'excellent personal relationships with many COSEP leaders.'

The new Junta members had spelled out clearly that this moderate and progressive mainstream of the 'Generation of '44' – Pedro Joaquin Chamorro – UDEL tradition of anti-Somocismo stood firmly behind the FSLN still as the Revolution moved into a new phase. Their comments, and Cordova Rivas's own decisive shift away from the policies of the new Democratic Conservative Party, pre-empted any right-wing attempts to appropriate that tradition. Whatever the MDN's rhetoric about 'socialisation in liberty' or the Social Christians' professed desire for a 'Costa Rican' future, there was no room left now for ambiguity about the Right's commitment to national unity. After May 1980, the bourgeoisie had to stand up and be counted.

La Prensa: Mouthpiece for Reaction

A parallel split developed simultaneously in the media, appropriately enough over the future of the newspaper which Pedro Joaquin Chamorro had edited – *La Prensa*. *La Prensa* is owned by the Chamorro family, and its contradictory attitudes to the first nine months of the Revolution very much mirrored the political differences at the heart of the family: the conservative general manager Jaime, the progressive pro-FSLN editor Xavier, and the aggressively right-wing son Pedro Joaquin Chamorro Barrios, who best typifies the new political drift of *La Prensa* since April 1980. 'I've defended freedom of speech,' he told an interviewer in February 1980. 'They [the FSLN] say I defend the freedom of the bourgeois press. I think that's best – their freedom of speech is 100% controlled, a freedom directed at Marxifying the country and turning the people into sheep . . .'[18]

Although the great majority of the journalists, like Danilo Aguirre and Pablo Emilio Barreto, were politically sympathetic to Xavier Chamorro, *La Prensa* was from the beginning a natural outlet for the views of the bourgeoisie, and the paper published in full (usually as paid advertising space) each major statement by COSEP, the PCD and other right-wing parties. The foreign news pages, meanwhile, presented a view of the world heavily coloured by the Western news agencies. All this contrasted sharply with the strongly pro-government editorials, which gave support for the Literacy Crusade, praised the government's handling of the CAUS strikes and hailed the unity talks of progressive parties as a 'transcendental step forward'. From March onwards, a major shift of emphasis was apparent. Front-page coverage of MDN and other right-wing meetings was stepped up, and the foreign page gave enthusiastic reports of the 'reforms' of the Salvadorean military/Christian Democrat Junta. The news content in general ceased to represent the majority view of *La Prensa*'s journalists.

The inevitable split was precipitated by union action on 19 April. *La Prensa*'s work force presented demands for a *convenio colectivo* with management, including a call for formal union representation on the paper's editorial council. Xavier Chamorro supported the workers' demands, thereby bringing the family polemic into the open, and the remaining members of the board decided that the time was ripe to fire him. *La Prensa* printed its final edition on 20 April. At lunchtime that day, with the following morning's edition already set up, two board members arrived with a 'last minute news story'. It contained the news of Xavier Chamorro's 'resignation', categorically denied by the editor himself. The union (STLP) immediately called a strike to demand his reinstatement. The STLP communique, delivered by its president Trinidad Vasquez, noted that the strike had nothing to do with the union's demands the previous day. The only question at issue was the dismissal of Xavier, which the workers described as 'the final chapter in a series of pressures, threats and insults which members of the board have been hurling at him for several months'. They declared, too, that the editor represented, together with Pedro Joaquin Chamorro, 'the central pillar of our newspaper, in all its technical, intellectual and moral aspects'. Finally, they condemned the activities of newly appointed board members who were breaking the traditions of *La Prensa* as a progressive newspaper, 'people who never wrote a word against Somoza and now furiously attack the Revolution'.

Despite the intervention of Labour Minister, Virgilio Godoy, and three members of the FSLN National Directorate, at the request of Violeta de Chamorro, the management proved intransigent. COSEP threw itself into the fray, accusing the striking workers of 'seriously endangering the free and pluralist character of our Revolution'. The strike went on. On the 28th, Xavier Chamorro gave a press conference to announce that he had withdrawn his shares in *La Prensa* and would use them to start up a new paper. 95% of *La Prensa*'s work force would be joining him to found *El Nuevo Diario*, which would be run as a cooperative with full worker participation in editorial decisions.

It took *La Prensa* a month to assemble a new work force which would bring the paper back on to the streets. As for *El Nuevo Diario*, it has maintained a line of critical support for the Revolution, and has used its own editorials to attack *La Prensa* for betraying the traditions of Pedro Joaquin Chamorro: the claim that *La Prensa* embodied the tradition was denounced as 'an immense historical falsehood, a great lie, because the truth is that those of use who fought *Somocismo* as journalists, at the risk of our lives, are those who now produce *El Nuevo Diario*.'[19] *La Prensa*, meanwhile, is on a collision course with the FSLN. New press laws prohibit the publication of economic stories which are not supported by official government statistics, after a rash of rumours about shortages and production shortfalls. These are only the start of the conflict, however. Humberto Ortega repeated that press freedom was not to be confused with the right to print counter-revolutionary propaganda: 'We are sure that, if this newspaper continues to behave as it has done, lending itself to the most reactionary domestic and foreign interests, the Nicaraguan people will make it into a paper read only by those who line up with the counter-revolution. But if it seriously damages the revolutionary process, the Junta will take legal steps to control the license which masquerades as press freedom.'[20]

Ortega's optimism about *La Prensa*'s declining sales is perhaps ill-founded. The paper has a well-established and efficient distribution network and continues to outsell both *Barricada* and *El Nuevo Diario*. Few Nicaraguans buy more than one daily paper, *La Prensa*'s traditional values are deeply ingrained in readers' minds, and the hatred of Somoza's *Novedades* has left a strong subconscious resistance to official government newspapers. Furthermore, Nicaragua's papers are published at different times of the day: *La Prensa* in the early morning, *El Nuevo Diario* at lunchtime, *Barricada* in mid-afternoon. *La Prensa* is aware of these advantages, and has used them as the basis for an increasingly subtle ideological fight against the FSLN. Its techniques, and its role in a deepening class struggle, chillingly recall those of *El Mercurio* before the Chilean coup and the Jamaican *Daily Gleaner* in the months leading up to Michael Manley's election defeat. These techniques go much further than acting as a simple mouthpiece for right-wing views. They extend through lay-out juxtaposition of stories, use of pictures, sensationalising trivial incidents which will reinforce an ideological position, printing false information. Foreign news coverage is highly selective, its main aim to portray a 'free world' under threat from Marxism. Its letters pages are full of attacks on the Revolution, with no attempt at authentication. Rumours and distorted stories about the Sandinista mass organisations, and above all the armed forces, are the daily fare of *La Prensa*'s front page, with the clear object of undermining public confidence in the institutions created by the FSLN.[21] This campaign of provocation – what Galeano called 'the bacteriological warfare of the Right'[22] – has so far met with an angry but measured response from the FSLN, which realises perfectly well the dangers of being goaded into action which could be portrayed as an attack on press freedom. But as long as *La Prensa* continues, it acts as the frontline for the right-wing assault on the new society and as the best single focus for uniting the divided factions of the bourgeoisie.

Rallying The Right

The parties of the Right have now abandoned their crude early tactic of building political support by masquerading as Sandinistas, an approach which added little to their membership and brought a premature confrontation with the FSLN. In the months immediately following the war, the name 'Sandinista' was adopted haphazardly by salesmen, shopkeepers and entrepreneurs, sometimes naively and sometimes with clearly ulterior motives. The Social Democrat Party (PSD), in particular, incurred the wrath of the FSLN by its attempts to add the word 'Sandinista' to its title: 'These groups now say they defend the legacy of the General of Free Men, Augusto Cesar Sandino. When they ought to have taken this name they did not, because they knew a bullet would await them if they had resisted during the struggle. The FSLN did not shrink from the bullets of the Somoza regime.'[23] The Frente followed this up with a decree on 13 September 1979 prohibiting the use of the name 'Sandinista' by anyone but the FSLN itself, its members and related organisations. Briefly the bourgeoisie fought back, with COSEP claiming that the 'party-state confusion' could be avoided 'if the decree could be suspended . . . [and instead] making this adjective a generic term denoting nationality and applying to all those groups who fought against the dictatorship.'[24]

. A different approach is dictated today. The period since May 1980 has seen intense efforts by each of the bourgeois parties to establish a solid national party structure. Often moving into unpoliticised areas, each has seen its membership grow, and while none of the parties is large, both the MDN and PCD have shown signs of building a useful social base. Despite their growth, it is still the economic interest group – COSEP – which remains the dominant voice of the bourgeoisie, and the Frente has taken care to prolong this state of affairs by directing its dialogue with the private sector at COSEP, rather than at any of the right-wing parties. It was COSEP, for example, which was called on to form a commission with the FSLN to dicsuss the political situation in the wake of the Robelo resignation. COSEP speaks as a united institution on behalf of its six-member organisations, but there is no doubt that some divergence exists among these six groups over the strategy which ought to be adopted against the FSLN. The big landowners of UPANIC are very different in class character from the urban bosses of the Chamber of Construction or the young entrepreneurs of INDE. INDE and the Chamber of Commerce would be very reluctant to ally themselves with any armed anti-Sandinista project. Their battles have been 'civic' ones designed to undermine state institutions like ENABAS. The Chamber of Commerce has attacked ENABAS for food shortages and set up the parallel private distribution agency ACAPROBAMA. INDE has sponsored cooperatives parallel to those of the state, using outlets like the Cooperativa El Socorro in Diriamba to accumulate private sector profits and win over unorganised small traders. To a large extent, UPANIC represents the older traditions of rural power. Its members are in daily confrontation with the agrarian reform programme, and several have been charged and convicted of active collaboration with terrorist bands of former National Guardsmen. Cattle ranchers, in particular, have frequently been implicated. Interestingly, it was Jorge Salazar, president of UPANIC, who became COSEP's most vocal spokesman in recent months on the 'crisis of relations' between the private sector and the FSLN.[25]

Of the parties, the MDN remains the likeliest focus of private sector discontent, though it has failed to provide the effective leadership which Robelo aspires to. FSLN propaganda has tried with some success to associate Robelo with Somoza in picking up the fallen banner of crude anti-Communism, and the content of Robelo's speeches since his resignation has shown the accuracy of this. The first — and still most notorious — was a speech in Matiguas on 10 May. The choice of location could hardly have been accidental. Matiguas is a small town in the interior of Matagalpa, settled during the 1970s as part of Somoza's counter-insurgency campaign and a traditional centre of support for the dictatorship. Here, Robelo attacked the Literacy Crusade, then in its sixth week, as 'Communist' (the area around Matiguas is 70% illiterate). The Council of State, he repeated, was 'totalitarian', and the MDN was determined to remain 'openly opposed to the reign of terror which Communism implants in countries which it oppresses, submitting them to an intolerable police state.'[26] Does this mean that the MDN would happily use arms to get rid of what they now see as a regime moving rapidly towards 'Communist dictatorship'? Individual MDN members have been implicated in armed plots, but the party itself has issued strong condemnations of armed raids like that on Quilali in August, and Robelo himself continues to hold up countries like Costa Rica and Venezuela as his ideal. There are strong hints that the MDN and PCD power bases are beginning to overlap. Although Robelo disclaimed any intention of linking up with the Democratic Conservatives when he led his party out of the Patriotic Front of the Revolution, the MDN has managed to plan meetings in traditional Conservative strongholds such as the *departamento* of Granada.

The PCD, meanwhile, has built up a national structure around regional committees in Granada, Boaco, Carazo, Rivas, Masaya, Bluefields and Matagalpa. It boasts of its ability to attract 500 peasant supporters to its meetings in the remote rural zone of Nueva Guinea, and well-armed military training camps and anti-Communist propaganda schools are believed to exist in the same area, operated by former National Guardsmen and even some deserters from the FSLN's Frente Sur. Internally, the party is still at odds. Many PCD supporters, headed by Cruz and Cordova Rivas, remain inside the government, still an important area of understanding between the FSLN and the private sector. But on the other extreme of the party, the classic language of Somocismo is common. One Diriamba delegate to a PCD conference in Chinandega reacted like this when asked his attitude to the FSLN:

> Communism! Totalitarianism! That's what we have in Nicaragua now,
> my friend. This country is overrun with Communism: its full of
> Russians, Cubans, East Germans, the whole red horde . . . And nobody
> realises. This isn't what Nicaragua wants. It's part of the international
> Communist conspiracy and it's all being imposed from above.
> Nobody has any choice, there's no freedom any more. No-one knows
> what is going on except the *comandantes*. It's all being done in secret.
> But let me tell you one thing. We're going to smash this Communist
> vermin into the ground, by whatever means necessary, like the true
> *machos* we are.[27]

Any right-wing party is likely to have members like this, but the new aggressive tone is reaching the PCD leadership too. At the same regional conference in Chinandega on 3 August, PCD Coordinator Clemente Guido led the attack on the FSLN: 'We did not fight to exchange one military dictatorship for another . . . Nicaragua has not yet begun to see the door to democracy.'[28] It is hard to see how much longer the PCD can reconcile this kind of attitude with the presence of two of its members in the Junta.

The Social Christians have a roughly similar strength to the PCD. The PSC was part of the Latin American wave of Christian Democracy. Founded in 1957, it built up a certain strength among the middle class and the peasantry, but saw much of this eroded with the breakaway of its progressive wing to form the PPSC. The Social Christians' main hope of influence lies not only in building the party within Nicaragua but in exploiting its valuable international alliances with Christian Democracy. Venezuela and Costa Rica are useful friends, especially since both governments have shifted their support away from the Nicaraguan Junta to follow a line close to that of the US State Department, especially in giving unconditional support to the military/ Christian Democrat Junta in El Salvador. The relative strength which it enjoys in the trade unions through the CTN, and regionally through the CLAT, also gives the Social Christians a degree of leverage.

The PSD is the youngest and most insignificant of the right-wing parties. Formed on an openly anti-Sandinista platform on 23 September, 1979, it is shunned by international Social Democracy, and despite the massive publicity afforded to it by *La Prensa* managed to draw only 200 supporters to its inaugural rally. In presenting itself as a reformist party under the slogan 'Sandinismo Si, Comunismo No', uncannily similar to ex-president Urcuyo's cry from Guatemala of 'Somocismo No, Comunismo No,' it has offered little which the MDN cannot already provide. Its guiding lights are older Conservative dissidents from the generation involved in the Olama y Los Mollejones invasion and the Jinotepe-Diriamba barracks attacks of the 1950s, but there is no evidence that it, or the PSC, has been actively involved in any armed initiative against the FSLN.

The Frente's announcement of an extension to the agrarian reform programme on 19 July, the defiance of right-wing calls for elections and the suggestions that Nicaragua will move closer in 1981 towards planned centralisation of the economy indicate the Sandinistas' sense of strength in the face of a still disarrayed bourgeoisie. In the words of Comandante Victor Tirado of the National Directorate:

'The neo-Somocistas are anti-government, anti-Frente Sandinista; in a word, they are pro-nothing, because they lack any solid and consistent political ideas or programmes. Up to now, all they have done is to unleash campaigns of rumours, insults and gossip against the Sandinista Government. But where are their practical proposals for dealing with the problems of unemployment, illiteracy, health care and social inequalities? Where is their cooperation, where have they taken any action to provide solutions?

All that the right-wing parties have in common is a crude and virulent anti-Communism, and the most skeletal of programmatic agreements – the demand for elections, a weighting of the economic system in favour of private enterprise. They have come up with no common tactical line. Bourgeois political commentators like Pedro Joaquin Chamorro Barrios touch on the futility of the right-wing parties remaining divided; Alfonso Robelo attends a conference in Panama with leaders of the PSD. But this is as far as it has gone.

The question implicit in this analysis of the right-wing parties is to what lengths they would now resort to change the government. The debate over elections and the future configuration of the state has become a battle which goes far beyond demands for a simple modification of the existing balance of power. In comparing the Frente with Somoza, describing Sandinista power as a totalitarian military dictatorship, the right-wing bourgeoisie is openly accusing the FSLN of illegitimacy. It is also tacitly declaring that the changes of restoring capitalist rule by 'civic' means are closed off. The initial resistance of the private sector was an attempt to wring economic concessions and win a larger slice of state power. From there, it has become a rejection of the very basis of the Sandinista state. Further economic sabotage is likely only to provoke further (if at this stage reluctant) nationalisation. The logical next step is to see private sector revolt as part of a strategy to overthrow the Sandinista state. Alfonso Robelo, and others like him, declare that they want to see a Costa Rica in Nicaragua, and there was initially no reason to doubt their sincerity. But the FSLN will not be deflected from its course by internal pressure. Other more powerful interests outside Nicaragua wish to see Sandinismo overthrown, and this is the context in which the actions of the Right should be seen. When Robelo withdrew from the Junta, a mass demonstration in the Plaza de la Revolucion brought a sea of banners denouncing him as 'traitor' or 'Somocista'. Those which read 'Robelo – Made in USA' were probably closest to the mark.

The Central American Dimension

Regional Terrorism

On 21 May, 1980, eleven days after Robelo's inflammatory speech in Matiguas, Georgino Andrade – a young peasant CDS coordinator, militiaman and Literacy Commission representative for the village of El Mancital in Chinandega – was seized by a right-wing gang, dragged into a cornfield, tortured for five hours and finally killed. Pedro Rafael Pavon, one of the murderers, received a thirty-year jail sentence, the maximum permitted under Nicaraguan law. He told the court that Georgino had been killed 'because he was a Communist'. All those like Robelo, who raise the banner of anti-Communism, said Tomas Borge at a rally to honour the dead brigadista, 'are the assassins of Georgino Andrade'.[29] Brigadistas returning home from the Crusade in August had lost seven of their numbers in right-wing sniper attacks. The worst incident came on 30 July, when an armed gang of 25 men fired on a Literacy Crusade boat from the Honduran Bank of the Rio Coco, killing three people and wounding three more. Those returning from the largely unprotected northern mountains told of the hostile propaganda put about by some local landowners, but re-affirmed their own resolve to carry on in the face of threats broadcast from the Somocista radio station *Volveremos* inside Honduras.

Also in May, a number of Boaco ranchers, including people associated with COSEP, were arrested on charges of arming and sheltering right-wing terrorists of the newly formed Fuerzas Armadas Democraticas (FAD). The National Guard might have been destroyed as an arm of the Nicaraguan state, but enough of its members escaped to make it a serious threat, and the tradition of the right-wing death squad is well-rooted in Central America. The Ministry of the Interior has made no attempt to play down the threat posed by these groups. In July, it emphasised the need to continue improving the technical and political capacity of State Security, and reviewed some recent successes against the FAD and the Fuerzas Armadas Anti-Communistas (FARAC). Terrorist raids had escalated during July, with agricultural installations in the north and west of the country a particular target. But the FSLM had dismantled an important band operating around Chinandega and Somoto, another led by former National Guard sergeant Santos Betanco in the region of Los Calpules, across from the Honduran border town of Danli, and several smaller groups in Matagalpa.[30] The phrase 'death squad' should not suggest that groups like the FAD and the FARAC operate on their own account. The aim of their attacks is not random terrorism, but a concerted effort to destabilise Nicaragua, provoke border incidents, provide pretexts for military intervention and prepare perhaps for a full-scale invasion at the right time. Captured FAD members have admitted receiving active support from the Honduran armed forces. The Honduran military may be split, but despite the progressive sympathies of some younger officers and the election victory of the Liberal Party in April 1980, the hardline military Right around General Policarpo Paz Garcia remains in control and receives military assistance from the United States. In November 1979, secret police of the Honduran DIN arrested two Nicaraguan Embassy staff in

Tegucigalpa and beat them up, charging them with espionage. At this point, Managua's friendly relations with the short-lived reformist Junta which had replaced General Carlos Humberto Romero in October were useful, and the two governments issued a joint statement deploring the 'irresponsible attitude of groups in the Central American region who are trying to create artificial conflicts with the new Nicaragua'. But when the Salvadorean Junta collapsed only ten weeks later, Nicaragua was once more isolated and Honduran provocation continued at such a pitch that the Sandinista Air Force remained on almost permanent alert during the middle months of 1980. Aside from the military implications, aggression by Nicaragua's northern neighbours has damaged the declared intention of Plan 80 to build on existing bilateral trading agreements with Honduras and multilateral agreements with El Salvador and Guatemala, and the collapse of the Dalvadorean economy in 1980 has reduced the Central American Common Market to a shambles.

The military regimes of Central America are terrified by the boost which their own guerrilla and popular organisations have been given by the Sandinista Revolution. In Guatemala, the country's four guerrilla groups have gained combat strength and popular support in the majority Indian population and the Democratic Front Against Repression (FDCR) has built a unified bloc of political parties, civic groups and labour organisations. In El Salvador, the threat to the Right was even more immediate. The popular organisations of the Left, which had grown steadily since their formation in the mid-1970s, came together at the beginning of 1980 to form the Revolutionary Coordination of the Masses (CRM) and were joined by the Salvadorean Communist Party. Within three months, their military wings had overcome the historic divisions of the country's guerrilla movement to form a joint military command and the mass organisations had joined with Social Democrats, Christian Democrats and the progressive Church to form the Revolutionary Democratic Front (FDR), which laid claim to support from at least 80% of the Salvadorean people. Given the previous fractured state of the Salvadorean Left, it was arguably an even more remarkable achievement than the creation of Nicaragua's National Patriotic Front under FSLN leadership in 1979. The response of the region's *gorila* regimes was an internal military clampdown financed by the USA, and an anti-Communist propaganda war against the Nicaraguan Revolution, in which the Salvadorean, Honduran and Guatemalan press fed its readers with a regular diet of stories of alleged Sandinista atrocities, mass executions and brainwashing of the people.

With the FSLN victory, the Central American Defence Council CONDECA fell apart, its nerve centre removed, and the ten-year-old split between Honduras and El Salvador still unhealed. A new military strategy was desperately required by the USA and its regional allies. It was inevitable that the leadership of any new programme of regional military containment should pass to Guatemala; the Salvadorean regime was staggering, Honduras was too weak. Guatemala would be the last bastion of the old-style Central American Right; it had, after all, been like Somoza's second home. While Guatemala took its place at the head of the 'drive against Communism', Honduras and El Salvador had to be brought together again. Within this strategy, the remnants of Somoza's National Guard became a crucial element, directed from Guatemala City by Anastasio Somoza Portocarrero, the dictator's son, and Pablo Emilio Salazar ('Comandante Bravo'). As many as 3,000 former Guardsmen were believed to have joined the regular armies or right-wing paramilitary forces of Guatemala and El Salvador, with almost as many again in camps along the Honduran-Nicaraguan border. Guatemala City serves as headquarters for the National Guard's Frente Patriotico Anti-Comunista (FREPA), the terrorist group which claimed responsibility for a light-plane attack on the Sandinista barracks in Leon and bombings of the Nicaraguan embassies in San Salvador and the Honduran capital, Tegucigalpa, during the July 1980 anniversary celebrations. Joint military operations in the region, directed principally at destroying the Left in El Salvador, were intensified. The presence of Salvadorean and Guatemalan troops at the side of Somoza in the Nicaraguan conflict a year before pales into insignificance beside the new levels of military cooperation.

Honduras has been unduly neglected in most analysis of the new military containment, but its role is a vital one. Although the Honduran Left remains weak, the military government of Policarpo Paz Garcia was quick to recognise that its own survival was directly threatened by the fires around it. Accordingly, Paz Garcia visited Washington in March 1980, and his talks with the Carter administration were rapidly rewarded with $3.9 million worth of lethal military equipment. Washington made it clear that the Honduran military were expected to become 'a bulwark of anti-Communism against the pressures of popular revolt'.[31] Old resentments against El Salvador became secondary in the face of this popular revolt, and press reports soon called attention to the brutal consequences of joint operations between the Honduran and Salvadorean military. These estimated that between 325 and 750 Salvadorean peasants had been massacred while trying to escape from counter-insurgency operations into Honduras, trapped on the banks of the Rio Sumpul which forms the border between the two countries by a human wall of Honduran troops. General Paz Garcia had authorised the free use of Honduran territory by Guatemalan troops as well. 'There is nothing extraordinary in this,' commented a high-ranking member of the Honduran armed forces. 'Guatemalan soldiers can enter and leave Honduras as and when they please. It's already a matter of standard practice.'[32]

The Central American Right did not need to wait for the Reagan election to launch its campaign for the military suppression of the Left. The Carter Administration, though beset by foreign policy splits between the White House, State Department and Pentagon, had already thrown in its lot with the Right in its last six months of office, sunk as it now was in the renewed throes of a Cold War mentality in the wake of Nicaragua, Iran and Afghanistan. To many observers within the Administration itself, Carter had already laid the foundations for the expected hard-line of the Reagan years,[33] by giving in during the last weeks of his administration to the position of those like National Security Adviser, Zbigniew Brezinski, who sought a military solution in Central America, and overriding the lingering human rights concerns of Secretary of State Edmund Muskie and other Washington liberals.

From Carter to Reagan: The Options for the Nicaraguan Right

The FSLN needs the victory of the popular forces in El Salvador, and since the precipitate collapse of the short-lived reformist Junta which took power there in October 1979, it has given its full and vocal solidarity to the FDR and the unified guerrilla forces who, in the summer of 1980, adopted the name 'Frente Farabundo Marti de Liberacion National' (FMLN), finding in Marti a historical figure embodying the same nationalist aspirations as Sandino. But while the solidarity of the Nicaraguan people with the Salvadorean struggle is absolute, the FSLN and Government of National Reconstruction have had to exercise caution, aware of the dangers of any visible involvement in El Salvador, and they have given considerable publicity to cases of Nicaraguan combatants prevented by the government from leaving to fight alongside the FMLN. Daniel Ortega had already outlined the risks in a speech to the United Nations even before the fall of the Romero dictatorship in Salvador in 1979:

> Some North American representatives claim to have been informed by the Government of El Salvador and by Salvadorean businessmen that we Sandinistas are mounting military operations in that country to bring about the fall of the regime. Senator Stone, for example, asserts this and leaps to the defence of Salvadorean democracy. And he says that he will demand greater vigilance over Nicaragua by the United States Government. We see all this as a provocation: to justify economic, political and even military pressure against Nicaragua.[34]

Just as the Frente needs the breathing space which it will gain from the victory of the Left in El Salvador, so the Nicaraguan Right now depends on its defeat. The most influential sectors of the local bourgeoisie, including Alfonso Robelo, would ideally have liked the same solution for Central America as envisaged by the liberals in the Carter State Department: rule by a pro-US 'democratic centre', a model which Washington briefly hoped the October 1979 coup might bring about in El Salvador. That model, which had promised agrarian reform and respect for human rights, causing the Carter Administration to breathe a large sigh of relief and restore economic and military assistance, lasted for only three months, unable to challenge the real power in the country wielded by the murderous military right-wing establishment.[35]

Its failure, and the effective extinction of the 'democratic centre' as a political species in Central America and the Caribbean, ushered in policies which embodied all the schizophrenia of the Carter years, a mixture of reform and repression to counter the threat of revolution in the USA's own traditional backyard. Schizophrenia yes, but one which invariably and fatally came down on the side of repression. In the Caribbean especially, this involved the rapid dismantling of an incipient anti-imperialist bloc headed by Jamaica, Grenada and Nicaragua, and the reassertion of the USA's traditional military rights over its *mare nostrum* by the creation of a Florida-based military task-force. It brought rapid deployment exercises for US troops stationed in Puerto Rico and the Panama Canal Zone and the naval manoeuvres of Solid Shield 80. For Cuba, it entailed renewed US hostility, with·allegations of Soviet combat brigades on the island (quickly retracted when proven to be groundless), the mock invasion of the American base at Guantanamo (which the US still maintains in defiance of Cuban sovereignty) and a major propaganda exercise over the Cuban refugee exodus of April 1980. It has meant the isolation of the tiny revolutionary island of Grenada in the eastern Caribbean, with US pressure on other Western governments not to provide aid to build an international airport on the island — on the grounds that it would be used as a Cuban staging-post. In Jamaica, the victim was the social democratic government of Michael Manley, destabilised by the CIA and defeated by the right-wing Edward Seaga who promised a return to free market capitalism and the expulsion of all Cuban personnel on the island. Nor did the smallest islands escape, with Barbados sending troops to quell a local revolt in St. Vincent, left-wing politicians subverted in tiny St. Lucia, and post-hurricane aid for Dominica withheld until Prime Minister Oliver Seraphine sacked left-wing members of his Cabinet.[36] 'The United States and the Caribbean have come to understand each other much better,' noted US Ambassador Sally Shelton in Barbados.[37] The consolidation of an anti-Cuban axis, with Barbados and Jamaica as twin poles and Venezuela as regional overseer, is something which Carter may look back on as one of his minor but important 'successes'.

In El Salvador, the USA tried during 1980 to weave reform and repression into a single package, with nationalisation of the banks and an agrarian reform programme carried out to a background of the Vietnamisation of the countryside, the creation of 'strategic hamlets' and 'free-fire zones', master-minded by US official Roy Prosterman who a decade earlier had put together something similar for the Thieu regime in Saigon. The strategy depended on the credibility of defending a 'democratic centre' supposedly trapped between the uncontrolled violence of the extreme Right and the Communist terrorism of the Left. In practice, it meant propping up a regime whose shreds of a popular base disappeared with the assassination of Archbishop Oscar Romero by right-wing gunmen in March 1980, through regular trans-fusions of economic and 'non-lethal' military aid, while the security forces set about annihilating the Left and Centre. Only weeks before his departure from the White House, Carter accepted the inevitable consequences of his policies, and restored US supplies of 'lethal' military hardware. By then, many senior members of the outgoing administration had refused to go on accepting the Right-Left-Centre myth, and stated clearly that such an impression had only been created by largescale US Government manipulation of the national and international media.[38] Commenting on the overwhelming proportion of trade unionists and peasant activists among the 10,000 dead in El Salvador during 1980, one State Department official asked wryly: 'Do you think the Left is going in for a great collective suicide?'[39]

The Salvadorean model of limited social reforms and military containment had manifestly failed in less than a year. The agrarian reform programme, designed as much as anything to win some limited power base for the Christian Democrat rump in the San Salvador Junta by directing itself primarily at the richer peasants uncommitted to the popular organisations,[40] has done nothing to alter fundamental patterns of land tenure, and the repression which accompanied its early stages has left the Salvadorean countryside a wasteland of burnt-out farmhouses controlled by an ever stronger and more popular Left. While allowing this to go on unchecked, the Carter Administration continued to agonise over the options remaining for the US Government and the Central American bourgeoisie. There were two, and both were cited in a July 1980 analysis by the *Latin America Weekly Report*. On one hand, the US military establishment argued that Central America was now a 'Soviet target', in terms which clearly justified United States support for any Central American regime as long as it was anti-Communist. The alternative was to 'allow the Left to come in from the cold',[41] the logic of that being to sit back and allow the expansion of Nicaragua's revolutionary democracy. It is extraordinary in retrospect that such arguments were still taking place in Washington's tortured foreign policy conscience as late as July 1980, when the die had already been clearly cast — military aid to Honduras, repression in El Salvador, subversion and militarisation of the Caribbean. Months before Reagan set foot in the White House, the USA had committed itself to holding the line against any repeats of the Nicaraguan Revolution.

This anti-Communist option, which remained to be formalised with the Republican presidential victory in November 1980, is the one which now faces Robelo and his ilk. They have already shown clearly enough that they reject the consequences of 'letting *Sandinismo* in from the cold', and the National Guard leadership in exile is not unaware of this. Although the private fantasies of some sectors of the FAD, FREPA and FARAC — the three principal right-wing terrorist groups — may run to reinstating *Somocismo,* the leadership of the National Guard fully recognise the existing balance of forces within Nicaragua. *Somocismo* is not an option for them, unless the whole of Central America were to be turned into another Vietnam by direct military intervention by the USA, and the remains of the Guard be plausibly promoted as the military instrument — indeed the only instrument — of a hostile bourgeoisie unable to rid itself of *Sandinismo* by any other means. But this involves projecting a new identity for the National Guard which breaks with forty-five years of historical association with the Somoza dynasty. The Nicaraguan middle class retains a deep and genuine hatred for Somoza and his military machine, yet it has no other armed force available, and recognises that, ultimately, only armed force will dent *Sandinismo* in Nicaragua. The convergence is a long shot, but it is not impossible as class polarisation in

Nicaragua deepens. It is a chilling prospect.

The first hints of such a convergence came in May 1980. Immediately after Robelo's anti-Communist rally in Matiguas, Radio Volveremos in Honduras began to broadcast propaganda in support of Robelo. On the night of 26 May, an armed band of twenty right-wingers attacked the TELCOR communications office in the small village of San Jose de los Remates in the *departamento* of Boaco, north-east of Managua. They then surrounded the Sandinista police station, announced that Boaco had fallen to insurgents, and opened fire. In the ensuing four-hour gun battle in driving rain, one policeman died. Such incidents are not uncommon in the mountainous interior, but this time there was a new element. The survivors reported that the terrorist group had launched their attack to shouts of 'Viva Robelo! We don't want Communism here'. The new 'Somocista-Robelistas'[42] have gained sympathy from the right-wing bourgeoisie as evidence grows of their links with local landowners and businessmen. After the arrest of nineteen members of the FAD in Boaco, the Nicaraguan Bishops' Conference expressed its disquiet, and *La Prensa* launched a feverish campaign accusing the FSLN of repression against the private sector. When the nineteen Boaco counter-revolutionaries were placed on trial on 9 August, it emerged that twelve of their number were landowners and merchants.

Former Guardsmen have also collaborated in large-scale cattle smuggling across the Honduran border, first from private ranches in collusion with their owners, and then from INRA farms. MIDA estimates that up to 300,000 of the country's 2 million head of cattle have been lost in this way. While the FSLN fails to consolidate its support in remote rural areas of the north and east, and while the old relations of production are not touched by INRA in these backward areas, the Right will also be able to recruit with some success among local peasants. The Ministry of the Interior confirmed this:

> The leaders of these counter-revolutionary groups, the FAD and the FARAC, recruited many peasants for their operations. They told the *campesinos* that the new Sandinista Government did not believe in God and would steal their farmlands. The *campesinos*, ignorant of politics, believed their lies ... Their other members are former Somocista Guardsmen, common criminals and embittered former members of the Sandinista armed forces. According to them, these counter-revolutionary organisations stand for a democratic regime 'without Communism'.[43]

If the Nicaraguan bourgeoisie paid close attention to the activities of these groups and their gradual shedding of a Somocista identity, it also waited anxiously for the results of the November 1980 US presidential elections. Although the Carter Administration had set the pattern of support for the Right, there were still many Central American soldiers and right-wing businessmen who regarded Carter's Washington as 'tainted by Communism', and the terrorist Right – whether in the Presidential Palace in Guatemala

City or in the border camps of Honduras – must regard a Reagan victory as a green light. Also in the back of the minds of the Nicaraguan private sector was the likelihood of Republican economic sanctions against the Sandinista Government and even a trade embargo, although 'this would be more difficult for the USA to impose than in the case of Cuba. Nicaragua's export markets and commodities are more diverse than those of Cuba. At the same time, an embargo on sales to Nicaragua could affect industrial inputs and cut the level of luxury imports even more drastically than the government's taxes on luxury consumption. This would be against private sector interests, which presumably the USA would be interested in bolstering.'[44]

At the same time, the private sector could hardly have missed the signal from the Republican Party in its Platform on Latin America, unveiled at the Party Convention in Detroit in July 1980, a week before the anniversary of the Revolution: 'We deplore the Marxist Sandinista takeover of Nicaragua and the Marxist attempts to destabilise El Salvador, Guatemala and Honduras. We do not support United States assistance to any Marxist governments in this hemisphere, and we oppose the Carter Administration's aid programme for the government of Nicaragua. However, we will support the efforts of the Nicaraguan people to establish a free and independent government.' Whether it welcomed the prospect of a Reagan victory or harked back nostalgically to the democratising mid-term policies of Carter, the Nicaraguan bourgeoisie realised that if the threats implicit in the Republican programme were carried out, it would find itself merely a bit player in a much larger Central American drama.

Notes

1. In his article on possible CIA destabilisation tactics in Nicaragua, Philip Agee noted that 'strikes in key industries, promoted by the CIA and I supported by local and international unions, could impede reconstruction and create a climate of tension' (retranslation from the Spanish version in *El Trabajador*, March 1980).
2. These campaigns are most actively represented by the editorial line of *La Prensa* since April 1980, three privately owned Managua radio stations, and successive communiques and proclamations from the private enterprise group COSEP.
3. The tactics of ideological warfare by the Right were dealt with extensively by Carlos Nunez, in a speech to students of journalism at the National Autonomous University (UNAN), reprinted as *La Reaccion y sus Ejes de Enfrentamiento Ideologico*, Managua, SENAPEP, Serie Orientacion Sandinista, No. 17, 1980.
4. Most accounts of the Simon Bolivar Brigade episode are notoriously unreliable. The majority of Western press reports have been confused about the exact political origins of the Brigade, referring to it merely as 'Trotskyist' or 'Maoist'. Most left-wing commentaries on the other hand have sought to defend one or other sectarian position of their respective

357

authors. The article 'Imperialism Launches Propaganda Drive Against Sandinistas', in the 3 September 1979 edition of *Intercontinental Press*, while admittedly tendencious, probably offers an account of events which is as factually correct as any.

5. FSLN Party Organisation Secretary Carlos Carrion, in *Barricada*, 28 January 1980.
6. This description of events around the Frente Obrero strikes is based on conversation with Carlos Fernando Chamorro, director of *Barricada*, interviews with trade unionists and accounts in both *Barricada* and *La Prensa*, all in February 1980.
7. *Barricada*, 3 February 1980.
8. *Barricada*, 28 January 1980.
9. FSLN Direccion Nacional, *Ayer, Unidad Nacional para lograr el Triunfo. Hoy, Unidad Nacional para mantener la Victoria*, communique to the people of Nicaragua, 23 April
10. MDN, *Ideario Politico* (Managua, Editorial Aleman, January 1980) p. 1.
11. *Ibid.*, p. 10.
12. *Ibid.*, p. 12.
13. *La Prensa*, 10 March 1980.
14. *La Prensa*, 12 March 1980.
15. 'Robelo makes his Bid to lead the Private Sector Backlash' in *Latin America Weekly Report*, 2 May 1980.
16. *Barricada*, 23 April 1980.
17. *Barricada*, 20 May 1980.
18. Interview with Pedro Joaquin Chamorro Barrios of *La Prensa*, Managua, February 1980 (used by kind permission of Reggie Norton).
19. *El Nuevo Diario*, editorial, 11 July 1980.
20. Humberto Ortega, speaking on Radio Sandino's 'Linea Directa' programme, 10 July 1980.
21. For a detailed and well-documented report on *La Prensa*'s tactics, see *Intercontinental Press*, 24 November 1980.
22. Eduardo Galeano, *Open Veins of Latin America*, (New York, Monthly Review Press, 1974) p. 160.
23. Statement by FSLN representatives in West Germany, September 1979.
24. COSEP Communique, 14 November 1979.
25. In November 1980, after the completion of this text, Jorge Salazar was killed in an exchange of fire with Sandinista security forces near Managua. He was believed to have been carrying arms in connection with a plot to overthrow the government. A number of senior figures within COSEP were subsequently implicated in this plan.
26. *La Prensa*, 11 May 1980.
27. Interview with Dr Raul Estrada of the Democratic Conservative Party, Managua, August 1980.
28. *La Prensa*, 4 August 1980.
29. *Barricada*, 24 May 1980.
30. *Patria Libre*, Managua, Ministry of Interior, No. 5, July 1980.
31. Syndicated article by US columnist Jack Anderson, 23 March 1980, quoting talks between Major General Robert L. Schweitzer, US Army Strategy Director, and the Honduran military regime.

32. Cable from Raimundo Riva Palacio, correspondent for the Mexican newspaper *Excelsior,* 28 November 1980.
33. Dissent Paper by outgoing officials of the State Department, Department of Defence, CIA and other US government agencies, Washington D.C. Dissent Channel, November 1980.
34. Daniel Ortega, address to the United Nations General Assembly, 28 September 1979.
35. Tommie-Sue Montgomery, 'US Policy and Revolutionary Process — the Case of El Salvador', unpublished working paper, May 1980.
36. *Latin America Regional Report,* RC-80-01, 18 January 1980.
37. *Ibid.*
38 Dissent Paper, op. cit.
39. Quoted in *Latin America Weekly Report,* WR-80-15, 18 April 1980. .
40. Interview with Salvadorean priest, former press secretary to Archbishop Romero and member of the progressive Church organisation CONIP, London, August 1980.
41. *Latin America Weekly Report,* WR-80-28, 18 July 1980, quoting (a) Major General Robert L. Schweitzer, (b) William M. LeoGrande and Carla Anne Robbins, in *Foreign Affairs,* Washington D.C.
42. *Barricada* coined this term in its 30 May 1980 edition.
43. *Patria Libre,* Managua, Ministry of the Interior, No. 6, August 1980.
44. Valpy Fitzgerald, interviewed in *Latin America Regional Report,* RM-80-03, 21 March 1980.

Postscript

Somoza is dead, killed in a machine-gun and bazooka attack in the
Paraguayan capital of Asuncion. Ronald Reagan occupies the White House,
put there by a little more than 26% of the American electorate. COSEP and
the right-wing parties have walked out of the Council of State, serving notice
that they are no longer prepared to debate state power from the inside. From
grumbling opposition, the right-wing bourgeoisie has moved on to become the
spearhead of foreign intervention.

Like its allies in the local bourgeoisie, the new Reagan Administration has
made it clear that its objective is the overthrow, not the modification, of the
Sandinista state. Open hostilities on the part of COSEP, the MDN, the Social
Christians and Democratic Conservatives began within a week of Reagan's
election in November 1980, and the Nicaraguan people were not slow to draw
the necessary conclusions. The right may have chosen to go its own way and
abandon the principles of national unity, but the national unity which really
counts — the solidity of the mass movement — has only been strengthened by
the assaults of the past three months. *Poder Popular* — Power to the People;
Un Solo Ejercito — A Single Army. These are the chants which ring out today
in every demonstration. And the words are matched with action. As in the
insurrection itself, Nicaraguans are again a people in arms. The militias,
60,000 strong only a few months ago, have now grown to three times that
number. The Brigada Ezequiel sweeps the northern border to combat the
incursions of National Guard terrorists; other militia units watch over the key
productive centres of the economy. The confidence of the people in their
eventual victory is unswerving, as is their faith in the leadership of the FSLN.
Political education may still have a long way to go, but the mass organisations
are solidly structured at a national level, further steps have been taken
towards eventual labour movement unity, the Sandinista party is being built
not only in the state, but in the trade unions, the farms and the *barrios*. *Plan
81* assumes a normal' development of the economy in the next year, but
Nicaraguans know and accept that its contingency plans for a war economy
are more likely. If there is a danger, it is not that the people will abandon
the Revolution, but that they will want to take it too far too fast, overtaking
the careful timetabling of the FSLN in their anger at the internal
provocations of the Right and the interventionism of the new administration

360

in Washington. Factory workers denounce the slightest hint of economic destabilisation by their bosses. The young students of the Sandinista Youth, newly politicised by the five months of the Literacy Crusade, represent a wave of revolutionary energy which may not be easily channelled. The FSLN has made it clear that while anarchy in the streets will not be tolerated, however just the popular grievances, the actions of the people against reaction will be endorsed, no matter what form those actions may take. It is a difficult and delicate balance.

Nicaragua today is a country under seige. The rhetoric of Reagan's foreign policy advisers in the months leading up to the November 1980 presidential election is now the policy of the US administration towards the region. Intervention is clearly on the agenda. US military advisers and new lethal hardware have been shipped to El Salvador, while continuing American support for the military rulers of Guatemala and Honduras is assured. Even the thirty-year democracy of Costa Rica is not safe, with the Americans fearing the existence of a stable base for the activities of the Left in the region. In January, a band of former National Guardsmen in that county attacked the left-leaning radio station *Radio Notieias del Continente* in San Jose. The Carazo Odio Government, committed politically to the El Salvador Junta, has begun to crack down on the activities of Guatemalan and Salvadorean militants in Costa Rica. Senior Costa Rican policitians question the very survival of their system.

But — apart from El Salvador — it is the destabilisation of Nicaragua that is uppermost in Washington's mind. Within days of taking power, Reagan had announced the suspension of the remaining US $15 million in aid not disbursed by the Carter Administration. This is the first step. Other forms of economic aggression will follow: withholding of food aid, a blockade of Nicaraguan export markets, pressure on international finance institutions not to make capital available. Supposed Nicaraguan involvement in El Salvador will be used as the excuse for this economic aggression. At the same time, the USA will encourage the ever more virulent anti-Communist propaganda and economic sabotage of the Right within Nicaragua, and manipulate international media coverage to distort, discredit and isolate the Revolution. They will hope thereby to sow doubt in the minds of friendly governments, and to drive the FSLN into war communism and internal repression of opponents. This, Washington believes, will fire popular discontent with the Sandinista Government and provide the basis for an anti-FSLN uprising. Having stagemanaged this economic and political destabilisation, a military invasion from beyond Nicaragua's borders will then be launched.

It is a strategy which is shared by the terrorist Right in Honduras and Florida, and since the death of Somoza in September 1979 one of the most significant developments has been the emergence of a new anti-Sandinista force in exile which has adopted an explicitly non-*Somocista* platform. The new group calls itself the Union Democratica Nicaraguense (UDN), and its leader is none other than Jose Francisco Cardenal — the same Cardenal who fled into exile in May 1980, denouncing his appointment to the vice-presidency of the Council of State as 'a hellish conspiracy of the Communist machine'. Cardenal claims to have several hundred armed men at his disposal, and to have rejected the aid of National Guards who seek to restore a Somoza-style military dictatorship. There are signs that his requests for assistance have not fallen on deaf ears in Washington.

Yet this strategy to overthrow *Sandinismo* is likely to come seriously unstuck. The open splits on major policy statements by Reagan Administration officials in their first weeks of office suggest that the divisions between the State Department, Pentagon, CIA and Department of Defence may not be a passing phenomenon of the Carter era, but something built much deeper into the fabric of American government. If the aggressive rhetoric of the Georgetown University ideologues continues to hold sway, Washington will have difficulty in persuading Nicaragua's Western friends to abandon the Sandinistas. Already Western social democracy has shown that it will not swallow US support for genocide in El Salvador, and the Socialist International has closed ranks behind Nicaragua by announcing the formation of a high-ranking Committee for the Defence of the Nicaraguan Revolution. US policy will also find it difficult to bring the Nicaraguan bourgeoisie into line. Carter's aid package was destined in the main for the private sector, and a cut-off of financial assistance by Reagan will alienate significant sectors of COSEP and the MDN. Many businessmen will see this as a repeat of US policy towards Cuba in 1960, 'driving Nicaragua into the arms of Moscow' and abandoning the local bourgeoisie to its fate.

But, above all, Washington's hostility will run up against the resolve of the Nicaraguan masses to defend their victories. '50,000 of us died to get rid of Somoza,' said one CDS member in January 1981. 'And if it takes five times that number of dead to defend our country from the Reagan terrorists, then we're prepared for that too.' Jaime Wheelock, speaking the same ie month to the First International Conference of Solidarity with Nicaragua, made it clear that the FSLN felt the same way: 'We know all too well what the value of this revolution is, and we shall preserve our national sovereignty . . . Nicaragua may be swept away and destroyed, its fields may be turned into salt and ashes, but it will never be conquered.'

January, 1981

Select Bibliography

Nicaragua is very little documented. My main written sources have been the Nicaraguan press (*Barricada, La Prensa, El Nuevo Diario*); pamphlets, manifestos and internal documents of the FSLN; manifestos and communiques of other political organisations (FAO, UDEL, MPU, COSEP etc); and the Latin American press, in particular *Granma* and *Bohemia* of Cuba, *Alternativa* of Colombia and numerous Mexican newspapers. In English, the most reliable sources of information are the Latin America Weekly and Regional Reports of London, and the NACLA Reports on the Americas (New York). This list, therefore, is for the general reader who wants to locate the few serious books and major articles on the Nicaraguan Revolution, and with few exceptions is limited to material readily available in Europe and the USA.

Books and Pamphlets
Amnesty International: *The Republic of Nicaragua*, London, AI, 1977.
Black, George and Bevan, John: *The Loss of Fear: Education in Nicaragua Before and After the Revolution*, London, Nicaragua Solidarity Campaign/ World University Service, 1980.
Blandon, Jesus Miguel: *Entre Sandino y Fonseca*, Managua, Impresiones y Troqueles, 1980.
Camejo, Pedro and Murphy, Fred (eds): *The Nicaraguan Revolution*, New York, Pathfinder, 1979.
Crawley, Eduardo: *Dictators Never Die: A Portrait of Nicaragua and the Somozas*, London, C. Hurst, 1979.
CSUCA: *Estructura Agraria, Dinamica de Poblacion y Desarrollo Capitalista en Centroamerica*, San Jose Costa Rica, EDUCA, 1978.
Debray, Regis: *A Critique of Arms*, London, Penguin, 1977.
Debray, Regis: *The Revolution on Trial*, London, Penguin, 1978.
EPICA Task Force: *Nicaragua: A People's Revolution*, Washington D.C., EPICA, 1980.
Fonseca Amador, Carlos: *Escritos*, Managua, SENAPEP, 1979.
Gilly, Alfonso: *La Nueva Nicaragua: Anti-Imperialismo y Lucha de Clases*, Mexico City, Ed. Nueva Imagen, 1980.
IEPALA: *Nicaragua: El Pueblo Frente a la Dinastia*, Madrid, Instituto de Estudios Politicos para America Latina y Africa, 1978.
Latin America Bureau: *Nicaragua: Dictatorship and Revolution*, London, Latin America Bureau, 1979.
Lopez, J., Nunez, O., Chamorro, C.F., Serres, P.: *La Caida del Somocismo*

y la Lucha Sandinista en Nicaragua, San Jose, EDUCA, 1979.

Martin, Megan and Willett, Susie (eds): *Women in Nicaragua,* London, Nicaragua Solidarity Campaign, 1980.

Millett, Richard: *Guardians of the Dynasty,* Maryknoll, Orbis, 1977

Ministerio de Planification: *Programa de Reactivacion Economica en Beneficio del Pueblo (Plan 80),* Managua, SENAPEP, 1980.

Ministerio de Planificacion: *Programa Economico de Austeridad y Eficiencia,* Managua, MIPLAN, 1981

Nunez, Carlos: *Un Pueblo en Armas (Informe del Frente Interno),* Managua, SENAPEP, 1980.

Ortega, Humberto: *50 Anos de Lucha Sandinista,* Managua, SENAPEP, 1980.

Ramirez, Sergio (ed): *El Pensamiento Vivo de Sandino,* San Jose, EDUCA 5th edition, 1980.

Selser, Gregorio: *Sandino, General de Hombres Libres,* San Jose, EDUCA 2nd edition, 1979.

Tefel, Reinaldo A.: *El Infierno de los Pobres: Diagnostico Social de los Barrios Marginales de Managua,* Managua, El Pez y la Serpiente, 3rd edition, 1976.

Tijerino, Doris: *Inside the Nicaraguan Revolution,* Vancouver, New Star Books, 1979.

Torres Rivas, Edelberto: *Interpretacion del Desarrollo Social Centro-americano,* San Jose, EDUCA, 5th edition, 1977,

Wheelock Roman, Jaime: *Diciembre Victorioso,* Managua, SENAPEP, 1979.

Wheelock Roman, Jaime: *Imperialismo y Dictadura: Crisis de una Formacion Social,* Mexico City, Siglo XXI, 3rd edition, 1979.

Wheelock Roman, Jaime: *Raices Indigenas de la Lucha Anti-Colonialista en Nicaragua,* Mexico City, Siglo XXI, 1974.

— *La Revolucion a Traves de Nuestra Direccion Nacional,* Managua, SENAPEP, 1980.

— *Nicaragua: Combate de un Pueblo, Presencia de los Cristianos,* Lima, Centro de Estudios y Publicaciones, 1978.

Articles

Garcia Marquez, Gabriel: 'Sandinistas Seize the National Palace', *New Left Review,* London, No. 111, September-October 1978.

Jung, Harald: 'The Fall of Somoza', *New Left Review,* London, No. 117, September-October 1979.

Petras, James: 'Whither the Nicaraguan Revolution?' *Monthly Review,* New York, Vol. 31, No. 5, October 1979.

— 'Nicaragua Patria Libre' *Casa de las Americas,* Havana, No. 117, November-December 1979.

Ministerio de Cultura: *Nicarauac,* Managua, Nos. 1, 2, 3.

North American Congress on Latin America (NACLA): 'Nicaragua', *Latin America and Empire Report,* New York, Vol. X, No. 2, February 1976.

NACLA: 'Nicaragua in Crisis', *Report on the Americas,* New York, Vol. XII, No. 6, November-December 1978.

NACLA: 'Nicaragua's Revolution', *Report on the Americas,* New York, Vol. XIV, No. 3, May-June 1980.

NACLA: 'The Pentagon's Proteges', *Latin America and Empire Report,* New York, Vol. X, No. 1, January 1976.

Index

365